My dear Ash

For you
respect & ...muration.
Cheers!

Henry (and Kris)
8/12/2000

# GLOBALIZATION OF CHINESE BUSINESS FIRMS

# Globalization of Chinese Business Firms

Edited by

Henry Wai-chung Yeung

and

Kris Olds

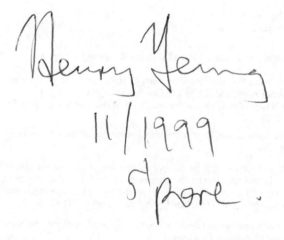

First published in Great Britain 2000 by
**MACMILLAN PRESS LTD**
Houndmills, Basingstoke, Hampshire RG21 6XS and London
Companies and representatives throughout the world

A catalogue record for this book is available from the British Library.

ISBN 0–333–71629–9

First published in the United States of America 2000 by
**ST. MARTIN'S PRESS, INC.,**
Scholarly and Reference Division,
175 Fifth Avenue, New York, N.Y. 10010

ISBN 0–312–22805–8

Library of Congress Cataloging-in-Publication Data
Globalization of Chinese business firms / [edited by] Henry Wai-chung
Yeung and Kris Olds.
    p.   cm.
Includes bibliographical references and index.
ISBN 0–312–22805–8 (cloth)
1. Corporations, Chinese.   2. International business enterprises–
–China.   3. Family-owned business enterprises—China.   4. China–
–Foreign economic relations.   I. Yeung, Henry Wai-Chung.   II. Olds,
Kris, 1961–  .
HD2910.G56   1999
338.8'8951—dc21                                                          99–39487
                                                                              CIP

This book is printed on paper suitable for recycling and made from fully managed and
sustained forest sources.

10   9   8   7   6   5   4   3   2   1
09  08  07  06  05  04  03  02  01  00

Printed and bound in Great Britain by Antony Rowe Ltd, Chippenham, Wiltshire

# Contents

*List of Tables*                                                    vii

*List of Figures*                                                  viii

*Acknowledgements*                                                  ix

*Notes on the Contributors*                                         xi

1   Globalizing Chinese Business Firms: Where are
    They Coming From, Where are They Heading?                        1
    *Henry Wai-chung Yeung and Kris Olds*

PART 1   GLOBALIZATION OF CHINESE BUSINESS:
         THEORETICAL PERSPECTIVES

2   What is Chinese about Chinese Family Business?
    and How Much is Family and How Much is Business?               31
    *Gordon Redding*

3   Reciprocity and Control: The Organization of
    Chinese Family-Owned Conglomerates                             55
    *Gary G. Hamilton*

4   The Dynamics of the Globalization of
    Chinese Business Firms                                         75
    *Henry Wai-chung Yeung*

5   Globalization, Institutionalization and the Social
    Foundation of Chinese Business Networks                       105
    *Hong Liu*

6   Internationalization of Ethnic Chinese-Owned
    Enterprises: A Network Approach                               126
    *Haiyan Zhang and Daniel Van Den Bulcke*

PART 2   MANAGING CHINESE BUSINESS ACROSS
         BORDERS

7   Transplanting Enterprises in Hong Kong                        153
    *Siu-lun Wong*

8   Bridging the Continents: the Roles of Los Angeles Chinese
    Producer Services in the Globalization of Chinese Business    167
    *Yu Zhou*

9   Chinese Business Networks and the Globalization
    of Property Markets in the Pacific Rim                        195
    *Katharyne Mitchell and Kris Olds*

10  The Internationalization of Singaporean Firms into China:
    Entry Modes and Investment Strategies                        220
    *Chia-Zhi Tan and Henry Wai-chung Yeung*

11  Failures and Strategies of Hong Kong Firms in China:
    An Ethnographic Perspective                                  244
    *Alan Smart and Josephine Smart*

PART 3   IMPLICATIONS

12  Epilogue                                                     275
    *Henry Wai-chung Yeung and Kris Olds*

*Bibliography*                                                   279
*Name Index*                                                     309
*Subject Index*                                                  316

# List of Tables

1.1 Leading Chinese business firms among the top 50 TNCs
from emerging markets, ranked by foreign assets, 1995    3
1.2 Major ethnic Chinese transnational corporations from
East and Southeast Asia    4
1.3 Distribution of ethnic Chinese outside China    7
1.4 Ethnic Chinese in East and Southeast Asia, 1995
1.5 Financial statistics of the 500 largest public companies in
Asia controlled by ethnic Chinese, 1994    7
1.6 Multi-disciplinary research into
'overseas Chinese' business    8
4.1 Sources of foreign capital in China, 1979–93    91
4.2 Listed members of the Charoen Pokphand
Group, Thailand    93
4.3 World-class hotels owned and controlled by
Chinese business firms from Hong Kong    94
4.4 Characteristics of Chinese business firms in
their globalization process    98
8.1 Chinese occupational patterns in Los Angeles County    172
8.2 Chinese-owned financial institutions headquartered
in Los Angeles County    184
10.1 Estimated overseas Chinese population of
Hainan origin, by country    223
10.2 Singapore's contracted FDI value and number
of projects approved in Hainan (in US$million)    224
10.3 Hainan's realized foreign investment from
Asian countries (in US$million)    224
10.4 Investment strategies of Singaporean firms in Hainan    236
11.1 Provincial distribution of foreign capital in PRC (1996)    246

# List of Figures

| | | |
|---|---|---|
| 1.1 | World map | 6 |
| 2.1 | Business dealings between the major ethnic Chinese in Asia, 1990–4 | 39 |
| 4.1 | A network spectrum of different forms of organizing international production | 97 |
| 6.1 | Impact of networks on the internationalization of the firm | 132 |
| 6.2 | Investment scenarios of Chinese-owned multinational enterprises from a network perspective | 140 |
| 9.1 | Pacific Place on the former Expo '86 site (North Shore/False Creek) | 208 |
| 10.1 | Location of Singaporean investments in China | 228 |
| 10.2 | Modes of entry of Singaporean investments in Hainan | 230 |
| 10.3 | Hainan Zilong Group Co. | 231 |
| 11.1 | Number of failures per 10 000 firms in Hong Kong, 1981–92 | 253 |

# Acknowledgements

This collection originates out of cross-border collaborative research into Chinese business firms and their global operations that has been under way since 1992, though the book itself has more recent origins. We first contacted almost all of our authors in April 1996 to discuss the possibility of contributing to this volume, and they have all since been very supportive of the project. One of the difficulties we faced was the geographical spread of the two editors and the contributors, and we did not have the good fortune to host a conference through which papers could be collated for publication. However, everyone eventually submitted quality chapters, and we hope all have forgiven us for the constant e-mail messages we sent. In short, we are extremely thankful to our contributors for their kind agreement to participate in this venture.

Macmillan has been a wonderful firm to work with, being both supportive and patient with our slow progress through the production process. The production process was slowed down by Kris Olds' two overseas moves, in 1996 and 1997, and the review process we instituted. We adopted a double review process in which we invited one of the contributors to evaluate anonymously another manuscript submission. In some cases when the subject area did not fit, we had to turn to an external reviewer for constructive comments and suggestions. Both of us also went through each submission and offered critical feedback. These comments and suggestions were then consolidated and given back to the contributors for possible revisions of their chapters. The revised chapters were further edited by us to ensure consistency of format, usage of terms and cross-referencing. We hope our contributors will not find their chapters appear too different from their original manuscripts.

At the National University of Singapore (NUS), we would like to thank the Department of Geography and the Faculty of Arts and Social Sciences for the research and administrative support that has made our editorial task more tolerable. In particular, we wish to acknowledge the exemplary editorial support provided by Elen Sia, whose employment was funded by the NUS via an ongoing research project – RP970013: 'Singapore's Global Reach'. Kris Olds would also like to acknowledge support via the Vancouver Centre for the Study of Immigration and the Metropolis <http://www.riim.metropolis.net/>, which is funded by the Government of Canada. Of course, we bear the usual responsibility for any editorial mistakes and errors. Henry Yeung also wants to thank his wife, Weiyu, for her understanding of why he often had to stay in the office on Saturday afternoons; Kris Olds would like to thank Janice Haller for all her generous support.

HENRY WAI-CHUNG YEUNG
KRIS OLDS

# Notes on the Contributors

**Gary G. Hamilton** Ph.D. is a Professor in the Department of Sociology, University of Washington at Seattle. He specializes in historical/comparative sociology, economic sociology, and organizational sociology. He also specializes in Asian societies, with particular emphasis on Chinese societies. He has previous held teaching positions at the University of California, Davis, and Tunghai University in Taiwan. His most recent research and publications have emphasized the comparative analysis of Asian business networks. He is the recipient of a Fulbright Fellowship, a Guggenheim Fellowship, and has been selected for a year's fellowship at the Advanced Center for the Behavioral Sciences at Stanford University. He has published numerous books and articles, including most recently *The Economic Organization of East Asian Capitalism*, with Marco Orru and Nicole Biggart (1997); *Asian Business Networks*, editor (1996); and *Cosmopolitan Capitalism: Hong Kong and the Chinese Diaspora at the End of the Twentieth Century*, editor (1999).

**Hong Liu** Ph.D. is an Assistant Professor in the Department of Chinese Studies and Assistant Director of the Centre for Research in Chinese Studies, National University of Singapore. He is an editor of the Hong Kong-based *Asian Review* and a specially-invited research fellow with Peking University. He has published more than twenty articles on the Chinese Diaspora, Sino-Southeast Asian relationships, and Chinese business networks in such journals as *World Politics*, *Journal of Southeast Asian Studies*, *The China Quarterly* and *Indonesia*.

**Katharyne Mitchell** Ph.D. is an Associate Professor in the Department of Geography at the University of Washington, Seattle. Her work focuses on the movement of people and capital across the Pacific, particularly the migration of wealthy Hong Kong Chinese to the cities of Vancouver and Seattle. She has published her work in a number of journals, including *Transactions of the Institute of British Geographers*, *Antipode*, *Economic Geography* and *Urban Geography*, and has a book forthcoming entitled *Transnational Migration and the Politics of Space*.

**Kris Olds** Ph.D. is a Lecturer in the Department of Geography, National University of Singapore. He has recently worked at the University of

Bristol, University of British Columbia, and held visiting appointments at Tongji University and the Chinese University of Hong Kong. His research interests include globalization and urban change, Pacific Rim cities, migration, and the social foundations of economic processes. He is the lead editor of *Globalisation and the Asia Pacific: Contested Territories* (1999); and author of *Globalization and Urban Change: Capital, Culture and Pacific Rim Mega-Projects* (forthcoming).

**Gordon Redding** Ph.D. is Affiliate Professor of Asian Business at the Euro-Asia Centre, INSEAD. He was previously founding Director of the University of Hong Kong Business School and spent twenty-four years in Hong Kong, teaching and researching Asian business. His main work has been on Chinese capitalism and his current interests are comparative systems of business and the operating problems of multinationals attempting globalization.

**Alan Smart** Ph.D. is Associate Professor of Anthropology at the University of Calgary. He has conducted research in Hong Kong and China since 1982. He is the author of *Making Room: Squatter Clearance in Hong Kong* (1992) and articles in the *International Journal of Urban and Regional Research*, *Society and Space*, *City and Society*, *Critique of Anthropology*, *Cultural Anthropology*, *International Journal of the Sociology of Law*, and numerous edited volumes.

**Josephine Smart** Ph.D. is Associate Professor of Anthropology at the University of Calgary. Her research is on informal economies, foreign investment in China, Asian immigration to Canada, gender relations and development in post-1978 China, and, more recently, NAFTA and its impact on the social and economic restructuring of three North American cities. She is the author of *The Political Economy of Street Hawkers in Hong Kong* (1989) and her work has been published in *International Journal of Urban and Regional Research*, *Critique of Anthropology*, *Anthropology of Work Review*, *Asian Journal of Public Administration*, *Canadian Journal of Development*, *Canadian Journal of Regional Science*, and in numerous edited volumes.

**Chia-Zhi Tan** graduated from the National University of Singapore with a B.A. Hons degree (majoring in Geography). His main research interests cover broadly ethnic Overseas Chinese investment in China, geography of transnational corporations, and the Geographical Information System. He conducted research field trips in Hainan Province,

China, in 1998, investigating the motivation behind Singaporean investment there. Currently, he is a web specialist in Temasek Polytechnic, managing the corporate Internet and Intranet.

**Daniel Van Den Bulcke** Ph.D. is Professor of International Management and Development at the University of Antwerp (RUCA) in Belgium. He is also a Fellow of the Academy of International Business. He is the author of many books and articles on foreign direct investment issues and the activities of multinational enterprises, especially in Europe and in Asia.

**Siu-lun Wong** Ph.D. is a Professor in the Department of Sociology, the University of Hong Kong. He has been the Director of the Centre of Asian Studies, the University of Hong Kong since 1996, and Pro-Vice-Chancellor of the University since 1998. His research interests include the study of entrepreneurship, business networks, migration, social indicators, and the development of sociology in China. He is the author of *Sociology and Socialism in Contemporary China* (1979); and *Emigrant Entrepreneurs: Shanghai Industrialists in Hong Kong* (1988). He is also the co-editor of *Hong Kong's Transition: A Decade After the Deal* (1995); and *Hong Kong in the Asia-Pacific Region: Rising to the New Challenges* (1997).

**Henry Wai-chung Yeung** Ph.D. is an Assistant Professor in the Department of Geography, National University of Singapore. His research interests cover the theories and the geography of transnational corporations, Asian firms and their overseas operations and Chinese business networks in the Asia-Pacific region. He has conducted extensively research on Hong Kong firms in Southeast Asia and the regionalization of Singaporean companies. He is the author of *Transnational Corporations and Business Networks: Hong Kong Firms in the ASEAN Region* (1998); editor of *The Globalisation of Business Firms from Emerging Markets*, 2 vols (1999); and co-editor of *Globalisation and the Asia Pacific: Contested Territories* (1999).

**Haiyan Zhang** is a Research Assistant at the University of Antwerp-RUCA. He is the author of several articles on the business activities of the Chinese and Overseas Chinese, in particular on their international investment operations and management. His research interests also include issues of foreign direct investment and the management of international joint ventures in emerging markets.

**Yu Zhou** Ph.D. is Assistant Professor in the Department of Geology and Geography, Vassar College. Yu Zhou received her Bachelor and Master degrees in Geography at Beijing University, P. R. China, and Ph.D. in Geography at the University of Minnesota in 1995. She has done research on ethnic economies in American cities, particularly the use of Chinese ethnic networks in various economic sectors among Chinese immigrant-owned firms in Los Angeles and New York.

# 1 Globalizing Chinese Business Firms: Where are They Coming From, Where are They Heading?

Henry Wai-chung Yeung and Kris Olds

> Chinese-owned businesses in East Asia, the United States, Canada, and even farther afield are increasingly becoming part of what I call the *Chinese commonwealth*. (Kao, 1993, p. 24; original italics)

In a widely-read *Harvard Business Review* article, John Kao (1993) concluded that Chinese business and its 'worldwide web' will become a major force in the global economy in the next millennium. Similarly, Joel Kotkin argued in *Tribes: How Race, Religion and Identity Determine Success in the New Global Economy* that by the early twenty-first century, 'the Chinese global tribe likely will rank with the British-Americans and the Japanese as a driving force in transnational commerce' (Kotkin, 1992, p. 9). Despite the 1997/8 Asian economic crisis, it appears that current thinking in global business reveals a serious reappraisal of the economic potential of Chinese business and its associated organizations and institutions. The Weberian thesis on the inherent limits to the growth of Chinese business and societies has been subject to fundamental challenges by recent studies (for example, Hamilton, 1996a; Whyte, 1996; Olds and Yeung, 1999). Scholars of contemporary Chinese business affairs have been forced to recognize the economic success of the 'overseas Chinese'[1] and their business firms in the host countries throughout East and Southeast Asia. Once established in host countries, Chinese business firms have extended their business operations and 'bamboo networks' across national boundaries, forming an increasingly global web of economic relations. These developments underscore the significance of a recent phenomenon in Chinese business – the globalization of Chinese business firms.

Economic globalization involves 'not merely the geographical extension of economic activity across national boundaries but also – and

1

more importantly – the *functional integration* of such internationally dispersed activities' (Dicken, 1998, p. 5; original italics). In affinity with Dicken, we define globalization as the growing functional and territorial integration of cross-border activities by business firms from specific countries.[2] The globalization of Chinese business firms therefore involves the spanning of activities across different countries and regions, as well as enhanced material and perceptual integration of these activities for strategic economic purposes. Ethnic Chinese-owned and controlled business firms from three of the four 'Asian dragons' (Hong Kong, Taiwan and Singapore) and other Southeast Asian countries (Indonesia, Malaysia, Thailand, the Philippines) are entering increasingly into the regional and global marketplace. As shown in Table 1.1, some ten Chinese business firms were included in the top fifty transnational corporations (TNCs) from emerging economies in 1995, and Table 1.2 gives further information on the shareholding and activities of these leading Chinese business firms from East and Southeast Asia. Some of the firms have been globalizing their domestic operations and setting themselves up as global competitors in business fields such as electronics and garment manufacturing, property development, financial services, hotel chains and so on.[3] It is likely that some will grow further, competing head-on with major transnational corporations (TNCs).

This book takes these recent trends as a starting point, and examines various aspects of the globalization of Chinese business firms. In particular, the contributors focus on two major issues: theoretical perspectives on the globalization of Chinese business firms; and the management and strategic practices of ethnic Chinese transnational corporations. The theoretical underpinning of this book draws on insights from international business, organizational sociology, international political economy, and economic geography to develop an integrated and interdisciplinary approach to our understanding of Chinese business firms and their overseas activities. It brings together contributions from leading researchers of Chinese business based in North America, Western Europe and Asia. It raises insights into the processes underlying the globalization of Chinese business firms, and the implications of this phenomenon.

In the remainder of Chapter 1 we shall first evaluate the importance of Chinese capital in East and Southeast Asia in order to familiarize readers with the nature and extent of Chinese capitalism. This is followed by a critical review of existing studies of Chinese capitalism and Chinese business firms, a review which serves to chart the direction of future research. In the final section of the chapter, a general synopsis of the book is given.

Table 1.1   Leading Chinese business firms among the top 50 TNCs from emerging markets, ranked by foreign assets, 1995 (in US$ millions and number of employees)

| Ranking (for assets) | Name of TNC | Economy | Industry | Assets Foreign | Assets Total | Sales Foreign | Sales Total | Employment Foreign | Employment Total | Index[a] |
|---|---|---|---|---|---|---|---|---|---|---|
| 1/52[b] | Daewoo | South Korea | Diversified | 11946 | 28898 | 8202 | 26044 | 28140 | 38920 | 48.4 |
| 4 | First Pacific Co Ltd | Hong Kong | Diversified | 3779 | 6821 | 4694 | 5250 | 33467 | 45911 | 72.6 |
| 7 | Hutchison Whampoa | Hong Kong | Diversified | 2900 | 11699 | 1632 | 4531 | 16115 | 29137 | 38.7 |
| 19 | New World Development Co Ltd | Hong Kong | Diversified | 1161 | 12396 | 471 | 2159 | 33550 | 45000 | 35.2 |
| 20 | Citic Pacific | Hong Kong | Diversified | 1070 | 5094 | 694 | 1401 | 7900 | 11500 | 46.4 |
| 26 | Acer Group | Taiwan | Electronics | 665[c] | 3645 | 2494 | 5825 | 4324 | 15352 | 31.7 |
| 31 | Tatung Co Ltd | Taiwan | Electrical equipment | 813 | 2929 | 1083 | 3100 | 9543 | 27254 | 32.6 |
| 35 | Genting Bhd | Malaysia | Properties | 692 | 2283 | 62 | 982 | – | – | 18.3 |
| 37 | Wing On Intl Ltd | Hong Kong | Retailing | 576 | 1344 | 40 | 366 | 1435 | 4006 | 29.9 |
| 42 | Creative Technology | Singapore | Electronics | 405 | 661 | 1175 | 1202 | 2048 | 4185 | 69.3 |
| 47 | Formasa Plastics | Taiwan | Chemicals | 327[c] | 2326 | 241 | 1650 | – | 3449 | 10.4 |

*Notes:*   The South Korean conglomerate, Daewoo, is included for comparative reasons. The table excludes government-linked corporations in Singapore (e.g. Singapore Telecom and Keppel Corporation) and Taiwan (e.g. Chinese Petroleum).
[a] The index of transnationality is calculated as the average of foreign assets to total assets, foreign sales to total sales and foreign employment to total employment.
[b] Data refer to the ranking among the world's top 100 TNCs.
[c] Data refer to 1994.
*Source:*   UNCTAD (1996a, table I.13; 1997, table I.8).

4

*Table* 1.2   Major ethnic chinese transnational corporations from East and Southeast Asia

| Company/group name | Major shareholder (ethnic Chinese) | Country of origin | Estimated net worth[1] (US$bn) | Major operations abroad |
|---|---|---|---|---|
| Cheung Kong Holdings | Li Ka-shing | Hong Kong | 5.8 | Husky Oil (Canada) Pacific Place Project (Vancouver) |
| Cathay Life Insurance | Tsai family | Taiwan | 7.5 | NA |
| Hong Leong Group | Kwek Leng Beng Quek Leng Chan | Singapore Malaysia | 2.0 2.1 | CDL Hotels (worldwide) |
| Salim Group | Liem Sioe Liong | Indonesia | 3.0 | First Pacific Group (HK) |
| Lippo Group | Mochtar Riady | Indonesia | 6.0 (assets) | Lippo Banks (worldwide) |
| Kerry Group | Robert Kuok | Malaysia/Hong Kong | 2.1 | Shangri-la Hotels (Asia) TVB International (Asia) |
| Charoen Pokphand Group | Chearavanont family | Thailand | 5.3 | CP Pokphand (HK and China) Telecom Asia (Asia) |
| Fortune Tobacco | Lucio Tan | Philippines | 1.7 | Eton Properties (HK) |

*Note:*   1. See source.
*Source:*   East Asia Analytical Unit (1995, table 6.1).

## THE ORIGIN AND IMPORTANCE OF ETHNIC CHINESE BUSINESS IN EAST AND SOUTHEAST ASIA

> Since the 1500s, southern China has served as a springboard for emigrants to Vietnam, Thailand, Indonesia, and elsewhere in Southeast Asia. These overseas Chinese [*sic*] have developed a bamboo network that transcends national boundaries. This informal array of complementary business relationships extends throughout the region, where entrepreneurs, business executives, traders, and financiers of Chinese background are major players in local economies. (Weidenbaum and Hughes, 1996, pp. 23–4)

Ethnic Chinese have indeed had a significant presence in East and Southeast Asia for a very long time (see Figure 1.1). The commercial influence of these Chinese merchants overseas dates back at least to the third century AD, when official missions were despatched to countries in the then South Seas (*Nanyang*). These missions were followed by Buddhist pilgrims, and later, during the Sung dynasty, by traders (Hodder, 1996, p. 1). After Chinese trade from Fujian and Guangdong to the south was legalized and licensed in 1567, stable and distinct Chinese communities became a feature of Southeast Asia (Reid, 1997, p. 41). In the mid-seventeenth century, there were communities of 3000 to 5000 Chinese in the major port cities in Java, Siam (Thailand) and Vietnam. By 1700, ethnic Chinese were unrivalled as the pre-eminent commercial minority in Southeast Asia and were 'the quickest to exploit the opportunities of the new commercialism because they were uninhibited by feudal tradition or landholding and because they had the necessary international contacts to move capital and goods across boundaries' (Reid, 1997, p. 43). These ethnic Chinese made a major economic contribution to the Southeast Asian region long before the nineteenth century (Dixon, 1991; Chan and McElderry, 1998). Some of them also became immensely powerful in both the colonial and indigenous governments in Southeast Asia of the time.[4]

As shown in Table 1.3, there are now some 55 million ethnic Chinese living outside China. The majority of them (91 per cent), however, live in Asia. Table 1.4 offers a detailed breakdown of the distribution of ethnic Chinese in East and Southeast Asia in 1995. Measured in absolute terms, Taiwan, Thailand and Malaysia have the largest ethnic Chinese population. In terms of ethnic distribution, Taiwan, Hong Kong and Singapore exhibit the largest concentration of ethnic Chinese. These ethnic Chinese contribute considerably to the dynamic economic systems of Asia

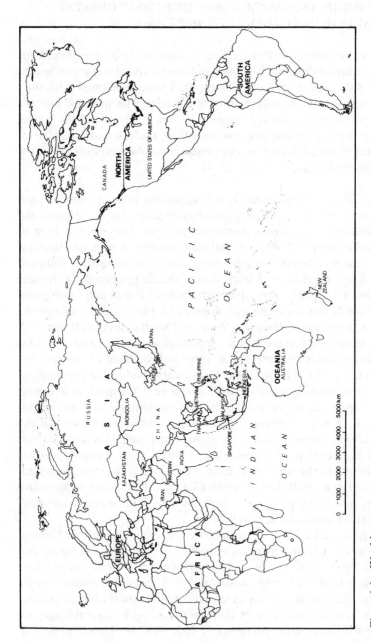

*Figure* 1.1  World map

*Table* 1.3    Distribution of ethnic Chinese outside China

| Region | Ethnic Chinese population (millions) | Percentage of total ethnic Chinese population |
|---|---|---|
| Asia | 50.3 | 91.3 |
| America | 3.4 | 6.3 |
| Europe | 0.6 | 1.1 |
| Africa | 0.1 | 0.2 |
| Oceania (including Australia) | 0.6 | 1.1 |
| **Total** | **55.0** | **100.0** |

*Source*:    East Asia Analytical Unit (1995, table 1.1).

and serve as a catalyst for regional economic growth. The World Bank estimates that the combined economic output of ethnic Chinese outside mainland China was about US$400 bn in 1991 and up to US$600 bn by 1996 (Weidenbaum and Hughes, 1996, p. 25). Through family, clan and dialect ties, they have virtually created a 'nation' without borders which generates a GDP only fractionally less than that of mainland China (*Asia, Inc.*, 1996; see also Table 1.4). Today, the collective 'funds' of these Chinese in the region (excluding Hong Kong and Taiwan) are conservatively estimated at US$400 bn (Hodder, 1996, p. 3).

In terms of their ownership of economic assets in the domestic economies, ethnic Chinese dominate. Table 1.5 presents some financial statistics of the 500 largest local public companies controlled by these

*Table* 1.4    Ethnic Chinese in East and Southeast Asia, 1995

| Country | Population (in millions) | Percentage of total population | Contributions to GDP (in US$bn) | Percentage of total GDP |
|---|---|---|---|---|
| Taiwan | 21 | 99 | 255 | 95 |
| Hong Kong | 6 | 98 | 120 | 80 |
| Singapore | 2 | 76 | 62 | 76 |
| Malaysia | 6 | 32 | 48 | 60 |
| Thailand | 6 | 10 | 80 | 50 |
| Indonesia | 8 | 4 | 98 | 50 |
| Philippines | 1 | 1 | 30 | 40 |
| Vietnam | 1 | 1 | 4 | 20 |

*Source*:    *The Economist*, 9–15 March 1996, p. 10.

*Table* 1.5    Financial statistics of the 500 largest public companies in
Asia controlled by ethnic Chinese, 1994

| Country | Number of companies | Market capitalization (in US$bn) | Total assets (in US$bn) |
|---|---|---|---|
| Hong Kong | 123 | 155 | 173 |
| Taiwan | 159 | 111 | 89 |
| Malaysia | 83 | 55 | 49 |
| Singapore | 52 | 42 | 92 |
| Thailand | 39 | 35 | 95 |
| Indonesia | 36 | 20 | 33 |
| Philippines | 8 | 6 | 8 |
| **Total** | **500** | **424** | **539** |

*Sources*:    Wu and Duk (1995a, table 3); see also Wu and Duk (1995b), and
Weidenbaum and Hughes (1996).

Chinese in seven Asian countries in 1994. Together, they control some
500 of the largest public companies in these Asian countries, with total
assets amounting to more than US$500 bn. These statistics exclude
many more privately-controlled Chinese business firms throughout the
Asian region. Some estimates also report that ethnic Chinese control
up to 80 per cent of Indonesia's corporate assets (and running 160 of
the 200 largest businesses), 40–50 per cent of Malaysia's corporate
assets, 90 per cent of Thailand's manufacturing, and 50 per cent of
Thailand's services (Wu and Duk, 1995a; Weidenbaum and Hughes,
1996). In 1995, every reported Indonesian billionaire was ethnic Chinese. In Thailand, ethnic Chinese control the four largest private banks,
of which Bangkok Bank was (until recently) one the largest and most
profitable in the region. In the Philippines, ethnic Chinese control over
a third of the 1000 largest corporations (Weidenbaum and Hughes,
1996, p. 25).

The economic power of these Chinese business conglomerates and
their extensive networks across the region have propelled the outward
movement of capital from their 'home' countries, forming an intricate
pattern of cross-border investments in Asia and beyond. Kraar (1993,
p. 87) notes that 'the strongest overseas Chinese [*sic*] have huge conglomerates with global reach. This is not some quaint ethnic side-show;
the Overseas Chinese [*sic*] are increasingly the main event in Asian
business today'. According to some boosters, the ethnic Chinese outside mainland China are effectively recreating an ancient empire, this

time as a twenty-first-century economic superpower. *Asia, Inc.* (1996) concludes that 'they have become merchant mandarins, parlaying for peace and prosperity. And, in the process, rebuilding an ancient empire'. While such statements are somewhat overblown and laden with ideological agendas, they contain realistic elements when one looks at indicators such as foreign direct investment (FDI). In mainland China, for example, since its open-door policy in 1979, ethnic Chinese from abroad have invested more than US$50 bn into various sectors, accounting for about 80 per cent of total realized FDI. At the time of writing they have formed more than 100 000 joint ventures in China (Weidenbaum and Hughes, 1996, p. 27). In Guangdong Province alone, investments from ethnic Chinese abroad account for around a quarter of gross output value of all industries (Ramstetter, 1996, p. 81). In 1993, ethnic Chinese investors from Hong Kong, Macao, Taiwan and other Asian countries contributed some RMB$85.4 bn to the gross output value of all industries in Guangdong Province (RMB$371.67 bn). These figures are very significant, given that, in 1995, mainland China was the largest recipient of FDI among *all* developing countries. UNCTAD (1998) estimates that at US$45.3 bn in 1997, inward FDI to China accounted for 11 per cent of total global FDI (US$400 bn), and 30 per cent of total FDI into developing countries (US$149 bn). In short, ethnic Chinese business firms, of all sizes, have played a critical role in the contemporary development of economies and regions in East and Southeast Asia. Such firms are also beginning to have a significant impact in selected cities (for example, London, Vancouver, Sydney, Los Angeles, New York) and certain sectors (for example, property, hotels, ports, banking) outside Asia.

## RESEARCHING 'OVERSEAS CHINESE' BUSINESS: TOWARDS A MULTIDISCIPLINARY ENDEAVOUR?

Although the 'overseas Chinese' have been a subject of study for a long time (see Wang, 1981; 1991; Suryadinata, 1997; Dirlik, 1997; Ong, 1997), studies of 'overseas Chinese business' are of relatively recent origin. This latter strand of literature is summarized in Table 1.6. In the late 1990s, Chinese business has become the subject of multi- and interdisciplinary research. In this introductory chapter, we shall briefly summarize the key themes of this literature and evaluate their usefulness in order to set the intellectual context for a book on the globalization of Chinese business firms. These themes are: (i) the spirit of 'overseas

Table 1.6 Multi-disciplinary research into 'overseas Chinese' business

| Discipline | Key author | Analytical category | Key explanations |
|---|---|---|---|
| Business | • John Kao | • worldwide web of Chinese business | • increasingly stretching beyond their Confucian-style family ventures |
| | • Linda Lim | • Chinese business strategies | • low cost, low profit margin and high turnover volume strategies for competition |
| | • Victor Limlingan | • spirit of Chinese capitalism | • Chinese values and beliefs lead to a strong tendency towards co-operation |
| | • Gordon Redding | • bamboo networks | • the role of bamboo networks in facilitating the creation of a new economic superpower in Asia |
| | • Murray Weidenbaum | • Chinese business system | • the role of the institutional foundations of Chinese family firms |
| | • Richard Whitley | | • different business recipes and different characteristics of business systems |
| Geography | • Rupert Hodder | • the 'Chineseness' | • no such thing as 'Chineseness' because definitive components of Chinese 'culture' are not peculiar or unique to 'overseas Chinese' |
| | • You-tien Hsing | • globalisation of Chinese business firms | • the role of political connections in facilitating Chinese business firms in China |
| | • Katharyne Mitchell | • the changing role and configurations of Chinese business networks | • personal relationships and business networks are necessary mechanisms of transnational operations by Chinese business firms |
| | • Kris Olds | • the role of the state and political-economic alliances | • cross-border operations of Chinese business firms set within the context of globalization |
| | • Henry Yeung | | • 'Chinese' business networks being reshaped by non-Chinese international business actors in a globalizing era |

| Discipline | Authors | Concepts | Arguments |
|---|---|---|---|
| History | • Raj Brown<br>• Wellington Chan<br>• Arif Dirlik<br>• Hong Liu<br>• Anthony Reid | • Chinese institutions and organizations<br>• family business<br>• Chinese capitalism | • the historical antecedents of Chinese institutions and organizations<br>• the social role of family business – as a socialization process<br>• Chinese capitalism is a localized, not a generalized, phenomenon<br>• Confucian discourse and cultural explanation of the East Asian economic miracle are driven by political ideologies |
| Sociology and Anthropology | • Susan Greenhalgh<br>• Gary Hamilton<br>• Thomas Menkhoff<br>• Donald Nonini<br>• Aihwa Ong<br>• Alan Smart<br>• Josephine Smart<br>• Tong Chee Kiong<br>• Wong Siu-lun<br>• Souchou Yao | • 'overseas Chinese' capitalism<br>• familism<br>• business networks and personal relationships<br>• social capital and social construction | • Chinese capitalism is socially organized, centred around the family firm<br>• business networks as important institutional forms to circumvent hostile host country environments and support economic success<br>• Chinese networks as a form of social capital<br>• strong entrepreneurial tendency of Chinese business |

Chinese' capitalism; (ii) Chinese business systems; and (iii) political-economic alliances in Southeast Asian countries. It must be noted that these themes are interrelated and by no means exhaustive. Some of them, though not conclusively reviewed in this chapter, are taken up by contributors to this volume.

**The Spirit of 'Overseas Chinese' Capitalism**

One of the most influential approaches in the study of Chinese business considers 'overseas Chinese' capitalism as an alternative economic institution that differs from Western capitalism. This is the so-called 'cultural' explanation of the East Asian 'economic miracle'. Redding (1990), for example, argues that 'overseas Chinese' capitalism is essentially an economic culture characterized by a unique capacity to co-operate. The 'overseas Chinese' are united by their deep sense of being ethnic Chinese who have not left China psychologically, or some ideal and romanticized notion of Chinese civilization (Redding, 1990, p. 2). 'Overseas Chinese' capitalism is not based on an elite system (as in Japan, for example) or rests on an explicit political system (for example, the USA), but rather is predicated on a household economy that is well adapted only to its sociocultural milieu. The spirit of 'overseas Chinese' capitalism is therefore a 'set of beliefs and values which lies behind the behavior of Chinese businessmen' (Redding, 1990, p. 79). Chinese values lead people to treasure relationships with one another. In classical Confucian thought, a person exists only in relation to others. There is thus no independent existence in society as such. The key to the Chinese socialization process is to achieve harmony and balance through good interpersonal relationships (*guanxi*). Good relationships are based on co-operative behaviour among members of the community (King, 1991). To highlight the importance of co-operation in Chinese social thought, Hamilton (1991b, p. 51) contrasts Western philosophical thought that 'the economic conception of a self-interested rational economic actor is not universal fiction; it is a European fiction, entirely a product of Western enlightenment thought that was enacted through political legislation and embodied in economic institutions'.

These beliefs and values are perceived to have significant impact on the nature of 'overseas Chinese' capitalism (Hamilton, 1996a; Redding, 1996; Hefner, 1998; see also Redding's Chapter 2 in this volume):

1.  Certain values surrounding authority in Chinese culture (for example, Confucianism) foster the stability and adaptiveness of the family firm.

2. Chinese values legitimize a distinct form of co-operation between organizations.
3. Chinese values retain long-term legitimacy because of their grounding in Chinese ethics.
4. Economic exchange and growth is enhanced by intra-organizational stability and inter-organizational co-operation.
5. There is no tight linkage between a set of state-supported institutions and the organizational principles of business.
6. Kinship relationships are very important in Chinese organizations.

In particular, the family provides the central foundation upon which Chinese social organizations and institutions are constructed. The family becomes the central unit of social thought and world view among the Chinese, thanks to the influence of Confucianism, which guides and shapes the role of family, compliance and social order. This phenomenon, known as familism, refers to the centrality of the family as a fundamental unit of social and economic organization among the Chinese. Some scholars of Chinese capitalism argue that it is familism that gives the 'overseas Chinese' their sense of 'Chineseness'. The cultural approach explains the success of 'overseas Chinese' capitalism through the role of familism and the Chinese socialization process.

Other recent studies of Chinese capitalism, however, cast doubt and considerable criticism on such conventional wisdom (for example, Nathan, 1993; Greenhalgh, 1994; Hodder, 1996; Dirlik, 1997; Ong, 1997; Yao, 1997). They suggest that the recent interest in and discourse on 'Chinese capitalism' as an alternative paradigm of development is little more than an essentialist invention of a new post-socialist and post-revolution discourse on *global capitalism*:

> Chineseness is no longer, if it ever was, a property or essence of a person calculated by that person's having more or fewer 'Chinese' values or norms, but instead can only be understood only in terms of the multiplicity of ways in which 'being Chinese' is an inscribed relation of persons and groups to forces and processes associated with global capitalism and its modernities. (Nonini and Ong, 1997, pp. 3–4)

Dirlik (1997, p. 308), for example, argues that the characteristics of 'Chineseness' may be the *effect* of the development of global capitalism. He suggests four main reasons why the prevailing discourse on Chinese capitalism may be wrong. First, the notion of 'Chineseness' is rather vague and contestable (see also Hodder, 1996). There are different self-images among the various Chinese populations in East and Southeast Asia. These individuals are presented and treated in analysis as a unidimensional phenomenon – 'the Chinese'. This line of thought is particularly problematic because 'it creates and legitimises the notion of "the Chinese" as a distinct entity which can be explained by the implicit application of laws and forces which are presumed to exist' (Hodder, 1996, pp. 12–13). Second, the Confucian revival in East Asia (for example, in Taiwan and Hong Kong) and Southeast Asia (for example, in Singapore) represents a 'Weberizing' of Confucianism because the dominant discourse suppresses the 'dark side' of Confucianism (that is, authoritarianism and gender-bias). Third, kinship ties are not unique to the Chinese. As argued by Maurice Freedman some four decades ago (Cited in Wong, 1988, p. 132), the crucial distinction between Chinese and Western economic behaviour is not that of kin and non-kin, but of personal and impersonal. That Chinese individuals tend to personalize their economic relations and kinship is just one of the possible bases for this solidarity. Finally, business networks among the ethnic Chinese may simply be a transitional strategy that emerges in unique circumstances (for example, hostile host environments).

Given the nature of the debates, there are no immediate solutions to what are fundamental epistemological differences in the conceptualization of 'Chineseness' and 'overseas Chinese' capitalism. Granting some validity to both sides of the argument, we shall examine in this book the extent to which Chinese business firms are socially and culturally unique in their globalization strategies and processes. We shall also devote some attention to the question of how such uniqueness, if it exists, may contribute to Chinese firms' success in establishing themselves in the Triad regions. The focus is not on whether Chinese business firms are distinctively 'Chinese', but rather on whether and in which ways the globalization of Chinese business firms may be different from counterpart firms based in Japan, Western Europe and North America (see Yeung's Chapter 4 in this volume). This theme therefore represents a new direction in research on Chinese business firms in that we examine whether and how 'Chineseness' can operate across national boundaries in both Asia and beyond. This brings us to the second theme in multidisciplinary literature on Chinese business – Chinese business systems.

## Chinese Business Systems

Whitley's (1992; 1998) business system approach offers a potentially fruitful avenue for understanding the nature and organization of Chinese business firms. He argues that 'different kinds of business and market organization develop and dominate different market economies as a result of major variations in social institutions and constitute distinctive business systems' (p. 7). As such, the focus is not so much on culture *per se*, but rather on the institutional structures of particular business systems that are socially constructed over time (and space, according to Hamilton, 1996a). The organization of business firms, as a result, is largely shaped by these institutional structures (Hamilton and Kao, 1990). Perhaps the most well-known characteristic of the Chinese business system is the role and extensive influence of *business networks* or 'bamboo networks' (Hamilton, 1991a; Menkhoff, 1993; East Asia Analytical Unit, 1995; Redding, 1995; Wong, 1995; Castells, 1996; Weidenbaum and Hughes, 1996; Zhou, 1996; Peng, 1997; Yeung, 1997a; 1998b; Haley *et al.*, 1998; Keister, 1998; Tong and Yong, 1998). Personal relationships (*guanxi*) are the most important mechanism for implementing co-operative strategies in Chinese business networks, although their importance obviously changes over time and differs by geographical and sectoral (for example, property) context (see Guthrie, 1998; Tsang, 1998; Smart and Smart's Chapter 11 in this volume). The reliance on personal relationships, however, is not restricted exclusively to this practice by the Chinese (see, for example, Björkman and Kock, 1995; Lewis, 1995; Windolf and Beyer, 1996; Lane and Bachmann, 1998; Olds and Yeung, 1999). Hodder (1996, p. 52), for example, argues that '*Guanxi*' (or reciprocity) is not a 'thing', or 'variable' or 'channel'. It does not characterise 'the Chinese', nor is part of a cultural mantle by which individuals can be identified as 'Chinese'. On the other hand, we argue that co-operative relationships in Chinese business are largely embedded in personalized business networks, whereas their Western counterparts tend to enter into co-operative relationships based on firm-specific business strategies. In short, interpersonal relationships continue to serve as the foundation for co-operative relationships in Chinese business networks.

Cooperative strategies are not new, but they are increasingly used by Chinese business firms in the network formation process. In the Chinese business system, co-operative strategies are *endemic* because the formation of Chinese business networks is itself a concrete manifestation of the underlying role of co-operative relationships. Business networks are very useful institutional means of implementing co-operative strategies and enhancing 'institutional thickness' in any business systems.[5] In the context of Chinese business networks, 'institutional thickness' can be generally represented by (i) the strong cultural and social embeddedness of business networks in personal relationships (*guanxi*);

(ii) high levels of personal and social interaction among actors in these networks; (iii) collective representation through trade and commercial associations and informal business groupings; and (iv) the quest for mutual benefits by which all parties in a network gain through co-operation.

Yeung's (1997a; 1997b; 1998b) empirical study of Hong Kong-based Chinese business firms and their cross-border operations in Southeast Asia has shed some empirical light on this complex issue of ethnic business systems and cross-border co-operative operations. The study identified three main network strategies pursued by Chinese business firms from Hong Kong: (i) co-ordinating intra-firm relationships to internalize entrepreneurship; (ii) entering inter-firm networks to extend friendship and accomplish business ambitions; and (iii) co-operating with extra-firm 'political patronage' to enhance the competitive advantage of local operations. At the intra-firm level, co-operative relationships are exploited by Hong Kong Chinese business firms to internalize entrepreneurship that would otherwise be lost. At the inter-firm level, Chinese business-people tend to come together to share business interests and develop personal relationships. Transnational operations are one possible institutional means by which they implement co-operative relationships. At the extra-firm level, co-operative strategies are underpinned by personal relationships between Chinese businessmen and top politicians in host countries. The process of politicizing business through extra-firm networks and political-economic alliances is particularly important in many Southeast Asian countries that lack well-defined legal systems and institutional structures (see below). Extra-firm co-operative relationships become an effective means of enhancing the competitive advantage of firms.

Another important characteristic of the Chinese business system is the *entrepreneurial tendency* of ethnic Chinese (see Mackie, 1992a; Chan and Chiang, 1994). Entrepreneurship is defined as a pro-business quality willing to undertake calculated ventures under reasonable risks and uncertainties. Historically and culturally, Imperial China was relatively frugal and self-centred in its economic relations with the outside world. Contemporary Chinese people, however, are experienced migrants and tend to form socially-organized networks to provide emotional and personal support. To a Chinese entrepreneur, setting up an overseas venture is very challenging, but the social significance of network exploration and formation makes the venture attractive in its own right. This argument applies to those ethnic link-based investments by Chinese businessmen, particularly in their hometowns in China (see Chapter 11 in this volume). Another element of Chinese entrepreneurship rests on the greater likelihood of internalizing external markets. Within the 'overseas Chinese' psyche, there is a deep-seated and culturally embedded desire for self-ownership and autonomy in decision-making (Bond, 1986; Redding, 1990). Although the family serves as a significant binding and centripetal force, Chinese entrepreneurs prefer to be their own bosses. There is a famous Chinese proverb: 'Better be the beak of a cock than the rump of an ox' (cited in Wong, 1988, p. 101). It is not surprising that the 'overseas Chinese' are well known for their entrepreneurial spirit. A rule of thumb in Chinese entrepreneurship is that a senior (sometimes a former employer) is obliged to help a junior to set up his/her own business if the latter is proven to be entrepreneurial enough. This unwritten 'cultural rule' is unthinkable in Western business because of culturally-embedded individualism and competitive behaviour (Hamilton, 1991b).[6] It must be emphasized, however, that this breed of 'juniors' is strictly limited to trusted members of the 'family'. Through this culturally-specific process of 'family-ization' (Chan and Chiang, 1994, p. 297; also Smart and Smart, 1993), 'outsiders' are socialized into the family to form an exclusive and elitist inner circle of relations:

> Clear boundaries are drawn between those business members who are in the family, and therefore are more trusted, from those who are not, and therefore cannot be totally or readily trusted but must be co-opted *gradually* by the family-ization process and through marriage alliances (Chan and Chiang, 1994, p. 354; original italics).

In short, the institutional approach to the study of Chinese business firms has provided us with a useful contingency model for understanding the dynamic characteristics of Chinese business firms when they transverse national boundaries. The challenge of the institutional approach for this book is to understand how Chinese business systems are shaped by different institutional structures in different countries (see Yeung's Chapter 4 and Wong's Chapter 7 in this volume). This is an important issue in understanding the nature of the globalization of Chinese business firms. It also has important implications for examining the transferability of Chinese business systems to countries or regions with fundamentally different institutional and/or cultural structures. It is imperative, for example, to evaluate the success of Chinese business firms in managing business networks and relationships over *space*. The manageability of cross-border business networks will determine the strategies and processes of their globalization, and the success or failure of the worldwide web of Chinese business (see Zhou's Chapter 8 and Smart and Smart's Chapter 11 in this volume).

## Political-Economic Alliances in East and Southeast Asian Countries

Related to the institutional explanation of Chinese business firms is a strand of literature focusing on the ways in which 'overseas Chinese' business firms integrate themselves into the host countries. This approach takes into account the local specificities of host countries and examines how ethnic Chinese successfully assimilate into local cultures and institutional environments (Limlingan, 1986; Cushman and Wang, 1988; Yoshihara, 1988; Jesudason, 1989; 1997; McVey, 1992; Hicks, 1993; Brown, 1995; Suryadinata, 1995; Hsing, 1998). The empirical focus of this literature is the hostility and discrimination faced by the 'overseas Chinese' in many Southeast Asian countries, and their political-economic coping strategies.[7] These studies of cross-border flows of ethnic Chinese capital from mainland China to East and Southeast Asia combine both cultural and institutional perspectives to arrive at a coherent explanation of the economic success of the 'overseas Chinese' in Southeast Asia. Their main argument is that ethnic Chinese in East and Southeast Asia are able to overcome host country hostility through kinship-based co-operation and political-economic alliances with host country power-brokers.

Host-country hostility contributes as much to situations of imperfect competition as to the deep-seated sense of self-protection and closely-knit social organization among ethnic Chinese diaspora in Southeast Asia (see Lynn, 1998). Historically, dynasties in China did not provide security to individual livelihoods because of the belief in family as the central unit of Chinese social structure. The family was, and is, the ultimate source of support and resources. Over centuries, a strong sense of co-operation has been developed in the Chinese business system, in particular along the family and kinship structures (see Redding's Chapter 2 in this volume). When a massive outward exodus of ethnic Chinese occurred in the late nineteenth and early twentieth centuries, they faced one of the greatest dilemmas in their social life – how to overcome formidable hostility in host countries. Naturally, these ethnic Chinese, particularly in Southeast Asia, turned to their inward-looking mode of social and institutional support – family and business networks based on co-operative and particularistic ties. These particularistic ties function as means of achieving 'closure' to outside competitors and to overcome their 'siege mentality' (Yoshihara, 1988; Redding, 1990) or 'trader's dilemma' (Menkhoff, 1993).

Anti-Chinese sentiments remain strong and pervasive in the political ideology and public discourse associated with many Southeast Asian countries (Yoshihara, 1994; Lim, 1996a; Yeung, 1997a; 1999a). With the exception of Singapore, the post-independence Southeast Asian region has been filled with anti-foreign and anti-Chinese capital sentiment (Mackie, 1988; Yoshihara, 1988; 1994; McVey, 1992). During the 1950s and 1960s, virtually all Southeast Asian countries were in an embryonic stage of industrialization. Anti-Chinese sentiment was rather deeply rooted in Indonesia and the Philippines (Robison, 1986; Mackie, 1988; Suryadinata, 1988; Yoshihara, 1994). In the Philippines, for example, the Chinese were seriously discriminated against under the Retail Trade Nationalization Law enacted in 1954, since most small-scale Chinese businesses were in retail and wholesale trade. In Thailand, the Chinese were able to assimilate themselves into the Thai economy and Sino-Thai businesses experienced rapid growth under Thai political and, often *de facto*, military patronage (Suehiro, 1985; 1992; Mackie, 1988; Yoshihara, 1994). In Malaysia, the Chinese established themselves under a more favourable political and ethnic climate because of the political coalition between the Chinese and the Malays (Jesudason, 1989; 1997).

The 1970s saw the emergence of a major ethnic backlash in Indonesia, Malaysia, and, to a lesser extent, in the Philippines and Thailand. The regulatory regime was much more restrictive. Domestically, pressure was exerted to allow a greater share of national economic wealth to indigenous people, known as *pribumi* in Indonesia and *bumiputra* in Malaysia. In Malaysia, for example, the New Economic Policy (NEP) was launched in 1970 to eradicate poverty in general and to strike a better balance in the ethnic distribution of wealth (Jesudason, 1989). In order to achieve the latter objective, the Industrial Coordination Act of 1975 required all manufacturing establishments above a certain registered capital to be licensed under the Ministry of Trade and Industry. The initial minimum threshold for the shareholders' fund was M$100000, but this was raised to M$250 000 in 1977 in an amendment to the act and recently increased further to M$2.5 m. It was hoped that through restricting both Chinese and foreign equity ownership, *bumiputra* ownership of the Malaysian corporate sector could eventually be increased from 2.6 per cent in 1970 to 30 per cent in 1990.

From the 1980s onwards, the attitudes of these Southeast Asian countries changed towards more a vigorous promotion of inward investments. The ethnicity issue has not disappeared completely – it has instead been supplemented by an increasing influx of foreign capital. Ironically, a large proportion of this foreign capital originates from societies dominated by the ethnic Chinese – for example, Hong Kong, Taiwan, and Singapore. Uneven development continues to be a prominent feature in the contemporary economic landscapes of many Southeast Asian countries (Jomo, 1988; Yoshihara, 1988; Jesudason, 1989; Kim *et al.*, 1992). Recent ethnic-inspired riots in Indonesia demonstrate that the issue of ethnic and regional inequality remains central to the stability and continual growth of many Southeast Asian countries. Ethnic-biased economic policies aiming at improving the economic well-beings of the *pribumi* in Indonesia and the *bumiputra* in Malaysia have effectively forced many ethnic Chinese business firms to reconsider their future growth strategies.

Ethnic Chinese business firms in Southeast Asia have responded to ethnic-biased economic policies in two basic ways: (i) establishing political-economic alliances; and (ii) globalization through diversification. First, many ethnic Chinese in Southeast Asia have entered into patron–client relationships with ruling military and political leaders. It is commonly acknowledged that the rise of Liem Sioe Liong in Indonesia, Robert Kuok in Malaysia, Lucio Tan in the Philippines, and Chin Sophonpanich in Thailand has been to a certain extent attributed to their close relationships with key politicians and military leaders in respective countries. They were often offered either privileged access to monopolized markets and resources, or outright political protection against the tide of discriminatory practices at the state level. They therefore benefited from these political-economic alliances by establishing themselves quickly in key domestic industries (for example, banking, property development, manufacturing).[8]

Second, upon consolidating themselves in their domestic economies by the 1980s, many Chinese business firms in Southeast Asia began considering the diversification of operations abroad in search of new investment opportunities; opportunities that were often denied in their home countries as a result of state regulations. This represents a new phase of development in the business history of Chinese firms in that they are increasingly operating across national boundaries to become diversified transnational corporations. Well-known examples are the Salim Group from Indonesia; the Kuok brothers and the Hong Leong Group from Malaysia; the Charoen Pokphand (CP) Group and Bangkok Bank from Thailand; and the Sy Group from the Philippines (see Table 1.2; also Yeung, 1998c, 1999b). In doing so, their strategies and processes of globalization are also shaped by the changing configurations of Chinese business systems and institutional structures of their 'home' countries as well as an increasingly global competitive environment (see Olds and Yeung, 1999; and Redding's Chapter 2 and Yeung's Chapter 4 in this volume). These issues are the central concern of this volume.

## ISSUES FOR RESEARCH INTO THE GLOBALIZATION OF CHINESE BUSINESS FIRMS

Today, Chinese business firms are becoming increasingly important players in the global economy. There are, however, only limited studies that focus specifically on emerging Chinese business firms. Most of these studies are concerned with either the nature of Chinese business and its practices, or the operation of Chinese business firms in their *domestic* contexts (see, for example, Limlingan, 1986; Redding, 1990; Menkhoff, 1993; Brown, 1995; Weidenbaum and Hughes, 1996). Few studies are concerned with the *global* operations of Chinese business firms. There are some studies that focus on issues related to globalization, especially those that emphasize the cultural politics associated with the transnationalization of the Chinese people (for example, Ong and Nonini, 1996). However, these studies are not very relevant to understanding the management and organization of Chinese business firms in the global economy.

Given such an intellectual context, this volume aims to fill both theoretical and empirical gaps in our understanding of the globalization of Chinese business firms. It focuses not only on the global and regional operations of Chinese business firms; but also on the numerous implications for those interested in the management, organization and regulation of these firms. More specifically, several chapters contribute to the theoretical debate about transnational corporations (see Dunning, 1993a; 1993b; 1997; Casson, 1995; Caves, 1996; UNCTAD, 1996b; Yeung, 1998b). These chapters argue that globalizing Chinese business firms may be organized and operate differently from their American, European and Japanese counterparts. This may help to revise current theories of TNCs and FDI. Dunning, for example, noted recently that 'until the late 1970s, scholars usually considered cooperative forms of organizing economic activity as *alternatives* to hierarchies or markets, rather than as part and parcel of an organizational *system of firms*, in which inter-firm and intra-firm transactions complement each other'. (Dunning, 1995, p. 463; original italics). In this regard, our contributors pay special attention to the role of ethnic business networks in the global operations of Chinese business firms, and their transferability to other contexts. Second, this volume presents much needed empirical analyses of the globalization of Chinese business firms. Most business case histories are concerned specifically with American, European and Japanese TNCs (for example, Bartlett and Ghoshal, 1995). Given the emergence of the 'Chinese commonwealth' in the global economy, it is important to learn more about the emerging corporate power and competitive strength of Chinese business firms. While this volume represents a major statement, it does not claim to be definitive. The structure of the book represents various 'cuts' through its themes rather than watertight distinctions and contributions. In particular, our contributors focus on two major themes in order to better understand the globalization of Chinese business firms: first, the theoretical perspectives on the globalization of Chinese business firms; and second, the management of Chinese business across borders.

## Globalization of Chinese Business Firms: Theoretical Perspectives

In the first part of this book we look at how the globalization of Chinese business firms can be conceptualized through various theoretical perspectives. As discussed earlier, there are several approaches to the study of Chinese business (for example, cultural explanation, business system approach, and institutional analysis). These approaches are re-examined critically by Gordon Redding in Chapter 2. Redding examines the extent of 'Chineseness' in Chinese business firms, and the role of the family in the operation of these businesses. In particular, Redding argues that Chinese business firms remain largely 'Chinese', even though many have become global geographically. To him, these Chinese business firms are unlikely to compete directly with global corporations in high-tech and high-value-added activities: this is because of the 'organizational slack' resulting from their growth trajectories in the 'soft' conditions of their home countries.

Chapter 3, by Gary Hamilton, however, reverses the argument and postulates that the 'bee' really can fly. To him, Chinese family-owned conglomerates have been misunderstood as 'ersatz' and 'hollow' by researchers adopting Western-centric perspectives. Drawing on some lessons from the recent Asian economic crisis, he argues that many ethnic Chinese-dominated economies of Asia have been relatively less damaged precisely because of their flexible business firms and institutional environment. To him, these firms and institutions are capable of flourishing in the next millennium under globalization. After offering a comparative analysis of the Chinese family firm as an object and a process, Hamilton defines five major trends in the globalization of Chinese family enterprises. He argues that the sociology of the Chinese family firm explains these recurring patterns better than alternative Western-centric explanations.

These contrasting assessments of Chinese business firms under globalization by Redding and Hamilton are followed in Chapter 4 by Henry Wai-chung Yeung, who offers a theoretical discussion of the global and regional dynamics of Chinese business firms and the globalization strategies of Chinese business firms. He argues that, in order to explain the globalization of Chinese business firms, we need to pay special attention to the dynamics of firm-specific strategies and the changing contexts in which these business firms are embedded and their strategies implemented. Yeung is less concerned with how distinctively 'Chinese' such firms are, and more with the global, regional and national contexts (and changing institutional configurations) that shape the globalization of Chinese business firms. His chapter also introduces an evolutionary model of the geographical expansion of Chinese business firms and maps their spatial growth over time.

The next two chapters are concerned with the social organization of Chinese business firms in their transnational operations. Using an institutional perspective in Chapter 5, Hong Liu expands on arguments by Redding and Yeung to incorporate the important role of chambers of commerce and other voluntary social institutions (*shetuan*) in the globalization of Chinese business networks. To Liu, these voluntary associations were traditionally organized under the principles of native place, kinship or dialect. In today's globalizing era, these Chinese *shetuan* are often perceived by the younger generations of ethnic Chinese as 'relics of a suffering past' (Liu, 1998b, p. 585). What they have forgotten is the vital role of new forms of such associations in facilitating the cross-border operation of Chinese business firms and their networks. Liu's chapter therefore opens an interesting window through which we can understand better how the globalization of Chinese business firms is embedded in these social institutions. Chapter 6 by Hai-Yan Zhang and Daniel Van Den Bulcke then proposes an analytical framework for analyzing the internationalization of Chinese business firms (see also Van Den Bulcke and Zhang, 1995). This framework is developed from a business network perspective, adding a new dimension to our understanding of the processes of globalization among Chinese business firms.

**Managing Chinese Business Across Borders**

Another significant issue in the globalization of Chinese business firms is how to manage transnational operations across national boundaries. This is, of course, not a unique problem for Chinese business firms (see Bartlett and Ghoshal, 1989; Humes, 1993). It is, however, important to learn whether Chinese business firms do have a unique way of managing their cross border operations. In this section, we first examine the different mechanisms through which Chinese business practices have been 'transplanted' successfully to other countries, and the international transferability of the competitive advantage of Chinese business firms. This is an important issue because, as Hu (1995, p. 85) has pointed out, Chinese business firms have experienced differential success in penetrating American and European markets, but succeed more often (in a relative sense) in Asia. If their competitive advantage is not transferable outside their 'home' countries, particularly to developed countries in North America and Western Europe, Chinese business firms may face serious problems in their globalization drive, and the worldwide web of Chinese business will remain a dream. Chapter 7 by Siu-lun Wong offers a general discussion of Chinese transplants overseas and examines the international transferability of Chinese business in Asia. To him, the successful transplant of Chinese business firms abroad is a result of, and sustained by, a rich cultural tradition in paradoxical, but favourable, institutional contexts. By examining four aspects of the evolution of Chinese business transplants in Hong Kong (from Shanghai to Hong Kong, from Hong Kong to Shanghai, from overseas to Hong Kong, and from Hong Kong to overseas), Wong's chapter sheds light on the 'ingredients' necessary for the successful international transfer of Chinese business firm to new locations.

Other chapters are concerned with the different mechanisms through which Chinese business has been transplanted and managed successfully in North America and Asia.[9] They provide very useful insights into the *modus operandi* of Chinese business in different political and sociocultural contexts. The next two chapters (Chapters 8 and 9) examine the mechanisms and institutions through which Chinese business firms operate in the USA and Canada. Complementing Hong Liu's institutional analysis of the globalization of Chinese business, Yu Zhou develops her earlier studies and examines the functions of small Chinese-owned producer services firms in Los Angeles (see also Zhou, 1995, 1996, 1998a). She argues that these small, privately-owned and decentralized Chinese service firms play key roles in connecting immigrant economic activities with international circulation of information, goods and capital. Three types of producer services are examined in the chapter: accounting, banking; and computer distribution. Zhou analyses the characteristics of each type of producer services, the problems faced by emigrant Chinese business firms in using such services from mainstream American firms, and the growth and operation of Chinese producer service firms in response to the need of these emigrant Chinese business firms. Together, these producer services act as a crucial enabling mechanism that smoothes the expansion of Chinese business into specific localities in the USA. The chapter therefore makes an important contribution to the wider producer service literature and ethnic (immigrant) economic literature.

In a similar way, the Chapter 9 by Katharyne Mitchell and Kris Olds provides an up-to-date assessment of the investment and management and practices of Hong Kong property tycoons in Vancouver (see also Mitchell, 1995; Olds, 1995, 1998, 2000). After discussing the nature and operation of Chinese business networks, and the globalization of property markets (particularly in the Pacific Rim) they use a case study to show how Chinese entrepreneurs gain access to quick and reliable information in distant locations. The case study highlights the critical role of cosmopolitan Chinese actors who effectively act as 'bridges', blending knowledge and business practices derived from both sides of the Pacific. They also argue that the manner in which information is shared between members of such trans-Pacific networks is both more particularistic and more flexible than in non-Chinese business firms; a business style which might lend advantages to Chinese firms operating within heavily regulated local property markets.

In Asia, China has been the leading destination for 'overseas Chinese' investments. Chapter 10 by Chia-Zhi Tan and Henry Wai-chung Yeung provide some empirical evidence to support Yeung's earlier chapter in which the globalization strategies of Chinese business firms were outlined. Based on personal interviews with Singaporean Hainanese investing in Hainan, China, Tan and Yeung argue that these investments are often embedded in the social and ethnic ties of their Hainanese owners with their ancestral homes in China. As a result, these Singaporean Hainanese often adopt particular entry modes and strategies. For example, they tend to enter into co-operative relationships with their counterparts from Hainan, and their operations are often orientated towards the local Hainan market. The chapter is also placed in the context of Singapore's ongoing regionalization drive, through which the Singapore government intends to encourage Singaporean investment in China.

Ethnic Chinese investments in China, however, are often beset by problems. In fact, the problems of cross-border operations faced by Chinese business firms have even more important implications for international business decision-makers and managers. Chapter 11 by Alan Smart and Josephine Smart presents an in-depth ethnographic study of the problems and strategies of Hong Kong firms operating in China. It complements their earlier studies of the role of personal relationships and kinship in the operations of Hong Kong firms in China (for example, Smart and Smart, 1991, 1993). They rightly point out that most studies of Chinese business revolve around 'success', both for the firms concerned and for the host countries where the firms are located, without examining the implementation of business strategies by these firms and the conditions for and/or against their implementation efforts. They argue that 'the economic success of a firm is strongly influenced by the complex interplay between management know-how and socio-cultural knowledge as played out in the daily decision-making processes and operational management undertaken by key individuals in the firm' (p. 244). The chapter focuses on three important and inherently risky strategies: (i) the reliance on social connections when investing in the 'frontier regions' of capitalism where legal foundations and property rights are not clearly defined; (ii) the employment of kin in key positions within Chinese business firms; and (iii) the issue of conflicts and tensions in the internal organization of these firms.

**Implications and Future Research Agenda**

This book represents an attempt to examine a relatively novel process – the globalization of Chinese business firms. The book therefore raises more questions and issues than it answers. Some of these questions and issues are discussed in the last chapter of the book – the Epilogue. In this chapter, Henry Wai-chung Yeung and Kris Olds draw together some general threads from the diverse chapters that are contributed by this interdisciplinary team. While this is not an easy task, the Epilogue does lay out some critical themes worth pursuing in future research on the globalization of Chinese business firms.

**Notes**

1.  The term 'overseas Chinese' may be contentious to some scholars of ethnic Chinese who are living outside mainland China. The term is related to the Chinese term *huaqiao* (Chinese national abroad) which has been criticized sharply in Southeast China for its implications that Chinese people born abroad with status as citizens in another nation are still Chinese in essence, and *huaren* (ethnic Chinese) has become more politically acceptable. The term 'overseas Chinese' is usually used to include *huaqiao, huaren*, and residents of Taiwan, Hong Kong and Macau (*tong bao*), who are considered to be compatriots living in parts of the territory of China temporarily outside mainland Chinese control. See Wang (1991) for an authoritative account of the origin and status of ethnic Chinese living outside mainland China. Throughout this book, authors will generally refer to 'ethnic Chinese' or to specific groups (for example, Hong Kong entrepreneurs) rather than 'overseas Chinese' in their discussions of research materials. But references to the literature sometimes require reference to 'overseas Chinese' to be clear.
2.  As a material process of global economic interpenetration, globalization contains certain illogic(s) (Jessop, 1999) and is often mystified and deployed through political discourses – in particular, neoliberalism – to create its own conditions of existence (Yeung, 1998a; Kelly, 1999). This book does not intend to delve into such a debate on the politics and discourses of globalization (see Boyer and Drache, 1996; Hirst and Thompson, 1996; Mittelman, 1996; Sassen, 1996; Cox, 1997; Scott, 1997; Dicken, 1998; Weiss, 1998; Doremus *et al.*, 1998; Olds *et al.*, 1999). Instead, it focuses on the *material processes* of how particular types of business firms – Chinese business firms – are globalizing themselves.
3.  Several detailed case studies have been published on the globalization of leading Chinese business firms from Asia in different sectors: Acer from Taiwan (Hobday, 1998; Mathews and Snow, 1998) and Johnson Electric from Hong Kong (Ellis, 1998) in electronics; Li & Fung from Hong Kong in trading (Fung, 1995; Magretta, 1998); CP Group from Thailand in agribusiness (Handley, 1997; Brown, 1998; Pananond and Zeithaml, 1998; Suehiro, 1998); and Cheung Kong from Hong Kong in property development (Olds, 1998).
4.  Examples include Thio Thiau Siat in Sumatra and Penang; Tan Seng Poh in Singapore; Loke Yew in Kuala Lumpur; Khaw Soo Cheang in South Thailand; and Oei Tiong Ham in Java (Reid, 1997).
5.  The notion of 'institutional thickness' is borrowed from Amin and Thrift (1994, p. 15) who define it as 'the combination of factors including interinstitutional interaction and synergy, collective representation by many bodies, a common industrial purpose, and shared cultural norms and values'. They have also identified four dimensions of 'institutional thickness': (i) strong institutional presence; (ii) high levels of interaction amongst the institutions in a local area; (iii) the development of sharply-defined domination and coalitions through collective representation; and (iv) the development of a mutual awareness.
6.  Many authors emphasize that contracts still play the most important role, even in co-operative ventures, among Western firms (see Lewis, 1995; Willcocks and Choi, 1995).

7. Hsing's (1998) study is an exception in terms of empirical focus. She looks at how Chinese business firms from Taiwan were able to establish themselves successfully in China through complicated political-economic alliances with local and provincial authorities.

8. The recent Asian economic crisis of 1997–8 has thrown these practices seriously into question. To many neoliberal observers, the evils of the Asian economic crisis are argued to be corruption and 'cronyism' which originated from the self-interested and utility-maximizing behaviour of state officials and business people (for example, Lim, 1997; Rosenberger, 1997; Emmerson, 1998; Haggard and MacIntyre, 1998; Yeung, 1999a). At least in Southeast Asia, many of these business people are ethnic Chinese in origin.

9. For a recent study of ethnic Chinese and their activities in Europe, see Benton (1997).

# Part 1
# Globalization of Chinese Business: Theoretical Perspectives

# 2 What is Chinese about Chinese Family Business? And How Much is Family and How Much is Business?

Gordon Redding

## INTRODUCTION

The questions posed in the title are a way of identifying the main contending models of cause and effect that may be used to explain the phenomenon labelled 'Chinese family business'. Simply put, these are (i) the culturalist position which would argue for the primary determinants being Chineseness and the associated transfer of values into stable patterns of action; (ii) theories which begin with the premise that the family stage of organizational emergence is consistent across cultures and that Chinese family business is the same as other family business; and (iii) more complex theories of the emergence of business systems which bring into play a much wider set of determinants, principally those of surrounding institutions, but also allowing for societal embeddedness, borrowing and constant adaptation. The considerations are then used to reflect on the issue of the globalization of the Chinese family enterprise. Another model exists based on the universalist and 'under-socialized' assumptions of economic theory; but as this tends to be based on selected and isolated 'facts' and is weak in dealing with complex interactions, reciprocal determinacy and multiple patterns of causation, it will be left out of this account. Instead, the focus will be on work that has dealt with the Chinese family organization as the unit of analysis and attempted to explain why it is so.

This now begs the question: what is the Chinese family business? The answer is far less clear than might at first be supposed, not because of a lack of clarity in defining the original form which became so visible in the early years of the twentieth century in the countries surrounding the

South China Sea, but because thirty years of rapid and sustained growth in those areas since the 1960s has led to differentiation in the form, so that it now appears in several shapes. In addition to this kind of proliferation, there has also been, since 1979, the emergence of China as a field for new forms of enterprise helped by a lifting of the dogma which so stifled familism after 1949 and in consequence hindered the rebirth of Chinese family business in its country of origin.

In order to place a boundary around the overall category of interest here, it is proposed that its most significant identifying feature is its capitalist nature. This means that forms of enterprise not included are those in centrally planned economies or organizations that are otherwise not directly influenced by market forces in the fields of capital, labour and demand. Taking Berger's (1986) consciously value-free definition of capitalism as 'production for a market by enterprising individuals or combines with the purpose of making a profit' (p. 19), this defines the boundary within which it is possible to categorize the following components:

i.    the 'traditional' small and medium enterprise found throughout the region, the management of which is centred on a particular family or two of Chinese ethnic origin;

ii.   the emerging large family business groups which take on many of the characteristics of the multinational enterprises apparently so legitimate as role models: the true extent to which this copying and borrowing changes organizational character remains an under-researched and significant question;

iii.  the large business groups or corporations supported by governments in Taiwan and Singapore, are virtually entirely Chinese in personnel and ownership, and run as capitalist businesses; and

iv.   the newly emergent private sector businesses in China that are responses to the increasing tendency for market forces to prevail in some sectors of the economy (Zhang and Sjoberg, 1992): there is, of course, a continuum here, with smaller organizations tending to follow the family model quite clearly and larger ones having to adjust to residual constraints of regulation by taking hybrid forms. The direction of movement is, however, consistently towards the capitalism defined above, at least in recent years, and is likely to continue under the conditions announced as policy in late 1997. The boundary between the private sector and that of the collective/town and village enterprise sector is blurred as the latter begins to exhibit the effects of marketization and the urge to profit.

It would be possible to produce a finer-grained and more complex set of component units but, for the purposes in hand, this rough set will be adequate. Two other points need making: first, there is some artificial exclusion by not taking alliances into account, especially alliances with Western or Japanese firms which often provide technical expertise and marketing skills, but are seen as a special topic outside the question of Chineseness. It does reflect a possibly culturally influenced capacity for co-operation and this will be discussed later. The organizational alliance as an analytical category, however, introduces too many new issues that are at a tangent to the concerns of this chapter and can only properly be treated separately. Second, it is very important to take on board the notion of change in a system in perpetual adaptive motion, and to accept that although certain fundamental historical influences may continue to shape organizations, what is being shaped is capable of reinventing itself and appearing in new guises. Arguably, under those guises, certain deep-seated traits remain distinctive and contribute to the adjustment process itself.

## THE CULTURALIST APPROACH

Those who argue for culture as a prime determinant of present-day business behaviour tend to follow a rationale that identifies certain societal values as being representative of a set of people, and seek connections between these values and consistent patterns of organizational behaviour. Much of the impetus for this school of thought has been through the successful assault by the Japanese on Western markets in the 1970s and 1980s. It was apparent that Japanese organizations were different from Western ones in ways that required subtle explanation. Much of such explanation has been couched in cultural terms, and the fascination with Japanese culture has been assisted by the clear nature of its boundary, the identifiable formative influences in its history, and the relative strength and consistency of its expression in daily life and work by the Japanese (Morishima, 1982; Ouchi, 1981; Pascale and Athos, 1981; Vogel, 1979; Rohlen, 1974).

Much of the literature on Japanese culture and management avoids the demonstration of cause and effect connecting values and behaviour, and retires to a position of asserting such connections. But there are enough studies to leave a strong case standing. There is also enough accumulated practical observation in the real world for people to accept that there is something distinct about Japanese organizations, even though its nature is not always explicit. The formidable competitive strength of Japanese business and the consequent importance of understanding its origins have served to enhance the claim of culturalists to be taken seriously. In recent years it has also become fashionable in some political quarters to identify Asian success with Asian values, a movement associated particularly with advocates such as Lee Kuan Yew. Although this has some scholastic base in, for example, the work of Tu (1984) in Singapore, it is essentially a convenient political counter to a perceived imbalance in the publicizing of societal ideals, with Western ideals having had such a strong run of secular acceptance and legitimacy, especially via such conduits as the world of finance and an international youth culture purveying Disney or pop music and so on. The need to re-establish Asian values and to contrast them with those of the West is part of a mental landscape that includes an assumption that they are determinants of economic and social progress.

The work of Hofstede (1980, 1992), in identifying the core dimensions of culture seen universally, and thus the categories for describing national variation, was built successfully on a long tradition in anthropology and sociology. Its key contribution has been to prevent research from endless attempts to define culture as an object of study and to move investigation forward towards the study of effects. There is, however, a dilemma inadequately addressed in much research – the mixing of analysis across different levels. Hofstede's dimensions capture an aggregate of individual responses. A figure on a scale is taken to represent the 'collective programming of the mind'. But a variable that is essentially psychological in origin connects uneasily with variables studied under organizational levels of analysis, or even more so with national performance data. Tracing the steps in the middle – going, in other words, from the psychological predisposition of individuals to behave in a certain way through the maze of organizational characteristics to outcomes such as performance, and even more so to the performance of numbers of organizations seen collectively – is a notoriously difficult intellectual task. Correlation is not causation. Methodological individualism of this kind will always remain controversial until it can be linked to a convincing theory of institutionalization to carry the concepts from the psychological level to the sociological. As one progresses through such logics, there is a constant accumulation of new aspects to be taken into account, and a resultant weakening of the role of culture in determining outcomes. This is not to say that culture disappears; rather, it takes its place in a queue of determinants, each claiming a place in the total explanation.

In the context of Chinese culture and its behavioural effects, the work of Bond (1996) remains dominant, and his massive *oevre* of detailed empirical studies provides ample evidence of connections from culture into many aspects of social behaviour. These include relationships, identity, the workings of power and influence, sources of motivation, communications, co-operation and face. He has also contributed usefully to understanding by making accessible the work of many other scholars, such as those in Taiwan and China, in the same field. Work such as this leaves little doubt that culture must be accounted for in explaining organizational behaviour, but it tends to stop short of explaining organizational *performance*, an elusive-enough challenge for even the most multidisciplinary of projects (Campbell *et al.*, 1970 ). Attempts to make such a linkage are usually in the form of outlines of hypothetical connections. These are often the concluding summaries of empirical work in the area of values which try to move the field forward to the next stage of enquiry. An example here is the general framework for a connection between Chinese cultural values and organizational–economic responses proposed by Redding (1990); so too is the parallel framework offered to explain the efficiency of the system of network capitalism in general (Redding, 1996) and its particular Hong Kong manifestation (Redding and Tam, 1993). Other examples of contributions to this development have been those of Kao (1993) in his analysis of bamboo networking, Hamilton (1996), in a general statement on Chinese capitalism and its workings; Lim and Gosling (1997), in a consideration of the role of minority status; and the summaries by Mackie (1992a, 1995, 1998) of the reasons for ethnic Chinese regional success.

Within China itself, an authoritative review by Wang (1994) concludes that the evidence for cultural influence working via groupism, shared ideals of harmony, equality and social commitment certainly exists, but the influence of economic reform was greater on management practice and organizational performance. In a centrally planned economy, even one changing rapidly, this is perhaps not surprising. But it does lead one naturally to the idea that the embeddedness of economic action in society in a larger sense introduces a wide array of determinants. This point will be returned to after first considering the question of more universal theory.

## UNIVERSAL THEORIES OF FAMILY BUSINESS

Although the managerial revolution in the West saw the significant separation of ownership from control and the move towards professionalizing the management function (Burnham, 1941; Berle, 1954 ), it is neverthe-less still normal for the initial stage of the growth of a firm to be under family ownership and control. The small and medium sectors of advanced economies have remained as highly significant contributors to national wealth, especially since the 1980s. The function of entrepreneurship has led to much research interest in this field, and family business as such is also treated as a field of academic study and teaching, with pro-fessorships devoted to it. The 'entrepreneurship movement' was also given a boost by the revival of free market political philosophies in the 1980s in the developed world.

It is, of course, not inevitable that entrepreneurship means family control. Many entrepreneurs will not employ family members. In search-ing for the differences that might make Chinese family business distinct from other forms of family business, this is precisely the kind of variable at which one is tempted to look. An equally important field in which Chinese family business might be distinguished from other subsets of the general type is in the field of networking and the extension of the boundaries of the firm beyond those of the legal entity. The doyenne of universalist analysis of the firm, Edith Penrose (1995, p. xx), remarked that:

> business network is very different from a cartel of independent firms in its structure, organization and purpose. It is clear that this type of organization is likely to continue to spread for some time and con-tinue to engage in a competition very different from that analysed between firms in so-called free markets. This may call for changed views about the behaviour of markets and the effects of 'free market' competition.

In what sense, then, might it be possible to argue that Chinese family business is just like family business elsewhere? Alternatively, what claims might be made for its distinctiveness as an analytical category ?

The most obvious points of evidence on which Chinese family busi-ness might be considered the same as family business anywhere are the Chief executive officer as owner, the employment of family members in key positions, a family monopoly over strategy-making, and a relatively low level of formalization associated with small or medium scale. An out-come of such factors combined is the problem of transition to a larger and more professionally managed enterprise, as this latter form usually demands the development of decentralized decision-making and the adoption of more structured systems of control. A further common feature of the family business in general is the transition problem between generations, as the legitimacy earned by the performance of one generation is difficult to transfer to the next, and effective co-ordination may break down. The saying about rags to riches and back again in three generations occurs in different forms in many cultures and is not a monopoly of the Chinese mental universe, even though it is firmly, and justifiably, embedded there.

These features are visible on the surface, but there are also more qualitative features which mark out businesses based on family and derive from that basis of ownership and control. First, they are the strength of managerial dedication to the enterprise which comes from the dependence of family security on its success. Second, there is the efficiency in decision-making and speed of response which comes from the concentration of both knowledge and decision power in one person. Third, there are lower transaction costs within a business network of such firms as compared to situations where business dealings are more contractual and more formalized. This can apply not just in transactions of buying and selling, but also in the exchange of information and the processes of financing. Somewhat more nebulous, but still arguable in many cases, is the retention of employee loyalty in systems that are essentially paternalistic.

These may be taken as universals for family business anywhere, albeit with variations from firm to firm in their intensity and their modes of expression. But there are at least two aspects in which Chinese family business may be said to be distinct compared to Western patterns of family enterprise: (i) Chinese family enterprise has not so far entered the transition to professionalism and public ownership which is such a common feature of Western economic evolution, even though arguably it has had plenty of time to do so; and (ii) the personalism used in cementing stable market relations between enterprises, in general conditions of mistrust, seems to reflect norms and values about co-operation that are distinctly Chinese and highly developed in the secular culture of Confucianism. The obvious special case of comparison is with Jewish family business. Analysing 'the two most prominent entrepreneurial minorities in the modern world', Chirot (1997, p. 3) argues that one must always take into account the stark and simple fact of a massive objective difference: that is, the Chinese operating in Nanyang have on its northern edge the world's most highly populated homeland. Despite a large number of apparent similarities in values and organizational behaviour, there are also other, more subtle, differences between the two types that prevent the easy transfer of arguments about causation from one to the other (Chirot and Reid, 1997).

The choice by the regional ethnic Chinese of a route to growth and wealth without copying the Western managerial revolution is visible in the retention of familism even on a large scale. It is tempting to see a connection applicable in most of mainland Asia Pacific between the patrimonial structures of those societies (Jacobs, 1985) and the tendency to retain familism as the dominant structural principle for societal authority. Connected with this is, of course, a subsidiary issue of growth and wealth *for whom*, but that is for a separate agenda. The avoidance of public ownership is visible in the shareholding data that display persistent family control in large enterprises throughout the region (Elvis, 1998; Ko, 1998). Techniques for the retention of family control via the use of positions in the organizational structure have been described by Hamilton and Kao (1990). By operating in industries that do not require extensive strategic delegation or very complex co-ordination, a family can build scale and some scope to very large size. It is also arguable that the nature of the business environments of Asia, the majority of which are characterized by high levels of uncertainty and the need for much co-optation of political support, makes the owner-dominated form of business very well adapted to handle the search for profitable opportunities. The personalism which marks the distinctly Chinese form of trust-bonding is visible in Figure 2.1 which shows business dealings between the major ethnic Chinese in the region between 1990 and 1994. Here we see a system designed for (i) the local identifying of opportunity; (ii) the gathering of capital to take it; (iii) the sharing and hedging of risk internationally; (iv) the probable sharing of rare and strategic information; (v) the local provision of political clearance if needed; and (vi) the maintenace and enhancement of the mutual assistance that is currency of the network.

The distinctiveness of the Chinese family business lies in the combination of internal features and external circumstances which have led to its flowering on this scale. It does not lie in the overlap of family and enterprise *per se*. In that sense, it looks largely the same as other forms of family capitalism. But in its development towards modern forms of Chinese capitalism, it has learned how to grow and still retain family control; it has also developed the art of alliance building to an unusually high level. In both of these aspects, one must acknowledge the role of insecurity in explaining the persistence with which both adaptations have been pursued. The insecurity is that of an ethnic minority, generally non-assimilated and yet successful in wealth terms, coming from a society in which the combination of totalitarianism and patrimonialism left a historical legacy of suspicion of any source of

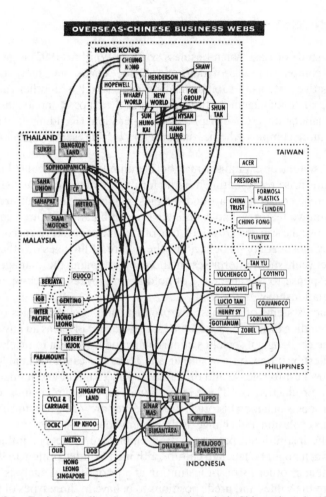

*Figure* 2.1    Business dealings between the major ethnic Chinese in Asia, 1990–4
*Notes*:    1. Publicly announced joint business deals between 1990 and 1994, at
value of over 10 million US dollars.
2. Note that one or two cases are not ethnically Chinese but are treated
as members of the net for this analysis.
*Source*:    S. G. Redding (1995) 'Oversease Chinese networks: understanding
the enigma', *Long Range Planning*, 28, 1, 61–9.

security except the family. The continuing reminders of this stark social
separation have accumulated to another high peak as the Asian regional
crisis of 1997–8 worked its way through society to the grassroots, especially in Indonesia.

## BUSINESS SYSTEM THEORIES

In his study of East Asian business systems, Whitley (1992) argues for more complex models of determinacy to explain the emergence of alternative systems of capitalism. This accords well with other calls for comparative management to escape from the traps of monocausalism and inadequate cross-disciplinary co-operation (Redding, 1993). In these more complex schema, the logic may be represented as follows:

1. A system of capitalism may be identified by a particular kind of enterprise representing it in the form of an ideal type. Such a form will be constructed around the most commonly found and representative features, and is defined as a combination of three components: the size and growth pattern of the kind of enterprise accounting for most economic behaviour; the nature of linkages or otherwise between such enterprises in the economy; and the management response to the challenge of holding employees in a co-operative relationship with the firm.
2. Such systems of business are products of a complex series of surrounding institutional influences; they have evolved as an answer to the challenge of societies undergoing modernization to resolve two questions: how best to gather and focus the capital available and how best to release and direct the supply of talent and human skill for productive use. These institutional responses are, in most cases, products of a long historical process. They are, of course, in continuous evolution and change as the system does.
3. The institutional pattern is itself embedded in deeper influences which might be labelled culture, although Whitley prefers to define them as other forms of institution at a prior level of analysis. They are the values and predispositions to behave in three types of social behaviour that are crucial to the organizing of economic action: the rules governing authority and how it is legitimized; the most natural sense of identity perceived by the individual; and the societal view of trust.

These cultural features run close to the empirically derived primary dimensions identified and labelled by Hofstede (1980) as power distance and collectivism. The issue of trust is, at least in part, arguably a behavioural outcome of identity. But it also encompasses the question of whether trust has been enhanced by moves to institutionalize it, as, for example, with commercial law. The availability of high levels of trust or 'social capital' is seen by some observers as being central to societal progress (Fukuyama, 1995; Putnam, 1993). In the case of Chinese capitalism, as argued above, it is the absence of societal trust that accounts for much of the behaviour in the networks. The particular way in which mistrust is surmounted owes much to specifically Chinese social ideals.

Under Whitley's formulation, the understanding of how Chinese family business has come to be as it is rests on a much more complex set of determinants than those found in previous accounts. It brings into play the workings of government policies, educational systems, financial systems, historical features of the development process, and the borrowing of organizational techniques from elsewhere. It does not eliminate culture, but places it in context as a conditioning factor shaping the fabric of the society that surrounds the enterprise. Culture thus shapes the institutions, and the institutions shape the business enterprises. This is a view based on multiple determinacy. No single cause is called upon to explain a current outcome. Instead, one is invited to consider much historical influence to understand how the multiple causes themselves have been interlocked. So too it is necessary to see influences flowing reciprocally, as the societal matrix is responsive to the world of business and reacts to it. An important epistemological assumption here is that the elusive social science goal of understanding (that is, as opposed to demonstration) is best served by coming to terms with the inner workings of such large entities as business systems, seeing them as discrete from each other, each with its own character, and seeing comparisons of deracinated components across such systems as being potentially misleading.

Analytical work of this nature cannot be handled within one discipline. Even though it will always rest somewhere in a main theory such as the sociology of firm behaviour, it requires acknowledgement of forces studied by geographers, economists, anthropologists, sociologists, historians, psychologists, political scientists and management theorists. It is only then that understanding can be reached. In a scholastic context where demonstrated connections and 'proofs' based on positivist epistemologies are now so dominant, and the rewards for multi-disciplinary work are consequently sparse, it is unlikely that new developments of this nature will emerge in quantity.

## HOW CHINESE IS CHINESE BUSINESS?

There are three sets of reasons for arguing that Chinese family business is a product of a unique set of forces and has become unique in itself, at

least as a type containing variety from firm to firm. These reasons are
(i) Chinese culture has seeped into it and continues to do so; (ii) the
social dynamics of the family play an important part in its nature, but in
ways that take on a Chinese flavour; and (iii) its particular historical circumstances are not replicated for other business systems. Here one has
in mind the immense symbolism of Chinese civilization as a co-ordinating social 'glue' in host environments. It may take on some of the characteristics of other systems and may in part be explicable in terms of
universally relevant forces acting on business organizations. But it is
not fully understood unless its particular circumstances are taken into
account. It needs to be examined on its own terms. What, then, are those
terms?

The impact of Chinese culture has worked through the two primary
determinants of social structures that affect the workings of organizations. These are, first, the rules that govern the stabilizing and legitimiz-
ing of authority, or the vertical dimension of order; and, second, the
rules that govern the stabilizing of co-operation, the horizontal dimension of order. In the Chinese case, the norms for vertical relationships
are inculcated via the Confucian ethic. This works by providing a very
clear set of principles for action, most of which surround the role of the
father figure as the pivot of the social system. The stability and constant
regeneration of the social system is achieved by the use of role training
and socialization built on the specific role prescriptions available. The
sanctions available to maintain compliance are connected with the psychological dependence of individuals on family identity and support.
This is enhanced by the general surrounding insecurity and the lack of
alternative foci of affinity and succour. Family identity is also strengthened by ideals of family perpetuity, the perceived importance of the
family's 'name' or reputation, and the long-standing tradition of extended
family support to members. These are outcomes of a social philosophy
of great antiquity and durability in China, in which the state is constructed
essentially from self-governing families. In this world view, the growth
of intermediary institutions that might deflect loyalty and dependence
away from the family has always been stunted. The resulting underlying
pattern reappears constantly after turbulent social upheaval and its
importance to the Chinese individual is regularly reinforced by his or
her observation of what life might be like without it.

In the organization, vertical structure is handled with a lack of form-
ality in terms of bureaucratic processes. Organization charts and job
definitions are replaced by social deference. People come into the organization pre-programmed to understand the hierarchy instinctively. The

style of leadership commonly adopted has a paternalistic flavour. The adoption of such a style by the owner sets the tone for other managers in less dominant positions to echo it in dealings with their own subordinates. This style can also bring with it nepotism. Often autocracy, as a discipline in the Confucian system, is very much a tradition. The spectrum of interpretation is wide, running from benevolent paternalism to harsh authoritarianism, with every shade existing in between. But the power relationships are never in doubt. Power rests in ownership and is legitimated by father-like behaviour. What makes this Chinese is not that it looks different in its practice from its Italian, French or Swedish equivalents, but that it rests on a specifically Chinese set of inner workings, rules, understanding about right and wrong, and expectations by the participants. These may have echoes in other societies, but they are only echoes and not close overlaps.

Similar considerations apply to the rules for horizontal order. The Confucian prescriptions of role behaviour, the absorption of which so predetermines the view of a person as civilized or not within the Chinese mind, include clear rules for the handling of friendship. Because society is generally seen with suspicion and mistrust, being what Lau (1982) has termed 'minimally integrated', the handling of friendship takes on strategic significance as a means to circumvent the problem of horizontal co-operation. Here again, the rules and roles are clear and well disseminated, and they have moral force. To lose one's reputation for trustworthiness is a most serious threat and to have achieved a high reputation for it is a basis for much honour. The moral strictures which surround the building of personal webs of connections remain in place because the webs are so necessary to the functioning of the society. Just as the society which gave rise to them has been Chinese, so too are the strictures themselves. The contrast with Mafia ethics governing horizontal relations is stark (Gambetta, 1988). The Mafia polices loyalty with great aggression and it approaches competitors in the same way. As a result, alliances within it tend to be fragile. The Chinese believe in never making enemies and are capable of very robust, long-standing and forgiving alliances.

One outcome of the Chinese perception of horizontal co-operation is the proliferation of network structures tying organizations together in strong but flexible alliances which form a basis for much of the success of Taiwan and Hong Kong, plus their hinterlands in OEM-based industry. Parallels come to mind in Silicon Valley, northern Italy and the British Midlands, where similar structures of adjustable networking provide flexible and speedy responses to the volatilities of demand and technology. But in none of these other cases is there quite the same kind of co-operativeness. On the surface, there is similarity; but under-standing requires going below that surface to the layer of motivation where the similarities break down.

One of the outcomes of the two primary cultural forces at work in the Chinese case is the inhibition preventing bureaucracy and the consequent perpetuation of personalism. Where power is legitimized by personal characteristics rather than by performance alone, and where trust is never entirely institutionalized but always also personalized, the growth of organizational scope is inhibited. The reasons for this are connected with the limits to organizational complexity introduced by the reliance on specific trusted employees to handle strategic matters. This inhibits organizational differentiation and decentralization of both vertical and horizontal kinds. Its effects are visible in the absence from world markets of household brand names originating in Chinese family businesses. The commonly referred to 'deal-making' mentality of the typical owner-man-ager tends to perpetuate mercantile capitalism in the system as a whole, and to inhibit large-scale industrial capitalism. OEM can make up for much of this gap, but the resulting pattern of industry outside that built with state sponsorship is arguably 'Chinese' in origin.

The institutional fabric of society in which modern economic organi-zations are embedded has a historic aspect as well as a modern form. Prior to the age of industrialization, many formative influences were at work to shape the way that patterns of business behaviour became adapted. Crucial among these was the patrimonial nature of the Chi-nese state and the consequent struggle of the merchant class to (i) work within a system in which government interference was often unpredict-able; (ii) deal with a status system in which the mandarin civil bureau-cracy was dominant; (iii) operate without clearly prescribed rights; and (iv) operate without reliable access to banking, business law or open information. The absence of a feudal tradition in which strong vertical bonding could lead to norms of loyalty and integration in society is marked, and illuminates one of the sharpest contrasts with Japan or Europe. The lack of decentralization typical of the patrimonial state also inhibited the emergence of a tradition of professional administra-tion below the level of that of the central state powers in the mandari-nate. Thus the idea of managerial skills as being worthy of acquisition in their own right was stifled. Administration in the world of business did not develop into the high status it acquired in Japan, whose feudal-based social history was so different.

The quality of administration within Chinese society historically was characterized by a proliferation of controls, all exercised by the mandarinate or other state officials, but with an absence of clearly codified specifications of rights and duties. Thus, interpretation of right and wrong was always a state monopoly, and outcomes of disputes were dependent on the mandarin's interpretation. State interference in the preserves of the businessman was always possible – for example, via taxes of various kinds, or by the non-negotiable announcement of what a vague law would be taken to mean. The status of the merchant traditionally was low. In such circumstances, a general sense of insecurity would be predictable, and with it the development of coping mechanisms. One of these was the extreme pragmatism in matters of money and the centrality of money in the value system, it being a surrogate for security. Such motivations would enhance the urge to control within the firm that is a common feature of managerial behaviour and would also explain the great care given to the cultivation of reliable surrounding bonds of connection and influence.

One of the features of Chinese tradition that has had a marked effect on organizations is the custom of partible inheritance. Unlike in Japan, where primogeniture allows family wealth to be preserved intact through generations, the Chinese tradition of constantly dividing it between heirs leads to the regular break-up of potential business dynasties. There are other reasons for this occurrence, such as internal family tensions that cannot be restrained after the loss of the uniting father role on his death. Both of these features tend to reinforce the tendency for Chinese business to form, grow, break up and reform, making the economy look like a constantly bubbling ferment of small pieces, with few large pieces surviving. That is not necessarily a negative situation, and in chosen industries it may well mean much higher overall efficiency than might occur with alternative structures. It may well account for the capacity of Hong Kong and Taiwan to produce national productivity gains ahead of Singapore, whose development policies began to marginalize the traditional family business sector in the 1970s and 1980s in preference to foreign multinationals. The Chinese firm itself, when viewed alongside the standard textbook ideal of progress by growth in scale, may fall short of Western ideals, although it is not a Western artefact. The unit of analysis that reveals its dynamism and efficiency is the collection of flexibly linked firms, membership of which may change over time for the good of the system as a whole. This is like the human body changing its cells, but continuing to function. As Penrose observed, a new theory of the firm may be needed to encompass this phenomenon.

The traditional institutions of Chinese society, some of which have been noted above, have left their traces. Closer to today's world lie another set of institutional influences whose role has been more direct. These are features of the industrialization process and they can only be described in particular political contexts because that is how they were formed and worked. The development histories of Taiwan, Hong Kong, Singapore and other Southeast Asian states have been very different from each other and they have left different economies in consequence. No explanation of the family businesses of Hong Kong, for example, is complete without taking account of (i) the government policy of 'positive non-intervention' adopted for several recent decades; (ii) the access via free market processes to information, standards, technology and price pressures from worldwide sources; (iii) the role of the traditional Western trading companies and Western-rooted banks in facilitating business; (iv) the weakness of the labour movement; (v) the provision of subsidized housing for half the population; and (vi) the form of education provided by the state and the resulting shape of the talent pool.

On the other hand, no explanation for Taiwan is complete without taking into account the effect of (i) fifty years of Japanese colonial rule; (ii) several decades of close ties with the USA; (iii) the involvement of the state in important sectors of the economy such as banking; (iv) the government's steering of industrial development – for example, in the creation of science parks; and (v) the role of advanced technical education in the USA for key players. One of the results is an industrial structure of a bipolar nature, with a number of huge firms and a vast number of smaller ones, many of which have subcontracting relations with the larger ones. Another outcome is a set of government–business relationships that are much closer and more active than those in Hong Kong, and which echo, if only faintly, the Japanese approach to political economy. No explanation for Singapore is complete without taking account of (i) the heavy involvement of the government in economic planning and direction; (ii) sponsorship of investment by large foreign firms; (iii) the shaping of the training and education infrastructure; (iv) government investment and risk-sharing in the economy; (v) the role of the Central Provident Fund in changing internal family dependencies; and (vi) the effects of subsidized housing on traditional social structures and attitudes. In other Southeast Asian states, various forms of crony capitalism have led to the selecting out of firms with high skills in political co-optation and the taking of the advantages that go with it. This is a risky game and requires agility to manage, as the 1997–8 crisis demonstrated. But when the data are in, they are likely to show a high level of survival capacity and risk hedging among those who adopted this set of opportunistic strategies.

Current institutional environments such as these are bringing change to these societies in ways that cause them to become different from each other. But the responses to such influences by family businesses have not been radical. Basic ideas about authority and co-operation remain both consistent and traditional among owner-managers throughout the Asian region as far as they affect the running of the firm (Redding, 1990). What these more modern institutional changes appear to have done is to reinforce the concern with personal control by the owner under the highly competitive environments induced by policies of *laissez faire*. Even in Taiwan and Singapore, where government involvement in the economy has developed strongly, it has still tended to leave the small-firm sector to its own devices and its own fate, and thus to perpetuate the traditional sense of anxiety about the longer term. The availability of access to viable commercial law does not appear to have altered Chinese beliefs in personalism as the guarantee of trust, or Chinese suspicions about the cost of lawyers.

The ensuing pattern of personal control perpetuates the tendencies to concentrate in particular fields and inhibits the growth of strong professional middle management and the decentralization of organizational power. Those firms that do expand tend to keep strategy-making as a family monopoly, to stay regional rather than global, to use alliances for the grafting on of competencies instead of growing them internally, and to rely heavily on the acumen of the owner in bringing into use the necessary capital and connections. Thus, the more fundamental firm characteristics are robust, and the overall climate of paternalism seems resilient in organizational cultures. Such resilience does not, however, mean that stagnation and adaptation take place to adjust to the conditions of modernization and successful development. The incorporation of technology by alliances, the use of a wider range of capital sources, some of which bring with them insistence on disclosure and adherence to international business norms, are two of the more obvious reactions (see Chapter 4 in this volume). This is still, however, a long way from a managerial revolution of the Western kind, in which radical shifts in ownership patterns are accompanied by important changes in managerial demographics, professionalization and empowerment.

## THE CHALLENGE OF GLOBALIZATION

Foreign direct investment into the Asia Pacific region in recent decades has been huge in quantity and has brought with it a wide array of influences (see the Introduction and Chapter 11 in this volume). So too have firms in the region connected increasingly with markets in the Western world and Japan. The two-way flows of communications have escalated to very high levels, and interdependencies have grown accordingly. The most dramatic manifestation of the new level of connectedness has been the international coalition to deal with the 1997–8 regional financial crisis. The work of the International Monetary Fund (IMF), among others, has brought in money for rescue operations, but in exchange for new patterns of conformity to what bankers see as universal norms of conduct especially in the fields of finance and risk management.

This process of decades of influence has also been affected by two other background features – knowledge codification and education – and by one specific business circumstance: the growth of strategic alliances. The codification of knowledge about organizing and managing economic activity has been a Western and, particularly during the twentieth century, a largely North American activity. The standard management textbook in any of the subdivisions of the field has tended to reach its most developed form in the USA, along with the institutions set up to convey such knowledge. Such institutions not only include business schools and degree structures, but also consultancy practices, the business media, and processes of professional training and certification. These forces of influence, often feeding off each other, have tended to spread the gospel of a certain acceptable way of organizing, even though there are constant shifts of emphasis and a proclivity to alter the details from time to time. 'Best practice' (and the inverted commas are important here) is more or less definable and regularly taken as authoritative in its original Western formulation.

The education of family business heirs is often a matter of exposing them to this paradigm. Many of them attend prestigious American or European schools of business or technology. They return to the firm with ideas that are often put to use in the family business. Illustrative examples here are the application of advanced stock control methods into a department store group by a returnee with a doctorate from Caltech in operations research, or a firm's entry into advanced telecommunications led by a returnee with a masters degree in electronic engineering. Other favourite educational fields are finance/accounting or the hard sciences. It is noticeable that none of this appears to change the most fundamental aspect of the firm's familistic nature, which is the retention of a monopoly on strategy-making by the owning coalition. Nor does it appear conducive to the spread of more participative management practices, or the retention of high-quality Western executives, although there are exceptions to this latter observation. In any case, it is an under-researched field and at the time of writing anecdotal impressions rather than data must be relied on. The general preference of the neutral professional outsider for avoiding the power dependencies of the Chinese family firm in favour of the more open systems of the Western multinational, is suggested by the high numbers of multinationals and the high levels of localization within them, at least at junior and middle-management ranks.

The growth of strategic alliances in the Asia Pacific region between large ethnically Chinese enterprises and foreign multinationals has been occasioned by the fertile combination of needs that are complementary. Generally speaking, what is normally needed by the outsider is a combination of (i) local market access; (ii) local political co-optation; and (iii) the ability to find and manage local skills. Such competences are commonly available from Chinese partners and usually in a well-developed state. What the Chinese firm is often seeking in return are (i) a major brand for local sale or access to Western/Japanese markets to sell what it makes; (ii) an injection of capital; and (iii) an injection of technical or managerial expertise, such as in production control, market research or financial systems. These competences are normally what the outsider would bring to the table. It is, then, not surprising that alliances have proliferated, and they have allowed many ethnically Chinese firms to transcend some of their organizational and technical limitations and to enter new fields, clearly visible examples being in telecommunications, pharmaceuticals, financial services, insurance, and hotels (see Chapter 4 in this volume).

The challenge of globalization now needs to be placed in context and against the simple empirical fact that the Chinese family business tends not to grow in scope even when it may grow in scale. Where it does extend beyond its normal range of organizational competence, it does so by alliance, not by the internal accretion of new organizational complexity and the internal differentiation of fields of action. A very important caveat here is that in certain contexts where markets are protected and the business environment is not fully open to world standards of competition, the demands for organizational efficiency and effectiveness are less and it is possible for conglomerate structures to grow on a large scale in such 'soft' conditions. Much organizational slack can be carried in circumstances such as this. These are in a sense the rewards of skilful political co-optation and they result from extremely well-judged strategic management of a kind not normally advocated or even discussed in the textbooks.

Even on this large scale, however, there is little decentralization of strategic decision-making power, and in most cases organizations retain a dependence on the intuition and accumulated industry knowledge of a single individual. Their growth in recent decades has tended to be regional rather than global. Apart from a spread of property investments internationally (see Chapter 9 in this volume) or of distribution facilities, they have not penetrated non-Asian markets or economies in any serious way except via membership of commodity chains and OEM. This is not to play down their record, which in fact has been formidable, but simply to say that the formula is not a repetition of the standard Western one – that is, the accumulation of increasing competence within the firm, the accretion of scale, the growth of the managerial skills needed for both differentiation and integration, and the decentralization of power via professionalism and objective control systems. There has been, for example (apart from the unusual case of Acer), no globally recognized consumer brand name emerging from a Chinese family enterprise. Three questions arise from this: Why is scope restricted? How are the limitations surmounted to achieve growth? How does the system adapt to perpetuate itself?

**Why is Scope Restricted?**

Mercantile capitalism is essentially deal-making. It rests on the search for capital accumulation via intelligent and/or opportunistic buying and selling. It is often set in a context where reliable cash-cows are incorporated into the firm as a source of stability and as a source of capital for risk-taking. This is an elegant combination. Arguably the deal-making works best in conditions where (i) decision-making can proceed at high speed; (ii) reliable information is a scarce and strategic resource; (iii) volatility or uncertainty provide opportunity spaces for exploitation; and (iv) opportunities exist for monopolies or oligoplostic cartels to be constructed to protect the cash-cows. This has been the environments in the region for some decades, and examples of the responses in operation have been the Hong Kong property cartel, the crony capitalism of several Southeast Asian states, and the covert business/military alliances that have often assisted the process of finding and taking opportunities in several countries.

In circumstances such as this, a concentration of organizational decision-making power is not only helpful, but necessary. Obligations have to be used and they only exist between individuals, as, for example, between ex-President Suharto and Liem Sioe Liong (see Chapter 4 in this volume). Also, the kinds of decision are often based on a judgement of risk and reward, which may take decades to nurture and much experience to learn from. Many ethnic Chinese CEOs have been working in an industry for forty or fifty years, and their awareness of its shifts and trends are highly informed. Lastly, much of the taking of such opportunities is a matter of the rapid focus of capital on one individual from among a group. That individual has to be 'magnetic' for such capital in the sense that s/he attracts it on the basis of his/her past record in deal-making and the subsequent sharing of benefits.

Organizations operating with such principles do not venture easily into unfamiliar fields, and their folklore is full of stories about the rash few who did. Sir Y. K. Pao with Dragonair, even the great Li Ka Shing with Husky Oil, and Sir Kenneth Fung's problems with his sons' experiments, are all object lessons to remind people of the value of focusing on what one understands. The end result is a high level of concentration on one field plus perhaps a related field – for example, property and construction – in the pattern of firm behaviour in the region. It is partly that the firm is dependent on one strategist and partly that the limitations on trust outside specific social ties limit the allocation of true responsibility to neutral professionals. These latter individuals might in other circumstances be leading ventures to proliferate the firm's fields of action, but here are constrained by the instinctive financial conservatism and the concern with control that so characterize the Chinese family boardroom.

### How Is Growth Achieved?

In the case of the large Chinese family firm, growth is achieved by a combination of opportunism in making capital gains plus the capture of cash-cows, usually in utilities or in a steady demand field such as food, commodities or transport. Rental from property is also a mainstay of these classic *rentier* capitalists. Opportunism is exercised overwhelmingly by property investment. Given the ease of entry, this has few international boundaries. It is, however, not a convincing case if one argues that having property in Toronto, Paris, London and Johannesburg, in addition to Hong Kong and Jakarta, makes a firm global in the normally accepted sense of the word (see Chapter 9 in this volume). Such investments can be made and sold from one desk with a good secretary, which can be located anywhere in the world. When Worldwide Shipping was the biggest company in the world in its field, it was still run in all its essentials with one map on the wall of the CEO's office and 200

administrators one floor below in central Hong Kong. Its global reach
was certainly geographical, but it is unconvincing to argue that it was
global in the sense that the firm incorporated highly diverse markets,
financial systems, employment practices, production systems, languages,
legal contexts and co-ordination challenges. Instead, a formula is sought
which can be standardized, and then replicated and operationally managed by subordinates.

Where real risks have been taken by large Chinese family firms, in the
form of heavy investments in industry – such as, for example, investments
in agribusiness and motorcycles by CP in China, these have been achieved
with high levels of government support. They also replicate a formula
perfected over decades, especially in poultry farming, and understood
on the basis of intense specialization combined with technical borrowing. With growth strategies of this nature, there is no doubt that Chinese family enterprises are capable of increasing their scale. But two
features conspire to prevent them from following the standard route to
the *Fortune 500* – first, the restriction of scope; and second, the retention of a family monopoly on strategy. In simple terms, even on a large
scale they remain family businesses. One could argue that this is not a
problem. By what logic are they *supposed* to become anything else? If
this introduces weakness in succeeding generations as the organization's psychological glue breaks down, they break up into sub-units, and
these sub-units then pursue growth to a comfortable size. So the system
in total continues to thrive on this version of creative destruction.

## System Adaptation

None of the several business systems of the ethnic Chinese are self-suf-
ficient or sealed against outside influence. Part of the process of their
evolution has been the incorporating of features from outside and
adaptation to such influences. Three of these influences could be argued
to have been liberating and two constraining. The liberating influences
have been (i) access to new capital via world financial markets, stock
markets and banks; (ii) access to world markets as trade has continued
to open – and crucially here the markets of the USA; and (iii) access to
new technology in both production and information and managerial
techniques in fields such as marketing, quality control, and accounting.
Examples of such influences at work are visible in the rationalizing of
the Hong Kong stock exchange in the late 1980s and its consequent
attraction of international investment; the transfer of technology into
the Taiwanese computer industry from the USA; the courting of multi-

nationals by the Singapore government; and the proliferation regionally of OEM in commodity chains reaching into Western markets.

What might be seen as constraining influences have been (i) the disciplines of disclosure that go with public accountability for capital use; and (ii) the internationalization of concern over 'uneven playing fields', cartels, corruption, cronyism, lack of democracy and lack of pluralism, all of which are seen by outsiders as contributing to the crisis of 1997–8 and all of which tend to create the kind of opportunity spaces that entrepreneurs are able to make use of. The steady increase in regulation, especially in financial markets, and the slow evolution of political empowerment, have meant that large regional enterprises have had to adopt new postures to be seen as legitimate. Typical adaptations have been detailed disclosure of public accounts, the conscious search for an image of professionalism and good management, and the employment of 'outsiders' in key positions at the interface with Western sources of capital or technology. Another adaptation in the cases of large firms, is the incorporation of a bank into the enterprise structure to act as a bridge into international capital markets. One of the main conduits of influence is the process of listing a firm: in this process, the firm is required to change, often quite radically, as a condition of listing. This price is paid because the listing itself makes family wealth suddenly both realizable and potentially expandable – attractions normally with great appeal to family members.

There are examples of firms that have combined Western structures of management, usually in discrete operating divisions, with Chinese control structures, to produce a hybrid form. Examples here would be the Hutchison group under Li Ka Shing, or First Pacific under Manny Pangilinan (and eventually Liem Sioe Liong). These are not pure types: they are not Chinese family businesses; and they are not Western-type multinationals either. They take the key characteristics of each and blend them. Such processes of adaptation are much more likely on a large scale rather than a small one, because the external pressures penetrate deeper via capital and technology provision and by alliances. In the small organization case, adaptation may be restricted to fields such as technology, which are fenced around within the organization. But as it is usually the large enterprises that expand internationally, this adapted form is worthy of note as a key vehicle.

The key to understanding the phenomenon is the structure for strategy-making in the enterprise and the related issue of control. Strategy tends to remain a family monopoly, and control remains centralized and tight. These are not normally given up; so whatever the organization grows into, it remains in its essentials a family possession, even under the conditions of hybridizing. It is not that large organizations are not produced – they patently are – but they are not outcomes of a Chinese equivalent to the managerial revolution whereby ownership becomes public, and control professional. They thus retain their inherent weaknesses, namely dependence on key individuals and fragility at times of succession. But, as argued earlier, *it does not matter*, because the system of Chinese capitalism as a whole remains robust. The understanding of Chinese family business is to acknowledge its changing nature, which is to say no more than that it is a normal social system. It has also to acknowledge that alongside Chinese culture there are a whole series of important determinants of its nature. Of these, the crucial ones are those institutions that have surrounded it during industrialization and modernization. But in the end, these too are embedded in Chinese culture and reflect the Chinese understanding of trust, identity and authority. The core system may have accreted new options and hybrids around it, but it has not yet changed deeply in its fundamentals.

# 3 Reciprocity and Control: The Organization of Chinese Family-Owned Conglomerates

Gary G. Hamilton

> Applying the generally accepted
> Aerodynamic principles it
> Became clear to them that
> Bees could not
> Fly.

> Wing-loading too high,
> Power-loading too high:
> No way.

> And since bees could not fly
> It followed obviously that they
> Could not collect pollen and nectar and
> Thus couldn't transmit
> Pollen from this flower to that.
> Therefore in a majority of instances
> Flowers couldn't exist.

> And just as obviously a bee that couldn't fly
> Couldn't exist.[1]

## INTRODUCTION

To poke fun at themselves and at their own branch of science, aeronautical engineers once proved that bees could not fly. With considerably more seriousness, organization specialists, applying sound principles of management, have demonstrated that Chinese family-owned firms cannot grow large and cannot undertake sizeable and complex projects. This reasoned conclusion leads to a second one: because Chinese firms cannot succeed in enterprises requiring scope or scale, those economies in which large Chinese family firms are found in some numbers must, therefore, be examples of 'ersatz capitalism' (Yoshihara, 1988) – speculative economies that are hollow at the core. This conclusion implies that an economy organized by Chinese firms cannot flower and bear the fruits of a capitalist way of life. Both conclusions, however, ignore the simple reality that Chinese family-owned firms do grow very large, that they do undertake sizeable and serious projects, and that the economies in which they exist have flourished in the last quarter of the twentieth century and will continue to flourish in the twenty-first. Like the allusion in Peyton Houston's wonderful poem, the impossibility of the existence of large Chinese family firms belies their success throughout much of the capitalist world. Clearly, there is a gap between theory and fact.

The financial crisis that humbled Asian economies in 1997 and 1998 made this gap even more obvious. The economies seemingly the most deeply affected by the crisis in East and Southeast Asian turn out, however, not to be Chinese-dominated economies at all, such as those in China, Hong Kong, Taiwan, or Singapore. Although these economies were certainly shaken, most of the firms and, more importantly, the basic economic institutions, remained sound. Instead, the big-firm economies of South Korea and Japan, the very epitome of capitalism in Asia, suffered the most, to their very cores, and sparing nothing – not even the banks, the biggest firms, or the integrity of the most prized economic institutions. The other set of hard-hit economies were those of Thailand, Indonesia and Malaysia, all economies that experienced huge inflows of foreign direct investments which created speculative property and manufacturing bubbles and encouraged firms to incur high debt levels. If ethnic-Chinese-dominated economies were really 'ersatz' economies, then this financial crisis should have revealed the fragility of large Chinese firms and/or Chinese-dominated economies. Instead, the very firms most susceptible to the currency fluctuations were those closest to the corporate ideal – the *chaebol* of South Korea and the bank-centred *keiretsu* of Japan, both consisting of large, state-of-the-art manufacturing and service-orientated firms.

The Asian crisis also reveals something else. It forces us to see that we cannot understand economies by looking solely at the nature of individual firms. We cannot understand the nature of individual firms unless we obtain a more encompassing view of how those firms fit into the organization of national, regional and global economies. The *chaebol* of South Korea have suffered greatly in the ongoing currency and credit crisis, not because their firms are large, but rather because the *chaebol* networks of firms are so heavily in debt to local and international banks and, through cross-shareholding, to other firms in the same network. The state has not only condoned this debt structure, it has actively encouraged it through its sponsorship of loan initiatives that guided *chaebol* into larger and ever more complex, capital-intensive manufacturing projects. Before the financial crisis, high levels of business group indebtedness and the state's control of the financial system were one of the means by which the state officials controlled the *chaebol*. With the crisis, however, this indebtedness, coupled with the bank's inability to extend credit any further because of a lack of liquidity, forced many *chaebol* firms into bankruptcy. In contrast, large Chinese-owned firms largely escaped bankruptcy because their economic strategies were relatively uninfluenced by state directives and their levels of debt were lighter and spread over a variety of financial sources, including substantial networks of co-owners. There is a good chance that most of the largest Chinese-owned firms will emerge from the Asian crisis on a sounder footing than they had before it occurred, but the same cannot be said of many of the largest firms in Japan and South Korea.

In this chapter, I want to rethink the conventional interpretations of the Chinese family firm and offer a new way to theorize it. I will argue that, when many management theorists think of the family firm, they think of the nature of families in general, and of Western families in particular. What they do not see is that familism in the Chinese context represents a way of organizing – a model of group formation – that can be quite flexible and may be applied to many different kinds of economic organization in many different contexts (see also Chapter 2 in this volume). In this chapter, I shall discuss the analytical dimensions of the Chinese family firm that make it an important, effective and highly resilient way of organizing spatially dispersed economic activities.

## THE CHINESE FAMILY FIRM AS AN OBJECT OF COMPARATIVE ANALYSIS

In the 1980s, journalists as well as academics raised the visibility of Chinese entrepreneurs by popularizing their achievements, calling them, among other things, the 'Lords of the Rim' (Seagrave, 1995; see also Abegglen, 1994; East Asia Analytical Unit, 1995; Fallows, 1995; Fukuyama, 1995;

Pan, 1991). Nearly every major news and business magazine (for example, *Time, The Economist, Far Eastern Economic Review*), and many newspapers (for example, *Los Angeles Times, San Jose Mercury, New York Times*) ran feature stories on Chinese entrepreneurs, valorizing the *guanxi* ties (personal connections) among them and the business networks founded on these ties. With the Asian business crisis of 1997, however, the tone of the articles about Chinese businesses changed almost overnight. The *guanxi* relationships that commentators had only a short time earlier praised so highly were now vilified. *Guanxi* suddenly became cronyism, and the economies where these relationships occurred were now used as examples of 'crony capitalism'. Amazingly, in the rush to criticize, all Asian firms were considered to be of the same hue. In regard to cronyism, Chinese networks from every location were tossed into the same conceptual morass as the Japanese and Korean networks.

The quickness to glorify (and the equal speed of the denouncement of) the interpersonal foundations of Chinese business suggests that most commentators have only a superficial understanding of Chinese business practices. One could criticize these analysts for failing to do their homework, but in truth there has been relatively little solid research on Chinese businesses. The relative absence of detailed empirical analyses of Chinese firms has encouraged analysts to adopt a general theoretical approach that often, relies, on making Eurocentric comparisons. As I alluded in Introduction, there is a substantial literature arguing that Chinese family firms are unsuitable organizations for advanced capitalist economies (for example, Yoshihara, 1988; Hwang, 1984; Redding, 1990; Fukuyama, 1995). This literature rests on assumptions about the intrinsic nature of capitalist enterprises that have been drawn from writings about the golden age of corporate capitalism in the USA (for example, Chandler, 1977, 1990). Held up against these models of Western capitalism, Chinese firms are found wanting. Family ownership, patriarchal authority, problems with succession, lack of professional management, weak employee loyalty, relative lack of research and development – these and other imputed traits convince many observers (for example, Redding, 1990, 1991; Fukuyama, 1995) that Chinese firms will remain small and temporary and will be incapable of generating a genuinely capitalist economy. Most specialists argue that in the next generation most Chinese businesses will either have to adopt Western corporate forms of organization and management (at which time, the theory goes, they will lose any distinctively Chinese quality) or be increasingly marginalized in a world of global corporations.

Although the conclusion reached from this comparison is widely held, the comparison itself is flawed on both sides. The Western side of the comparison is based on a now outdated conception of capitalist economies. The assumption is that what we call industrial capitalism is a relatively stable economic phenomenon, is global in its reach, and is compatible with only a few types of economic organization that are supposedly most efficient and capable of surviving in a competitive environment: namely, Western-style corporations. The most recent scholarship regarding the modern world economy, however, questions these assumptions. This research (for example, Hollingsworth and Boyer, 1997; Orrù et al., 1997) demonstrates that there are organizational differences among even geographically adjacent economies, such as the British, German and French forms of economic organization (at both the level of the firm and the economy as a whole), not to mention the differences between the more geographically dispersed Asian and Western forms of capitalism. This research (see, for example, Saxenian, 1994; Gereffi, 1994) also shows that organizational diversity exists in the same advanced capitalist locations – for example, in California's Silicon Valley, where large and small, local and foreign multinationals rub shoulders with recent startups. Finally, and most significantly, this research (see, for example, Piore and Sabel, 1984; Gereffi, 1994; Harrison, 1994) shows that a worldwide transformation in the global economy is under way, a transformation that is pushing firms towards the development of inter-firm networks and away from establishing vertically integrated production systems. If the vertically integrated corporation was ever such an organizational ideal that Chandler makes it out to be – and there are now plenty of studies questioning this conclusions (Fligstein, 1990; Roy 1997) – then that time has surely passed and new forms of organization, including inter-firm networks, have emerged. To compare the way Chinese firms operate in the late 1990s to a now defunct model of capitalist organization is surely a fallacious approach.

The Chinese side of the comparison is also flawed. Here, analysts assume greater coherence and more uniform qualities to Chineseness, the Chinese family, and the Chinese family firm than are in fact the case. In an interesting essay, Susan Greenhalgh (1994) argues that much of the literature about the Chinese family firm builds on an Orientalist view of the Chinese family. Citing her indebtedness to Said (1978), she writes (1994, p. 749) that an Orientalist discourse is 'a stereotype-filled discourse that constructs the Orient in terms of timeless essences and stresses the Orient's separation from and opposition to the West'. An Orientalist view of the Chinese family essentializes the traditional,

collectivist, and mutually beneficial nature of the Chinese family. Such
a view, borne of what Greenhalgh (1994, p. 749) calls 'armchair Sino-
logy', obfuscates the fact that at the core of the Chinese family are considerable inequalities in power between genders and between generations.
Even though specialists often represent the Chinese family firm as the
embodiment of an enduring, traditional and harmonious culture, the
Chinese family firm is in fact as Greenhalgh argues (1994, p. 750), a
'political infrastructure' in which 'power differentials ... lie behind the
disparities in economic roles and rewards in the family business'. To the
extent that Greenhalgh is correct, and I believe she is, then Chinese
family firms are not remnants of the past, but rather are active social
constructions in the present, constructions having economic as well as
social purposes. Viewed this way, Chinese entrepreneurs knowingly
draw on those institutional resources available to them, such as the
organizing principles for the Chinese family, to create economically
active groups that they can control on the basis of familial authority. In
this sense, families and family firms are not concrete phenomenon to
be analyzed as objects, but rather are processes to be understood
dynamically.

Although Greenhalgh's essay helps to de-objectify the Chinese family and situate any consideration of Chinese families in specific times
and places, it begs the question about interpreting the family as political
infrastructure. There may be 'no place beyond power' (Greenhalgh,
1994, p. 768, quoted from Kondo, 1990, p. 305), but we should ask, 'What
is this system of power that creates and legitimizes such power differences between the genders and the generations?' This question is important because these inequalities, by Greenhalgh's own admission (1994,
p. 769), constitute some of the most overlooked 'features of contemporary life' in Chinese society, widespread in their occurrence and pervasive in their effects. These inequalities obviously do not result from the
naked use of force, with elders and males exacting compliance in each
and every instance of activity. Instead, this is a system of power, in
which such inequalities are normatively (but not necessarily personally)
accepted as legitimate and are intersubjectively understood, regardless
of whether specific people consider the inequalities to be morally right
or wrong. Moreover, as a mode of organizing the economy, this system
of power is not restricted to family members alone, but cognitively situ-
ates, in an organized matrix of activity, those within and outside family-
owned firms.

If indeed both sides of the comparison are flawed, then research on
the Chinese family firm should not be based on a Western ideal of busi-

ness organization, however implicitly such a comparison might be made. The negative question about how and why Chinese firms depart from a Western ideal simply will not lead to a genuine understanding of how Chinese-owned firms do, in fact, operate in the late-twentieth-century world economy.[2] Instead, we should try to understand Chinese firms in their own right, including diversity among them – and then (and only then) begin to make contrasts with non-Chinese firms. This procedure is the only way to specify whatever, if any, distinctive features Chinese firms may have *vis-à-vis* other possible categories of firms.

## THE INNER AND OUTER MANIFESTATIONS OF CHINESE PATRIARCHAL CONTROL

If we conceive of Chinese firms as being organized through a system of power based on family organizational principles, then we should recognize from the outset that they are not in some way mirror images of Western firms. Instead, they rest on socially accepted organizational principles that have no necessarry correspondence to the organizational principles found in Western societies (Hamilton, 1994). Fei Xiaotong (1992 [1947]), one of founders of a non-Eurocentric social science, described the principles of Chinese social organization earlier and more insightfully than anyone else has done. His theory is not deduced from a general theory of society, but rather is drawn from a deep and specific understanding of Chinese society gained from many years of fieldwork and study. In order to theorize his understanding of Chinese society, he contrasts Chinese and Western patterns of social organization heuristically. This technique allows him to accent certain features of Chinese social organization that would be obscured were there no comparisons at all, or were the comparisons mainly to establish a universally applicable, variable-based theory of social organization (Fei, 1992, pp. 7–8).

According to Fei, as well as many subsequent researchers whose work supports Fei's theory (Chen, 1994; King, 1991), the organizational principles[3] of Chinese society are social and relational rather than personal and jurisdictional, as they are in the West. Recognizing that both Chinese and Western societies share all four characteristics, Fei argues that the basic building blocks of Chinese society consist of differentially categorized social relationships. Individuals in Chinese society evaluate who they are and how they manoeuvre in relation to others by cognitively juxtaposing their ongoing social interactions with a grid of predefined categories of social relationships that normatively define the identities and the social responsibilities of those with whom they are interacting. Fei calls this consensually validated framework of action '*chaxugeju*,' which I have translated as 'differential mode of association' (Fei, 1992). The characteristic feature of the differential mode of association is that every dyadic relationship between ego and another person is constrained by a distinctive set of normative expectations. Those relationships closest to ego, such as one's relationship to a father or mother, are the most precisely defined, the most demanding, and the most hierarchical. Those relationships less immediate, but yet still familiar, such as with a classmate or a person from one's hometown, are framed by qualitatively different sets of expectations. Those relationships still more remote from ego, such as the impersonal relationships between a storeowner and a customer, are constrained by still different sets of expectations. Fei uses an analogy to characterize this pattern of social organization, that of ripples resulting from throwing a rock into a pool of water. In this analogy, ego stands at the point where the rock hits the water. The resulting rings of ripples closest to where the rock hits the water are the strongest, signifying the sets of relationships that require the most attention. As the rings move further out they grow weaker, signifying sets of relationship that are less demanding. And the point where the rings disappear altogether signifies the end of moral demands on ego.

Kwang-kuo Hwang (1987), in theorizing the framework of action in Chinese society, has divided these sets of relationships into three categories. Those closest to ego are defined as 'expressive ties', indicating those relationships that are emotionally as well as normatively binding. Those relationships furthest from ego are defined as 'instrumental ties' and are governed by a utilitarian calculus. Between the two extremes, according to Hwang, is a large and extremely significant category of diverse relationships that he identifies as 'mixed ties'. Hwang, following colloquial Chinese, identifies an activated mixed-tie relationship by the term *guanxi*, literally meaning 'relationship' or 'connection'. Examples of such possible *guanxi* include relations between distant relatives, classmates, neighbours, colleagues, teachers and students, people coming from the same hometown, or any other particularistic trait of similarity. When activated, these relationships combine elements of both extremes, of a certain amount of expressiveness and a clear-eyed means –end orientation. If one or both of the parties to a mixed tie chooses not to engage in a relationship, the mixed tie is dormant, requiring few to nil demands on either person.

Should the two parties agree, a mixed tie relationship can be activated so that the tie between the two individuals is mutually constrained by what Hwang calls 'the rule of *renqing*' (Hwang, 1987, p. 953). *Renqing* literally means human emotion. As Hwang (1987, pp. 953–4) describes it, however, *renqing* has three different meanings that make it, when applied to a mixed tie relationship, into a very complex principle of interaction. First, it means an empathic understanding of the 'emotional responses of an individual confronting the various situations of daily life'. Second, it means a gift that one gives in recognition of the emotionally-defined situation of the other. Hwang (1987, p. 954) writes that 'in Chinese society, when one has either happy occasions or difficulties, all one's acquaintances are supposed to offer a gift or render some substantial assistance. In such cases, it is said that they send their *renqing*'. Third, *renqing* identifies a 'set of social norms by which one has to abide to in order to get along well with other people in Chinese society'. These norms are the rules of reciprocity. 'A good person', writes Yunxiang Yan (1996b, p. 123; see also 1996a) in her extensive study of *guanxi* and *renqing* in a Chinese village, 'always interacts with others (with whom you have a mixed tie) in a reciprocal way. This reciprocity is characterized by the obligation of giving, receiving, and returning gifts in the long run'. So significant are these norms of reciprocity and the social relationships they spawn that they form the organizational medium through which Chinese society is constituted (Fei, 1992; King, 1985, 1991; Kipnis, 1997; Hamilton, 1991b; Yan, 1996a and b; Chen, 1994; Lui, 1998). In the words of Douglas North (1990), this organizational medium provides the 'rules to the game' for Chinese society.

For the purposes of this chapter, the important point is that family relationships (defined as those within a household or *jia*) are defined in terms of *xiao* (filial piety or obedience) and not *renqing*. Close relationships with people outside the family are defined through rules of *renqing* and not *xiao*. Both *xiao* and *renqing* define sets of obligations, and hence both represent forms of authority, but the two sets of obligations are quite different. Whereas relationships defined in terms of *xiao* are hierarchical, the relationships defined in terms of *renqing* are, in principle, horizontal in nature. Applying this very brief discussion of the sociology of Chinese society to our analysis of the Chinese family, we can now define analytically the principal axis of power and authority. The head of the Chinese household, normally the eldest male, has a position of patriarchal authority *vis-à-vis* others within the household, but his patriarchal power does not normatively extend beyond the members of the household. Instead, the patriarch's connection to others outside the household is defined in terms of the norms of reciprocation. With this distinction between inner and outer aspects of patriarchal control in mind, we can now examine the intra- and inter-firm organization of Chinese family businesses.

## THE THREE-WAY DISTINCTION BETWEEN OWNERSHIP, MANAGEMENT AND CONTROL

The organization of Chinese businesses is shaped by the three-way distinction between ownership, management and control. In most small Chinese-run businesses, especially those with modest capital requirements, ownership, management and control are usually concentrated within a single family, even though some informal division of labour would probably exist between husband, wife and children. As Chinese-run firms grow larger and the business requirements become more complex, the three-way distinction between ownership, management and control becomes more formalized and is institutionalized in work routines and organizational design. Although it does not always work this way in practice, in principle, as firms grow larger and more complex, ownership is shared, management is segmented, and control is centralized.

### Ownership Networks

During the course of the nineteenth century, the practice of forming limited companies based on British corporate law was adopted in and diffused throughout China.[4] Since that time, most Chinese entrepreneurs have raised the capital required to start their businesses by splitting the ownership of firms between family and non-family members. The founder of the business might claim a founder's share, often 51 per cent, based on his willingness to use his own and his family's labour to run the business. The actual investment capital, however, might be raised from a network of people, including family members, more distant kinsmen, and usually friends (and friends of friends) who are linked to the founder through a series of connections. This practice allows the ownership of firms to be spread across the social landscape, to be an aspect of *renqing*, and to be based on the norms of reciprocity (Chen, 1995). Accordingly, at some later time, when another person in the interconnected networks needs investment capital, the founder of the first business would feel obligated, according to the norms of reciprocity, to invest money in that firm. This is so much the case that some analysts have viewed Chinese business networks as being founded on mutual indebtedness (Wickberg, 1965; Tien, 1953; Geertz, 1963; Mark, 1972; Limlingan, 1986, pp. 86–93; DeGlopper, 1995, pp. 204–14; Numazaki, 1991a, 1991b, 1997; Chen, 1994, pp. 75–106; Chen, 1995). The pool of shared capital is circulated within the interconnected networks, raising the capacity of everyone in the networks to succeed. Because each person's success depends on the trustworthiness of everyone else, the network rests on mutual reputation in the past, mutual trust and mutual surveillance in the present, and the possibility of mutual sanctions in the future. Although such ownership networks are personal, they are also strictly instrumental.

Studies of Taiwanese businesses provide some good examples of the structure of shared ownership. In Chen Chieh-hsuan's extensive research (1994, 1995; see also Winn, 1994) of small and medium-sized firms in Taiwan, he shows that most small businesses rely on capital raised by borrowing from one's network of family and friends. Sometimes local businesspeople use rotating credit associations to raise money; and sometimes they ask for personal loans from distant family members and from their networks of friends and colleagues. Entrepreneurs will engage in this practice even if they have sufficient money to start a firm, simply in order to establish a network of alliances built on reciprocity, which is cemented through building credit relationships. The same basic ownership structure also exists for the largest Taiwan business groups (Hamilton, 1997; Semkow, 1994). Every firm in a population of the almost 800 firms that make up Taiwan's 100 largest business groups is owned by a discrete set of owners.[5] Within individual business groups, there is considerable overlap among principal shareholders, but a remarkably little overlap among shareholders between business groups. This finding demonstrates, as Numazaki (1991a, 1991b) and others (Mark, 1972; Greenhalgh, 1988) also observed, the importance of personal networks in the growth of Taiwan's capitalist economy.

This manner of raising investment capital begs the question of whether the capital raised through family, friends and colleagues represents 'ownership' in the Western sense of the term. In the West, ownership connotes 'property rights' which confer the right of control. In the case of Chinese firms, control is distinguished from ownership. In fact, most owners in a limited partnership usually regard themselves as 'silent partners' who have a claim only on the money loaned (and on the relationship signified by the loan) and not on the actual control of the business.[6] The exceptions to this prove the rule. In recent times, this shareholder/

entrepreneur relationship has been altered by the development of equity markets institutionalized on the basis of Western laws, which specify the rights of the shareholders to control management. In such cases, founding entrepreneurs are very aware of the necessity to maintain 50 per cent ownership, and, while lacking the necessary capital, have developed a number of shareholding schemes to maintain control. The most common of such strategies is to pool borrowed capital in one or more privately-held, limited-partnership firms that in turn own enough publicly-offered shares that, when added to the founder's and the founder's family's shares, will give the entrepreneur undisputed control.

In this setting, therefore, ownership of shares does not confer property rights. What this system of shared ownership does confer, however, is a relational foundation for creating very complex networks that are themselves useful for other business purposes (Chen, 1994, 1995; Limlingan, 1986; Numazaki, 1991a, 1991b; Shieh, 1992; Jamann, 1994; Yeung, 1997b) Often, the principal investors will also be associated with the founder through other types of business relationships – for example, through subcontracting or distribution linkages. Equally important, a system of shared ownership based on reciprocity facilitates the flow of information about entrepreneurial opportunities, which helps to explain the speed with which Chinese production and distribution networks can shift the location of operations or product lines (Landa, 1994; Hsing, 1998; Pack, 1992).

**The Separation between Management and Control**

Making ownership a function of reciprocal networks separates ownership from the internal organization of family-owned enterprises. In family enterprises, where the boundaries between households and firms are ambiguous, hierarchical obedience based on the norms of filial piety (*xiao*) is the normative expectation. These expectations are most evident when the firms are small and use mainly the labour of household members. In such cases, enterprise management and control overlap with the principles of household management and control. Within families, wives often manage the households and track the accounts. Similarly, Kao Cheng-shu and his colleagues (Kao, 1999) shows that in Taiwan in small and medium-sized firms, the wife of the owner typically manages the labourers or keeps the firm's books; often doing both. The husband controls the allocation of resources; he decides where and how to invest, and he maintains his *guanxi* connections with his network of friends and colleagues, which is often a time-consuming and expensive activity. Several studies on corporate kinship units in South China show that a similar split between management and control occurs within lineage corporations too (Cohen, 1976; Faure, 1989). The eldest male members of the lineage control lineage resources and make long-term allocation of resources. Day-to-day management of lineage lands and enterprises is in the hands of junior members of the lineage.

The same distinction between day-to-day management and long-term control over resources also applies to large firms (Lasserre, 1988). In fact, the distinction goes to the core of how very large family enterprises typically are run. Management and control are institutionalized as two different kinds of tasks. On the one hand, day-to-day management requires a close relationship between employers and employees that duplicates the pattern of authority within households. Typically, this situation is best achieved in small groups, where the persons in charge (*laoban*) or their representatives forms fictive kinship ties with non-family members for purposes of control. To create such ties, the husband or wife may utilize generation and gender inequality as a way to increase the obedience of employees. Entrepreneurs may hire non-household kinsmen and the sons and daughters of friends and neighbours to enhance their management of work. Employment in such small firms can be very oppressive and exploitive to everyone concerned, particularly the family members of the owner, as Greenhalgh (1994) rightly notes (see also Gates, 1987; Shieh, 1992).

As firms grow larger or more complex, however, patriarchy becomes particularly onerous to those who have no relationship to the owner. In Taiwan, for example, high rates of employee turnover and the clear preference to own one's own firm is an indication of the tension between owners and non-family employees (Shieh, 1992). This problem of how to create a management structure in larger firms is typically solved in two ways. First, heads of the family businesses may segment their holdings by creating a number of small and medium-sized firms instead of one large firm. The entrepreneurs then create a management hierarchy that best suits each of the firms they own. This duplication of the management hierarchy (Hamilton, 1997) means that entrepreneurs would have distinct administrative positions in each firm. Second, should the firms be large enough (or the tasks complex enough), the entrepreneurs would possibly also hire trained managers to be in charge of day-to-day management. The segmentation of family holdings into several independent firms, and the lack of any unified command structure, make it very difficult for professional managers to assume a higher level of control than that of the management of labour and the work process.

While management is segmented, control over family resources is centralized. Owners typically take control of their firms by centralizing personnel and accounting functions, particularly the allocation of money (Lasserre, 1988; Semkow, 1994; Yeung, 1997). One businessman, quoted by Tong Chee Kiong (1991, p. 181), nicely illustrates this form of centralization:

> My father made all the decisions when he was alive. He formed a board to help run the business; this board made the decisions. But this was only in name. In actuality my father made all the decisions himself still, especially in non-technical matters like investment, getting loans, negotiations with banks, finance companies, suppliers and so on. But consulted the rest in very technical things. Anyway, he had the last say. After all, the business was his. Even when we, his children, had any suggestions, we had to go through our father's friends first because my father felt that as head of the family, he was to be obeyed at all times.

The centralization of major decisions and the control of budgets allow owners to assume personal, and perhaps patriarchal, control over family assets. This form of centralization gives heads of family businesses the deal-making capabilities for which the Chinese are so well known. It also helps to explain the flexibility and speed with which Chinese businesses can transfer assets and start new operations. Because the family head is also the person who has the responsibility of extending horizontal ties beyond the family, many of these transactions involve opportunities generated through networks of friends, and friends of friends.

Although an owner may assume personal control, these assets are not his alone. They are the long-term possessions of families and not individuals, and, if the patriarchal principle of inheritance is followed, the assets will be split equally among the entrepreneur's sons after his death (*fenjia*) (Wong, 1985). This principle of partible inheritance pushes heads of family businesses toward starting multiple firms, which can later be divided among the family, instead of expanding the size of existing firms. However, as I explain elsewhere (Hamilton, 1997), partible inheritance is only one of many pressures in Chinese-dominated economies that favour segmentation over concentration of assets. Ironically, the business strategy of 'not putting all your eggs in one basket' reinforces the importance of a centralized decision-making, which in turn supports the personal and patriarchal characteristics of Chinese business organization.

## The Tension between Inner and Outer Aspects of Family-Owned Businesses

As the preceding discussion makes clear, entrepreneurs face an ongoing tension between managing the labour and resources inside the firm and obtaining the resources and opportunities necessary for the family assets to grow outside it. On the one hand, Chinese entrepreneurs use the principle of *xiao* (best conceptualized in this context as 'obedience to patriarchy') to organize the inner (*nei*) realm of their business. Using the principles embodied in *xiao*, Chinese entrepreneurs want to manage and control their own businesses and the long-term fate of those businesses on an authoritative basis that is apart from both the demands of family members and business colleagues. If businesses grow large, entrepreneurs often elect to subdivide their firms, through creating internal divisions and hiring professional managers, or through starting independent firms that re-concentrate the entrepreneur's authority and create a new profit centre.

On the other hand, using their family-centred resources, Chinese entrepreneurs attempt to organize the outer (*wai*) realm based on the norms of reciprocity (*renqing*) in order to create, and maintain themselves within, wider structures of opportunity. In Chinese-dominated economies, this outer realm of inter-personal and inter-firm relationships is as important, if not more so, as an inner system of control, because it is in this outer realm that business people establish the business networks that make Chinese enterprises so dynamic. The success of large Chinese family-owned enterprises comes from their ability to solve these basic problems of internal and external organization of the firm: that is, to make this tension between the inner and outer business activities into a source of entrepreneurship. In the concluding section of this chapter, I want to illustrate how this tension is manifested when Chinese entrepreneurship has become more global in recent decades.

## CONCLUSION: THE GLOBALIZATION OF CHINESE FAMILY ENTERPRISES

Bees do fly, and Chinese businesses do grow large and complex, and do function well in the modern world. The size and complexity of Chinese businesses, however, are deceptive phenomena, largely because Western concepts of vertical and horizontal integration do not apply very well to the expansion of Chinese business. Conglomeration is a more appropriate concept, but that too does not clarify Chinese business strategy. The important dimensions of Chinese businesses involve the personal nature of the relationships both inside and outside the firms. Networks inside the firm embody the hierarchical patriarchal principle requiring personal obedience to the *laoban*. Outside the firm, collegiality and reciprocity define networks. These linkages, too, are highly personal. Therefore, when Chinese entrepreneurs want to expand their assets locally, they do not necessarily expand the size or geographical boundaries of their existing firms, but rather they diversify by starting new firms and creating new alliances. The form of expansion is perhaps best called 'opportunistic diversification' (Hamilton and Kao, 1990; Hamilton, 1997).

This same general strategy of investment is followed when the Chinese expand their business interests across national boundaries. In recent decades, Chinese entrepreneurs, considered as a group, have been major foreign investors in many Asian economies. For example, the Chinese outside China (including Hong Kong Chinese) have invested considerably more than any other group in China (Naughton, 1997). Before the 1997–8 Asian economic crisis, ethnic Chinese FDI (primarily from Taiwan and Hong Kong) equalled or exceeded Japanese investment in many Southeast Asian countries, and was considerably beyond the level of investment of the USA and the countries of Europe (Chung, 1997). The Chinese patterns of globalization, however, differ considerably from the patterns of Japanese and Western foreign direct investments. There are, of course, many variations within all these patterns, but there are also recurring themes. In this conclusion, I will list five of these recurring themes of Chinese global investments that have been observed in the last decade. The sociology of the Chinese firm, which I have outlined above, explains these recurring patterns better than alternative explanations.

First, the general pattern of FDI for Japanese and Western corporations is for the largest firms to globalize first. Smaller firms may expand later, if at all. The general pattern of FDI for Chinese firms is for the *small and medium-sized firms* to globalize first, to be followed later, if at all, by the largest business groups. This pattern of expansion for Chinese firms is particularly pronounced for Taiwan- and Hong Kong-based firms (Naughton, 1997; Dobson and Chia, 1997; Chen *et al.*, 1995; Hsing, 1998).[7] This pattern of globalization is largely explained by the fact that networks of small and medium-sized firms in Hong Kong and Taiwan can mobilize resources more quickly and respond faster to consumer demand than can large firms. As a consequence, they gradually became the primary export manufacturers, and the large firms gradually became the suppliers of intermediate parts and services for export production to the smaller firms (Hamilton, 1997; Liu *et al.*, 1993). When currency inflation after 1985 began to undermine the export competitiveness of Taiwan- and Hong Kong-based firms, the small firms quickly relocated to Southeast Asia, and in particular to the People's Republic of China, where they could employ less expensive labour (Hsing, 1998). The success of the small and medium-sized firms and the rapidity of their response are largely explained by the sociology of Chinese family firms. The success of the small and medium-sized firm sector arises from the Chinese capability of mobilizing entrepreneurial resources through horizontal networks (see also Chapters 4 and 6 in this volume). The rapidity of response is largely explained by the entrepreneur's centralized deal-making ability, which is a characteristic of an economy organized through patriarchally-controlled family firms.

Second, when Western and Japanese corporations expand overseas, they expand existing firms geographically and organizationally by creating branches, subdivisions or joint ventures. When Chinese entrepreneurs globalize, they start *new and independent firms*. These patterns of expansion for Chinese firms seem to be true regardless of whether these independent firms extend or relocate an existing business originally started elsewhere or represent a completely new business venture. In the new location, the firms typically constitute new sets of owners and often establish new sets of business alliances that will be useful in the future. While certainly not universally true, this generalization seems to hold for all sizes of firms. For example, the global expansion of the Charoen Pokphand Group (CP Group) is typical of most Chinese large enterprises groups (Brown, 1998; Hamilton and Waters, 1997; Yeung, 1999a). Owned by ethnic Chinese, the CP Group is the largest multinational business group in Thailand and one of the largest single investors in China. Before the group consolidated somewhat during the Asian economic crisis, it consisted of 250 companies worldwide, 130 of which were located in China (*Far Eastern Economic Review*, 23 January 1997, p. 38). The CP pattern of global expansion is to start new, independently-owned companies for each business venture in each location. The network of owners differs for each company, even though there remains a similar core set of owners across all companies, centring on the personal holdings of CP's chairman, Dhanin Chearavanont. A number of researchers (Chen *et al.*, 1995; Dobson and Chia, 1997; Hsing, 1998; Liu *et al.*, 1993) have observed similar patterns for smaller firms as well, but without noting their significance from a comparative point of view. This pattern arises as a consequence of the internal and external organization of Chinese firms. New companies represent distinctive sets of external (*wai*) alliances (and thus a distinctive network of owners) that the entrepreneurs put together from their social and economic community. Once established, however, companies also manifest the entrepreneurs' desire to establish their personal authority inside (*nei*) the company by creating clear relationships linking workers and managers to the entrepreneurs (see also Chapter 11 in this volume).

Third, most overseas investments take the form of *personal investments* rather than corporate ones. Therefore, very large family holdings are possible, even though the sizes of the constituent firms may be modest. The personal nature of deal-making and overseas investment has been noted by many observers of Chinese family enterprises (Lasserre, 1988; Redding, 1990; Numazaki, 1997; East Asia Analytical Unit, 1995; Sender 1991; Tong and Yong, 1998; and Kao, 1993). As explained above, the personal quality of many investments reflects the combination of centralized patriarchal control (*nei*) and of the entrepreneurial importance of external *guanxi* networks (*wai*) for creating economic opportunity. This pattern of investment tends to de-emphasize the importance of firms, and stresses the significance of family assets. The goal of the entrepreneur is to increase family assets and make them continue and increase across generations. The continuity and importance of firms is secondary to the continuity of family assets (see also Chapter 9 in this volume).

Fourth, because most overseas ventures represent distinct alliances, with capital or with labour, in the long run most overseas ventures will probably become *grounded in the local economy*. Several analysts (for example, Chen *et al.*, 1995; Dobson and Chai, 1997) have observed that when Chinese entrepreneurs invest in enterprises outside their home society, the new firms tend to 'assimilate' quickly into the local economy. In the case of Taiwan, entrepreneurs investing in Southeast Asia and China, researchers have found that, before moving, the entrepreneurs were involved in Taiwan-based networks of production. Once these entrepreneurs invested in a factory overseas, they could not fully duplicate the old network in the new location. Therefore the owners tended to develop larger and more vertically integrated firms in the new location (Chen *et al.*, 1995; Hsing, 1998). Even so, the entrepreneurs have to draw heavily on local labour, local capital and local connections to facilitate their control of the new economic environ-ment, and this local embeddedness quickly leads to lessening ties back to Taiwan and deepening relationships in the new locale.

Fifth, most Chinese entrepreneurs with extensive overseas invest-ments develop *diversified investment strategies* by investing in different kinds of projects in different locations. This strategy resembles the careful management of a portfolio of distinct investments rather than a strategy of creating a large corporate presence, which is characteristic of most Western and Japanese entrepreneurship. Many journalists and scholars have noted the global diversity achieved by all the heads of the largest Chinese owned conglomerates (Lasserre, 1988; East Asian Analytic Unit, 1995; Seagrave, 1995; Sender, 1991; Kao, 1993; Yeung, 1999a). For example, Y. K. Pao, Li Ka-Shing, Robert Kuok, Chin Sophon-panich, Dhanin Chearavanont, Wang Yung-chi, Tsai Wan-lin, and Liem Sioe Liong, to name just a few of the best known Chinese entrepreneurs, all have global investments in many firms and are listed among the world's richest men. Their assets, however, are not concentrated in any one firm, but rather spread across many firms in different business in many dif-ferent global locations. This same pattern is not the exception, but rather the rule for Chinese entrepreneurs who invest globally.

A sociology of Chinese business also helps to explain this pattern. In Chinese-dominated societies, the medium for organizing the economy is a family-centred system of social relationships. In such an economy, measures of economic success are the size and composition of family assets and their ability to be passed down through the generations. Diversi-fied assets are typically less risky than assets concentrated in one loca-tion. Long-term diversification is particularly advantageous, because partible inheritance practices undermine the short-term advantages of enlarging the firm to achieve economies of scope and scale. One key to successful diversification is to gain access to information, and material and fiscal resources through establishing and maintaining reciprocal relationships with a wide circle of friends and colleagues. These recip-rocal relationships, in turn, facilitate the development of many different kinds of business opportunity.

In this chapter, I have argued that the modal form of organizing Chi-nese family enterprises combines centralized internal controls within firms based on patriarchy, and external controls of the economic envir-onment through establishing resource-rich networks based on recipro-city. This form of enterprise is not a type of organization, but rather a mode of organizing. It is a process as much as a configuration. As a mode of organizing, it is highly flexible, suitable for both large and small firms. This family mode of organizing business is temporally dynamic; it adapts to changing business conditions and to changing times. Economically and geographically, it is expansive, capable of generating complex networks. As a rule, these economic networks are more attuned to commercial and light industrial endeavours than to heavy industry. But this type of networking has also been proved itself to be highly competitive in such globalized sectors as high technology, including the capital-intensive semiconductor industry (Zhou, 1996; Saxenian, 1998; see also Chapter 8 in this volume). It is clear, therefore, that Chinese family firms are not just temporary phenomena that will fade away with modernization and with the spread of Western science and technology, but rather will embody flexible techniques to establish what are, in the final analysis, essentially non-bureaucratic business organizations.

## Notes

1. 'Impossibility of the Bee', Petyon Houston, 1985.
2. For a discussion of the appropriate uses of negative questions in comparative, historical sociology, see Hamilton (1985).
3. I define 'organizational principles' in a very simple way as the institutional means or medium by which groups of people are put in contact with one another.
4. This conclusion comes from the dissertation research of Wei-Keung Chung, whose work is still in process. Also see Kirby (1995).
5. The ownership data examined in Hamilton (1997) was for 1983, but the same holds true in Taiwan at the time of writing (China Credit Information Service, 1998).
6. This is a very old practice that has continued into the late 1990s. See Anonymous (1887).
7. By contrast, in Southeast Asia, the largest Chinese-owned enterprise groups are the ones most likely to globalize, mainly because the largest groups form the linkage between local business and foreign ventures.

# 4 The Dynamics of the Globalization of Chinese Business Firms[1]

Henry Wai-chung Yeung

## INTRODUCTION

Globalization is a dynamic process through which activities at different places and regions are increasingly integrated on a global scale. Since the 1960s, the world economy has been globalizing to a much greater extent than before (Ohmae, 1990; Dunning, 1993b; Dicken, 1998; Hirst and Thompson, 1996). The basic driving force behind this ongoing process of globalization is transnational corporations (TNCs) and their cross-border foreign direct investment (FDI). To date, many ethnic Chinese business firms from Hong Kong, Taiwan and Southeast Asian countries have ventured into different locations within the Asia Pacific region. They are rapidly becoming major players in the regional marketplace. Recently, some of them are even globalizing their commercial and manufacturing operations to become a worldwide competitor in such business fields as electronics and garment manufacturing, property development, financial services, hotel chains and so on. The globalization of Chinese business firms from Asia has become more real than ever.

This chapter aims to examine the changing nature of this globalization of Chinese business firms. My argument is that the globalization of Chinese business firms can be explained by an amalgamation of multi-dimensional dynamic processes and cannot therefore be narrowed down to any single factor. In explaining the globalization of Chinese business firms, we need to pay as much attention to the *firm-specific strategies* as to the *changing contexts* in which these business firms are embedded and their strategies are implemented. As such, a comprehensive explanation of their globalization needs to examine the changing configurations of their operating contexts and globalization strategies. Another important point is that some of these configurations of contexts and strategies are *historically-* and *geographically-specific*. They are historically-specific because the globalization of Chinese business firms is very much a recent phenomenon (see Kao, 1993); they are geographically-specific in that Chinese business firms are largely associated with the overseas Chinese diaspora and their geographical concentration in several Asian countries. The configurations of explanatory contexts and strategies for the globalization of Chinese business firms therefore may not be applicable to explaining the globalization of other business firms. It is as important to examine their firm-specific strategies as to situate them in peculiar historical and geographical contexts.

This chapter is based on a detailed survey of the existing literature on 'Third World multinationals' (see Yeung, 1994a, 1994b) and overseas Chinese business (Redding, 1990; Brown, 1995; East Asia Analytical Unit, 1995; Hodder, 1996; Weidenbaum and Hughes, 1996; Orrù *et al.*, 1997; Haley *et al.*, 1998). The next section examines the changing dynamics of Chinese business firms by discussing the global, regional and national contexts of their globalization processes and the changing institutional configurations of Chinese business systems. The third section is concerned with the globalization strategies of Chinese business firms. A model of geographic expansion is proposed and the historical geography of the internationalization of Chinese business firms is analyzed. The section further considers the modes of their globalization and strategies for growth. The concluding section summaries the key points in the chapter and raises some research questions for future work on the globalization of Chinese business firms.

## THE CHANGING DYNAMICS OF CHINESE BUSINESS FIRMS

This section is concerned with the changing global, regional and national contexts of the globalization of Chinese business firms. This contextualization is extremely important because previous studies of Chinese business firms tended to examine the behaviour of individual firms outside the changing structural contexts in which they were embedded. I shall first examine how the global shift of economic activities since the 1960s and the emergence of the Asia Pacific region have provided a favourable contingent factor for Chinese business firms in Asia to globalize their operations. I then outline the changing institutional configurations of Chinese business systems in order to situate their globalization in a dynamic home-country institutional context. Finally, the organizational challenge to the globalization of Chinese business firms is discussed. I argue that globalization poses significant challenges to the traditional organizational structures of Chinese business firms. A dynamic process of organizational restructuring occurs when Chinese business firms operate across national borders and charter into unfamiliar territories.

## The Dynamics of the Globalization of Economic Activities

The globalization of economic activities is a relatively recent phenomenon. Since the 1960s, the global economy has become increasingly interdependent through cross-border flows of capital, goods and people. The role of transnational corporations in these cross-border activities is particularly important. The outward FDI stock by TNCs grew from a meagre US$129 bn in 1970 to US$1.1 trillion in 1988 (UNCTAD, 1994; table I.8). By the end of 1997, there were some 53 000 TNCs worldwide, controlling more than 450 000 foreign affiliates. In the late 1990s they had a combined outward FDI stock of more than US$3.5 trillion (UNCTAD, 1998). Along with the growing role of TNCs, the UNCTC (1992) has identified some other recent and long-standing developments in the global economy: (i) an increasing emphasis on market forces and a growing role for the private sector in nearly all developing countries; (ii) rapidly changing technologies that are transforming the nature of international production and the organization as well as the location of such activities; (iii) the globalization of firms and industries, whereby production chains span national and regional boundaries; (iv) the rise of services to become the single largest sector in the world economy; (v) regional economic integration, involving the world's largest economies as well as selected developing countries; (vi) an increasing tendency towards developing intra- and inter-firm networks on a global and local scale, and (vii) the adoption of a global competitive strategy towards future development of TNCs and the world economy.

The outcomes of this accelerated process of globalization are manifested in the increasing *global interdependence* of national economies and *Triadization*. In the former case, the economic fortune of countries is intertwined with the global shift of economic activities (Dicken, 1998). In the latter, three distinct regions have emerged as the leading centres of the global economy – North America, Western Europe and Asia (Ohmae, 1985; 1995; Lévy, 1995). Within the Asia Pacific region, ethnic Chinese and their groups of business firms have made a notable start in the internationalization of their diverse range of activities, particularly in recent decades. Their dynamics is supported not only by the emergence of global TNCs *per se*, but also by the changing market structures and institutional configurations in their home countries and region. The opening of China in the late 1970s and the regionalization of markets in North America and Western Europe in the 1980s prompted and accelerated the internationalization of Chinese business firms. Since the inauguration of the open-door policy in China in 1979, China has experienced remarkable economic growth. Meanwhile, its two immediate ethnic Chinese neighbours, Hong Kong and Taiwan, grew tremendously during the 1980s. The late 1980s witnessed the emergence of the Greater China zone, in which cross-border investments between Hong Kong and China, and between Taiwan and China, contributed to greater sub-regional integration between Hong Kong and Taiwan on the one hand and Southern China on the other (Luo and Howe, 1993; X. Chen, 1994; La Croix *et al.*, 1995; Ng and Tuan, 1996; Hsing, 1998). One of the leading forces in this process of sub-regional integration is represented by ethnic Chinese TNCs from Hong Kong, Taiwan and Southeast Asian countries. The opening of China and the subsequent emergence of the Greater China economic zone have therefore facilitated the regionalization of ethnic Chinese TNCs in the Asia Pacific region, in particular those from Hong Kong and Taiwan.

Another important trend in the global economy is the regionalization of markets in North America and Western Europe. The formation of the North American Free Trade Area (NAFTA) and the Single European Market in the early 1990s has created unprecedented opportunities for Chinese business firms from Asia to tap into emerging regional markets and centres of technological innovations in the West. As these ethnic Chinese TNCs have consolidated their foothold in Asia, they have begun to penetrate into markets in North America and Western Europe through international production and investment rather than international trade. This represents an important strategic move for Chinese business firms because in the interdependent global economy of the late 1990s, it is no longer sufficient to rely on exports in order to serve foreign markets. Customers are becoming more demanding and markets more volatile than before. This is especially the case for markets in North America and Western Europe because of intense competition from domestic and global firms (Moran and Riesenberger, 1994). The establishment of transnational operations, as a strategic tool, has become one of the most important competitive strategies for these Chinese business firms to secure a place in global competition.

In addition, one of the most significant competitive *dis*advantages of Chinese business firms is their lack of technological and managerial sophistication. In their drive to become major competitive players in the global economy, Singapore and Taiwan are very concerned with the technological and managerial capabilities of their national firms (see Mathews, 1997, 1999). These predominantly ethnic Chinese business firms are compelled to globalize their manufacturing and trading operations into the Triad regions in order to secure access to intangible technology and managerial expertise. Why are these ethnic Chinese-based national economies so keen in globalizing their domestic firms? One of the answers comes from their changing institutional configurations.

## Changing Institutional Configurations and Organizational Restructuring

Institutional configurations of business firms refer broadly to the relationships between state institutions, business systems and individual firms. In explaining the behaviour of individual firms, we have to examine not only their firm-specific motives and rationality, but also the broader institutional context in which these business firms are embedded (Hodgson, 1988; Granovetter, 1991). The understanding of this institutional context becomes even more important when the firm is involved in globalization and faces more institutional constraints (Whitley, 1994; 1998). First, the *changing institutional configurations of business systems* provide an important nexus through which the globalization of Chinese business firms can be examined. In his study of the institutional influences on the development of Chinese business firms, Whitley (1992, p. 198; see also Whitley, 1990) notes that the distinctive characteristics of Chinese family firms 'stem from the patrimonial nature of pre-industrial China and the dominant forms of commercial organization that developed there'. Some aspects of this patrimonial system included the lack of local power centres, the emphasis on moral worth as the basis of authority, the low integration of vertical royalties, considerable merchant insecurity, patriarchal authority in families, and equal inheritance.

The subsequent industrialization patterns and institutional environment in Taiwan and Hong Kong further influenced the evolution of these Chinese family firms. Some of these institutional influences were dominant and exclusionary state (Taiwan); distant state and low risk-sharing (Hong Kong); weak labour movement; and the establishment of trading and business networks. The aggregate result of these institutional influences on Chinese family firms was manifested in their distinctive organizational characteristics: (i) strong personal owner control; (ii) managerial specialization and entrepreneurial diversification; (iii) risk management by minimizing commitments and maximizing flexibility; (iv) limited inter-firm commitments; (v) personal links between firms; (vi) highly personal authority and low formalization of procedures; (vii) limited commitment to, and low mutual dependence on, employees; (viii) centralized decision-making and control, and weak middle management; and (ix) paternalistic and aloof management roles (see also Redding and Wong, 1986; Wong, 1988; Redding, 1990; 1995; M. Chen, 1995; Chapter 2 in this volume).

These traditional management practices, organizational structures and capital formation among Chinese business firms were relatively enduring and remained basically the same despite new challenges posed by the influx of foreign trade, technology and imperialism at the turn of the twentieth century in China (Chan, 1982; Chan and McElderry, 1998). This relative inertia in organizational change resulted in the low level of internationalization of Chinese business firms in their early stages of development (see below). Large Chinese business firms, whether having transnational operations or being exclusively domestically-orientated, existed as loose groups of affiliated companies throughout the early phases of their organizational development. Typically, these affiliated companies were linked through family relationships and interlocking directorates. The holding company format to consolidate control and ownership of large Chinese business groups did not become a reality until after 1949, mainly in Hong Kong, Taiwan and Singapore (Chan, 1995, p. 89). Business networks became the predominant organizational form of Chinese business firms in their domestic institutional context.

One of the most interesting dimensions of the Chinese business system is the role of *guanxi* (personal relationships) and business networks as the *institutional foundation of internationalization*. Chinese business firms are a complex species of institutions that carry with them distinctive organizational, social and cultural characteristics. At the inter-firm level, Chinese business firms and their activities are mainly organized around intricate webs of business networks sustained by the interpenetration of ethnic Chinese capital. This interpenetration of Chinese business networks is particularly pronounced in the transnational operations of Chinese business firms from Hong Kong and Taiwan (Smart and Smart, 1991; 1993; Mitchell, 1995; Hsing, 1996; Olds, 1998; Yeung, 1998a). Hodder (1996, p. 68) argues that 'social networks founded upon reciprocity and its soft-framed institutions may be constructed as an end in themselves, but they may also be directed towards the extension and institutionalization of trade'.

In their journey to globalization, however, Chinese business firms may experience changing configurations of business systems and institutional influences in host and home countries. In the first place, the role of ethnic Chinese *guanxi* and business networks may diminish when Chinese business firms move beyond the Asia Pacific region and venture into foreign markets/regions. As Brown (1995b, p. 9) observes, 'the importance of the Chinese networks still endures, but the complex changes they have undergone are crucial'. In their global operations, many Chinese business firms are linked increasingly with Western TNCs and host country national firms which grew out of different configurations of business systems and institutional contexts. Their business practices may be based more on professional management, formal contracts, price competition and competitive inter-firm relationships and so on. These practices have been characterized by the business historian, Alfred Chandler (1977, 1990), as 'managerial capitalism' in which there is a distinct separation between ownership and management of modern corporations. Many ethnic Chinese TNCs from Hong Kong, for example, have professionalized their management; and their foreign subsidiaries are also given substantial autonomy in decision-making and control. There is thus a tendency towards the convergence of alternative business systems and management practices when different business firms participate increasingly as key players in the global economy (see Whyte, 1996; Olds and Yeung, 1999).

In their domestic context, however, the role of *guanxi* and business networks in the regionalization of Chinese business firms within the Asia Pacific region may still be strong and indeed further reinforced when they enter into all sorts of co-operative arrangements with global corporations eager to make their presence felt in the region. Ethnic Chinese business firms can play a very significant role in the globalization of Western firms into the Asia Pacific region by providing vital business contacts, reducing economic risks and uncertainty, identifying the initiatives of nation-states and pooling capital and appropriate technology. For example, ethnic Chinese firms were important 'gate-keepers' in the privatization of major public-sector industries in Indonesia, Malaysia and Thailand during the 1980s and 1990s. In their study of the privatization of Thailand's telecommunications industry, Priebjrivat and Rondinelli (1994) note that Chinese business firms played a vital mediating role between state political and military elites and foreign giant telecommunication corporations. This discussion of the role of *guanxi* and business networks indicates that Chinese business firms may pursue dual management and organizational practices in their globalization processes: (i) increasing incorporation of Western management practices and organizational structures in host countries *outside* the

Asia Pacific region, and (ii) the continual exploitation of the role of *guanxi* and business networks *within* the Asia Pacific region.

Second, the *changing priorities and concerns of home countries* also significantly shape the globalization of Chinese business firms from Hong Kong, Taiwan and Southeast Asian countries. Research in international business studies has shown that the globalization of TNCs is to a large extent related to the changing conditions in and competitive advantage of their home countries (see Dunning, 1993b, 1997, 1998). As the home countries of ethnic Chinese business firms go through different stages of economic development and political change, it becomes necessary for these firms to respond to changing circumstances in the home countries by engaging in global operations. One of the most important driving forces from their home countries is the limits to future growth that can arise from either discriminatory state regulation or market saturation. The former condition is applicable to many Southeast Asian countries in which Chinese capital has dominated the domestic economy, for example, Indonesia, Malaysia, the Philippines and Thailand. In these Southeast Asian countries, Chinese capital is subject to discriminatory regulation and constraints imposed by host country nation states (Mackie, 1988; Yoshihara, 1988; Jesudason, 1989; McVey, 1992; Hodder, 1996; Brook and Luong, 1997; Hefner, 1998). Ethnic-based economic policies aiming at improving the economic well-beings of the *pribumi* in Indonesia and the *bumiputra* in Malaysia have effectively forced many ethnic Chinese business firms to reconsider their future growth strategies. Once they have grown to a certain size and organizational complexity, many of the Chinese business firms in Southeast Asia begin to branch into overseas markets in search of new investment opportunities that are denied in their home countries as a result of state regulation. Well-known examples are the Liem Group from Indonesia, the Kuok brothers and the Hong Leong Group from Malaysia, the Charoen Pokphand (CP) Group and Bangkok Bank from Thailand, and the Sy Group from the Philippines (see East Asia Analytical Unit, 1995; Yeung, 1999a).

Another compelling condition is market saturation in many ethnic Chinese-dominated societies, particularly the Asian Newly Industrialized Economies (NIEs) – Hong Kong, Singapore and Taiwan. In these economies, the leading Chinese business firms have outgrown their domestic economies. The search for overseas markets has become the only feasible strategy to sustain their capital accumulation and growth. With the exception of Hong Kong, the state has a significant degree of influence in chartering the developmental trajectory of these national economies (see Amsden, 1989; Wade, 1990; Appelbaum and Henderson, 1992; Fitzgerald, 1994). In Singapore, the corporatist state has traditionally depended on the influx of foreign capital to sustain its economic growth (Rodan, 1989). This economic strategy has not been abandoned. Instead, the state has recently launched a major regionalization drive to develop an 'external wing' of the economy (see Yeung, 1998b, 1999b). This regionalization drive is deemed to be necessary if Singapore is to succeed in growing beyond the limits of its domestic market and capturing the emerging markets of the Asia Pacific region. Major government-linked corporations are spearheading this regionalization drive (for example, the Keppel Group, the Sembawang Group, Singapore Technologies, and Temasek Holdings).

In contrast, this phenomenon of state-driven outward investment by Chinese business firms occurred earlier in Taiwan (from the mid-1980s), when the state relaxed its foreign exchange and foreign investment regulations (see C. Chen, 1986). Before that, the Taiwanese government actively promoted the emergence of 'national champions' in certain industrial sectors (for example, Formosa Plastics in plastics production, and Acer in computers) through granting subsidies and incentives, providing R&D infrastructure and protecting key domestic markets (see Amsden, 1989; Chang, 1990; Wade, 1990; Mathews, 1997). After 1985, the state has actively encouraged national firms to relocate their low-cost-orientated production facilities to other countries in the region and to secure strategic access to foreign technology in the Triad countries (T. J. Chen, 1992; 1998; X. Chen, 1996; Chen and Chen, 1998). In that respect, Chinese business firms from Taiwan have been much more successful in globalizing their operations beyond their national boundaries. By the end of the 1980s, more than half of Taiwanese FDI had gone to developed countries, particularly the USA (see Yeung, 1994a).

In the case of Chinese business firms from Hong Kong, their globalization is prompted not such much by any coherent state action, but rather by the changing political climate and inherently small size of the domestic market. It is true that Chinese business firms from Hong Kong have long been operating in Southeast Asia because of the overseas Chinese networks (see Yeung, 1996). But the drive towards globalization did not become a serious consideration until the so-called '1997 question' surfaced in the period leading to the 1984 Sino-British Joint Declaration which stipulated the return of Hong Kong to China on 1 July 1997. Since then, many leading Chinese business firms have stepped up their globalization process in response to ongoing industrial restructuring in Hong Kong, and political uncertainty (Ho, 1992; Chiu *et al.*,

1997; Yeung, 1999c). By 1996, the manufacturing sector had contributed to no more than 7.2 per cent of Hong Kong's GDP (Census and Statistics Department, 1998). A large proportion of Hong Kong's manufacturing industry has been relocated across the border in southern China. Some high-tech manufacturing Chinese business firms have ventured into the Triad countries in order to penetrate the highly competitive marketplace. Service-oriented Chinese business firms from Hong Kong are also globalizing to diversify their political risks (Yeung, 1999d). For example, Chinese business firms from Hong Kong are very active in cross-border mergers and acquisitions, involving some US$78 bn and ranked third worldwide after the USA and France in 1992 (*Economic News*, 2 February 1993). Many leading Hong Kong property firms have bought into hotel chains in the USA and Europe, and other Hong Kong firms are involved in high-profile acquisitions of foreign companies in the telecommunications (Microtell in Canada), oil and gas (Husky Oil in Canada), electronics (Sansui Electric in Japan); and retail and distribution (Harvey Nichols in the UK and the Singer Co. in the USA).

## GLOBALIZATION STRATEGIES OF CHINESE BUSINESS FIRMS

The above section has explained the dynamic context in which ethnic Chinese business firms are globalizing in the world economy. It is insufficient, however, to explain the globalization of Chinese business firms *vis-à-vis* this dynamic context alone. To understand fully the behaviour of these ethnic firms, we need to examine also their firm-specific strategies that are the *raison d'être* of their globalizing tendency. In this section, I first propose a general model of the geographic expansion of Chinese business firms in their globalization drive. The model is then used to map the geographic expansion of Chinese business firms in the twentieth century. It must be noted that this model is useful as an heuristic device, but not as a universal explanation in its own right. In fact, most Chinese business firms would not go through all stages of the model. There is thus no inevitability of Chinese business firms going through all stages. Instead, we shall find a mixture of these firms in every stage of the model, depending on the historical and geographical contexts of their formation and transformations. In this sense, the model is at best a *post hoc* rationalization of the experiences of globalizing Chinese business firms over the past two centuries.

Second, the modes through which Chinese business firms enter host countries are examined. The choice of different modes of entry is explained by differences in institutional contexts and firm-specific advantages. Finally, the strategies pursued by Chinese business firms in global competition and globalization are explained.

## An Evolutionary Model of the Geographic Expansion of Chinese Business Firms

In his seminal paper on the evolution of TNCs, Perlmutter (1969) notes that TNCs tend to evolve in three stages: from ethnocentric to polycentric, then to regioncentric and geocentric. Put in simple terms, the transnational firm starts as a domestic firm with one centre of activities. It serves the global market through exports and licensing (the ethnocentric stage). Over time, it grows beyond its national boundaries and establishes multiple centres of activities (the polycentric stage). At this stage, however, its different centres of activities are not integrated with the headquarters and remain largely decentralized. Each foreign subsidiary is run as a stand-alone operation. It is only at the final stage that the regional/global operations of the TNC are integrated within co-ordinated networks. There is no longer any trace of parent–subsidiary relationships. The TNC is now fully integrated globally and is equipped with global scanning capabilities and intra-firm co-ordination and control of international production. This has also been called the 'transnational solution' in Bartlett and Ghoshal's (1989) study of the evolution of leading global corporations, and 'differentiated networks' in Nohria and Ghoshal's (1997) study of the organization of value chains by multinational corporations. An example of this evolutionary globalization of an ethnocentric TNC is Eli Lilly and Company, an American pharmaceutical TNC (Malnight, 1995).

Although the model is relatively simplistic and idealized, it can be applied to the globalization of Chinese business firms, albeit with some modifications and context-specification. Weidenbaum and Hughes (1996, pp. 4–5) have constructed a three-stage model of the internationalization of Chinese business firms, as follows:

- **Stage 1**   Chinese business firms go literally from rags to riches when 'families created their own businesses, and in the process developed much of the modern private business sector throughout Southeast Asia – in Taiwan, Hong Kong, Singapore, Malaysia, Thailand, Indonesia, the Philippines, and, to a more limited extent, Vietnam'

(Weidenbaum and Hughes, 1996, p. 4). This is thus the phase of early firm formation and expansion.

- **Stage 2**   This is known as 'the duplication of the House of Rothschild phenomenon' (Weidenbaum and Hughes, 1996, p. 4), when Chinese business firms internationalize their operations throughout the region based on common grounds in family ties, language, culture and ethnicity. These common grounds are particularly important institutional means for internationalization in an area where formal business agreements are difficult to establish, let alone to enforce. Weidenbaum and Hughes (1996, p. 5) even argue that 'it is common for the father-CEO stationed in Hong Kong or Bangkok or Singapore to send one son to Shanghai, another to Taipei, a son-in-law to Manila, and a nephew to Kuala Lumpur'.
- **Stage 3**   Chinese business firms engage in massive investment and rapid penetration into the Greater China which completely surpass the efforts of their counterparts from the West.

It should be noted that their model is based on the experience of Chinese business firms investing in China. The model is therefore historically- and geographically-specific. In order to ensure the relative generality of the model, it is necessary to add further stages to account for the globalization of Chinese business firms into other destinations outside the Asia Pacific region:

- **Stage 4**   This is characterized by the worldwide web of Chinese business firms when these ethnic TNCs globalize their operations beyond the Asia Pacific region. At this stage, their worldwide operations are not yet fully integrated and their organizational structures remain largely polycentric. Their capabilities are embedded in their home country advantages and their ability to learn from partnership with global corporations in Asia.
- **Stage 5**   We witness the emergence of the global networks of Chinese business firms when they begin to integrate their worldwide operations within sophisticated networks. At this stage, Chinese business firms are increasingly transnational in that they no longer belong to a particular country of origin. They draw capital and finance from the global networks of Chinese and non-Chinese capital. Their decision-making is no longer personalized by the patriarch of the family, but is rather dependent on the collective consensus of global executives from the various centres of activities within the network.

It must be noted that Chinese business firms from different home countries may enter the model at different stages because of their locational advantages and disadvantages (for example, Hong Kong versus Malaysia). Early stages of the model are more applicable to traditional Chinese business firms, whereas the later stages are more relevant to 'newcomers' from Asian NIEs.

To date, only a selected number of Chinese business firms have reached Stage 4, and globalized their operations. Acer Computer from Taiwan is perhaps one of the best examples (*Far Eastern Economic Review*, 25 July 1996, pp. 74–80). It is now one of the top ten global manufacturers of personal computers. Its worldwide operations span some thirty-five countries in the Triad regions, but 66 per cent of its profits in 1995 came from Asia (*The Straits Times*, 26 March 1996). To date, however, there are very few truly transnational firms, irrespective of the country of initial origin (Hu, 1992). It is even more difficult to find a Chinese business firm that has fully transnationalized its operations. It will take many more years of globalization for Chinese business firms to reach the final stage of the evolutionary model of Chinese TNCs.

**Mapping the Growth of Chinese Business Firms over Space**

The historical geography of the globalization of Chinese business firms is extremely interesting in that four distinct phases of globalization can be identified: (i) early internationalization from China to other Asian countries; (ii) capital flows from China to Hong Kong/Taiwan and Southeast Asia in the late 1940s; (iii) two-way investments between Hong Kong and Southeast Asia over the next three decades; and (iv) globalization of Chinese business firms from Hong Kong, Taiwan and Southeast Asian countries in the 1980s and 1990s. The word 'phase' is used instead of 'stage' because I want to situate the globalization of these firms in their historical and geographical contexts, although each of them may be at different stages of the evolutionary model. In the *first phase*, internationalization occurred either when some Chinese capitalists established operations outside China, or when ethnic Chinese invested in their home country. An example is the Wing On Group, now based in Hong Kong (Chan, 1995). At the turn of the twentieth century, both Hong Kong and Shanghai experienced new challenges as the Chinese economy was buffeted by many new forces – rapid population growth, imported technology, foreign trade and Western imperialism among others. Chan (1995, p. 80) notes that 'by learning new managerial techniques, by planning out new strategies and by setting up appropriate organizations, [the Wing On Company] was one of the very small number of Chinese enterprises which responded successfully to these challenges'.

The Wing On Company's early success in internationalization can be explained by its multi-product marketing approach and its multi-unit organizational structure which provided critical support through access to new markets and sources of supply, a control mechanism to ensure consistency in quality, and an efficient distribution network. The first company of the Wing On Group, the Wing On Fruit Store, was established in Sydney in August 1897 by Guo Luo (1874–1956), one of the two founding brothers of the Wing On Company from a relatively wealthy peasant family in Zhongshan in southern China (Chan, 1995, p. 82). Guo Luo pursued a strategy of expansion through backward integration and diversification. He first secured his sources of fruit supply by setting up his own banana plantations in the Fiji Islands. He then diversified into trading in other products such as dried coconuts, sea shells, dried sea slugs, leather, plywood and other Chinese native products. By the early 1910s, Chan (1995, p. 83) notes that 'the company owned some eighteen plantations covering over 2,000 acres of land and employing more than 1,200 workers, as well as other banana plantations, almost 1,000 acres in size, in the Charters Towers area of Queensland, Australia'.

The return of the Guo brothers to Hong Kong and Shanghai was prompted by revolutionary ideas in the 1900s (Chan, 1995). They wanted to bring in modern management practices to revolutionize traditional Chinese business practices in China. They decided first to establish a modern department store in Hong Kong. The Wing On department store was opened for business in Hong Kong in August 1907, supported by a well-planned internal organization headed by family members. The department store existed as a separate affiliate or associated corporation of the Wing On Fruit Store in Sydney. The company then expanded swiftly to found the Jinshanzhuang in Sydney (1907), the Wing On Native Bank in Zhongshan (1910), a chain of Great Eastern Hotels in Guangzhou city (1914) and in Hong Kong and Shanghai (1918), and the Wing On Warehouse (1916) and the Wei Sun Knitting Factory in Hong Kong (1919). There were also several new affiliates, each with its own corporate charter and independent sources of capital: the Wing On Fire and Marine Insurance Co. Ltd of Hong Kong (1915), the Wing On Co. Ltd of Shanghai (1918), the Wing On Textile Manufacturing Co. Ltd in Shanghai (1921), the Wing On life Assurance Co. Ltd in Hong Kong (1925) and the Wing On Commercial and Savings Bank Ltd in Hong Kong (1933). There was no single holding company to consolidate control and ownership of this diverse group of Wing On companies. By the early 1920s, the Guo brothers 'had fashioned out a complex multi-unit organization that bound its subsidiaries and affiliates together through the use of interlocking directorships and inter-company loans whenever they were needed' (Chan, 1995, p. 89). The case of the Wing On Group indicates that before the Communist takeover in 1949, some Chinese business firms had already been actively involved in cross-border investment within the Asian region.

The *second phase of internationalization* coincides with the civil war and the Communist takeover in China during the late 1940s. This is the stage when disruptions in China caused massive outflows of capital from China to Hong Kong, Taiwan and Southeast Asia. In a landmark study of the role of these capital flows in Hong Kong's industrialization, Wong (1988) examines how political chaos in the 1930s and the founding of the People's Republic of China in 1949 led Shanghai's industrialists to seek alternative, safer locations for their businesses. This was a phase of 'involuntary internationalization', when Chinese capital fled in response to home-country conditions rather than business opportunities emerging from host countries. Many of these Shanghainese, in particular owners of cotton mills, chose to re-establish themselves in Hong Kong, where they found a favourable setting for the development of modern Chinese business firms. One example is the Rong Family which created the Shen Xin textile empire and dominated the Chinese textile industry. The eldest son of the family, Rong Hong-yuan, left Hong Kong in 1948 to set up the Bangkok Cotton Mill in 1950. But severe restrictions by the Thai government caused the mill to collapse into bankruptcy after a short period of operation (Wong, 1988, pp. 21–2). These 'emigrant entrepreneurs' played a major role in the subsequent industrialization of Hong Kong and contributed significantly to the importance of Hong Kong as a global textiles and garment co-ordination centre.

The *third phase of internationalization* witnesses significant two-way investments between Hong Kong and Southeast Asia throughout the following three decades (see Yeung, 1996). After more than a decade of industrialization in Hong Kong, by the end of the 1950s the textile industry had become one of the vital pillars of its economy. Hong Kong had become one of world's largest exporters of textile products. The same period nevertheless saw the imposition of quota constraints on Hong Kong's cotton textile products (Lau, 1991). Many Chinese textile family firms began seriously to consider their future growth strategies, and transnational operations seemed to be a viable solution to circumvent quota restrictions. Chinese textile business firms began to internationalize their operations in search of alternative non-quota production and domestic markets. For example, as early as 1951, Nanyang Cotton Mill Ltd had built a 10 000-spindle spinning mill in Argentina, where no Chinese had ever owned a factory, although the mill was eventually sold in 1960 (The Hong Kong Cotton Spinners Association, 1988, p. 92). By the 1970s, nearly all the Chinese textile firms controlled by the Shanghainese entrepreneurs in Hong Kong had diversified their investments to Southeast Asia, Canada, Latin America and parts of Africa (Wong, 1988, p. 39).

Another Shanghainese entrepreneur, Frank Tsao, with several Hong Kong friends, pioneered the first textile venture in Malaysia in 1958, known as the Textile Corporation of Malaya. The venture was established primarily for two reasons: first, Malaysia was an alternative production site to circumvent quota restrictions imposed on Hong Kong by developed countries in Europe and America. At that time, these developed countries did not impose any quota restriction on textile products imported from Malaysia. Second, Frank Tsao himself had extensive personal and family connections in Malaysia. At the personal level, the Textile Corporation had the industrial and financial support of several other leading Shanghai industrialists from Hong Kong and Malaysia – for example, Chow Wen-hsien and Chow Chung-kai from the Winsor Industrial Group in Hong Kong, and Robert Kuok in Malaysia. Frank Tsao has also been a personal friend of Mohammed Mahathir (the Prime Minister of Malaysia at the time of writing) since the independence of Malaysia (*Capital*, June 1994, p. 80).

Since then, Frank Tsao's textile and garment empire in Malaysia has expanded further to include Malayan Weaving Mills, the Textile Corporation and Malacca Textile. Frank Tsao's main business, however, was not in textiles, but in shipping. Together with Robert Kuok, Frank Tsao helped the Malaysian government to set up its Malaysian International Shipping Corporation (MISC) in the late 1960s. In the process, Frank Tsao was invited to be a shareholder of the national shipping line – albeit a small share of only 4 per cent. For his distinctive contributions to the Malaysian shipping industry, Tsao was given Tan Sri (a knighthood) by the Sultan of Malaysia. He now has a much higher shareholding in the Thai national shipping line, at an estimated 70 per cent at the time of writing (*Singapore Business*, February 1989, p. 21; July 1994, p. 28; *Forbes*, August 1992, p. 41). It is interesting to note that Frank Tsao, during the 1980s and early 1990s, was heavily involved in developing Singapore's largest private property development – the Suntec Convention Centre. The billionaire-club, chaired by Frank Tsao, has strong financial and personal support from many leading Hong Kong businessmen, including property magnates such as Li Ka-shing, Lee Shaukee and Cheng Yu Tung, and eminent industrialists such as Li Dak-sum and Anthony Yeh. The Suntec project is primarily a transnational project based on personal friendship and co-operative strategies among leading Chinese businessmen from Hong Kong (see Yeung, 1997a; 1998a).

In the *fourth phase, of geographic expansion* during the 1980s and 1990s, Chinese business firms from Hong Kong, Taiwan and Southeast Asian countries began to globalize their commercial operations into virtually every corner of the world. Perhaps the largest geographical destination of these cross-border investment flows from Chinese business firms is China itself. Since the initiation of its open-door policy in 1979, China has become one of the largest recipients of FDI. There is no doubt that this wave of FDI is sustained by overseas Chinese capital (East Asia Analytical Unit, 1995; Weidenbaum and Hughes, 1996). By 1994, the amount of cumulative realized foreign capital surpassed US$100 bn. This was spread across more than 167 500 foreign-invested enterprises, including wholly-owned companies, joint ventures and co-operative enterprises. As shown in Table 4.1, overseas Chinese business firms have 'out-invested' the USA, Japan and the European Union (EU) by a factor of more than five to one, contributing well over 80 per cent of

*Table* 4.1   Sources of foreign capital in China, 1979–93

| Source country | No. of enterprises | Percentage | Foreign investment (US$bn) | Percentage |
|---|---|---|---|---|
| Hong Kong | 106 769 | 63.7 | 47.5 | 69.1 |
| Taiwan | 20 612 | 12.3 | 6.4 | 9.3 |
| Macau | 4 188 | 2.5 | 1.9 | 2.8 |
| Singapore | 3 037 | 1.8 | 1.5 | 2.2 |
| Thailand | 1 361 | 0.8 | 0.8 | 1.2 |
| **Sub-Total** | **136 042** | **81.2** | **58.1** | **84.6** |
| United States | 11 554 | 6.9 | 3.7 | 5.4 |
| Japan | 7 096 | 4.2 | 3.3 | 4.8 |
| Other | 14 314 | 8.6 | 4.4 | 6.4 |
| **Total** | **167 500** | **100.0** | **68.7** | **100.0** |

*Source*:   East Asia Analytical Unit (1995, table 10.1).

both the number of projects and investment since 1979 (East Asia Analytical Unit, 1995, p. 197; see also Chapter 11 in this volume). To a large
extent, these flows of overseas Chinese capital from Taiwan and Southeast Asian countries to China are channelled through Hong Kong and
Singapore (Wu and Duk, 1995a; Low *et al.*, 1998).

Among the largest overseas Chinese investors, in terms of capital
invested and the number of companies they control in China, are two
from Southeast Asia: the Sino-Thai agribusiness group, Charoen Pokphand (CP) Group, and the Sino-Indonesian Oei family which controls
Indonesia's Sinar Mas Group. Whereas the CP Group controls more than
seventy operations in China, including its core agribusiness activities
and Shanghai real estate development, the Sinar Mas Group manages and
controls more than eighty companies in China, particularly in Fujian,
Zhejiang and Shanxi. Other leading overseas Chinese business firms from
Southeast Asia have made significant investments in China: for example,
the Sino-Indonesia Salim and Riady families and the Dharmala Group,
the Malaysian Kuok group, Hong Leong and Berjaya groups, the Sino-
Thai Bangkok Land Group, and the Singaporean Far East Group (East
Asia Analytical Unit, 1995, pp. 198–9).

The CP Group, now based in Thailand, is an interesting example of
the extent of its involvement in China. Today, it may be the single largest investor in China since its open-door policy began. The group was
founded some 70 years ago by two ethnic Chinese brothers, Chia Ek
Chor and Chia Seow Whooey, who arrived in Thailand in 1919 from
the Shantou region of Guangdong (East Asia Analytical Unit, 1995,
pp. 323–6; Hamilton and Waters, 1995, pp. 104–5; Weidenbaum and
Hughes, 1996, pp. 30–4). The CP Group started in the farm-seed business and moved into animal feeds and then into chicken farming and
processing with initial technical support from the US poultry giant,
Arbor Acres. Although the group's interests extend to petrochemicals,
motorcycle and automotive parts, real estate and telecommunications,
60–70 per cent of its revenue is still derived from agribusiness. During
the 1980s, the CP Group became Asia's biggest exporter of processed
and frozen chickens, mainly to Japan, China and Brazil. One of its largest ventures outside its agribusiness core is its stake in TelecomAsia, a
joint venture with the US telecommunications giant NYNEX. In all,
the CP Group now controls more than 280 affiliated companies, of which
only fourteen are listed on stock exchanges worldwide (see Table 4.2).
In 1993, the group officially reported US$5 bn in revenues. In 1995, the
Chearavanont family's wealth was estimated at US$5.5 bn, placing it
the 25th wealthiest in the world (Shikatani, 1995, table 4.1). The CP

*Table* 4.2   Listed members of the Charoen Pokphand Group, Thailand

| Name of company | Stock exchange | Market capitalization in Nov. 1994 (US$m) | Net profit in 1993 (US$m) | CP stake (per cent) |
|---|---|---|---|---|
| 1. EK Chor China Motorcycle | New York | 360 | 20 | 72 |
| 2. CP Pokphand | Hong Kong, London | 622 | 44 | 56 |
| 3. Hong Kong Fortune | Hong Kong | 107 | 0 | 64 |
| 4. Orient Telecom & Technology | Hong Kong | 896 | 12 | 51 |
| 5. CP Indonesia | Jakarta | 234 | 13 | 71 |
| 6. CP Prima | Jakarta | 198 | 6 | 92 |
| 7. CP Enterprise | Taipei | 132 | 2 | 30 |
| 8. Shanghai Dajiang | Shanghai | 141 | 17 | 44 |
| 9. CP Feedmill | Bangkok | 839 | 48 | 39 |
| 10. CP Northeastern | Bangkok | 60 | 3 | 59 |
| 11. Bangkok Produce Merchandising | Bangkok | 49 | 3 | 37 |
| 12. Bangkok Agri-Industrial Products | Bangkok | 118 | 4 | 73 |
| 13. Telecom Asia | Bangkok | 9 030 | 23 | 29 |
| 14. Siam Makro | Bangkok | 875 | 6 | 15 |

*Source*:   East Asia Analytical Unit (1995, table A7.1).

Group set up its first China venture, Conti Chia Tai, in Shenzhen in 1981 and was an early entrant into the China market. It now has operations in twenty-six of China's thirty provinces, indicating its broad interests in China and its geographic coverage. The group's total assets in China were estimated at US$1.3 bn in 1993 (East Asia Analytical Unit, 1995, p. 324). Its China investments are mainly conducted through its Hong Kong subsidiary, CP Pokphand, which controlled thirty-six very diversified businesses in China in 1993.

Another geographical indication of the extent of the globalization of Chinese business firms is the flow of ethnic Chinese capital to the Triad countries in North America and Western Europe. An emerging spatial division of investment is observed when Overseas Chinese FDI in these Triad countries originates largely from Chinese business firms based in Hong Kong and Taiwan, whereas most Chinese business firms from

*Table* 4.3   World-class hotels owned and controlled by Chinese business firms from Hong Kong

| Chinese business firms from Hong Kong | | Hotel | Location | Number of rooms | Total revenue ($m) |
|---|---|---|---|---|---|
| | | | | | *1992* |
| Hong Kong and Shanghai Hotels Ltd | 1. | The Peninsular | Hong Kong | 156 | 320 (HK$) |
| | 2. | The Kowloon Hotel | Hong Kong | 737 | 598 (HK$) |
| | 3. | The Peninsular New York | USA | 242 | 275 (US$) |
| | 4. | The Peninsular Beverly Hills | USA | NA | NA |
| | 5. | The Peninsular Manila | The Philippines | NA | NA |
| | 6. | The Palace Hotel, Beijing | PRC | NA | 29 (RMB$) |
| | | | | | *1993 (US$)* |
| Mandarin Oriental International Ltd | 1. | Mandarin Oriental | Hong Kong | 542 | 60 |
| | 2. | The Excelsior | Hong Kong | 905 | 50 |
| | 3. | The Oriental, Bangkok | Thailand | 393 | 39 |
| | 4. | Mandarin Oriental, Manila | The Philippines | 464 | 20 |
| | 5. | Mandarin Oriental, Jakarta | Indonesia | 446 | 20 |
| | 6. | Mandarin Oriental, Macau | Macau | 433 | 18 |
| | 7. | The Oriental | Singapore | 517 | 30 |
| | 8. | Mandarin Oriental, San Francisco | USA | 158 | 9 |
| | 9. | Hotel Bela Vista | Macau | 8 | 0.4 |
| | 10. | Phuket Yacht Club | Thailand | 110 | NA |
| | 11. | Baan Taling Ngam | Thailand | 49 | NA |
| | 12. | Mandarin Oriental (1994) | Mexico | 316 | NA |
| | 13. | Landmark Hotel, Surabaya | Indonesia | 150 | NA |
| | 14. | New Thai Island Resort | Thailand | 40 | NA |
| | 15. | Mandarin Oriental (1997) | Malaysia | 628 | NA |

| New World Development Co. Ltd | | | | 1993 |
|---|---|---|---|---|
| 1. | New World Hotels | Hong Kong | 1936 | NA |
| | | The P.R.C. | 3984 | NA |
| | | Southeast Asia | 319 | NA |
| | | Macau | 394 | NA |
| 2. | Ramada International Hotels | N. America | 21861 | NA |
| | | Europe/Mid East | 12481 | NA |
| | Stouffer hotels | Latin America | 4063 | NA |
| | Renaissance hotels | Asia | 3580 | NA |
| | Ramada hotels | Australia | 1994 | NA |

| Wharf Holdings Ltd | | | 1992 |
|---|---|---|---|
| | | | HK$1.7 billion |
| 1. | Omni The Hongkong Hotel | Hong Kong | 718 |
| 2. | Omni Marco Polo Hotel | Hong Kong | 440 |
| 3. | Omni Prince Hotel | Hong Kong | 402 |
| 4. | Omni Marco Polo Hotel | Singapore | 603 |
| 5. | Omni Houston Hotel | USA | 381 |
| 6. | Omni Parker House | USA | 550 |
| 7. | Omni Berkshire Place | USA | 450 |
| 8. | Omni Richmond Hotel | USA | 375 |
| 9. | Omni Ambassador East | USA | 300 |
| 10. | Omni Mandalay Hotel | USA | 420 |
| 11. | Dunfey San Mateo Hotel | USA | 300 |

Table 4.3 (*contd.*)

| Chinese business firms from Hong Kong | | Hotel | Location | Number of rooms | Total revenue ($m) |
|---|---|---|---|---|---|
| | | | | | *1993* |
| Hopewell Holdings Ltd | 1. | Grand Hotel Excelsior | Hong Kong | NA | HK$210 million |
| | 2. | Kowloon Panda Hotel | Hong Kong | NA | |
| Regal Hotels International Holdings Ltd | 1. | Richfield Hotels (171 hotels) | USA | 33350 | NA |
| | 2. | Regal Hotels (4 hotels) | Hong Kong | 2210 | NA |
| | | | PRC | NA | NA |
| | 3. | Regal Germany (20 hotels) | Canada | 900 | NA |
| | | | Europe | NA | NA |
| Shangri-La International Group | 1. | Shangri-La | Hong Kong | NA | NA |
| | | | Malaysia | NA | NA |
| | | | Singapore | NA | NA |
| | | | The Philippines | NA | NA |
| | | | PRC | NA | NA |

*Source:* Yeung (1998b, pp. 212–13).

Southeast Asian countries tend to engage in intra-regional investment (Yeung, 1994a). Some of the high-profile investments in North America and Western Europe by ethnic Chinese business firms from Hong Kong are Li Ka-shing's property development projects in Vancouver (see Mitchell, 1995; Olds, 1998; Chapter 9 in this volume) and the acquisitions of hotel chains by property-based Chinese business firms (see Yeung, 1998a). As is evident from Table 4.3, some of these Chinese property business firms are increasingly interested in expanding their corporate empires by acquiring hotels throughout the world: for example, New World and Wharf. Meanwhile, new hotel operations have emerged since the late 1970s – for example, Regal International and Shangri-La International (see also Go and Pine, 1995).

**Modes of Globalization**

The globalization of Chinese business firms has taken a great variety of organizational forms. The choice of different modes of entry into foreign markets therefore becomes an important issue in understanding their globalization processes. As shown in Figure 4.1 below, there are many ways of organizing transnational operations, from arm's-length market transactions (that is, exports) to fully-integrated vertical hierarchies (that is, FDI). Joint ventures and acquisitions are perhaps the most common organizational modes through which Chinese business firms globalize their operations (see Table 4.4). In fact, many overseas Chinese business firms in China are joining hands with local enterprises and state institutions (for example, the CP Group mentioned earlier). Acquisitions are also preferred by large ethnic Chinese business conglomerates to control their foreign subsidiaries. One of the best-known Chinese business conglomerates is the Liem Group from Indonesia (East Asia Analytical Unit, 1995, pp. 163–75; Yeung, 1999a). At the time of writing, the Liem Group has more than 400 affiliated companies

| Licensing | Alliances | Joint ventures | Family business |
|---|---|---|---|
| **Markets** ← | | | → **Hierarchies** |
| Franchising | Co-operative agreements | Subcontracting | Conglomerates |

*Figure* 4.1   A network spectrum of different forms of organizing international production
*Source*:   Yeung (1994c, fig. 1).

*Table* 4.4    Characteristics of Chinese business firms in their
globalization process

| Aspects of globalization | Characteristics |
|---|---|
| FDI motivations | • risk diversification<br>• production cost driven<br>• following customers |
| Location and partner selection | • existence of ethnic connections and networks<br>• preference of kinship or friendship |
| Business strategies and production structure | • low degree of multinationalization<br><br>• no clear sequence in overseas operations<br>• low physical integration between parent company and subsidiaries<br>• special business arrangements with low transaction costs |
| Ownership and control | • wholly-owned subsidiary or majority joint ventures<br>• dualism in organizational structure and control system<br>• highly centralized decision-making<br>• tight financial control<br>• preferential recruitment and promotion of kinship for top and key management positions |

*Source*:    Van Den Bulcke and Zhang (1995, table 12.2).

employing at least 135 000 people. In 1993, group sales were estimated
to be US$9 bn, accounting for some 5 per cent of Indonesia's GDP. The
expansion of the Liem Group can be divided into four phases: (i) entry
into manufacturing (1968–74); (ii) the development of banking (1975–
8); (iii) the cement business expansion (1977–81); and (iv) conglomerate diversification into unrelated businesses (1981–5). The group now
has interests in Singapore, the Philippines, Vietnam, Australia, the former Soviet Union, Germany and China. The group's major overseas
expansion arm is the First Pacific Company based in Hong Kong, which
the Liem Group acquired in the early 1980s. The First Pacific Group
now has operations in at least twenty-five countries. Acquisition is
often the preferred mode of entry by First Pacific. Over the fifteen
years following its acquisition by the Liem Group, First Pacific acquired
several leading banking and trading companies, included the nineteen-

branch United Savings Bank in California, Hagemeyer in the Netherlands (operating in twenty-one countries), Berli Jucker Co. Ltd in Thailand, Metro Drugs in the Philippines, and the First Pacific Davies (establishing a strong foothold in the Australian property services market).

Other co-operative strategies in globalization, such as informal networks and strategic alliances, have also been adopted by Chinese business firms. Chinese business firms from Hong Kong, for example, are particularly well-known for their exploitation of co-operative strategies in cross-border investments (see Yeung, 1997a; 1997b; Chapter 8 in this volume). Studies have shown that co-operative strategies of Chinese business firms from Hong Kong are manifested in at least three dimensions: (i) intra-firm internalization of entrepreneurship based on regional ties; (ii) inter-firm collaboration on the basis of personal friendship; and (iii) extra-firm co-operation with key 'political patronage' to create competitive advantage in transnational operations. The implementation of these co-operative strategies through Chinese business networks is made possible because of the social and institutional foundations of Chinese business systems described earlier. These co-operative strategies are also adopted by other Chinese family firms from Southeast Asian countries.

What, then, explains the choice of organizational modes in the globalization of these Chinese business firms? Two sets of explanations are relevant: (i) institutional contexts; and (ii) firm-specific advantages. In their domestic *institutional contexts*, many Chinese family firms from Southeast Asian countries face discrete discrimination in their home countries because of the state's narrowly-defined ethnic-based economic policies. Many of them decide to operate outside the home country in order to transcend the home-country limits to growth. At a result, foreign-based affiliates are used to offset accusations of capital flight. For example, the Liem Group diversified its capital assets outside Indonesia, not through direct acquisitions, but rather through its Hong Kong-based First Pacific Group (Weidenbaum and Hughes, 1996). Acquisitions are preferred over greenfield operations because of speed and risk factors.

Other components of the institutional context are host-country requirements. When Chinese business firms from Asia attempt to venture into unfamiliar marketplaces in North America and Western Europe, acquisitions are preferred because the open business environment does not give these Chinese business firms the competitive advantage they enjoy in the opaque Asian business environment. Rather, these open business fields in the West tend to intensify competition and accentuate the importance of economies of scale, particularly to new entrants from Asia. Acquisitions of existing operations in these Triad countries facilitate risk

minimization and experience-building which pave the way for subsequent major investment in the host countries. On the other hand, the
opaque business environment in China and some Southeast Asian
countries favours joint ventures between ethnic Chinese business firms
and local enterprises/state institutions. These Chinese business firms
may also team up with Western firms in order to establish themselves in
the host Asian countries. Chinese business firms from Hong Kong and
Singapore have long been promoting themselves as the 'gateway' between
the East and the West. For example, Peter Woo and his flagship companies in Hong Kong, Wharf Holdings Ltd and Wheelock & Co., have
striven hard to become a modern-day *compradore* in order to make a
bridge between Western firms and business in China (*Far Eastern Economic Review*, 23 December 1993, pp. 38–9; *Forbes*, January–February
1994, pp. 22–5). In Woo's opinion, China is too big for anyone to go in
alone. Mainland investment is all about partnerships, pooling resources
to help China to develop. He found Western firms very inefficient and
bureaucratic in making deals:

> Western businessmen go to [Beijing] when they want to do deals in
> China. But when I go to the US, I rarely go to Washington... Western
> companies take a long time to make decisions; they need a lot of law-
> yers. The bureaucracy is too heavy for this part of the world. Over-
> seas Chinese know not to create such deterrents. (quoted in *Far
> Eastern Economic Review*, 23 December 1993, p. 39)

The competitive advantage offered by his companies when going into
partnerships to invest in China is that 'We have the ability to network,
we have good people, we can give others credibility' (quoted in *Far
Eastern Economic Review*, 23 December 1993, p. 39).

*Firm-specific advantages* also play an important part in explaining the
choice of globalization modes by Chinese business firms. If a particular
firm's key globalization strategy is to secure technology and market
share in order to overcome its lack of firm-specific competitive advantage, it may choose to acquire directly-existing foreign operations. This
approach is particularly favoured by Taiwanese and Singaporean electronics firms when they globalize into the US market. For example,
as part of a strategy to reduce its dependence on OEM sales and to
build up its market position in the USA, Acer acquired Counterpoint, a
start-up firm that built a powerful minicomputer using multiple micro
processors, in 1987 for US$6 m (Hu, 1995, p. 85). In 1990 Acer paid
US$94 m for Altos Computer Systems Inc., a Silicon Valley firm with

an extensive network of distributors, to improve its distribution and market presence in America (Yeung, 1994a, p. 43).

When a Chinese business firm has gained sufficient firm-specific competitive advantage in its domestic countries, it may pursue a beach-head strategy for globalization. In this case, the firm may first engage in joint ventures with foreign firms to 'test the water'. The foreign joint venture operation also serves as a marketing and information gathering intelligence unit to prepare the parent firm for the eventual establishment of wholly-owned subsidiaries in the host countries. For example, in Singapore, state-owned Singapore Technologies formed a joint venture with Sierra Semiconductor Corp. of San José to make wafers for integrated circuits. They also took a major stake in Momenta Corp in Mountain View, to make pen-based computers (Hu, 1995, p. 85).

**Strategies for Growth**

In their globalization drive, Chinese business firms may face severe competition in different markets and constraints in different institutional contexts. How do they overcome these difficulties and constraints? What are their strategies for growth in order to capture globalization benefits? Three strategies clearly emerge as Chinese business firms are competing in the global marketplace: (i) sectoral specialization; (ii) diversification; and (iii) control strategies (see also Table 4.4). Most Chinese business firms tend to specialize in niche markets within particular sectors and industries. They are unable to produce sophisticated products with a strong brand name. Rather, most Chinese business firms prefer to operate in the interstices of the trading and subcontracting world. Many of the small and medium enterprises (SMEs) in Hong Kong and Taiwan specialize in parts of the production chains and international subcontracting networks which are essentially controlled by giant global corporations from the Triad regions. These ethnic Chinese SMEs may venture into other Asian countries in order to secure access to low-cost production sites and to meet the demands of their principal customers. Much of the cross-border investment from Hong Kong and Taiwan is of such an origin. To some extent, their cross-border activities represent at best a degree of regionalization rather than globalization because they have yet to develop a global presence and to integrate their worldwide operations.

*Diversification strategies* are particularly favoured by large Chinese conglomerates in the globalization process. They tend to diversify from their core businesses, which are often property development (for example, Cheung Kong from Hong Kong), finance (for example, Hong Leong from Malaysia and Singapore), agribusiness (for example, the CP Group from Thailand), and industrial production (for example, the Liem Group from Indonesia). Two reasons account for their diversification strategies: first, many Chinese business firms gain recognition through investments in real estate and trading businesses. They have subsequently become cash-rich and needed to reduce their risk of overdepending on the return on investments in these two volatile sectors. Diversification into other business fields poses attractive alternatives to spread their risks. Another reason for risk diversification is the pervasive threat of host-country governmental expropriation and ethnic discrimination as described above.

Second, diversification into different business activities is the option preferred by Chinese business firms because of their diverse networks of personal and business relationships. When a leading Chinese business person is approached by a friend or business associate from another industry for equity investment, an agreement may be reached to promote friendship and *guanxi* even though there is no obvious complementarity between their businesses. As a result, the diversification of Chinese firms into different business fields is often determined by social relationships, rather than by strategic necessity. For example, although the diversification of Thailand's CP Group from feed mills to poultry farming is seen as being logical it is much more difficult to rationalize why it has diversified into, and become so successful in, motorcycle manufacturing and telecommunications joint ventures (see Weidenbaum and Hughes, 1996).

In order to compete for growth over time, Chinese business firms must pursue certain *control strategies* that facilitate globalization. One key nexus of these managerial strategies in Chinese business firms is the role of control and co-ordination of their overseas subsidiaries. Control and co-ordination are important in sustaining the competitive advantage of TNCs and their overseas operations because of the difficulties in transferring their competitive advantage from home countries to host countries (Hu, 1995). If appropriate control and co-ordination are not exercised in the management of foreign affiliates, a TNC may eventually find its firm-specific advantages being eroded in an era of global competition. It was noted earlier in this chapter that the control and co-ordination of Chinese family firms is exercised firmly by the patriarch of the family. This is possible because of the sheer proximity of different business units within the same home country, or the presence of networks of personal and business relationships. When these Chinese family firms globalize their operations, it is questionable whether the patriarch can still exercise control and co-ordination over foreign subsidiaries to the same extent. There is not only the issue of geographic distance involved, but also the confrontation of new business environments. Some of these new business environments, such as in North America or Western Europe, may not justify tight control and co-ordination of local subsidiaries by their parent Chinese business firms in Asia. Faced with direct competition and open business fields, many foreign subsidiaries of Chinese business firms need to respond quickly and be able to adapt their organizational structures to allow for more local autonomy and decision-making. They can also absorb more local expertise through local partners and joint ventures, thereby building up new sources of competitive advantage to compete in the regional and global marketplace.

## CONCLUSIONS AND IMPLICATIONS FOR RESEARCH

This chapter has provided a general analysis of the changing dynamics of the globalization of Chinese business firms from Hong Kong, Taiwan and Southeast Asian countries. In particular, it has examined the changing structural and institutional contexts in which these Chinese business firms are embedded. In an era of accelerated globalization of economic activities, Chinese business firms continue to evolve from ethnocentric firms into large conglomerates capable of competing in the regional and global marketplace. In the late 1990s, the unique configuration of institutional and organizational contexts that explain the early characteristics of Chinese business firms has changed. Despite the ongoing Asian economic crisis, there are still many opportunities in the regional and worldwide economy, but the competition between firms is increasingly intense and global. Chinese business firms are therefore compelled to respond by globalizing their operations in order to secure a share in the worldwide marketplace.

As each home country of Chinese business firms enters a different stage of economic development and political change, these ethnic-based firms also move into different stages in their geographical expansion. This chapter has proposed a five-stage model to examine the dynamics of their globalization processes. It must be cautioned that not *all* Chinese business firms will conform to the model; each firm will have its own unique configuration of historical and geographical specificity. Different firms may also join the model at different stages. It is sufficient, however, to note that the model is useful in mapping the general patterns of geographic expansion experienced by most Chinese business firms. The chapter further concludes that the globalization of Chinese business firms is nowhere near complete. In fact, it has just begun, as leading Chinese business firms from Hong Kong, Taiwan and Southeast Asian countries have started to venture into countries outside the Asia Pacific region. Their globalization has become even more imperative in the context of the current Asian economic crisis.

In their drive towards globalization, Chinese business firms tend to prefer joint ventures and acquisitions as the main vehicles of foreign market entry. This preference can be explained by their relative lack of firm-specific competitive advantage (for example, technology and managerial expertise) and their unfamiliarity with host-country business environments. After all, many Chinese business firms grew out of a 'protected' institutional environment in which information flows were limited and monopolistic advantages maintained by business–state coalition. Moreover, many of these Chinese business firms choose to specialize in specific niche segments of production chains, for essentially the same reasons. For those with a large capital base because of monopolistic positions in their home countries, they exist in the form of giant conglomerates with diverse business interests and hundreds of affiliated companies. They prefer to diversify rather than to consolidate their business interests in view of the inherent risk factor in the Asian institutional environment. As their business horizons are increasingly global in scale, the future organizational characteristics of these Chinese business firms are likely to become more diverse and dynamic.

**Note**

1. I would like to thank Danny Van Den Bulcke and Haiyan Zhang for their helpful comments on an earlier draft of this chapter.

# 5 Globalization, Institutionalization and the Social Foundation of Chinese Business Networks*

Hong Liu

## INTRODUCTION

Globalization, defined as 'social, economic, cultural, and demographic processes that take place within nations but also transcend them' (Kearney, 1995, p. 548), has been a central characteristic of the world economy in the late twentieth century. Within this broad context, the globalization of Chinese business firms has constituted one of the dominant forces shaping the nature and characteristics of economic development in the Asia Pacific region, and it has enormous ramifications for the socio-political and cultural (re)configurations of the region (Dirlik, 1997; Yeung, 1999a; Olds and Yeung, 1999). It has been generally agreed that Chinese business networks have contributed significantly to the rapid growth of ethnic Chinese economic activities and the internationalization of Chinese business firms (Mackie, 1992a; East Asian Analytical Unit, 1995; Hamilton, 1996; Chapter 4 in this volume). In conceptualizing these networks, however, most studies seem to have placed an overriding emphasis on the informal, uninstitutional, or under-institutionalized aspects of business networking and to have paid little attention to formal institutionalization.[1] These networks are described as being 'composed mostly of family firms' and as something possessing 'no head, no organization, no politics, and no central "brain"' (see also Chapter 2 in this volume). While the notion that Chinese business networks are based on informal personal and family ties is largely sound, it nevertheless underestimates the significance of their institutionalized social foundation. As this chapter demonstrates, the recent globalization of 'overseas Chinese' social organizations, guided by the principles of locality and kinship and built upon their historical precedence of intensive cross-regional interactions, has provided an important foundation to sustain the formation and expansion of Chinese business networks in the global space-economy. These institutionalized linkages, in turn, serve as a transnational social sphere which facilitates the globalization of Chinese business firms.

This chapter is divided into four parts. It first summarizes a remarkable trend that has characterized the scene of Chinese diaspora communities since the 1970s, namely, the globalization of Chinese social organizations and their increasing transnational mobility. Second, it examines the institutional foundation and historical precedents of this recent phenomenon, pointing to the importance of formal inter-locality linkages among ethnic Chinese in the Asia Pacific region. Third, it analyses the impact of globalization on Chinese business networks, operating within two separate and yet closely related contexts: intra-diaspora linkages and the connections between the diaspora and their ancestral hometowns. Lastly, it briefly considers the theoretical implications and suggests the need to bring institutionalization into the studies of Chinese business networks.

## GLOBALIZING TREND

The globalization of the Chinese diaspora takes a variety of forms, such as the large-scale (re)migration of the ethnic Chinese population, the enormous investment in mainland China, and the extensive flows of cultures and ideas among different circles of the Chinese world (Wang, 1997; Ong, 1997; Tu, 1994). One of the most important vehicles of transnational mobility for the Chinese diaspora, which has been largely unknown to the English-speaking world, is the globalization of Chinese voluntary associations (*shetuan*).[2] This globalization is most obviously manifested in their worldwide gatherings, characterized by four major features: (i) their frequency and large scale; (ii) strong financial and political backing; (iii) their institutionalization; and (iv) their utilitarian functions as a social foundation of Chinese business networks.

First, *shetuan*'s world conventions are held frequently and with large attendance. Preliminary data show that nearly a hundred world conventions of Chinese *shetuan* have taken place since the 1960s, and particularly since 1980. For example, the Fifth Hakka International Reunion was held in Tokyo in 1980, with 1100 participants representing thirty-three associations worldwide. In 1991 more than thirty associations sent some 1000 delegates to the Sixth International Teochew (Chaozhou) Convention held in Paris. The First World Anxi Convention took place in Singapore in 1992, with 2000 delegates coming from different parts of the globe. The Third World Chinese Entrepreneurs Convention opened in Bangkok the next year with 1500 delegates, representing fifty-five Chinese chambers of commerce in twenty-three countries. In 1996, when the Second Fujian World Convention was held in Langkawi (Malaysia), about 2500 representatives took part in the gathering. More than 4000 Teochews from different parts of the globe gathered in Shantou (Guangdong) to hold their international convention in November 1997. The Asian financial crisis has not deterred these associations from holding their international gatherings. In 1998 alone, Hakka, Fuzhou, Jinjiang and Guangdong associations, to name just a few, held their respective international conventions. For example, the Third International Tong-an Convention was held in Malacca in November 1998, with more than 2500 participants from around the world. In the same month, several thousand people gathered in the Great Hall of the People in Beijing to hold the Fifth International Fuzhou Conference.

Second, these conventions are organized and patronized by prominent Chinese transnational entrepreneurs, with the blessing of many local political leaders. The membership roll of the International Association of the Fuzhou Corporation, for example, reads 'like a who's who of overseas Chinese business barons' (Pura, 1994). They include Malaysia's biggest timber tycoon, Tiong Hiew King; Hong Kong-based sugar and hotel magnate, Robert Kuok Hock Nien; patriarch of Indonesia's Salim Group, Liem Sioe Liong; and the chairman of the Indonesia's timber-based Djajanti Group, Burhan Uray. A deputy-speaker of the National People's Congress and two vice-chairmen of the Chinese People's Consultative Congress were present at the Second Tong-an World Convention (Tong-an, Fujian, 1996). National leaders were seen frequently at similar conventions held in Singapore, Malaysia and Thailand. Singapore's Senior Minister, Lee Kuan Yew, once argued that ethnic Chinese should build and maintain worldwide networks among themselves as a valuable tool for business advancement (cited in Lim and Gosling, 1997, p. 309). Canada's prime minister and a number of cabinet ministers attended the opening ceremony of the Fourth World Chinese Entrepreneurs Convention held at Vancouver in August 1997.

Third, the establishment of international co-ordinating entities and permanent secretariats usually follow the world conventions. Since 1984 the World Guan Association, a conglomerate of twenty-two Guan clan associations formed throughout the world by the 'overseas Chinese' whose place of origin is either in Guangdong or Fujian, has had a permanent association centred in Hong Kong (Woon, 1989). Following the 1988 First Fuqing World Convention, the International Federation of Fuqing Clans was formed with headquarters in Singapore. Its lifetime chairmen include Liem Sioe Liong, Rachman Halim (Tjoa To Hing), and Djuhar Susanto (Liem Oen Kian), all prominent ethnic Chinese tycoons. The Federation aims to provide 'planning, organization, and leadership' for its international constituent members.

Last but not least, these world conventions and the resultant international entities are explicitly and intimately linked to the creation and expansion of flourishing Chinese business networks. As will be detailed later, many of these interactions are sponsored and organized by international *shetuan*. They are carried out both among the Chinese diaspora and between them and their kinsfolk in *qiaoxiang* (the diaspora's ancestral hometowns), through such mechanisms as mutual visits, investment and trade fairs, joint holding companies, charitable works and investment projects.

The globalization of Chinese social organizations does not take place in a vacuum. As an integral part of globalization, it emerges against a backdrop of growing transnational mobility and the enormous flow of Chinese capital originated outside the mainland (Lever-Tracy *et al.*, 1996; Brown, 1998). Moreover, this globalization has had its institutional foundation rooted deeply in the historical evolution of the Chinese diaspora communities since the end of the nineteenth century.

## INSTITUTIONAL FOUNDATION AND HISTORICAL PRECEDENTS

As I have argued elsewhere (Liu, 1998b), there are two sets of factors explaining the dramatic rise of organized Chinese transnationalism. The first is concerned with *shetuan*'s internal structure (organization, leadership and membership), and the second the relatively favourable external environments prevailing in the Asia Pacific region (China's economic rise and political climates in Southeast Asia). Here we shall look at the two dimensions that are particularly relevant to the discussion of the social foundation of Chinese business networks and its relationship with globalization, namely, (i) the institutionalized vertical and horizontal linkages; and (ii) the historical patterns of Chinese associations' cross-national business-related activities.

**Vertical Representations and Horizontal Linkages**

Just like their counterparts in mainland China, Chinese diaspora associations were established for the purposes of mutual assistance, dispensing public charities, preserving Chinese culture, and fostering group identity. As a structural form, *shetuan* fulfilled a variety of changing functions, among them the establishment and consolidation of trade specialization by locality/dialect groups as well as the formation of domestic regional trading networks (Goodman, 1996). These practices were carried with them by Chinese immigrants and firmly re-established in their adopted lands. As the 1910 inaugurating statement of the Singapore Fuqing Association put it: 'Our association aims specifically at establishing business networks and promoting fellow-countrymen feelings' (cited in Liu, 1999b). *Kongsi* (limited partnership) is found extensively in Southeast Asia's Chinese business practices, while Singapore's Chinese businessmen tended to establish commercial organizations with their fellows from the same regions. The Chinese in Japan were inclined to form close business ties with fellow-provincials in other Asian nations, and relied on the compatriot clan associations for institutional arrangements of their economic activities (Wang, 1995; Cheng, 1985; Liao, 1997). Many associations were subsequently organized structurally to reflect this business-related function by dividing members into three types: individuals; commercial firms; and groups.

It is clear that *shetuan* took on a dual role. Vertically and within national boundaries, they articulated and represented the interests of a specific locality, clan and trade, and acted as a link between the (colonial) states and Chinese communities in general. Horizontally and beyond national borders, they constituted a nexus connecting various similar associations in other countries and *qiaoxiang*. For example, the Singapore Anxi Association undertook the following activities in the first month of 1940: holding wedding ceremonies for five couples; providing 200 certificates for those returning to China; arbitrating seven disputes among the members; and forwarding twenty letters to the Anxi municipal government (Anxi Association Minutes of Meetings, cited in Liu, 1999b). Throughout the first half of the twentieth century, the Singapore Chinese Chamber of Commerce (founded in 1906) served as a nexus for regional business networks in Asia, its networking orbit extending to mainland China, Indonesia, Malaya, Hong Kong and Japan (Liu, 1998a). It is because of these vertical/horizontal advantages that Chinese social organizations abroad were constructed as key institutional foundations building and sustaining the business linkages among a diverse spectrum of the Chinese diaspora in different parts of Asia (see Chapter 8 in this volume on the similar role of Chinese producer services in North America).

## Patterns of Linkages between Social Organizations and Business Networking

Two patterns of linkages existed between social organizations and business networking prior to the 1980s: the intra-diaspora linkages, and the connections between the Chinese diaspora and their ancestral hometowns. The Singapore Chinese Chamber of Commerce can be taken as an example of the first pattern. It provided various types of commercial information for its members and other Chinese merchants outside Singapore. The Chamber took on a variety of tasks in organizing the interests of Chinese business, and served as a spokesperson for Southeast Asian Chinese business communities as a whole. In the decade following Singapore's independence in 1965, the Chamber mobilized different commercial and political organizations in both Singapore and Malaysia to form extensive business networks. It successfully organized a cross-national campaign to counterbalance the monopoly of Western shipping conferences over the shipping business in Southeast Asia. This in turn helped the economic and trading activities of the Chinese in the two nations, which were heavily reliant on the exportation of raw materials such as rubber (Liu, 1998a, 1999a).

The patterns of business linkage between the Chinese associations and their *qiaoxiang* can be further divided into three sub-patterns: *shetuan* constituted simultaneously (i) as a forum to propagate official 'fund-raising' messages; (ii) as a means of accumulating actual capital for economic development; and (iii) as an agency to represent mainland Chinese companies. Because of their considerable influence, organizational capacities and broad membership base, associations were an indispensable stop for visiting Chinese officials, from the central and local *qiaoxiang* governments alike. In the 1930s, the vice-minister of the Ministry of Overseas Affairs urged the Singapore Anxi Association members to set aside some of their business profits for 'investment in China as an indication of supporting the nation'. Addressing the same Association, the consul of the Chinese embassy emphasized that 'overseas Chinese' had a long tradition of supporting China, which earned them the honour of 'Mother of the Revolution', and that it was their moral obligation to help the motherland (Liu, 1999b).

Partly inspired by this combined power of broad-based nationalism and local loyalty, Chinese social organizations were involved actively in efforts to raise funds for economic construction in *qiaoxiang*. In the 1947 Pan-Malaya Federation of Taishan Associations meeting, more than a quarter of the resolutions were concerned with the promotion of Taishan's economy. Resolution 5, for example, suggested that 'overseas Chinese' resources should be tapped for local economic development and that the county government should formulate detailed plans to encourage the Taishanese abroad to form corporations to invest in their hometown. More concrete fund-raising efforts were undertaken through the channel of associations. For example, during the 1930s, both the Fujian Economic Development Holdings Company and Hui'an Fishing Company were successful in raising funds by using the Singapore Hui'an Association as an effective venue.

Chinese associations abroad also served as an agency for companies in *qiaoxiang* and the mainland. In 1949, Hong Kong's Jiyou Bank provided the Singapore Tong-an Association with detail information concerning its clientele and marketing strategies, asking the Association's help in courting business with their fellows from the same region. In the 1920s, the Singapore Chinese Chamber of Commerce was the agent for sixteen major Chinese companies, including the Chinese Commercial Bank, Sin-Thai Shipping Company, and the Bank of China, some of which were located in *qiaoxiang* and/or had substantial business dealings with them (Liu, 1998a, 1999b).

**Enforcement Mechanisms of Business Trust**

In addition to these two patterns of direct support for business networking, Chinese social organizations also acted as an enforcement mechanism of business trust. It has been established convincingly that one of the enduring features of Chinese business practices is trust (*xinyong*), which helps to reduce transactional costs (the search for trading partners, costs of contract negotiation, enforcement and so on) (Mackie, 1992a; Landa, 1991; Tong and Yong, 1998). 'While monetary capital is limited, the capital of trust is boundless', a publication of the Singapore Chinese Chamber of Commerce declared, 'If a businessman does not abide by business ethic [which is the foundation of trust], he is just like committing suicide [*sic*]' (SCCC, 1931, p. 20). The question, then, is how to forge and sustain business trust, both personally and institutionally?

While it has been pointed out correctly that traditional Chinese values – Confucian ethics in particular – have been instrumental in the formation of business trust, this cultural element is more like 'software', or what Douglass North (1990, p. 4) calls 'informal constraints' (conventions and codes of behaviour).[3] Its effective operation requires a set of compatible 'hardware' or 'formal constraints' (institutions). Defined as 'any constraint humans devise to shape their interactions', institutions 'reduce uncertainty by providing a structure to everyday life'. As such, 'the institutional framework plays a major role in the performance of an economy' (North, 1990, pp. 25, 69). Such institutional hardware and formal constraints were, and continue to be, important in the colonial and post-colonial societies, where the legal infrastructure has been inadequate, and the lack of long-term agreements and non-existence of secure property rights has led to high transaction costs. Through formulating and sustaining proper codes of behaviour and supporting Chinese cultural values, Chinese social organizations have played a part in fostering a sociocultural ethic that was conducive to business trust. More importantly, they have served as a third-party enforcement mechanism encouraging business trust.

Let us take another historical example. During the early 1930s, the Singapore Chinese Chamber of Commerce worked closely with business and political organizations in Malaya, Singapore and China, and dealt successfully with a number of cases where business trust was being abused. In 1930, Tay Zinan, a businessman from Kluang (Malaysia), cheated two commercial firms in Singapore. On receiving the latters' complaints, the Chamber first appealed directly to Tay. But he took money and ran away to his hometown in Jieyang (Guangdong). Starting in December 1930, the case was formally filed with the SCCC, which then communicated with the two firms in Singapore, the Shantou Chamber of Commerce (which had commercial judicial control over Jieyang), the municipal government of Jieyang county, and the Court of Jieyang county. In addition to supplying details of Tay's whereabouts in China, the Chamber also suggested appropriate ways of handling this case. By the end of April 1931, Tay had been arrested and charged by the Court in Jieyang (SCCC, 1931, pp. 6–60). In a similar vein, the Penang Anxi Association in Malaya engaged in a series of concerted actions with its Singapore counterpart to deal with an embezzlement case involving a former manager at the Anxi Bus Company, in which Anxi fellows abroad had invested a substantial amount of money (Liu, 1999b).

It is clear that ethnic Chinese associations have taken advantage of their vertical/horizontal linkages and played an important role in the making of Chinese business networks characterized by their extensive regional interdependence (McVey, 1992; Brown, 1995). The existence of dense social/locality/kinship networks of interaction, in turn, helped to reduce the costs of transacting, thus facilitating the trading activities of the Chinese diaspora, both among themselves and between them and *qiaoxiang*. The recent globalization of these organizations has therefore built on the institutional foundation and historical precedents of social–business interactions that existed prior to 1980. Since the principal rationale for their globalization lies in seizing the expanding business opportunities worldwide, particularly in China, the associations' built-in business functions and vertical/horizontal linkages can easily be converted into promoting their new agendas of transnationalism.

Like their predecessors of the pre-1980 era, the contemporary globalizing activities of Chinese *shetuan* abroad are similarly guided by the principles of locality and kinship, and driven by a longing to expand business networks beyond national boundaries. There are, however, at least four structural differences. First, in terms of operating space, while the pre-1980 *shetuan* mainly undertook bilateral relations in the region of East/Southeast Asia, the internationalizing *shetuan* of the 1980s and 1990s have not only transcended national borders, but have also gone far beyond the Asian region and extended into North America and Europe. Two-way communications have been transformed into multi-dimensional networks. Second, in terms of membership, while the pre-1980 *shetuan* were primarily concerned with and bounded by their traditional obligations to their domestic members, new international associations have the specific purpose of reaching a cross-national membership who are keen to take advantage of expanding economic opportunities and renewing compatriot cultural ties. Reflecting this greatly expanded social space and needs, the leadership is composed of ethnic Chinese from various countries. Third, while the pre-1980 activities were represented primarily by higher levels of aggregation such as provincial-based associations, current *shetuan's* globalization is predominantly propelled by a new set of dynamic actors – namely, lower and county level associations, which collectively form their respective international *shetuan*. For example, the International Jinjiang Federation was formed in May 1997 and is composed of member associations from Asia, Europe, North America, Australia and South Africa. It has evolved from the Union of Jinjiang Societies formed in Asia in 1990, with members in Singapore, Malaysia, Indonesia, Macao, the Philippines, Taiwan and mainland China (Sinn, 1997). Lastly, the current wave of *shetuan* globalization is marked by a greater degree of institutionalization, with sophisticated agencies to carry out systematically their international missions and specific ideological justifications to legitimate and sustain this new pattern of organized Chinese transnationalism.

## REINVIGORATING OLD LINKAGES

Having established the observation that the globalization of Chinese social organizations has its institutional foundation and historical prec-edents, I now turn to the role of this globalization in the formation and expansion of Chinese business networks. Three patterns can be identi-fied: (i) globalization as a forum to establish contacts and to cultivate trust both intra-diaspora and between ethnic Chinese abroad and their compatriots in *qiaoxiang*; (ii) globalization as an institutionalized mech-anism to carry out investment and charitable works in *qiaoxiang*; and (iii) globalization as a cultural agency to shape (sub)ethnic identities and strengthening the symbolic capital of transnational entrepreneurs.

### Globalization as a Forum to Establish Contacts and Cultivate Trust

As discussed earlier, the notion and practice of trust historically were essential to Chinese business and they remain indispensable today. 'I think *xinyong* (trust) is the most important element in doing business,' said Liem Sioe Liong. 'This is the reason why I consider *xinyong* to be my second life' (*Rong Qing*, no. 22 [1994], p. 6). Contrasting the busi-ness practices of ethnic Chinese with those of Westerners, the manage-ment guru Peter Drucker comments: 'What holds the [ethnic Chinese] multinationals together is neither ownership nor legal contract. It is mutual trust and the mutual obligations inherent in clan membership' (Drucker, 1994).

An essential strategy of building and maintaining trust is through face-to-face interpersonal contacts. It is here that old linkages based on place of origin, kinship and dialect have a comparative advantage because they can be used as a foundation for establishing *guanxi* (personal rela-tionships), a concept that is embedded in Chinese culture. According to Mayfair Yang (1994, p. 111; my emphasis), 'Guanxi exchange can only be carried out between two parties who have established in one way or another, *a basis of familiarity*'. It has also been pointed out that in Chi-nese societies, 'the most common shared attributes for building net-works are locality (native place), kinship ... [and] surname' and that the nature of these shared attributes 'is quite elastic in the sense that they can be contracted and expanded' (King, 1994, p. 116). Therefore, in the same manner as what Pierre Bourdieu calls 'the social uses of kinship', old ties can effectively be reinvigorated to cultivate trust and *guanxi* for economic purposes. For one thing, a common heritage and shared traits are perceived as bridges through which strangers can get to know each other and to explore further the possibilities of forging business partnerships (see also Chapter 8 in this volume).

In his autobiography, Lin Tongchun, president of the Kobe General Association of Overseas Chinese and Chinese Chamber of Commerce, who has also been active in the International Federation of Fuqing Clans, recounted how the trading networks of Japan's Fujianese businessmen with their fellow-provincials in other parts of Asia constituted 'a key to their business success in the post-World War II era' (Lin, 1997, pp. 147, 199; personal interview). During the First Fujianese World Convention held in Los Angeles in 1994, a North American delegate put it emotion-ally: 'over the past several decades, we have been wandering around all over the world and have encountered numerous difficulties and set-backs. In a strange land, the only people we can turn to for help are those fellows originating from the same place' (cited in Liu, 1998b, p. 599). Udane Techapaiboon, a Sino-Thai tycoon, attributed in a somewhat romanticized and simplified manner the success of ethnic Chinese abroad to 'two unique Chinese traditions': kinship and native-place sentiment (*Guoji Chaoxu* [TIC Bulletin], nos. 18/19 [1996], p. 6). In a similar vein, Liem Sioe Liong believed that compared with other types of associ-ation, native-place association is a better basis upon which to establish close relationships. He declared that 'after all, we are all from the same county, speak the same dialect, and share common customs. By singing the same clan song, we can forge great unity among our fellow county-men' (*Rong Qing*, no. 22 [1994], p. 6).

While old linkages based on locality, kinship and dialect are condu-cive to the formation of business networks, 'Chineseness' (being Chinese and speaking Chinese) also plays a role. This is where one finds the rel-evance of trade associations such as Chinese chambers of commerce and their vigorous transnational mobility. The first World Chinese Entrepreneurs Convention (Singapore, 1991) was based on 'the com-monality of our ethnicity', as its organizing committee chairman put it (SCCCI, 1991, p. 19). During this and subsequent meetings, there have been constant emphases on Chinese culture's contributions to the suc-cess of the Chinese diaspora.

Chinese voluntary associations' globalization has provided not only the forums in which to establish and renew fellow feelings, but also various institutional channels to facilitate business ties. *Rong Qing*, the internal publication of the International Federation of Fuqing Clans, regularly issues member directories, in which the Fuqingese from all over the world supply specific information concerning their personal businesses and areas of possible co-operation with fellow countymen in other places. Modern technology is used for the same purposes. The World Chinese Business Network (WCBN) was formally launched by the Singapore Chinese Chamber of Commerce and Industry in 1995. Accessible through the Internet (http://www.wcbn.com.sg), this is a massive database containing information on more than 100 000 companies run by Chinese business people in fifty-three nations. The WCBN, according to its sponsor, 'aims at strengthening the networking of Chinese businessmen throughout the world. It is designed to help Chinese businessmen world wide in establishing contacts and exchanging information with one another in a speedy and systematic manner'. It is reported that the site receives some 500 000 hits in an average month (*Business Times*, 8 December 1995; *Lianhe Zaobao*, 12 August 1997).

These different methods of contact have bolstered and re-created the bonds based on real or imagined commonality in (sub)ethnicity, place of origin and kinship, and they are particularly instrumental in the early stages of business networking. After the people involved get to know each other better, shared attributes and backgrounds become less relevant and the *shetuan* connection is then pushed into the background. It is at this stage that the parties concerned are prepared to enter into more substantial discussions and actual business dealings (personal interviews with an entrepreneur who frequents such meetings). It is precisely in this connection that Dr Ling Liong Sik, chairman of the influential Malaysian Chinese Association and the country's Minister of Transportation, urged his fellow Fuzhouese who were attending the First International Fuzhou Conference to 'nurture fellow feelings, exchange business information, and establish trade credits through kinship-based friendship'.

**Globalization as an Institutionalized Mechanism for Investment and Charitable Works**

Social and business networks partially founded by Chinese voluntary associations and their international entities normally work through three major mechanisms: (i) the reaffirmation of *shetuan*'s long-developed business capacity; (ii) the setting-up of *shetuan*-based holding and investment companies; and (iii) the pooling of Chinese financial resources for infrastructure construction and charitable works in *qiaoxiang*. As mentioned earlier, Chinese voluntary associations historically had an inbuilt function to facilitate the formation and expansion of business networks. With their declining influence in some (Southeast Asian) domestic settings in the 1960s and 1970s, this function has been forgotten or played down. The worldwide gathering and resulting international entities provide a good opportunity to reaffirm and reinforce this business-related function that has been written into almost all of the constitutions of the international bodies of voluntary associations. Two of the four aims of the International Tong-an Association, for example, are directly concerned with expanding business linkages: 'liaising with fellow Tong-anese from all over the world for the purpose of promoting mutual relationship' and 'exchanging business information in all parts of the world for the purpose of promoting investment and trade' (Tong-an, 1994, p. 11). Similarly, the Constitution of the International Anxi Society specifies six objectives, four of which are about the methods and mechanisms for 'establishing a worldwide business networks of Anxiese' (Anxi, 1994, p. 98). And these conventions and codes of behaviour are followed closely in each international gathering. For example, during the 13th International Hakka Reunion, which attracted more than 3000 participants (Singapore, 1996), the majority of resolutions passed were concerned with the formation of Hakka-based business networks (Hakka, 1998, pp. 101–2).

In almost every *shetuan*'s world convention, the proposal of setting up clan-based holding companies is raised, debated and refined. This agenda is derived partly from the fact that many Chinese voluntary associations control vast financial resources. It is estimated, for example, that Malaysia's Chinese associations possessed a combined asset of M$10 bn (US$4 bn) in 1996 (*Sinchew Jitpoh*, 8 October 1996). To use these collective resources effectively, holding companies have to be established to circumvent regulations that prevent voluntary associations from engaging directly in commercial activities. Take the Guangxi International Association as an example. The idea of forming an International Guangxi Corporation was raised and discussed during the two world conventions in 1986 and 1988. In a 1993 Singapore meeting, Seng Lup Chew, honorary chairman of the Guangxi International Association, called for the establishment of internationally-based Guangxi investment and holding companies to invest in Guangxi and 'other profitable areas'. Other Chinese international *shetuan* followed the suit. During the First World Anxi Convention in 1992, Tong Djoe, chairman of the International Anxi Society and a prominent Sino-Indonesian tycoon, urged his fellow countrymen to form international conglomerates to invest in China. 'Blood is thicker than water,' concurred the chairman of Malaysian Selangor Anxi Association. 'For this reason alone, we should set up holding companies to invest in Anxi' (Anxi, 1994, pp. 26, 51–2). Participants of the First Feng Shun World Convention (Singapore, 1992) decided to raise S\$30 m (US\$18.4 m) to set up a Feng Shun Holdings Company which was to construct an 'overseas Chinese' new town, a hot spring recreation village in Feng Shun (Guangdong) and a 22-storey building in Guangzhou (*Lianhe Zaobao*, 7 December 1992).

A third mechanism uses the pooled financial resources of clans and individual members abroad to help infrastructure and charitable works in *qiaoxiang*. The booming economy of the south-eastern coast of mainland China creates an unprecedented need for infrastructure constructions that require large amounts of capital which cannot be raised by the local *qiaoxiang* governments alone (see Chapters 10 and 11 in this volume). It is at this point that 'overseas Chinese' capital, channelled partly through international *shetuan*, provides some essential support. During the 12th International Hakka Reunion held in Meizhou in 1994, Hakka from outside mainland China contributed some 70 million *yuan* (US\$8.1 m) to public and charitable projects. The International Tong-an Association has also been instrumental in fund-raising efforts to help construct the Lianhua Water Reservoir in Tong-an, begun in 1997.

*Qiaoxiang* also benefits directly from hosting the trade fairs and investment talks which constitute an indispensable part of convention schedules. In the Second Anxi World Convention (Anxi, 1994), some US\$20 m-worth of contracts and Memorandums of Understanding (MoUs) were agreed upon, while the Second Tong-an World Convention (Tong-an, 1996) witnessed the signing of contracts, agreements and MoUs with a total value of US\$160 m. During the Second Fujianese World Convention in Langkawi (Malaysia, 1996), to which the Fujian provincial government sent a large delegation led by the vice-governor, six investment projects worth US\$25 m were being set up (*Lianhe Wanbao*, 6 November 1994; *Lianhe Zaobao*, 5 December 1996).

In short, Chinese voluntary associations' globalizing activities have created tremendous and tangible economic results for both *qiaoxiang* and the Chinese diaspora. Anxi may be taken as a representative. According to official statistics, during the eighteen months after the holding of the First Anxi World Convention, more than 3000 Anxiese abroad visited their hometown for tourism and economic activities. They spent 49.5 million *yuan* (US\$5.7 m) in charitable projects (such as hospitals and schools), set up fifty-one factories worth of 92.4 million *yuan* (US$10.7 m), and contributed some US$64.8 m of additional capital to Anxi. This almost doubled the number of new factories and provided 4.6 times the amount of overseas Anxiese's investment. In 1997, Anxi's enterprises had increased their total output to ten times the rate of five years before (*Anxi Xiangxu*, 6 April 1994; Liu, 1998b).

**Globalization as a Cultural Agency in Shaping (Sub)Ethnic Identities and Strengthening Symbolic Capital**

The functions of the globalization of Chinese associations should not be judged entirely in economic terms; there are broader social and cultural ramifications involved. One of the major missions of *shetuan*'s globalization has been the preservation and promotion of specific local cultures and traditions. Together with business networking, this is another key agenda that has been written into the constitutions of nearly all Chinese international associations. Seminars or international conferences on concerned local cultures and the showcasing of popular (sub) cultures (such as food festivals and folklore dancing) constitute a major part of *shetuan*'s world conventions. These organized activities help to inject (or renew) public interest in traditional forms of cultural representation that might otherwise be forgotten or dying. By highlighting the uniqueness of concerned groups, Chinese diaspora's cultural affinities with their ancestral homes have also been forged or strengthened. The singing of Hakka mountain songs, for example, is considered to be 'invaluable for maintaining the Hakka identity'. While participating in the 9th International Teochew Convention in Shantou in 1997, an Indonesian-Chinese realized that 'dialect is a special kind of identity and sentiment'. After visiting their relatives living in the countryside during the same convention, Singapore Teochews were convinced that 'blood is after all thicker than water and the fellow sentiment cannot be separated by distance' (*Lianhe Zaobao*, 20 and 24 November 1997).

'The homeland is partly invented', writes anthropologist, Arjun Appadurai (1991, p. 193), 'existing only in the imagination of the deterritorialized groups'. For some Chinese diaspora, the globalizing process has helped to transform a cultural homeland from an imagined one into a reality. For historical reasons, Hakka ('guest people') lack a collectively recognized and identifiable hometown. Yew Sim Liong, a Hong Kong-based tycoon originating from Malaysia and the honorary chairman of the 13th Hakka International Convention in 1996, declared that 'after substantial research' he had identified the village of Shibi (in

Linghua, Fujian) as Hakka's Holy Land. A World Hakka Shrine has subsequently been established there and the Ting River claimed to be Hakka's Mother River (*Sinchew Jitpoh*, 1 January 1996). The reinforcement of Chinese (sub)ethnicity serves as a social foundation and cultural bond nurturing the growth of business networks. In the meantime, it facilitates Chinese transnational entrepreneurs' accumulation of symbolic capital and the collective consciousness of the international clan membership, which is made up mainly of people from small and medium-sized businesses.

As noted elsewhere (Liu, 1998b), the rapid globalizing activities of Chinese associations have been led and supported by Chinese transnational entrepreneurs characterized by their international-orientated outlook and extensive cross-national investments. They provide major financial backing to the holding of each international convention and the maintenance of subsequent international entities. To them, participating in this globalizing movement not only reaffirms their strong Chineseness or a sub-ethnicity based on locality and/or kinship, but it also strengthens their symbolic capital. According to Pierre Bourdieu, 'symbolic capital is a credit; it is the power granted to those who have obtained sufficient recognition to be in a position to impose recognition' (Bourdieu, 1989, p. 22). The financial patronizing of *shetuan*'s international gathering is therefore constructed as a strategy to seek and/or accumulate 'symbolic capital' and to further bolster up their credit and status. Indeed, where can one find a better occasion than a world convention – in which prominent Chinese transnational entrepreneurs, indigenous people and politicians from China, and fellow clan/kinship people are all present – to be seen and to know someone in strategic positions? As noted by Bourdieu, this symbolic capital can be converted into social and economic capital.

*Shetuan*'s globalizing movement has also had an impact on the Chinese diaspora's collective consciousness which has a historical base partly on real or imagined commonalties in (sub)ethnicity, dialect, kinship and place of origin. It is also shaped by the common diaspora background. As James Clifford (1994, p. 306) has pointed out, diaspora consciousness is constituted by 'the experience of discrimination and exclusion' and by 'a shared, ongoing history of displacement, suffering, adaptation, or resistance'. This shared past and culture, together with a history of dispersal and myths/memories of a real or symbolic homeland, becomes a strong glue bonding ethnic Chinese from different parts of the globe. Chinese associations' world conventions are perfect occasions to remember, renew and reinforce this collective past and ongoing present. The strengthening of sub-ethnicity provides an additional incentive for the forging of business ties among people with shared traits, because the younger generation of ethnic Chinese abroad joined clan associations partly to attract business opportunities. In the words of Chua Lew Kee, president of Singapore Ji Yang Cai Clan Association, 'Those who invest in China often find it easier to deal with others of the same surname or from the same locality' (*Sunday Times*, 17 April 1994).

Scholars find that Chinese businessmen abroad have an inclination to form partnerships with people of similar backgrounds in ethnicity, kinship, place of origin and dialect. According to a survey of Chinese entrepreneurs abroad conducted by John Kao of Harvard Business School, 52 per cent noted that more than half of their domestic working relationships and 39 per cent of their international business ties were with Chinese principals (Kao, 1993). Moreover, those involved in small and medium-sized businesses are particularly keen to take part in world conventions and concerned international bodies because, as a middle-aged Singapore Chinese entrepreneur who frequents such meetings said, 'they want to know somebody and to be known'. According to him, the participation of *shetuan* activities also provides a testing ground where a person's social and business abilities can be judged by his/her peers. These contacts are important first steps in selecting (and being selected for) potential business partners (personal interviews).

In brief, the globalization of Chinese voluntary associations has multidimensional functions. It not only revitalizes and regenerates old (and sometimes forgotten) linkages, but more importantly, it provides muchneeded spaces, forums and mechanisms to forge new international business and sociocultural networks. Without a doubt, Chinese entrepreneurs' foremost consideration in deciding the sites of their investments has been profitability and the economic opportunities available. Nevertheless, because real/fictive (sub)cultural affinities could facilitate significantly the formation and consolidation of effective personal and business relationships, shared sub-ethnic traits play an important part in directing a substantial amount of investment and charitable money to *qiaoxiang*. It is perhaps partly for this reason that even those who are not active players in Chinese associations' globalizing movement, such as Mochtar Riady (Li Wenzheng), chairman of Indonesia's Lippo Group, are similarly following the path of 'playing up local ties' by investing heavily in their ancestral homes (Faison, 1996; *Lianhe Zaobao*, 27 November 1992, 27 January 1993).

## CONCLUDING OBSERVATIONS

The globalization of Chinese voluntary associations, as I have argued, is a reworking of structural and cultural relationships in a multiple-dimensional global space. It has been constructed as a strategy of historical regeneration, social survival, economic expansion and cultural revitalization for traditional Chinese organizations. This flourishing globalization and the resulting multi-polarity diaspora networks have had a profound impact on the patterns of modern Chinese transnationalism and the socio-economic development of the Asia Pacific region, and *qiaoxiang* in particular. Although the ongoing Asian economic crisis has undoubtedly had a negative effect on the scale and pace of this globalization, the trend toward internationalization and transnational mobility still continues.

What are the theoretical implications of this case study concerning the interactions between the globalization of Chinese social organizations and the institutionalization of Chinese business networks? There are at least three issues that deserve further analysis: (i) the social foundation of business networks; (ii) the patterns of state–society linkages and economic performance; and (iii) the dialectic relationship between globalization and localization (see Chapter 12 in this volume). The first implication is concerned with the role of social organizations in the making and the expansion of Chinese business networks. While it has rightly been argued that family (business) and informal personal ties form the basic building blocks of Chinese business networks, the role of formal institutionalization built and facilitated by Chinese social organizations should not be overlooked. For one thing, unlike their Western counterparts, Chinese voluntary associations were formed with the specific agenda of promoting (cross-border) business ties with people of common backgrounds. Historically, in China as well as abroad, they were actively engaged in the forming and sustaining of ethnic-based business networks, linking Chinese people from different corners of Asia. These regionalized interactions became the historical precedents of *shetuan*'s current transnational mobility. In the transition to this globalizing phase, their business-related functions have been increasingly institutionalized: they have gained remarkable stability (symbolized by the formation of international *shetuan* entities) and have acquired well-cherished value (exemplified by the incorporation of commercial agendas into *shetuan*'s constitutions). Furthermore, in the process of procuring stability and value, Chinese social organizations' business linkages have been maximized by forging joint investments, facilitating business trust, and fostering the symbolic capital of transnational entrepreneurs.

Juxtaposed with and reinforcing personal informal networks, this formal institutional framework constitutes an important competitive advantage that distinguishes Chinese entrepreneurs from their Southeast Asian native counterparts. It thus buttresses the characteristics of Chinese capitalism in the region, which is considered as 'first and foremost a *network* capitalism ... [being] built from the ground up, not on the basis of legal contracts and the supervisory authority of the state but on particularistic relationships of trust' (Hefner, 1998, p. 12). Seen from a theoretical perspective, this institutionalization forms a central component of what Kenneth Arrow calls 'the social system' which is essential to the working of the economic system.[4] Indeed, in the process of *shetuan*'s globalization, the values of communications, shared social norms and the enforcement mechanisms are all being highlighted, strengthened and materialized.

The second implication is concerned with the place of voluntary associations in the overall configuration of state–society relationships and their links with economic performance in a globalizing era. It has been pointed out that the patterns of state–society linkages have a direct bearing on economic development in contemporary East and Southeast Asia. Since the 1970s, such societal forces as business associations have been increasingly assertive in determining the course of the region's politico-economic evolution. An institutionalist approach has emerged to explain this new phenomenon (Hawes and Liu, 1993; Unger, 1996; Nevitt, 1996), and the globalization of Chinese associations can be examined within a similar framework. For one thing, their structural strength of vertical/horizontal linkages has been revitalized to promote transnational business activities, thus reinforcing the collective bargaining power of the societal force as a whole. In line with the far-reaching impact of globalization, these cross-border movements may lead to the partial erosion of state authorities and the growth of civil societies. In the meantime, these increasingly important societal forces, including Chinese associations of various types, in fact constitute a bridge between state and society. This provides a counter-argument to Francis Fukuyama's assertion (1995) that Chinese societies are low-trust societies because they lack a strong and effective link between the state and society. Voluntary associations in effect have been an important institutional source in supplying sociocultural norms and enforcement mechanisms to support business trust.

Finally, it should be emphasized that the globalization of Chinese associations takes place against the backdrop of increasing localization. This case study may be seen as a complementary exercise to support the view that globalization in effect propels a return to the local and the familiar (Kearney, 1995; Wang, 1997; Cohen, 1997). These two simultaneous processes are in fact two sides of the same coin which should not be construed as dichotomies. The globalizing trajectory of Chinese social organizations is based on local and parochial entities and sentiments, such as regional associations, local cultures, dialects, renewed interests/reinvented memories of the place of origin, and the support from *qiaoxiang* authorities. The reinforcement of what Geertz calls 'primordial attachments' (Geertz, 1973, p. 259) has in fact served as a powerful dynamic to the Chinese diaspora's transnational mobility. This internationalizing process, in return, strengthens *qiaoxiang's* economic power and influence. It also helps to revitalize Chinese (sub)cultures and provides much needed impetus for the survival and expansion of traditional Chinese associations within national boundaries. This dual process of globalization and localization therefore provides a transnational social sphere that facilitates the expansion of Chinese business networks and the globalization of Chinese business firms.

### Notes

\* Some of the material used in this chapter has appeared in Liu (1998b).

1.  This paper follows Samuel Huntington's definition of institutionalization, which is 'the process by which organizations and procedures acquire value and stability' (quoted in Remmer, 1997, p. 35).
2.  A voluntary association is defined as 'any public, formally constituted, and non-commercial organization of which membership is optional, within a particular society' (Marshall, 1994, p. 557). It should be borne in mind that Chinese voluntary associations are different from those in the West. As Hamilton (1996a, p. 18) points out, 'Voluntary associations are clubs with members, with precise organizational boundaries, with some kind of governing body and specific purpose, and with written duties and responsibilities for the members. Chinese associations, however, are not so clear-cut as these, and not as well defined and neatly bounded. Rather, these Chinese groups focus on the relationships that bind members into a common identity and that form a moral community out of which a sense of duty and obligation arises.'
3.  Kenneth Arrow also argues that 'for there to be trust, there has to be a social structure which is based on motives different from immediate opportunism' (Quoted in Swedberg, 1990, p. 137). I am indebted to Professor Kunio Yoshihara for bringing to my attention important theoretical insights articulated by North and Arrow, both of whom are Noble Prize-winning economists.

4. According to Arrow (quoted in Swedberg, 1990, pp. 139–40), all three elements of the social system are needed for the economic system to work: 'the element of communication, such as codes, symbols, and understanding; the element of shared social norms, which is the reasonable expectation that the norms will be followed even if it would be profitable not to follow them at least in the short run; and thirdly, the existing institutions for enforcement, which themselves operate outside the market system and are needed for enforcement purpose'.

# 6 Internationalization of Ethnic Chinese-Owned Enterprises: A Network Approach

Haiyan Zhang and Daniel Van Den Bulcke

## INTRODUCTION

Research into ethnic Chinese-owned enterprises[1] has identified social and business networks as powerful determinants of the economic success of Chinese entrepreneurs in Southeast Asian economies (Redding, 1995; Brown, 1995). In recent years the network concept has frequently been used to explain typical organizational structures as well as the internationalization process of ethnic Chinese-owned multinational enterprises (CHMNEs) (Kao, 1993; Yeung, 1997a). There seems to be a general agreement in the literature that the corporate governance and business system of Chinese enterprises are greatly affected by the social and personal relations of their entrepreneurs (Redding, 1990; Whitley, 1990, 1991, 1992). Hence, a better understanding of how these entrepreneurial networks of CHMNEs might assist in reducing transaction costs and substitute for deficiencies in their resource-based ownership advantages is a relevant research topic. An important concern in research about the internationalization process, strategic setting, control and organization is also to find out how and to what extent these social and personal networks affect CHMNEs in their building of successful cross-border inter- and intra-firm linkages.

The main purpose of this chapter is to suggest a conceptual framework to analyze the extent and patterns of the dynamic interaction between entrepreneurial and business networks in the internationalization process of CHMNEs (see also Chapter 4 in this volume). The chapter is structured as follows: in the second section, the internationalization of firms is explored from the perspective of transaction cost economics (TCE). The shortcomings of the TCE approach are discussed before the network concept is introduced in the third section. The business

126

network is analysed as a hybrid form between market governance and firm hierarchy, while the social network of entrepreneurs is considered to have an impact on the business transactions of firms. In the fourth section, the salient characteristics of ethnic Chinese-owned enterprises are examined in relation to the network approach. The penultimate section examines the interactive patterns of business and entrepreneurial networks in the internationalization process of CHMNEs, while the concluding section summarizes the main arguments of the chapter and emphasizes some possible implications for existing studies on the internationalization of firms.

## MARKETS OR FIRMS: THEORETICAL PERSPECTIVE OF TRANSACTION COST ECONOMICS

Most widely accepted theoretical approaches on the internationalization of firms (for example, Buckley and Casson, 1976, 1988; Casson, 1990; Rugman, 1980; Hennart, 1982, 1988, 1990; Teece, 1986) are basically derived from transaction cost economics (Williamson, 1975, 1985). The principal tenets of this so-called 'internalization model' suggest that the lack of and/or the imperfection of markets, especially for intermediate goods, makes it often impossible or inefficient (that is, more expensive) for a firm to serve a foreign country via the market – for example, by exporting or licensing agreements. Internal structures are established as an alternative to markets in order to remove many hindrances. The replacement of markets by hierarchically structured M-form corporations lowers costs that are normally connected with the negotiation and enforcement of contracts to manage business transactions. Compared to market transactions, however, hierarchies provide 'agents' with weaker incentives to maximize profits and normally incur additional bureaucratic costs for controlling and co-ordinating intra-firm exchanges (Buckley and Casson, 1976, pp. 33–4). Therefore, the strategic decision process and the choice of an organizational structure in cross-border business transactions are functions of two main factors. First, there are economic benefits that can be derived from internalizing transactions within the firm. Second, there are bureaucratic costs associated with managing M-form corporations. It is postulated by the transaction cost perspective that the difference between relative benefits and costs leads firms to choose either a market approach or internal vertical integration, or possibly horizontal diversification (Jones and Hill, 1988, p. 160).

Although the TCE in general provides a powerful explanation of the emergence and development of multinational enterprises (MNEs), a growing number of studies on international business and organization have challenged the TCE-based views. Three main critical limitations have been recognized. First, since the simple dichotomy between market transactions and internalization within the firm represents only two transaction forms among a number of possible economic arrangements, it would seem that the TCE cannot sufficiently explain when the economic exchanges take place within a hybrid structure. The expansion of new business organizations – such as co-operative agreements on supply, distribution and marketing, non-equity consortia for R&D, or co-production and strategic alliances – shows that the 'monolithic' structure of the traditional MNEs has changed (Van Den Bulcke, 1995, p. 27). Also, the affiliates or production units of MNEs tend to increase their independence *vis-à-vis* their parent companies or/and other subsidiaries, while structural decentralization results more often in the formation of new organizational set-ups, such as networks (Nohria and Eccles, 1992) or 'heterarchy' (Hedlund, 1986), and 'transnational' mindset's (Ghoshal and Bartlett, 1990). Thus clusters or networks of cross-border internal and external relationships tend to be regarded as a hybrid form that combines aspects of both market transactions and hierarchical administration (Casson and Cox, 1992; Florin, 1996).

Second, it is argued that the transaction cost approach takes the transaction as given rather than as a value-generation process (Demsetz, 1988). The 'historical heritage' and the consequent inertia inside the firm are not considered in detail (Fladmoe-Lindquist and Tallman, 1992). From the internationalization perspective, TCE is not concerned with the competitive advantages that could be created during cross-border business transactions – that is, the *'transitional ownership advantages'*. Yet these advantages are quite different from asset-based ownership advantages because they are derived from the internationalization process itself. The third shortcoming in TCE is that it does not sufficiently appreciate the social context and cultural dimension that could affect international business transactions. A link between the cultural context and the technical concept of transaction cost is generally absent in TCE. However, empirical research has shown that the cohesion which exists in particular societies may enable the reduction of transaction costs because of the existence of high levels of trust among members of a society (Buckley, 1991; see also Chapter 2 in this volume). More explicitly, Boisot (1986) has developed a conceptual framework to analyze the cultural aspects of organizational phenomena. He shows that the choice between markets and hierarchies cannot be reduced to a simple choice between an external and an internal transaction. Cultural variables may act as catalysts in such a way that they can influence how firms grow and expand abroad.

The above criticisms are mainly derived from the 'rediscovery' of corporate networks based on social groupings in general (Casson and Cox, 1992) and the recognition of networks and dense ties between entrepreneurs in Southeast Asian economies in particular (Biggart and Hamilton, 1992). While the paradigm of TCE implies that economic actors are rational and autonomous, and that they seek their self-interest independently of social relations, social networks of entrepreneurs in Southeast Asia link firms into integrated production clusters of a myriad small manufacturers from Taiwan and Hong Kong as well as the Korean *chaebol*, the Japanese *keiretsu* and the Chinese conglomerates. The tremendous growth of the Asian economies in recent decades and the success of Asian corporations in establishing their leading regional positions reveal that the market- and firm-based TCE is too limited to explain the business networks of Asian corporations, because it is too strongly rooted in the Anglo-Saxon experience (Castells, 1996, p. 190).

## NETWORK AS A BUSINESS SYSTEM

In the recent development of TCE, two important modifications to the traditional 'market hierarchy' structure are adopted. First, the 'hybrid' mode, including different transaction forms, is introduced in the 'dichotomy' structure of 'market hierarchy' (Williamson, 1991). Second, the institutional environment is analyzed as a network with an evolving social structure (Williamson, 1993). From this conceptual framework, two extra dimensions could be added to the traditional TCE – that is, hybrid forms of business transactions and cultural and social factors that can be analyzed in terms of trust or social network (Casson and Cox, 1992).

### Network as an Alternative to Markets and Firms

The term 'network' in this chapter refers to the hybrid type of transaction form that combines aspects of both market governance and hierarchical authority.[2] The introduction of this concept is mainly based on the discussion about business transactions that require a new and more 'network-like' organizational structure and consist of a fluid, flexible and dense pattern of relationships (Nohria and Eccles, 1992; Forsgren,

Holm and Thilenius, 1994). The network concept is quite different from the TCE in explaining the ownership-specific advantages of firms, organizational structure, inter- and intra-firm relations, and corporate control and co-ordination systems.

First, the network approach suggests that the interdependence among firms and within an industrial network is of great, and increasing, importance (Johanson and Mattsson, 1988). The competitive advantages of a firm are based not only on its '*internal assets*', such as financial capabilities, product and process technology, marketing expertise, organizational knowledge, proprietary rights and brand names, but also on the resources controlled by other firms. The access to these '*external resources*' through its network relationships and position can generate value for the firm and serve to give it access to other firms' internal assets. However, the access to the network is not simply given, as it itself emerged over time as the result of previous co-operation. As the development of a network position takes time and effort, and its present position defines opportunities and restrictions for the future strategic development of the firm, the firm's actual position in the network can be considered as consisting of partially controlled intangible assets.

Second, the network approach has extended a firm's boundaries to include co-operative modes, such as joint ventures, licensing and other long-term co-operative agreements, in inter-firm relationships. 'Make or buy' thus becomes 'make or co-operate'. The make or co-operate decision is made in the context of a concrete network as opposed to a transaction within an abstract market. Such a co-operative form is quite different from the market hierarchy governance, as it is developed around trust rather than the opportunism that is the basic assumption of the TCE approach (Florin, 1996). The emergence of such a co-operative network is a 'value-generation' process, as it is formed gradually through the accumulation of inter-firm ties, and it provides these firms with opportunities and benefits.

Third, the control and co-ordination mechanism within the business network is quite different from that of markets and hierarchies. While price incentives and administrative authority are two dominant forms of control in market transactions and hierarchical governance, respectively, reciprocity norms and trust are considered to be important factors in explaining the duration and stability of the network structure. The organizational structure and control system in the network are particularly distinct from markets and hierarchical arrangements in their heavy reliance on reciprocity, collaboration, complementary interdependence, a reputation and relationship basis for communication, and an informal climate orientated toward mutual gain (Larson, 1992, p. 76).

**Entrepreneurial Network**

An entrepreneurial network is defined as a set of linkages that connect, directly or indirectly, the entrepreneurs to their social groups that are in general based on affection, friendship, kinship, authority, and economic and information exchanges. The new institutional approach has recognized that non-economic governance and mechanisms, such as clans and trust, may serve to increase economic efficiency in exchange relationships (Ouchi, 1980) and to solve the co-ordination problem (Casson, 1995, p. 47). An entrepreneurial network is considered as a source of competitiveness because it provides entrepreneurs with information, business opportunities and resources in term of social capital (Burt, 1992, pp. 57–9), knowledge (Sohn, 1994, pp. 299–302) and governments' favourable attitudes and decisions (Boddewyn, 1988, pp. 348–57). The resources in a social network are different from 'traditional' tangible assets (Burt, 1992, pp. 57–9) because they are intangible and jointly developed and owned by its members. No one player has exclusive ownership rights to this social capital, of which the value remains in intensive exchanges.

As a vehicle for knowledge exchanges and gaining experience, an entrepreneurial network is also assumed to be able to provide not only information about business opportunities for value creation, but also a basis for trust and compatibility of business philosophies. The information gained through a network may help in the initial steps that partners take when entering into a co-operative arrangement, while high trust can sustain an equilibrium of honesty and openness to avoid opportunistic behaviour and to encourage partners to share their tangible and intangible assets (Casson, 1995, pp. 52–3). However, trust itself is costly to create and it has to be developed over time as social bonds strengthen through shared norms and/or similar values (Larson, 1992, pp. 82–4).

**Network Interactions in the Internationalization Process**

Different from the paradigm of TCE, business transactions that take place in the network approach cannot be considered exclusively as 'rational' and 'unsocial' (Biggart and Hamilton, 1992). The interaction between business and entrepreneurial networks suggests that the internationalization of firms is not a simple matter of transferring value-added activities abroad through the market or the firm, but consists of a much more complex and varied set of relationships between economies, institutions and firms (Whitley, 1992, pp. 249–55). Implicit in TCE is the notion that the choice between a 'hierarchy' or a 'market' should enable a reduction of transaction costs that are usually related to collecting information, negotiating contracts and solving conflicts. Information costs are therefore crucial in the approach as they are connected not only with decision-making, but also with the implementation of decisions. Such information particularly concerns 'uncodified' and 'undiffused' knowledge which is embedded in social structures and cultural contexts (Boisot, 1986). This knowledge not only yields a reduction of the risks involved in going abroad, but also provides a vehicle for acquiring internal and external resources and opportunities for combining them (Eriksson *et al.*, 1997, pp. 342–6). The propensity or the ability of a firm to 'transplant' its value-added activities abroad is largely determined by the firm's perception of, and capability to support, information costs. Since entrepreneurial networks may provide information and experiential knowledge, the development of and access to these networks are considered as essential drivers for the internationalization process (see also Chapter 4 in this volume). The possible impact of entrepreneurial networks and business networks on the internationalization of firms and their outcomes are illustrated in Figure 6.1.

The upper left quadrant of the figure represents a situation in which the contacts of the firm with foreign markets are generally limited to occasional and recurrent transactions, such as the purchasing of standard equipment and materials (Williamson, 1985). The firm has little know-

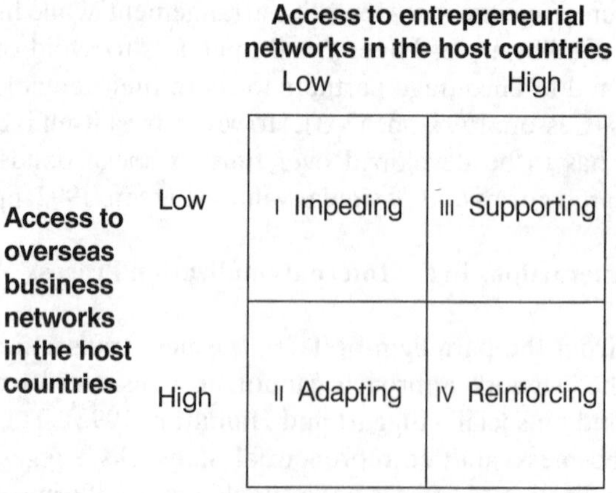

|  |  | **Access to entrepreneurial networks in the host countries** | |
|  |  | Low | High |
| **Access to overseas business networks in the host countries** | Low | I Impeding | III Supporting |
|  | High | II Adapting | IV Reinforcing |

*Figure* 6.1   Impact of networks on the internationalization of the firm

ledge about foreign markets and cannot count on utilizing network relationships to gain such knowledge, because the business and social networks are not 'internationalized'. For a firm that is used to operating in a local environment where social relations and cultural preference are strongly interfaced with business decisions, the lack of an entrepreneurial network in the host country might impede its ability to locate abroad. The greater a firm's lack of foreign business expertise, the higher the perceived cost of the internationalization process will be (Eriksson *et al.*, 1997, p. 344). In this situation, there is usually no incentive for the firm to 'internalize' its transactional activities, given the high information costs combined with an unfamiliar environment. Even if internationalization becomes necessary, the firm tends to follow a sequential process in order gradually to develop its position in a foreign business network. For example, the firm will tend to initiate its first investment abroad by using agents or commercial offices rather than subsidiaries, in order to minimize the needs for knowledge development and to benefit from the position reached by local firms in their own networks (Johanson and Vahlne, 1977). An alternative strategy, especially for large firms that are resourceful in the home market, could be the acquisition of an existing company abroad in order to gain direct access to local networks. However, since such an operation requires a large investment and is more risky, smaller firms are unlikely to be able to use this mode of penetration for their first investment ventures abroad.

The lower left quadrant of the figure reflects the situation in which frequent international transactions occur in different business environments and/or with partners who do not share the same entrepreneurial network. Because the firm has intensive exchanges with business networks abroad, it has already acquired experience and relationships in foreign markets. The connections with foreign business networks, for example, via exports or subcontracting, may be considered to some extent as a driving force for a firm to establish a production unit abroad. The firm's move can be 'pulled out' by the 'leading' firm of the network, especially when it needs to maintain and/or to adjust its position in the value-added chain. Such so-called 'follow-up' investment may be beneficial from the special position that the firm occupies in its business network – that is, its highly specialized activities in the networked production chain. The need for the firm to develop its own network in a foreign market is less necessary, because it can use already established relationships in both domestic and foreign markets. All these factors allow lower entry costs into foreign markets. However, the need for co-ordination and transaction costs in such a business network is likely to be high because of the lack of a common entrepreneurial network to provide trust and efficiency for co-ordinating different parts of the network. The economic logic of a business network will normally oblige firms to adapt to each other and to respect similar 'rules'. Yet, the firm with a dominant position in a network is more likely to 'impose' its managerial practice – that is, to reproduce its domestic patterns of economic organization – in the host country. A company with a weak position, however, will have to adapt its procedures when it moves abroad.

When a firm moves to a country where it can rely on a shared entrepreneurial network, the situation may change completely. The upper right quadrant of the figure presents the case in which, while the firm has few, if any, business activities abroad, it has experience and knowledge of foreign markets because of its access to local entrepreneurial networks. The existence of an entrepreneurial network abroad generally can support the investing firm with market information, while the similarities in cultural background and business practices will allow it to reduce bargaining, contractual and maintenance costs in its business transactions. These factors could change the internationalization process – that is, because the firm will tend to move into foreign markets without necessarily following the traditional steps of the internationalization process. This illustrates a high correlation between low transaction costs and a high degree of community cohesion.

The lower right quadrant of the figure refers to a situation in which the firm is linked both to highly internationalized business and to entrepreneurial networks. Multiple affiliation is important in the development of business networks by entrepreneurs. The wider the range of affiliation of entrepreneurs, the larger will be their personal networks of trusted contracts (Casson, 1995, p. 54). The cohesion and consistency of both business and entrepreneurial networks between home and host countries results in a mutually reinforcing and integrated business environment. The intensive personal relations and trust-based co-operation does not only provide control and co-ordination, it also enhances the effectiveness of network forms in business transactions.


## CHINESE BUSINESS SYSTEMS IN THE NETWORK PERSPECTIVE

Recent studies of Chinese business systems in East and Southeast Asia (for example, Whitley, 1990, 1991; Redding, 1990; Brown, 1995) have identified a number of distinctive characteristics of ethnic Chinese-owned enterprises, compared to other Asian or Western business organizations. First, business networks of CHMNEs are found to be strongly based on the social relationships of their entrepreneurs and consist mainly of (i) intra-firm internalization of entrepreneurship on the basis of ethnic ties; (ii) inter-firm collaboration on the basis of personal friendships; and (iii) extra-firm co-operation with key 'political patronage' (Yeung, 1997a, pp. 34–45). Second, while ethnic Chinese entrepreneurs still rely on a closed family circle to manage their tangible assets, they are increasingly obliged to open their family businesses to 'outsiders' in order to achieve further expansion (Kao, 1993, p. 33; see also Chapter 9 in this volume). These characteristics can be summarized by a network approach with two specific dimensions.

**Chinese Business Networks**

On the basis of the network approach in the earlier section, ethnic Chinese enterprises in Southeast Asia can broadly be divided into four categories in relation to their organizational form and market orientation. The first category (that is, the 'paternalistic' firm with local market orientation) is the dominant form of Chinese business organization in Southeast Asia (Whitley, 1990, pp. 59–61), notably in ASEAN-4 (Thailand, Indonesia, the Philippines and Malaysia). Most of these U-form enterprises specialize in a single product or market segment. Although their culturally-specific advantages such as strong ethnic emphasis on entrepreneurship allow them to have access to cheap capital and information through extended family and social networks, they have few connections with the international market. The inter-firm relations they have with other enterprises in the local market are not very stable and often subject to change (Redding, 1990, pp. 205–6). Yet they are very concerned with developing personal ties and creating mutual obligations with their business partners. A shortcoming of these enterprises is their inability to undertake major strategic transformations in rapidly changing business environments because these require strong ownership advantages in terms of technology and marketing knowledge. As for other indigenous firms, their competitiveness is often based on location-related factors – for example, the comparative advantages and disadvantages of their home countries, especially in the context of governments' import substitution policies (see Chapter 11 in this volume).

The 'generic' expansion of family enterprises with a U-form structure often leads to the creation of 'entrepreneurial conglomerates'. The emergence of this second type of enterprise is strongly linked to the ability of the entrepreneurs to create and enhance family business resources and to implement an appropriate strategic setting facing the changing business environment (Limlingan, 1986, pp. 62–3). The rapid growth of Chinese family businesses in Southeast Asia is both a cause and an outcome of the establishment of partnerships between Chinese entrepreneurs themselves on the one hand, and with government institutions and local indigenous enterprises on the other. These conglomerates are strengthened when entrepreneurs invest in each other's businesses beyond their initial agreement and show their commitment to the long-term future of the relationship. Although the term 'pariah entrepreneur' has become somewhat outdated for describing the position of Chinese entrepreneurs in Southeast Asia (Mackie, 1992b, p. 177), it still indicates the motives for which Chinese entrepreneurs may have opened up their family businesses to external capital, even when there are risks of losing control. In ASEAN-4 countries as well as in Taiwan, a significant number of large Chinese family enterprises have established permanent relations with the civil and military authorities by creating joint ventures with government institutions or directly with important personalities. Such 'political alliances' allow Chinese entrepreneurs to benefit from favourable conditions in terms of credit allocation, obtaining quotas for importing and exporting goods, enjoying monopolistic positions in specific sectors, access to public markets, and receiving government protection against competition.

Chinese entrepreneurial conglomerates are quite distinct from the Japanese *keiretsu* and the Korean *chaebol*, as they are usually diversified into a large number of unrelated activities ranging through banking, trading, real estate and manufacturing. This mode of organization has been called a 'golden diamond' structure (Lasserre, 1988, p. 122). However, the diversification pattern of their product portfolio is linked more to the opportunities these sectors offer than to their strategic design. These groups are in most cases still under the leadership of a 'father-manager' who exercises control over the strategic decisions of the business units through his personalized relations with his 'key' managers. The major source of value added in these groups emanates from the ability of the entrepreneur to leverage financial and human resources, to establish political connections, to conclude special deals with governments and business partners, and to improve loyalty and discipline within the business units. Entrepreneurial conglomerates usually expand by acquiring an increasing number of companies rather than by expanding existing companies, therefore the overall business groups may be large, but their individual subsidiary companies are likely to remain small.

The intra-firm linkages within these conglomerates are very limited, especially in terms of the transfer of technology and integrated production, because their activities are extremely diversified. However, the stand-alone operations of subsidiary companies within the Chinese entrepreneurial conglomerates are in general organized around the group's 'flagship' company, which is most often structured as a holding company. Because of the establishment of an internal capital market and the centralized configuration of financial resources, different business units are highly integrated. In addition, the direct control over the managers through entrepreneurial networks assures a high strategic commitment and co-ordination between different business units.

The third category of enterprises consists of the so-called Asian 'mobile exporters' (Wells, 1992): that is, a group of small- and medium-sized firms based mostly in Taiwan and Hong Kong. As compared to the traditional 'paternalistic' firm in the ASEAN-4 countries, these companies have access to a highly internationalized production and/or market network. They have generally developed and expanded their linkages with foreign companies in the context of export promotion policies, despite some variations with regard to their network positions (for example, as local subcontractors for leading MNEs, or as exporters through agents established abroad). These enterprises often rely on the strategic direction of the production and market network to which they are connected. The access to a highly internationalized network through subcontracts for processing, assembly and original equipment manufacturing (OEM) activities and the specific position in the networked production system constitute the main ownership advantage of this group of enterprises.

The fourth type of ethnic Chinese-owned enterprises emerging recently are the 'regional and global players' which are often integrated industrial groups or diversified conglomerates (Redding, 1995, pp. 65–8). Although the number of these enterprises is rather small, they have become extremely visible primarily through the strategic alliances among them and with Western MNEs in order to establish regional and global operations. These strategic alliances result mainly from tremendous inter-firm exchanges of capital, information and market resources (Redding, 1994, p. 115). The business relationships between these Chinese firms and Western groups may be competitive as well as co-operative. While local Chinese enterprises can serve as a cultural facilitator for foreign investors in Asia, the contribution of technology and capital from their Western partners is regarded as being crucial for the transformation of Chinese family enterprises. These contributions have allowed

traditional Chinese businesses to be transformed into more open structures and to be integrated into the production networks of industrial
countries.

## Chinese Entrepreneurial Networks

The entrepreneurial network is an important dimension of the Chinese
business system. Chinese entrepreneurial networks are generally based
on five types of social relations that extend beyond the family – namely,
kinship, surname, residence, origin and contract (Serrie, 1985, pp. 272–
7).[3] The most important characteristic of this structure is the principle
of hierarchy on the one hand and the nature of substitution in network
formation on the other. Different types of social relations – that is, kinship, residence and contract – are organized in a 'hierarchical' structure, while the family is the 'core' organization of Chinese social networks
and the relationship of residence predominates in contract associations.
However, these hierarchical relations can be complemented by horizontal extensions. For example, with regard to the relationship of residence, the widening circles of affiliation include the larger neighbourhood,
perhaps a village, a region, a similar dialect and so on. All these social
units can be substituted for each other. The structural *hierarchy* and
*substitutability* therefore constitute the foundation of Chinese entrepreneurial networks.

Hierarchy is the basic component of Chinese firm structure within
which authority is supported by the mutual self-interest of group members. Resource allocation and configurations are concentrated within
the hands of the family chief, whose authority is strictly related to his
'paternal' position. Because of the concentration of devoted family members in the decision-making process, Chinese family enterprises are perceived to have a perfectly working structure for rapid resource mobilization
and allocation. The hierarchical structure of Chinese family enterprises
is more distinctive and more evident than that of Western family enterprises as the position of each family member in the former type is determined by social order. This provides Chinese family enterprises with an
efficient and less costly control system. The usual identification of the
personal interest of the entrepreneurs with that of the enterprise allows
more flexibility and efficacy in the decision-making process. The personalized 'leadership' and family loyalty provide these firms with high
flexibility in case of business reorganization. Yet, the motivation and
the initiative of the employees in such structures may largely be limited,
while the growth of family enterprises may be handicapped by the limits

of family resources in terms of financial capabilities and management resources (Wong, 1985).

And, it is in extending the network links beyond the immediate family that Chinese business networks differ from those emanating from other cultures. Rather than utilizing the hierarchically structured family to support an extension of the network, more broadly-based ethnic and regional ties are relied upon. There is a tendency for people within one regional grouping, such as the Hokkien or the Teochew, to specialize in a certain range of occupations and activities (Redding, 1990). Because of the critical nature of external needs on the one hand and of the traditional lack of a legal structure able to enforce agreements on the other, a strong ethic of trust has developed among entrepreneurs who share the same social network. One outcome of this networked social structure is efficiency in economic transactions, because business links among these firms for supplies, labour, customers and information are founded on a basis of mutual trust among their managers. The horizontal extension of the entrepreneurial network provides small-scale family firms with mutual co-operation based on ethnic and regional links.

Lastly, the extension of social relations to Chinese ethnic communities and networks that are spread out over the Southeast Asian countries may generate 'infrastructure'[4] (for example, similar business practices, cultural climate); production factors (labour, sourcing, distribution, capital); and market segments (for example, ethnic products) for their overseas expansion. The geographical dispersion of Chinese ethnic groups has provided Chinese entrepreneurs with additional resources and a basis to develop their domestic and regional business networks (see Chapter 5 in this volume). Also, personal experience as recent immigrants may provide some special abilities (for example, flexibility and adaptability) to those entrepreneurs which allow them to cope better with new business environments when they extend their businesses abroad.

## THE INTERNATIONALIZATION OF CHINESE BUSINESS NETWORKS

Based on the network approach and the specific characteristics of the four groups of Chinese-owned enterprises described above, their internationalization is analyzed through four scenarios that are likely to reflect the development path and the main characteristics of CHMNEs based in Southeast Asia (Figure 6.2).

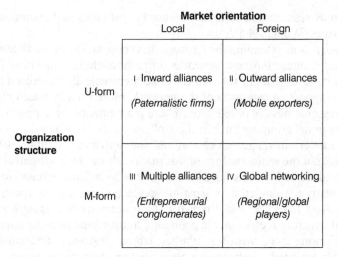

*Figure* 6.2   Investment scenarios of Chinese-owned multinational enterprises from a network perspective

## Scenario I   Inward Alliances

Most ethnic Chinese enterprises in Southeast Asia tend to be small in size and have only limited resources. This is often the case for local market-orientated 'paternalistic' firms, which, from a practical point of view have few ownership advantages or exchanges with business networks connected to foreign markets. The propensity of these companies to spread out abroad is quite low, but their role in the inward investment operations of other Chinese enterprises is very important, as they link up these inward investors with local businesses and entrepreneurial networks.

### Inward alliances with ethnic Chinese investors

Extended Chinese families are frequently dispersed over extensive geographical areas. This geographical dispersion of family members and ethnic groups in Southeast Asia constitutes a very important base and provides resources for Chinese entrepreneurs who want to develop their regional operations. First, the presence of family members and an ethnic community abroad has allowed Chinese immigrant entrepreneurs to start businesses with network support in terms of both tangible and intangible assets. This network support provides a basic element in the growth and evolution of many Chinese entrepreneurs in Southeast Asia. Second, the ethnic community in Southeast Asia was the targeted market segment for the first 'market seekers' from Hong Kong and Taiwan when they started their overseas activities during the 1960s. Yet, market-seeking investments by ethnic Chinese and other investors in ASEAN-4 countries has expanded into a much larger flow since the late 1980s as a result of the growth of local markets. Third, low production costs and geographical proximity, combined with the cultural and ethnic backing of the Chinese community, made Southeast Asian developing economies an attractive offshore production location for ethnic Chinese manufacturing firms that wanted to avoid export quotas in the 1970s and subsequently to lower production costs (Wells, 1992). The mutual trust and strong commitment between local Chinese partners and inward Chinese investors have allowed the latter to lower entry and operating costs in the host economies. This can be illustrated by the case of many Taiwanese enterprises operating in the ASEAN countries, and more recently by ethnic Chinese investment in the coastal region of mainland China (see Chapters 10 and 11 in this volume).

## Alliances with Japanese and Western investors

The inward dimension of the internationalization of Chinese enterprises into Southeast Asia can be also illustrated by their linkages with Japanese and Western investors. The traditional role of Chinese traders and entrepreneurs as 'middlemen' between indigenous and Western enterprises in Southeast Asia can be dated back to the colonial period (see Chapter 1 in this volume). After the Second World War, American and Japanese, as well as European manufacturing companies moved successively into the Southeast Asian region for resource- and/or market-seeking purposes. During their moves into these markets, local Chinese companies served as partners not only to link them to local production and distribution networks, but also to connect them with government institutions. Around 90 per cent of Japanese joint ventures in Southeast Asia are with local Chinese entrepreneurs (East Asia Analytical Unit, 1995, p. 245). This proportion is higher than the already high proportion of Chinese businesses represented in these local economies – for example, 65 per cent in Malaysia, 40 per cent in the Philippines, and 80 per cent in Indonesia and Thailand (Lim, 1991, p. 37). Inward foreign investment has served to decrease the dependence of Chinese enterprises on local sources of support and to increase their political and financial leeway (Mackie, 1992b, p. 183). Recently, alliances with ethnic Chinese entrepreneurs have been used not only to target local markets or specific industries, but also to enter into third countries and to establish a substantial presence in the region. Yet this latter type of alliance has been in most cases agreed with large Chinese enterprise groups and entrepreneurial conglomerates (for example, the CP Group, Salim Group, Lippo, Hong Leong and Robert Kuok) rather than with small local market-orientated companies (Redding, 1995, p. 68).

### From inward to outward alliances

Linking up with local Chinese businesses and entrepreneurial networks allows inward ethnic Chinese and foreign investors to identify business opportunities, to substitute in some cases for the lack of ownership advantages specific to investing firms, and to have a better understanding of the local business environment. The alliances with these investors also strengthen the competitive position of local Chinese enterprises in terms of technology and marketing expertise, and allow them to benefit from their 'foreign company' status for political and tax incentives. This latter aspect was very important for ethnic Chinese enterprises in ASEAN-4 countries, especially in the 1960s and 1970s, when they were constrained by discriminatory policy measures by the government against the expansion of the local Chinese community. The alliances with inward ethnic Chinese and/or foreign investors allowed these firms to acquire joint venture status and to avoid discriminatory measures. These inward linkages also allowed local Chinese enterprises to connect with their partners' business networks, thereby facilitating their own future expansion abroad. This can be illustrated by the case of Chinese enterprises in Taiwan and Hong Kong. The links these companies as local partners had forged with American and Japanese MNEs in the early offshore production stage which later developed into more complete regional production networks. These companies moved their production activities abroad as 'mobile exporters' or follow-up investors. Thus the dependence of ethnic Chinese enterprises on the strategic moves of leading companies in the 'internationalized' network is a major factor that has contributed to the dynamic interaction between and gradual switching from inward to outward internationalization of Chinese enterprises.

The connection of local Chinese firms with 'foreign' Chinese investors through joint venture agreements extends their family-owned businesses into a more open structure, including cross-border inter-firm linkages and mutual equity participation. Yet the strong links with inward Chinese investors can reinforce Chinese 'cultural' practices when doing business. For example, throughout Southeast Asia, Taiwanese investors in particular have shown a strong preference for clustering their projects together with local Chinese businesses. This tendency could keep other local and foreign companies out, resulting in an 'isolated' position (Lim, 1991, p. 16). These reinforcing effects in inward-linking investment could be considered as an obstacle for Chinese firms when moving into the next strategic stage: that is, regional integration or globalization.

### Scenario II   Outward Alliances

This scenario analyses outward manufacturing investment by Chinese companies that are strongly linked with, or integrated into, foreign business networks. This especially concerns the outward internationalization of the so-called 'mobile exporters'. Since the early 1980s, the business environment for export-orientated firms in Taiwan and Hong Kong has deteriorated because of increasing labour and land costs and appreciating currencies, at least until October 1997. These changes in the business environment require a fundamental transformation of the family business in terms of ownership, organization and management. However, these changes would normally stretch most of these companies beyond their available resources and reach the limits of their family structure. Large investments are needed to restructure different industries to upgrade the technology and/or to merge into larger units to achieve economies of scale and scope. Because of the inability to undertake substantial restructuring in home markets, these companies tend to move all or part of their production activities to Southeast Asian countries. This strategic move enables them 'to avoid or delay transformation by providing location specific advantages that prolong their firms' specific advantages and enable them to continue with their traditional business practices' (Lim, 1991, pp. 21–2).

The advantages of these companies are clearly related to their connections to a highly internationalized business network. This means that they had already acquired experience and set up relationships in foreign markets during the inward internationalization stage when they were involved in supplying foreign production/markets. Outward investment by these enterprises can be considered as follow-up operations. In a sense, they are 'pulled out' of the home country by the 'flagship' firms of the business network in which they have taken part as subcontractors, suppliers or even joint ventures. Overseas expansion of these enterprises is often related to the 'special position' they have acquired in the supplying networks – that is, their highly specialized subcontracting activities in the whole networked production chain of MNEs, or their reputation for meeting the standards and schedule of foreign buyers (Wells, 1992, p. 182).

The investment of 'mobile exporters' is often directed to Southeast Asian economies because of their lower production costs and geographical proximity. Production facilities in these countries are used to serve export, rather than local, markets, as in the case of ethnic market-seekers. The need for these enterprises to develop local business networks in the host country is therefore less important because their activities are mainly linked with export markets in Europe and North America rather than with the local economy. They are usually located in export processing zones and rarely rely on local sourcing and distribution networks. However, these companies may find in Southeast Asia a culturally and socially congenial host business community – that is, an ethnic Chinese community, which provides them with the necessary support to obtain special incentives or to conform to the requirements of host country investment regulation (Van Den Bulcke and Zhang, 1995, p. 236).

## Scenario III  Multiple Alliances

This scenario is concerned with outward investment by large Chinese family enterprises/groups (for example, entrepreneurial conglomerates from ASEAN-4 countries). It principally reflects the 'replication' of business networks by large CHMNEs in multiple locations with the strong support of local Chinese entrepreneurial networks, especially in Southeast Asian economies. Outward investment by these enterprises dates back to the 1960s and 1970s when the economic domination of ethnic Chinese firms became a matter of political and social concern, which resulted in a whole range of hostile reactions and policies from their home countries (Wu and Wu, 1980, p. 39). As ethnic Chinese enterprises in these countries were more sensitive than indigenous firms to frequent changes in government policy, they tried to diminish and to diversify their political risks by investing abroad.[5] Ethnic relations and personal contacts, especially dispersed family members in different countries, were considered to be a very important factor in the decisions of these early 'risk-driven investors'. As a result, most of this investment was directed to less hostile countries with a strong cultural and social backing, such as Taiwan[6], Singapore, Hong Kong and even some states in the USA with large concentrations of Chinese immigrants. Although such early investment was sometimes qualified as 'flying capital' because is was carried out through informal channels such as family connections and was concentrated in real estate and other non-manufacturing sectors, it served as the first basis for Chinese entrepreneurs to explore overseas opportunities (see Chapter 8 in this volume). A number of these companies developed into investment holdings for overseas expansion, especially those established in Hong Kong and Singapore.

During the last two decades, the propensity of Chinese entrepreneurial conglomerates from ASEAN-4 countries to invest abroad has increased significantly as a result of substantial changes in their firm-specific and location-specific factors (see also Chapter 4 in this volume). First, these companies have diversified into the manufacturing sector in the context of import substitution policy of their home countries. Second, with the 'linking up' process, they have also diversified their ownership structures by creating joint ventures with foreign and inward ethnic Chinese investors, and established links with indigenous companies and local governments. The successful achievement of business and ownership diversification has reinforced the competitive position of these companies in the domestic market and allowed them to accumulate the necessary resources to spread abroad. Third, because of the growing rivalry since the beginning of the 1980s between Asian developing economies to deregulate foreign direct investment (FDI) and sectoral and market liberalization there have been increasing opportunities for ethnic Chinese companies to benefit from incentives and advantages as 'foreign investors' by investing in neighbouring countries. This trend can be illustrated by increasing intra-regional FDI in Southeast Asia.

The geographical dispersion of ethnic Chinese entrepreneurs, coupled with a strong preference for internalizing the cost of business services, has affected the location decisions of Chinese conglomerates, which tend to replicate their business networks through cross-directorship, cross-shareholding and joint ventures with ethnic Chinese entrepreneurs in host economies. This can be regarded as a creation of a miniature version of their business networks in Southeast Asian economies. The rapid market penetration and low-cost moves of Chinese conglomerates into multiple locations are related to two major factors. First, most of these operations are undertaken with the strong support of entrepreneurial networks. The networked social relations provide these companies with market niches, low-cost information and such ethnic resources as labour, capital and access to local business networks. Second, the financial arm of these companies – for example, the investment holdings and banks they established in Hong Kong and Singapore, provide ready access to reliable sources of funds. Yet the different business units of these companies are dispersed in multiple locations without intensive intra-firm integration because of their very diversified business activities. This obliges Chinese conglomerates to increase intra-firm co-ordination and determines their next strategic move towards regionalization and/or globalization.

## Scenario IV     Global Networking

This scenario illustrates the growing trend of a number of large Chinese business groups to create regional or even global strategic partnerships and linkages with indigenous, ethnic Chinese as well Western companies. The global network set up by CHMNEs consists of cross-border alliances between leading Chinese and non-Chinese business groups in establishing a regional presence, expanding ethnic Chinese businesses beyond Asia, and creating value-added networks on a worldwide basis. The alliances between leading Chinese business groups in Southeast Asia are typically used to co-operate in the financial field rather than to carry out integrated production. This intangible and flexible relationship, based on mutual understanding and the use of similar management practices, has allowed ethnic Chinese enterprises to benefit from an efficient network for acquiring capital and information without being part of a rigid structure. This type of alliance is quite different from the hierarchically organized paternalistic firm, or from the loosely integrated entrepreneurial conglomerates (Redding, 1995, pp. 66–7). They have broken away from their heavy dependence on such location-related factors as low production costs, highly protected markets and strongly reliable entrepreneurial networks. Increasingly, non-Chinese enterprises, especially Western MNEs, have recognized the benefits of establishing relationships with leading Chinese business groups, either to develop business interests in the region or to gain access to third markets (East Asia Analytical Unit, 1995, pp. 246–7). Alliances with Western companies have also provided these Chinese companies with access to new technology, modern management expertise and global production networks. Compared to previous investment scenarios, these Chinese enterprises have acquired substantial organizational skills that allow them to establish workable alliances with Western MNEs. This networking process has been accelerated as these firms compete with each other for larger shares in the region's growth (Redding, 1995, p. 68).

Compared with the successful achievement of strategic alliances between leading Chinese and Western groups in Asia, the attempts by Chinese enterprises to expand into Western countries have met with mixed success. A number of large groups that used to operate in relatively highly structured business environments, such as Hutchison Whampoa from Hong Kong and Acer from Taiwan, have encountered few problems when establishing a presence outside Asia. These companies have accumulated knowledge in operating in different environments, and established multiple relationships with foreign companies in both domestic and foreign markets. However, companies that used to rely more heavily on ethnic entrepreneurial networks and on labour-intensive technology face many difficulties in reaching their targets when they expand into the highly structured markets of Western countries. For example, the lack of firm-specific advantages and the disconnection from entrepreneurial networks have been the root cause of the failure of Thailand-based Unicord's acquisition of Bumble Bee Seafoods and the take-over of Ramada by Hong Kong-based New World Development in the USA. In both cases, the ethnic Chinese buyers paid too high a price for the acquired company and underestimated the difficulties of operating in the American market (East Asia Analytical Unit, 1995, p. 249).

Globalization is a big challenge for ethnic Chinese-owned enterprises and requires more linkages between Chinese, indigenous and foreign enterprises because of the growing scale and complexity of their business operations. It is expected that the more advanced Chinese enterprises will incorporate and rely more on non-Chinese capital, on non-Chinese and non-family members as employees and in managerial and professional positions, as well as on non-Chinese partners. This is a development process that will reduce the ethnic character of Chinese business in Southeast Asia progressively and thereby help it to overcome its present ethnic limitations in operating on a global scale (Lim, 1991, p. 30).

CONCLUSION

The framework presented in this chapter has analyzed the internationalization of CHMNEs from a network perspective. The interaction between business and entrepreneurial networks has been analyzed to emphasize different possible scenarios of internationalization of CHMNEs and the evolving nature of the different stages involved. In particular, the linkages between inward and outward investment on the one hand, and ethnic Chinese and Western enterprises on the other have been studied on the basis of network interaction. This chapter has several specific implications for international business research *vis-à-vis* the TCE approach. First, the study of the internationalization of firms has to extend beyond the firm itself in order to include its business network.

The network position of a firm is important because it provides additional resources and determines the strategic direction, process and timing for expanding abroad. The growing interaction and links between Chinese, indigenous and Western companies in Southeast Asia and their multiple networked relationships will certainly affect the future attitude of Chinese enterprises towards globalization.

Second, while most previous studies have emphasized the importance of social and cultural factors in the growth and internationalization of Chinese-owned enterprises, the interaction of these factors with business transactions under different circumstances (for example, location and partners) has not been analyzed systematically. The consideration of the social and cultural background of entrepreneurs in a network approach allows US to understand different strategic settings and outcomes of their internationalization behaviour in different business environments. As indicated in this chapter, entrepreneurial networks have had a positive effect on the internationalization of CHMNEs in the inward linking and multiple replication stages, but the high dependence on these social and ethnic links is also considered as a hindrance to their expansion beyond Southeast Asia.

Third, the linking up of inward and outward investment within a perspective of network creation and expansion provides possibilities of considering internationalization as a value-creating process. The development path of many Chinese enterprises in ASEAN countries shows that linking up with inward ethnic Chinese investors can provide them with basic elements of their further internationalization. This is one of their specific advantages compared to their indigenous counterparts. As far as globalization is concerned, inward investment by Western MNEs in Southeast Asia, and their alliances with local Chinese enterprises, will certainly influence these later firms when they spread into Western countries.

## Notes

1. Although a growing number of enterprises from mainland China are also involved in the internationalization process, they have been excluded from this study.
2. The network concept used in this chapter is quite different from the definition of organizational networks in which the MNEs are conceptualized as a network of exchange relationships among different organizational units, including relationships between both headquarters and different national

subsidiaries as well as relationships between national subsidiaries and external customers, suppliers and regulators with which different units of the MNEs must interact (Ghoshal and Bartlett, 1990, pp. 609–10).

3. The kinship organization recruits members through birth or marriage, and may be expanded beyond the level of the family into clans or lineage, while surname organizations are open to all persons of a given surname, as an extension of kinship. The residence organization is based on the territorial proximity of its members, including traditional neighbourhoods and villages. As far as the origin of the organizations is concerned, district and dialect associations in the commonalities of former residence include people rooted in a wider area beyond the original neighbourhood or villages. The contractual organizations are free of prior connections that extend from family or domicile. They recruit members on the basis of common interest and serve needs of subsistence, credit, politics, religion, education, culture, sports and so on (Serrie, 1985, pp. 272–7).

4. Entrepreneurs are embedded in social structures that influence their perception and interpretations of organizational reality and regulate their access to or control over valued resources. Redding (1990, pp. 143–6) argues that the management value of Chinese entrepreneurs is determined not only by the political, economic and social factors of their environment, but also by several fundamental principles of Chinese culture, such as paternalism, personalism and insecurity. The impact of these cultural factors can be observed at three levels of society: the self, relationships and the organization: 'At the level of the self, the Confucian stress on role compliance is capable of producing high levels of self-confidence and a subsequent urge to control one's fate, a drive which is reinforced by and able to counteract surrounding insecurity. At the level of relationships, family coalitions counteract the problem of mistrust by the use of extensive networking. At the level of the organization, the patrimonial atmosphere is used to counteract problems of employee loyalty and bonding, by creating personalistic obligation ties'.

5. This consideration should be restricted to the analysis of their early overseas investments, because considerable changes in economic policies and relaxation in the official attitudes of these countries have taken place since the 1980s. However, anti-Chinese civil disturbances in Indonesia in May 1998 resulted once again in increasing insecurity among Chinese entrepreneurs, who began to move their business abroad.

6. For example, between 1952 and 1983, more than half of Taiwan's inward FDI was provided by ethnic Chinese abroad.

# Part 2
# Managing Chinese Business Across Borders

# 7 Transplanting Enterprises in Hong Kong

Siu-lun Wong

Hong Kong is a haven for entrepreneurs of all shades,[1] as it provides a congenial environment for the transplanting of enterprises. By definition, the act of transplanting involves mobility and diversity. It entails the coexistence and cross-fertilization of indigenous and foreign ventures. As a haven, Hong Kong has attracted innovators and risk-takers, not only from China but also from all over the world. As soon as Hong Kong became a British colony and a trading port in 1842, it drew into its fold Parsees and Jews, Portuguese and Muslims, Scots and Eurasians, all competing fiercely in business (Faure, 1997). After the Second World War, Hong Kong took over in popular imagination the mantle from Shanghai as a proverbial paradise for adventurers. For example, in the American movie *Prizzi's Honour*, made in the 1980s, when the couple of professional killers found themselves being cornered by their own Mafia family, Kathleen Turner playing Irene said to Jack Nicholson, as Charley, 'Let's go to Hong Kong. Let's make a run for it while there's still a chance. I know someone there who can give us a new face, a new identity, even a new set of fingerprints. We can disappear and start a new life.'

In this chapter, I shall not deal with the transplanting of European or Indian enterprises. I shall confine myself to the Chinese ones. It is as well to remember that Chinese enterprise transplants have a long history in Hong Kong. They grew into a formidable economic force there soon after British colonization. Chinese merchants who moved to the colony to trade became very successful. In the early 1880s, Sir John Hennessy, the then governor, drew the attention of the Legislative Council to the massive transfer of property worth nearly HK$ 2 m from European to Chinese hands in the short span of seventeen months between January 1880 and May 1881. Because of their economic prowess alone, Governor Hennessy argued, the views of the Chinese merchants had to be taken seriously by the colonial government (Chan, 1991, p. 107). For the Chinese merchants, Hong Kong was a safe haven where they could escape from the stifling hand of political authority and the dead weight of social conformity. It stood for 'the other China', which offered hope to all kinds of dissidents. In particular, it provided a sanctuary for those who were less stridently vocal, like many of the businessmen who were deviants of a sort when they engaged in innovative activities, who just wanted to be left alone, to make money and lead a life of their own choosing.

These businessmen, coming from Guangdong and other parts of China, often brought with them capital, personnel, or even organizations. But most important, they brought with them innovative ideas, the seeds from which their enterprises grew. This elusive asset, which we may call entrepreneurship, has been thrown into relief by Mr W. H. Chou, managing director of the Winsor Industrial Corporation. In an interview, Chou described himself as a man of ideas rather than a man of action. After migrating from Shanghai to Hong Kong in 1947, he and his partners created an integrated textile production venture, which became the mainstay of the Winsor Corporation. But he also tried out other ideas in numerous fields. Besides the more conventional investments in property development and shipping, he was one of the local pioneers in the production of instant noodles, washing powder, prefabricated building materials and Chinese herbal medicine against cancer and heart disease (*Next Magazine*, 14 January 1994, pp. 128–34).

The seeds of innovation sown by these men of ideas flourished in the milieu of Hong Kong as they had once flourished in the environment of the Chinese treaty ports before the Second World War. It is probably at the level of ideas and entrepreneurship that we shall find the clearest linkage between business and culture. Nowadays, it is generally accepted that a connection exists between the two spheres. However, not so long ago, the dominant view among the Chinese political and intellectual elite was that business was business, culture was culture, and the two did not mix. The market was seen as a jungle where the ruthless thrived. Let us recall how the anthropologist, Fei Xiaotong, himself a Western-educated liberal, criticized the Chinese businessmen in the treaty ports in 1946, on the eve of the Chinese Communist victory. He said:

> [To] such ports a special type of Chinese was attracted. They are known as *compradors* ... They are unscrupulous, pecuniary, individualistic, and agnostic, not only in religion but in cultural values. Treaty ports are ultra-urban. They are a land where the acquisition of wealth is the sole motive, devoid of tradition and culture ... From this group a new class is formed ... But, being reared in a cosmopol-

itan community, they are fundamentally hybrids. In them are manifest the comprador characteristic of social irresponsibility (Fei, 1946, pp. 646–7).

Pushing such sentiments to their logical extreme, the Chinese Communists proceeded to purify treaty ports such as Shanghai after their victory. The result is well known. In the words of the historians Frederic Wakeman Jr and Wen-hsin Yeh, 'Cosmopolitan Shanghai had become securely Chinese' (Wakeman and Yeh, 1992, p. 14). During the Maoist era, the new class of bourgeoisie was overthrown and destroyed, and private business transplants were cut down and eradicated.

With the hand-over in 1997, Hong Kong has reverted back to China as a Special Administrative Region (SAR). Chinese leaders have reassured the people in Hong Kong time and again that circumstances have changed, that the Shanghai experience will not be repeated in the territory. Notwithstanding all the good intentions in the world, will Hong Kong lose its cosmopolitan character as a community? Will the Hong Kong ethos, so hospitable to business innovations and transplants in the past, be dissipated? Can the Hong Kong brand of capitalism thrive within the new framework of 'one country, two systems'? There are no ready answers to these questions, of course. But if we can come to a valid understanding of the role played by Chinese culture and tradition in the business success of Hong Kong in the past, if we can point out why the diagnosis of treaty port culture by Fei Xiaotong and his contemporaries was mistaken, then we may have some clues as to the possible future development of the territory.

I shall argue that Chinese business enterprises as found in Hong Kong are by no means culturally shaky and rootless. Rather, they are nourished and sustained by a rich and supple cultural tradition in a paradoxical, colonial context. Their strength and vitality derive from the fact that they are in fact organic outgrowths of an evolving business tradition. More specifically, my thesis is that there exists a four-way interconnection among entrepreneurship, cultural tradition, migration and colonialism (or host institutional context) which are mutually reinforcing. And it is this potent combination of forces that has generated the dynamism for Hong Kong as a key centre for the globalization of Chinese business. Let me substantiate my argument by examining four aspects of the evolution of the Hong Kong business community: namely, the transplanting of enterprises (i) from Shanghai to Hong Kong; (ii) from Hong Kong to Shanghai; (iii) from overseas to Hong Kong; and (iv) from Hong Kong to overseas (see also Chapter 9 in this volume).

## SHANGHAI TO HONG KONG TRANSPLANTS

The post-war development of Hong Kong owed a great deal to the influx of entrepreneurial talents from Shanghai. Many of the Shanghai entrepreneurs who fled to the territory in the late 1940s became pioneers in textile production, shipping and other industries. As an economic elite brought up in the leading industrial area in China before the war, these entrepreneurs were mainly Western-educated and cosmopolitan in outlook. But in their business practices, as I have discovered in my research on the Hong Kong cotton-spinning industry (Wong, 1988), they were heavily influenced by Chinese traditional values, as shown in their reliance on family and regional solidarity. Their entrepreneurship was deeply rooted in tradition.

The interrelationship between entrepreneurship and tradition is best demonstrated in the phenomenon of the family firm, the dominant mode of organization among the Shanghainese and other local Chinese business ventures. The Chinese family firm as found in Hong Kong has four major characteristics (Wong, 1985, 1997; see also Chapters 2 and 3 in this volume). First, family solidarity is of crucial importance in the ownership of the enterprise. But this does not necessarily entail family dominance in management or nepotism in personnel matters. The family firm is in fact very flexible in format and has the potential to incorporate professionals as managers and bureaucratic procedures in recruitment and promotion. Second, the wax and wane of the business enterprise is affected by the life-cycle of the family. Typically, it would go through an emergent phase, a centralized phase, a segmented phase, and a disintegrative phase. These developmental phases tend to coincide with the succession of generations. For the economy as a whole, we should expect to find energetic and prosperous family firms coexisting with sluggish and declining ones at any given point in time, as they are evolving through different stages of their life-cycles. Third, the economic order in Hong Kong is built on the basis of an organic integration between personal trust and system trust. In upholding personal trust, family reputation plays an important role. But the Chinese family is not a durable entity. It will be reconstituted with the passing of each generation. Therefore, personal trust and family reputation cannot be taken for granted and need to be maintained and renewed constantly, thus absorbing much of the attention of the entrepreneurs. Fourth, although familism is the cohesive force in the internal ownership of the enterprise, it is not very important in mediating external affairs with other organizations. Inter-firm relationships are built on a multiplicity of personal ties, such as regional connections, 'old-boy networks', and former employer–employee relations. The family is not all there is to Hong Kong Chinese business and its significance should not be exaggerated.

The economic potential of traditional Chinese values such as familism, pragmatism and personal trust is often not fully appreciated by observers, who tend to look at them in isolation and to assume that they are static in nature. In fact, these values are highly adaptable. Their adaptability becomes most apparent in the process of migration, when they are being transposed to a new environment. In the case of the Shanghainese cotton spinners, their business success cannot fully be understood without taking into account the fact that they are migrants. Their entrepreneurship, besides being steeped in tradition, is also closely linked to migration. When we say that the Shanghainese entrepreneurs are migrants, we need to distinguish between two types of people on the move: namely, the sojourners and the refugees (Reid, 1996). Before the Second World War, Hong Kong was essentially a city of sojourners. The border was permeable. Many Cantonese traders, artisans and peasants went to Hong Kong to look for economic opportunities and to make a living, regarding their stay in the colony as temporary. Their homes were in their native villages in Guangdong. When they made enough money, they would send it back home. When they met with adversity, they would return home for shelter. Should they die in Hong Kong, their bones would be transported home for burial.

But in the post-war period, the situation changed in a fundamental way. When the Shanghainese entrepreneurs arrived in the territory, they came as refugees and not as sojourners. They were more resourceful, as they had been members of the economic elite in Shanghai before they escaped. They were not looking for economic opportunities in Hong Kong. Instead, they were running for their lives. They were fleeing from political violence and a Communist regime that was hostile to private business. They were more vulnerable than previous sojourners, as they had no safety nets to protect them if things did not work out in Hong Kong. Perforce, they had to be more self-reliant and more determined to succeed. This reinforced their family cohesion. It also pushed them to look beyond the family and to mobilize whatever social networks were available to ensure their own survival and to establish footholds in the new environment. But most important of all, they had uprooted themselves and had given up hope of returning home in the foreseeable future. This set them apart from the sojourners, who yearned to have their business success recognized and celebrated in their native communities by turning their wealth into status and power. As refugees who were not homeward bound, the Shanghainese entrepreneurs were more inclined to reinvest their business profits for expansion and diversification. There were fewer temptations for them to convert their economic capital into social or political capital, because Hong Kong was not their home. Furthermore, the colonial situation in Hong Kong prior to 1997 was not conducive to such conversions.

This brings us to the connection between entrepreneurship and colonialism. When they arrived in Hong Kong, these Shanghainese met barriers preventing them from entering civil service jobs and professional careers. Their credentials and qualifications were not recognized by the colonial government. With the more secure bureaucratic and professional channels of mobility closed to them, they had to take risks in the volatile business world. The impact of colonialism on entrepreneurship also worked at a more subtle level. Paradoxically, colonialism in the territory acted to preserve traditional Chinese values and to facilitate migration. The Hong Kong government extolled a *laissez-faire* philosophy, not only in the economic sphere but also in the social and cultural arenas. Practising a policy of indirect rule, the colonial government remained aloof from the local Chinese community. It was not keen to intervene in the social affairs of the locals as long as they kept the peace (Lau, 1982). But it was vigilant against Chinese political agitators and social reformers, and did not hesitate in making them unwelcome in the territory. For their part, out of a sense of pride, Chinese political activists and intellectuals were not drawn to the colony unless they had to go into exile. Therefore, Hong Kong was relatively free of the reformist zeal and anti-traditional fervour that engulfed the Chinese mainland from the beginning of the twentieth century.

But after 1949, the Hong Kong government had to practise more than indirect rule. They also had to contend with the new dimension of the Communist threat across the border. The reluctance of the government to popularize the use of *Putonghua* and simplified Chinese characters, and its quiet decision to uphold the Confucian content in the local Chinese curriculum were probably part of a long-term strategy to foster a separate cultural identity in Hong Kong to resist the Communist challenge. Similarly, its policy of tolerance towards refugees coming from the mainland from the 1940s up to the late 1970s was clearly inspired not just by humanitarian concerns but also by ideological considerations.

If the analysis so far on the Shanghai to Hong Kong enterprise transplants is not mistaken, then we can establish the existence of a four-way interconnection among the phenomena of entrepreneurship, cultural tradition, migration and colonialism that were mutually reinforcing.

After the end of colonialism in 1997, significant changes might well occur in the areas of migration and cultural policies, and consequently the forces affecting entrepreneurship too. It is quite likely that pockets of tension would emerge in the Hong Kong SAR. Anti-traditional sentiments and reformist zeal might well arise; anti-immigrant emotions and demands to protect indigenous rights might well surge; and anti-colonial feelings and the insistence on removing credential barriers might well grow. Then the environment for enterprise transplants might well take a turn for the worse. The robust entrepreneurship we have seen for so long may weaken. But none of these, I believe, is inevitable so long as the policy-makers in the SAR are able to keep a clear head and come to grips with the full implications of the change in sovereignty for business activities. Fortunately for Hong Kong, the Chinese mainland has gone through an economic transformation since the 1970s. Its dynamic growth has attracted many Hong Kong entrepreneurs to invest there and the transplanting of enterprises has apparently reversed its direction. I shall not be able to deal with the full scale of this relocation of Hong Kong business to the Chinese mainland in this chapter (see Chapter 11 in this volume). Instead, I will concentrate on the Shanghainese entrepreneurs.

## HONG KONG TO SHANGHAI TRANSPLANTS

Judging from the scattered information available, the Shanghainese entrepreneurs in Hong Kong do not seem to be particularly enthusiastic about going back to Shanghai to invest. On the whole, they are testing the waters rather gingerly. This is in sharp contrast to the multitude of small local Cantonese industrialists who flocked to southern China to set up subcontracting operations. Since the beginning of economic reform in China, Hong Kong has provided the main bulk of its foreign investment. However, only a small portion of this investment has been channelled into Shanghai. As the economist Y. W. Sung (1996, p. 185) points out, in the fifteen years from 1979 to 1994, 'cumulative utilized foreign investment in Guangdong was 4.1 times that in Shanghai'. In a 1994 sample survey of foreign-invested industrial firms in Shanghai, it was found that 30.9 per cent of them came from Hong Kong. But 'being a Shanghainese' was not among the top five major motives for investing in Shanghai (Nyaw, 1996, pp. 254–6). Thus it appears that the Shanghainese in Hong Kong are even more hesitant than foreign investors such as the Japanese spinners, who have been establishing joint ventures and subsidiaries in Shanghai in the recent years.

Their lack of enthusiasm to return to Shanghai to invest can be attributed partly to the fact that Shanghai is not exactly their home community. Most of them are infact natives of Suzhou, Wuxi, Ningbo and other townships and villages in Jiangsu and Zhejiang. Shanghai was once the place where they lived and where they made their mark as entrepreneurs. Now, after a lapse of more than forty years, they have few social linkages there to draw them back. Therefore they tend to be more pragmatic in evaluating the economic potential of Shanghai. And, in pragmatic terms, it might be more attractive for them to try out experimental ventures in townships close to their native villages where there is cheaper land, more abundant labour and better terms offered to external investors. The caution shown by the Shanghainese entrepreneurs in returning to Shanghai is also partly related to the suffocating concentration of state enterprises still found in that city. I have argued elsewhere that we can discern two patterns of entrepreneurship in contemporary Chinese communities (Wong, 1996b). One may be called the mainland pattern, with state ownership and huge bureaucracies as its hallmarks. This was exemplified in Shanghai during the Maoist era. The other may be labelled the external pattern, with family ownership and flexible subcontracting networks as its key characteristics. This was embodied in Hong Kong during the post-war period.

Deng Xiaoping's economic reform has led to a blending of the two patterns, especially in southern China. But the transformation of state enterprises in Shanghai and other large industrial cities to the north remains one of the most intractable problems of market transition. In comparing the relative merits of the two patterns of Chinese entrepreneurship, we have to acknowledge at least one major advantage of the external pattern as found in Hong Kong. It is what the economist Joseph Schumpeter has called 'creative destruction'. In recent years, the Hong Kong economy has undergone a structural transformation. The manufacturing sector is shrinking. Its contribution to GDP was reduced from 23.7 per cent in 1980 to only 9.2 per cent in 1994. Meanwhile, the service sector is growing dramatically. By 1994, it accounted for 83.4 per cent of Hong Kong's GDP (Enright *et al.*, 1997, p. 13; see also Howlett, 1997, pp. 49–54). In this process, many industrial operations, including the cotton-spinning mills, are in decline. But these enterprises can be closed or phased out quickly with relative ease. In contrast, the gigantic state enterprises in Shanghai simply refuse to die even though they have been suffering from a haemorrhage of losses for a long time. Thus the durability of an enterprise is not necessarily a strength when the collective well-being of an economy is concerned, particularly when the economy has to renew itself from time to time.

So these are some reasons why the Shanghainese entrepreneurs are less than enthusiastic to return to Shanghai. But the most important reason, it seems to me, is that Shanghai still lacks an entrepreneurial culture conducive to private business. This is manifested, for example, in the Shanghai residents' attitude towards self-employment. In a survey conducted in 1987, it was found that self-employed occupations were the least preferred options by Shanghai respondents as desirable jobs for their sons. Less than 1 per cent of the sample opted for this choice. In contrast, when the same question was posed to respondents in South Korea, 30 per cent of the sample indicated that they would prefer their sons to be self-employed (Chu and Ju, 1993, pp. 296–7). In Hong Kong, the 1988 social indicators survey has revealed that starting one's own business was regarded as the best mobility channel, chosen by 41 per cent of the sample (Wong, 1991, p. 164).

The absence of a thriving entrepreneurial culture in Shanghai, even after two decades of economic reform, has many causes. The burden of past practices of central planning is no doubt responsible. But less obvious, yet equally important, are the stifling effects of social policies (many of which are still in force), which act wittingly or unwittingly to repress the entrepreneurial urge among Shanghai residents. Foremost among these social policies was the attempt by the Chinese Communist Party (CCP) at 'taming the shrew' after 1949. Shanghai was singled out for special treatment as the symbol of bourgeois capitalism. It was made to admit its guilt and atone for its sins. The capitalists were punished and expelled from the city, together with the prostitutes. The city was forced to yield a major part of its earnings to the central government for redistribution (White, 1989). The CCP's attempt at purification was so relentless that it succeeded in breaking the bourgeois spirit and destroying the cosmopolitan identity of the city. Now the CCP realizes that it went too far during the Maoist era and wants to reverse course to revive Shanghai as an entrepreneurial city. But the trauma suffered by the Shanghai community runs deep. The broken spirit and damaged identity will take a long time to heal. Other social policies, such as strict migration control, job allocation, the creation of the work unit or *danwei* system, and drastic birth control measures, all contributed to dampening the entrepreneurial spirit in Shanghai. But this is not the place to elaborate on them (see Wong, 1996c). Suffice it to say that, for the reasons mentioned above, I do not think that it is likely that Shanghai will overtake Hong Kong as a city of thriving private entrepreneurship in the near future.

So far, I have focused on the reasons why the Shanghainese entrepreneurs in Hong Kong are not eager to transfer their enterprises back to Shanghai. But for Hong Kong entrepreneurs as a whole, it is well known that a massive relocation process has occurred, so much so that the economic boundary between the Hong Kong SAR and the Chinese mainland is becoming blurred. This growing economic integration has generally been regarded as beneficial and inevitable. However, we should not lose sight of the potential costs involved. First, the integration will entail a drastic change in the size of the Hong Kong economy, thus altering its share in the world market and affecting its competitiveness. Hong Kong investors in the mainland will generate latent capital–labour conflicts (see Chapter 11 in this volume). Future economic sanctions imposed on China by other countries for political reasons will have a direct effect on the SAR. Hong Kong will easily be drawn into the tug of war that is developing between the SAR and the regions within China. There will also be increasing pressure on Hong Kong to redistribute its economic surpluses as a matter of fairness to other regions with which it deals in business terms.

In view of these potential costs, it would be unwise for Hong Kong to abandon its policy of upholding a distinct economic boundary and spreading its risks widely. But another major reason why Hong Kong should maintain its economy as a separate entity is that it has to ask itself the question: does the SAR want to remain a haven for 'overseas Chinese' capital in the future? Hong Kong has long served as a refuge for Chinese entrepreneurs overseas, and this takes us to the phenomenon of the transplanting of overseas enterprises in Hong Kong.

## OVERSEAS-TO-HONG KONG TRANSPLANTS

For over a hundred years, Hong Kong served as the main port for people from various parts of China to go overseas. The money earned by the ethnic Chinese abroad was then channelled back as remittances to China through Hong Kong (Sinn, 1995). After 1949, particularly when private business was collectivized in China, the flow of these overseas remittances back to the home communities ceased. Instead, these funds were deposited or invested in Hong Kong for safe-keeping or as flight capital. Thus this 'overseas Chinese' capital played a significant part in the post-war economic development of Hong Kong (Szczepanik, 1958).

Other than funds, business ideas and people were also transferred from ethnic Chinese communities abroad to Hong Kong. In terms of business ideas, the most notable example is, of course, the development of the Wing On Company. The company was founded in 1907 by the Kwok brothers, who created one of the first modern department stores in Hong Kong modelled on those they had observed in Sydney, where they began their business careers (Shanghai Academy of Social Sciences, 1981; Chan, 1995). In terms of people, large numbers ran for cover and took shelter in Hong Kong when struck by political calamities in various parts of Southeast Asia – for example, when racial violence broke out in Indonesia in 1959; when banks and other enterprises were nationalized in Burma in 1963; in Kampuchea in 1975; and in Vietnam in 1954 and 1978 (Chang, 1989, p. 9).

Some of these ethnic Chinese abroad, particularly those from Indonesia, first went back to China for nationalistic and other reasons. Then they suffered tremendously through the Cultural Revolution. When opportunities arose in the late 1970s for these returned ethnic Chinese to leave China, most of them seized the chance. By the end of 1976, it was estimated that about 250 000 of them went to settle in Hong Kong, with another 25 000 in Macao (Godley, 1989, p. 349). Among them were doctors, scientists, engineers, teachers, writers, athletes, musicians, artists, and former cadres. Even after the door of Hong Kong was firmly closed to illegal immigrants in 1980, a steady trickle of them still managed to enter the territory through the daily quota of legal immigrants from the mainland. Like the Shanghainese who came before them, their credentials and qualifications were not recognized in Hong Kong. Quite a number of them thus went into business and became the new rich in the territory (Chen, 1990; He, 1992).

Let me highlight just two aspects of these 'overseas Chinese' transplants in Hong Kong. The first relates to their refugee mentality. This is well articulated by Yung Ching-ching, a former film actress who started another career as an insurance executive after marrying a film director. Accounting for her determination to succeed in the business world, she said:

> I came to Hong Kong when I was eleven months old. My father was the richest man in Vietnam. When Vietnam fell [to the Communists], our spinning mills, our banks, all were gone. The world is too precarious. Nothing lasts. Any possession can be taken away from you, by political changes or by riots. All of a sudden, everything can disappear. The only thing that cannot be taken away from you is your

knowledge. I hope my children will work hard on their studies (*Next Magazine*, 5 November 1993, p. 7; my translation).

From her reflections, we can see more clearly that the obsession with education and qualifications among the Hong Kong inhabitants is not just a matter of their Confucian heritage. Psychologically, it is a matter of a burning anxiety that infects all the refugees and their offspring in the community.

The other aspect of the overseas Chinese transplants in Hong Kong relates to their mixed and ambivalent identities. Who exactly are they? Are they Fujianese, Indonesian, overseas Chinese, *Ah Chan*, *Biu Suk*, or *Heungkong Yan* (Hong Kong people)?[2] The problem of their multiple identities is, of course, not unique. It is only more acute, serving to pinpoint the common psychological tension that is pervasive in Hong Kong as a community of migrants. The tension generated by these multiple identities must have a bearing on the bustling business activities and entrepreneurial vigour found in the territory. More recently, these multiple identities have been made even more complex through large-scale emigration, with Hong Kong people becoming Canadians, Americans and Australians.

## HONG KONG TO OVERSEAS TRANSPLANTS

Since the signing of the Sino-British Joint Declaration in 1984, emigration from Hong Kong has increased steadily. In the early 1990s, it reached a high level of about 60 000 persons leaving the territory per year. Many of them were young, educated professionals, managers and technicians. The story of their relocation and adjustment abroad is too lengthy to be told here (see Skeldon, 1995). As far as the theme of this chapter is concerned, it is worth noting that these emigrants have started another process of enterprise transplants, this time outwards to English-speaking countries. The force that propels them to become entrepreneurs abroad is familiar. Their qualifications and work experience are not readily recognized in Canada, the USA, or Australia. They therefore venture into self-employment and small business (Lever-Tracy *et al.*, 1991; Skeldon, 1994). In addition, the multiple identities they possess help them to create extensive business networks. These networks are valuable resources and can be regarded as a form of business capital. We may therefore say that many of these emigrants are rich in network capital (Wong and Salaff, 1998).

On a macro level, the proliferation and expansion of these individual stocks of network capital contribute to the formation of a collective asset for Hong Kong as a whole. The dispersal of emigrants and the spread of transplanted enterprises abroad enhance the role of Hong Kong as a cosmopolitan business centre by intensifying its global linkages. However, network capital is not endearing in its nature. In the attempt to optimize benefits, entrepreneurs would have to adopt an instrumental approach in cultivating personal relationships. They would appear to be too cunning, and too manipulative in turning ends into means. As innovators, they tend not to respect existing social boundaries and conventions, and tend to mix the sacred with the profane. Particularly in the eyes of many intellectuals, they are not to be trusted because they are seen to be deviants and upstarts, newcomers and intruders, speculators and exploiters. These prejudices and hostilities are deep-seated and it will take time for them to be soothed in a society. As a community of migrants, Hong Kong has built up a tradition of tolerance and hospitality to business transplants and immigrant entrepreneurs. But in the destination countries of the recent wave of Hong Kong emigrants, the host populations may not be as receptive, if only because they are having so many new immigrants entering in so short a period of time. Therefore the real danger for Hong Kong is not brain drain or capital flight. It is the spectre of a backlash against its business transplants abroad and the perils of too rapid a process of globalization.

## CONCLUSION

Hong Kong is a key node in the extensive Chinese business networks throughout the world. For that reason, it commands our special attention when we seek to understand the dynamics of the process of globalization of Chinese enterprises. The entrepreneurial vitality of Hong Kong, as I have tried to demonstrate in this chapter, is closely linked to its openness to migration, its cultural tradition pertaining to commercial activities, and its special political and social framework. As an academic, I find it fascinating to observe how entrepreneurs make large amounts of money both within and outside the territory. Of course, this is not to forget that many of them lose money too (see Chapter 11 in this volume). Watching from a safe distance, I cannot help marvelling at the diversity of their endeavours and the rapidity of their rise and fall. I also cannot help realizing how little we really know about that elusive quality we call entrepreneurship, and how urgent it is that we should try to capture and record it systematically in its full colours, through detailed case studies, before it changes beyond recognition. It has often been said, somewhat dismissively, that the business of Hong Kong is business. But for students of Chinese entrepreneurship, this should be regarded as a positive statement as it would place us right in the middle of an exuberant garden of private enterprise. It would enable us to explore that multifarious world of business transplants and their creative destruction, to unlock the mysteries of their vitality, and to reveal the dynamic forces that are shaping the growth of Hong Kong and its entrepreneurial ventures abroad.

## Notes

1. An earlier version of this chapter was presented as a Hong Kong Lecture at the University of Hong Kong on 25 November 1995. For this revised version, I wish to thank Henry Yeung, Kris Olds and the anonymous reviewer for their comments and suggestions.
2. *Ah Chan* and *Biu Suk* are local Cantonese slang used in Hong Kong to refer to new arrivals from the Chinese mainland.

# 8 Bridging the Continents: The Roles of Los Angeles Chinese Producer Services in the Globalization of Chinese Business

Yu Zhou

## INTRODUCTION

Since the 1970s, 'globalization' has become a buzzword to describe and explain current world economic affairs. The overuse use of this term, however, often disguises the complex nature of globalization. Vast disparities exist in different parts of the world in technology, politics, economics and legal institutions, as well as in language, culture and social norms, all of which have to be overcome in the millions of small and large transactions that comprise the globalization process. Globalization has been made possible not only by the progress in transportation and communication technologies, but also by the growing presence of a sophisticated institutional infrastructure that provides services to bridge these international differences. Among these services, producer services – sometimes referred to as business services – stand out as the key components of this institutional infrastructure. Producer services are services mainly orientated towards organizations rather than individuals, including a large variety of service types. The broadest definition of producer services includes financial, legal, general management, innovation, development design, administration, personnel, production technology, maintenance, transportation, communication, wholesale distribution, advertising and selling (Marshall, 1988). Together, they make up one of the most rapidly growing sectors in advanced capitalist economies and play prominent roles in co-ordinating and controlling economic activities. The rise of globalization has been accompanied by the rapid growth and internationalization of producer services (Dicken, 1992). As in the case of the manufacturing sector, the providers of

international services are dominated by large transnational corporations (TNCs) headquartered in the developed countries. Examples of
these are American Express in financial services, Big Six in accountancy,[1] AT&T in telecommunications, and Mitsubishi in general trading.
While recognizing the formidable force of large TNCs, whose enormous financial and human power spans across geographical, political, and
cultural boundaries, I argue that they are not the only capable players.
In particular, the role of immigrant-run producer services deserves a
closer look because they provide an alternative form of global guidance
by forging numerous small, but enduring, linkages between their host
and origin countries. Because these businesses tend to be small, they
are far more attentive to the needs of smaller-sized enterprises engaging
in the globalization process.

As the various chapters in this volume show (see especially Chapters
10 and 11), the globalization of Chinese business, rather than being
always dominated by major TNCs, may also be marked by a large number
of small-to-medium-sized firms coordinated through dense webs of personal networks (Goldberg, 1985; Hamilton and Biggart, 1988). The small
size of these firms and the many informal transactions among them raise
an interesting problem for the globalization of Chinese business. Small
firms are usually unable to afford the specialized services provided by
large transnational service corporations. Yet they desperately need such
expertise in dealing with international businesses, since they are even
less likely to be equipped with in-house experts. This chapter looks into
the operation of small, Chinese-owned producer service firms in Los
Angeles as a key agent to solving this dilemma.

Since 1965, changes in US immigration policy have led to the rapid
growth of Asian immigration. Between 1970 and 1990, the Chinese population in the Los Angeles metropolitan area increased by more than six
times – from 40 798 to 245 033 (US Census of Population, 1990). Large
amounts of financial investment from Chinese societies in Asia also
arrived through various channels such as family or company transfers,
and foreign direct investment. As a result of this influx of Chinese
population and investment, the Chinese-owned producer service firms
have emerged as a vital sector of the Chinese ethnic economy in Los
Angeles, with abundant Chinese-operated banks, accounting firms,
legal offices, real estate agencies, advertising firms, trading companies,
and travel agencies.

Since producer services are extremely heterogeneous, only a sample
of the sectors can be examined in this study. After a broad overview of
the development of ethnic Chinese producer services in Los Angeles,

I shall provide a more detailed analysis of three types of producer services where ethnic Chinese presence is substantial: accounting, banking, and computer distribution firms. Each sector is different from others in terms of inputs, products, production methods, institutional organization, capital requirement, and human resource dependency. Together, however, they demonstrate the multiple roles played by Chinese producer services within different spheres of the globalization of Chinese business. The firms examined are generally small, privately-owned, and most have been established since the 1980s. At first glance it may seem that they are part of an enclosed ethnic economy operating within immigrant enclaves, but my research found that they play key roles in connecting immigrant economic activities to the international circulation of information, capital and commodities. The information in this chapter was collected during field work over two summers in Los Angeles, in 1992 and 1993. During those two summers, I conducted two questionnaire surveys of all identifiable Chinese-owned accounting and computer firms located within Los Angeles County, and also interviewed about sixty Chinese entrepreneurs, employees, journalists and informants related to these sectors. Other documentation such as bank financial reports, Chinese-language newspapers, the Chinese yellow pages and some commercial directories were also collected and analyzed.

## THE DEVELOPMENT OF CHINESE PRODUCER SERVICES IN LOS ANGELES

Producer services are often seen as privileged sectors in advanced capitalist economies as they require a highly skilled and educated work force and offer high-paying jobs (Daniels, 1985). The rising importance of producer services has been widely documented and has generated considerable discussion among scholars (Beyers, 1991; Coffey and Bailly, 1991; Daniels, 1985; Hansen, 1990; Harrington, 1995; Sassen, 1988, 1989; Walker, 1985). Most studies on producer services in the USA, however, concentrate on mainstream firms run by highly educated white professionals. Virtually no studies have paid attention to immigrant-run enterprises of a similar nature. Research focusing on immigrant economies also tends to ignore these sectors because they are not known to offer larger employment bases, which presumably are central to ethnic economies. In short, both the producer-service literature and the immigrant-economy literature offer little information about immigrant producer services.

Despite their invisibility in the literature, however, I argue that immigrant-run producer services provide key functions for the development of the ethnic economy in general, and international operations in particular. Immigrant-owned producer services are run by individuals possessing cross-cultural knowledge, backgrounds and connections, thus providing inexpensive but valuable channels for international transactions. It is these businesses that connect the external resources to the local ethnic economy (Y. Zhou, 1998a). The development of Chinese-owned producer service firms in Los Angeles is a response to the growing sophistication and maturation of the ethnic economy, and to its soaring demand for international connections.

While being little documented, immigrant-operated producer services have existed in the major Chinese communities of North America for some time. For example, the widely documented rotating credit systems are, in effect, informal financial organizations serving the financial needs of ethnic businesses (Light, 1972; Min, 1987). Studies of many large Chinese communities also indicate the existence of firms engaged in financial, real estate, accounting and legal services (Wong, 1988; M. Zhou, 1992). In most cases these firms were few, small in size, informally structured, serving multiple purposes, and often run on a part-time basis (Waldinger; 1986). In addition, these services were usually confined exclusively to their own communities, with little interaction between them or similar firms in mainstream society. As was the case for other social organizations in various Chinatowns, Chinese producer services were very much segregated from the rest of the society. Since the mid-1970s, this picture has changed dramatically for Chinese communities, especially that in Los Angeles. As the injection of new immigrants and capital intensified, isolation became increasingly hard to maintain (Tseng, 1994a; Fong, 1994). The rapid growth of the ethnic economy in size and sophistication gave rise to a demand for higher-quality services to link ethnic firms with mainstream institutions and business activities at the international level. Rather than depending on the well-established mainstream producer services of Los Angeles, the Chinese community has developed its own system of producer services, run primarily by immigrants. Since the early 1990s, the system has become so comprehensive that few business needs have to be met outside the community. A Los Angeles Chinese business leader described the situation as follows:

When you come to Los Angeles to do business, you are immediately provided with all kinds of business services operated by other

Chinese. So I don't have to worry about how to find a banker who is willing to check my credit history in Taiwan, a forwarder who can contact my suppliers and their forwarding companies to speed up the shipment, an accountant who knows our financial practices, an attorney who speaks my language and helps me to understand American laws, etc. I don't know where else in the world outside of Chinese societies that you can find a business environment as convenient for the Chinese as Los Angeles. (Interview quoted in Tseng, 1994a, p. 82)

Today's Chinese producer services in Los Angeles are drastically different from their earlier predecessors. They tend to be specialized, professionally-run, have extensive interactions with mainstream firms, and are regulated by mainstream institutions. According to Aldrich and Zimmer, on the formation of ethnic enterprises, two conditions have to be met for the development of ethnic producer services (Aldrich and Zimmer, 1986). First, there should exist a large number of underserved enterprises, representing demands and opportunities for entrepreneurs to enter the producer service sector. Second, entrepreneurs should possess the skills and economic resources necessary to establish such firms. Given the skill-intensive nature of producer services, the local presence of both financial and human resources is critical. Both conditions were well met in Los Angeles, thanks to the emergence of two immigration flows.

Earlier Chinese immigration to the USA was dominated by homogenous male labourers, with little or no education, coming from rural regions in Guangdong Province and speaking Cantonese. Since the immigration reform in 1965, the educated urban professional population has comprised a growing share. Although the flow of unskilled labour remains significant, those who engage in unskilled non-agricultural occupations in Los Angeles have never been much over 30 per cent of the employed Chinese population since 1970. In contrast, the majority of the Chinese population in Los Angeles are professionals, with the managerial, professional and speciality occupations accounting for 33.1 per cent, and other white-collar occupations, such as technicians or clerks, accounting for another 37 per cent of the employed Chinese population in Los Angeles in 1990 (see Table 8.1). The presence of this large professional population has pulled the Chinese community forcefully out of social isolation while at the same time pushing ethnic economic activities beyond their traditional labour-intensive domain. Well-equipped with education, expertise and experience, the professional population is the brain power behind the development of Chinese producer services.

*Table* 8.1   Chinese occupational patterns in Los Angeles County

|  | 1970 (%) | 1980 (%) | 1990 (%) | L.A. (%) |
|---|---|---|---|---|
| *Persons (aged 16 and over)* | 100 | 100 | 100 | 100 |
| Managerial and professional speciality occupations* | 35.6 | 33.9 | 33.1 | 27.6 |
| Technical, sales and administrative support occupations | 24.8 | 33.7 | 37 | 32.3 |
| Service occupations* | 15.6 | 13.8 | 12.1 | 12.3 |
| Farming, forestry and fishing occupations | 0.1 | 0.5 | 0.3 | 1.2 |
| Precision production, craft and repair occupations | 4.1 | 6.4 | 6.4 | 11 |
| Operators, fabricators and labourers | 19.6 | 11.7 | 10.8 | 15.6 |
| Unclassified | 0.2 | 0 | 3 | 0 |

*Notes*:    * The share of Chinese working in both professional and service occupations experienced a slight decline from 1970 to 1990, while technical, sales and administrative support increased dramatically. Given the fact that the Chinese population has increased sixfold during this period, the slight decline in population share does not indicate a decline in service establishments.
*Sources*:    US Bureau of Census (1990) *Census of Population*, PUMS 5 per cent sample, 1970 and 1980 data; 1990 data tabulated by the author.

Another group of people instrumental to the growth of Chinese producer services are the wealthy entrepreneurs or business people from Taiwan and Hong Kong, migrating primarily for political reasons. They have been migrating since 1970, but mainly during the 1980s. While their total number may not be very large, they have brought about the most fundamental changes in the Chinese community of Los Angeles. The shifting of the political wind in the 1970s and 1980s in East Asia were mainly responsible for this wave of immigration. The visit to China in 1972 by US President Richard Nixon, and the later establishment of official ties between the USA and the Peoples' Republic of China in 1979, were seen as a severe blow to Taiwan's security. The wealthy elite, upper-class Taiwanese, fearing an eventual takeover by mainland China, found various ways to transfer their capital as well as their families out of the country, mainly to their long-time superpower ally – the USA. This was reinforced by the Sino-British Joint Declaration in 1984 that Hong Kong would be returned to China in July 1997, which had similar effects on Hong Kong's capital and elite.

Beyond politics, the economic dynamism and growing globalization of Chinese economies inside and outside China are also responsible for the population and investment flows. East Asian countries were among the fastest developing nations in the world from the 1970s up to the recent Asian financial crisis. China, Taiwan, Hong Kong – the three Chinese societies – are among the top trading partners of the USA. These countries have generally excelled in developing export-orientated economies for whom the USA is the single largest technology source and market. Liu and Cheng (1994) argue that US military and political involvement in Southeast Asia created a cultural hegemony among the Asian middle-class population, deeply penetrated their values, and established their Western orientation. The growing trade ties further strengthened this relationship and provided many incentives for Chinese business people not only to move their families, but also to set up their businesses in the USA. Following the elite, some of the growing and prosperous middle class in Taiwan and Hong Kong also chose to migrate to the USA to escape the social and environmental ills brought on by rapid industrialization and political instability. With rocketing property values, sustained prosperity and relaxed monetary policies since 1986 in Taiwan, the more recent migrants are capable of bringing increasing amounts of cash to the USA (Tseng, 1994b).

Since the late 1970s and throughout the 1980s, the outflow of capital from East Asia to North America has been astonishingly heavy. Although the majority of Hong Kong money ends up in Canada or San Francisco, Los Angeles is the most popular destination for the Taiwanese (DeMont and Fennell, 1989). Of Taiwanese immigrants in 1990, 22 per cent declared that they intended to reside in Los Angeles (Waldinger and Tseng, 1992). The attraction of Los Angeles is its existing Taiwanese population, and its gateway location to the rest of the USA (Y. Zhou, 1998b). Los Angeles is the largest port and business service centre for Pacific Rim trading in the USA. The export-orientated economy in Taiwan familiarized many Taiwanese with Los Angeles, who then preferred it as a migration destination. According to an estimate by the Taiwan government, more than US$1.5 billion flowed from Taiwan into the Los Angeles area alone between 1985 and 1987 (Tseng, 1994b). A local branch of a Taiwanese bank in 1992 (the First Commercial Bank) reported that every month it processed US$10 m in transfers to Taiwan and received US$35 m from Taiwan (*Chinese Daily News*, 11 February 1992, p. C2). This capital flight has flooded the local municipalities where the Chinese have a strong hold. For example, Monterey Park, a middle-class neighbourhood with about 30 per cent Chinese population, has received so much capital since the 1980s that, as of 1990, each resident had an average of US$32,000 in bank deposits in twenty-two financial institutions within the city (most of which are Chinese-owned), a result of 17.2 per cent annual growth in bank deposits since 1981 (Fong, 1994).

The long-term impact of the financial crisis in Asia since 1997 is still too unclear to be assessed systematically. Yet a preliminary observation in Los Angeles in 1998 suggests that although capital from South Korea dried up almost instantly, there are few such signs for Chinese capital. In fact, the Asian financial crisis further validates the fear of instability that motivated many Chinese to move their families and investments abroad in the first place. The general experience among the bankers in Los Angeles has been that if the other side (Asian side) was doing well, the money and population flow to the USA would slow down and even reverse, but if the other side was doing poorly because of political instab-ilities, such as the mainland China military exercise over the Taiwan strait in 1993, the flow to the USA would intensify. The Asian financial crisis, while it did not stem from political confrontation, heightened a similar sense of insecurity and the urge for investment diversification. The USA, with the world's most powerful economy, continues to draw immigrants and investment. It also needs to be noted that among all major Asian economies, Chinese economies in mainland China and Tai-wan are still among the least damaged by the financial crisis. It is there-fore still possible for immigrants to move their wealth into the USA.

Supported by this international capital, the new immigrants act very differently from their predecessors. Unlike professional Chinese, who depend on their educational resources to climb the social ladder in the USA, a good many recent immigrants came to America with the inten-tion of doing business. Unlike earlier immigrants who had to accumu-late not only petite capital, but also necessary business knowledge and skills from menial work, these recent business people came with capital and extensive business experience from their countries of origin. Some of them were able to start large-scale businesses such as hotel/motels or shopping-complex developments soon after arrival (Tseng, 1994b). It was the presence of these investors that caused the boom in real estate and commercial activities in the San Gabriel Valley, Los Angeles during the 1980s. In 1989 alone, 60 per cent of the shopping/retailing property transactions handled by companies in the San Gabriel Valley, totalling US$800 m, was invested by the Chinese. In 1991, 65 per cent of the ware-house purchasing in the San Gabriel Valley was Chinese-related (Tseng, 1994a). The rising apartment buildings and condominiums in Monterey Park and Alhambra, and the transformed commercial strip stretching for mile after mile along Garvey, Valley and Atlantic Boulevards, are testimony to Chinese investment power (Fong, 1994).

This group of people and the commercial activities associated with them also constitute the main base of Chinese producer services. Since many of them establish their businesses within a short period after arriving the USA, they have little understanding of the American commercial environment, and are also handicapped by language and cultural barriers. Being used to far more *laissez-faire* types of capitalist economies, they found their new environment full of traps and puzzles. They desperately needed services that provide a bridge between their activities and mainstream society. As their businesses expanded into diversified and unfamiliar fields, their needs for producer services also grew, not only in volume, but also in sophistication. Mainstream firms are ill-equipped to meet such demands because of the peculiar cultural and language characteristics of these entrepreneurs, which has left a market niche to be filled by Chinese-immigrant-run producer services.

It should also be noted that Chinese producer services grow during a period when the mainstream society experiences a rapid development of producer services. Los Angeles, as a world city, has become the prime location for headquarters and regional headquarters of TNCs and financial institutions in both the US and Asia, whose activities require extensive support of producer services (Ong and Azores, 1994). In addition, many vertically integrated corporations also started to disintegrate into smaller and more specialized units, a trend particularly visible in high-tech manufacturing and producer services. Disintegration amplifies the need for external transactions, thereby stimulating the establishment of free-standing producer service firms (Coffey and Bailly, 1991; Scott, 1993). The proliferation of producer services in mainstream society is echoed within immigrant communities. Chinese enterprises, during the process of interacting with mainstream firms, feel the pressure to adopt prevailing institutional structures and transactional routines, leading to an increase in demand for such services within the Chinese community. Several sectors have grown more rapidly, reflecting the primary interests of overseas capital: banking, real estate development, hotels/motels, and trading (Tseng, 1994a). To accommodate and assist such development, more general types of producer services, such as accounting, legal services, advertising and travel agencies have also become booming areas in the 1990s.

In short, the growing size and sophistication of a minority ethnic economy, fuelled by the presence of an immigrant professional and entrepreneurial population with international connections, have stimulated the development of ethnic producer services. It would not be an exaggeration to say that the growth of Chinese producer services from the very beginning was rooted in the globalization of Chinese business. The economic restructuring of the larger society only reinforced this growth. In the following section, I examine three producer service sectors, each of which has a substantial presence of Chinese firms and provides a unique function as a bridge to the immigrants' home countries and their destinations. For each sector, I shall identify its unique characteristics, the problems facing immigrant enterprises in using services from mainstream institutions, and the growth and operation of Chinese producer service firms. I shall highlight in particular the international linkages fundamental to the growth of each sector as well as the role each plays in the globalization of Chinese business.

## ACCOUNTING

I went to the US in the 1970s from Taiwan, pursuing an MBA degree, majored in accounting. When I graduated in the 1980s, the [US] economy was in recession. I could not decide whether I should stay here or go home. Eight of us fellow students drove in a big car, travelled as nomads to Los Angeles. When we arrived, some stayed with relatives, those of us who didn't have relatives rented apartments here. Although it was not easy, soon all of us managed to find jobs. Our path is similar to many other people: first we were hired by a company and then we got green cards. I worked at different accounting firms until 1985, Chinese and Jewish firms. After 1985, I went to Price Waterhouse, one of the so-called Big Eight [Big Six in 1992 after merger]. I did expatriate taxes for US green-card-holders who were assigned by their companies to work abroad. I am interested in this area and got the job at the Taiwan Price Waterhouse. At that time, there were only three Big Eight associates in Taiwan. Six people did taxes; I was the only Chinese. Our clients are big companies such as IBM, AT&T, and DuPont. In 1987, I came back to the US and continued to work at accounting firms. I had an old client in the hotel supply business who asked me to become a shareholder in his company. This introduced me to the business world. Since I still had some old clients, I never left accounting entirely. At the end of 1990, my partner, who was a schoolmate of mine, and I decided to open our own accounting firm. I left my other business to my wife and other partners and started this accounting firm. (Interview No. A-6)

The above quotation briefly exemplifies the path of a Chinese accountant in Los Angeles. While he had American accounting training and work experience, he also maintains extensive linkages to international operations and to the local ethnic economy. It is this set of connections and those with positions like his that enable Chinese accountants to provide cross-cultural services to Chinese businesses in Los Angeles. Accounting is a basic component of any business operation, regardless of size and sector. Chinese accounting firms have the longest history of operations in Los Angeles among the three sectors discussed below. In central-city Chinatown, bookkeepers had long been assisting other small firms with bookkeeping and filing tax returns. Since the demand was fairly small, most bookkeepers were part-time, often operated a small shop, and did accounting in their spare time or in the tax season. Before 1970, hardly any Certified Public Accountants existed in Chinatown because most of the demand was for basic services. According to the founder of a Chinese bank, Henry Hwang, who was the first Chinese immigrant to open a CPA firm in Chinatown in the 1960s, he had only US$50 in business per month in the early stages of his operation. Until the mid-1970s, existing Chinese accounting services could hardly be called professional services because most service providers did not undergo professional training. Most formally-trained Chinese CPAs launched their careers in mainstream firms rather than in Chinatown.

The growth of Chinese accounting services has followed the boom of Chinese businesses in Los Angeles since the late 1970s. As money kept flowing in after the late 1970s, new business ventures mushroomed all over the western San Gabriel Valley. These new investors were in great need of accounting and consulting services. A majority of Chinese businesses are small in size and relatively inexperienced, and are likely to operate within a more stringent budget and face tougher competition as new players in unfamiliar fields. Subcontracting accounting work to independent firms is seen as advantageous for them since it not only saves overhead costs, but also enables Chinese entrepreneurs to use the expertise of accountants to overcome their unfamiliarity with the business environment. Mainstream American firms, accustomed to their own cultural environment, were poorly adjusted to the needs of emerging ethnic markets. Not only is there a lack of trust between Chinese entrepreneurs and mainstream firms, without which it is impossible to conduct accounting business, there is also the major problem of communication between people of markedly different languages and business cultures. Just imagine explaining, in a language he or she does not quite understand, US tax laws to a client who has no prior business experience in the USA.

Chinese accountants, many formerly employed in mainstream firms, know such problems at first-hand and understand that they can only be solved by cross-cultural services. Equipped with bicultural and bilingual backgrounds, they can provide adequate services for newly arrived Chinese business people. They responded cautiously to these new opportunities at first. In the late 1970s, a few Chinese CPAs started to open offices in the rising Chinese business centre in Monterey Park. It became clear in the early 1980s that Chinese CPA firms, estimated at fewer than twenty, were still not sufficient to meet the demands of a vibrant ethnic economy. As recalled by one interviewee: 'Until the middle of the 1980s, there was a lot of demand for accounting in the community. If you were a CPA, you had no problem finding clients. They would come to you' (Interview No. A-7).

Although still small in number, Chinese accounting services at this point started to operate a lot more like professional accounting firms. They were mainly full-time firms, often with CPAs. They generally targeted Mandarin-speaking Taiwanese; some of their projects involved investment consultancy and financial planning that went beyond simple bookkeeping and personal tax returns. Between 1985 and 1993, the number of Chinese-operated accounting offices mushroomed. Seventy-two Chinese accounting firms were listed in the *Chinese Yellow Pages* published in 1985, a considerable increase compared to just a few years before. In 1993, the same publication listed 196 CPA firms, and another thirty-nine bookkeeping and tax services. My survey shows that only slightly more than 10 per cent of current firms have been in existence since the 1970s; 63 per cent of the firms opened in the 1980s; and 23 per cent of the firms opened in the 1990s. Thus, in a decade or so this once-empty field suddenly became crowded and extremely competitive.

The growing interest in serving ethnic markets is also related to the frustration that Chinese CPAs experienced in mainstream firms. Chinese CPAs commonly complained of the lack of promotion opportunities in such firms because of their minority or immigrant backgrounds, the so-called 'glass ceiling' problem. There has also been a growing sense of insecurity when the mainstream economy shows signs of recession. As Asians, they are afraid that they will be among the first to go in the case of a cutback. Two quotes from interviews illustrate this problem:

Chinese accountants are usually considered good employees technically. You probably will get fast promotion at the beginning, but at a certain point it will stop. It is extremely rare for the Chinese to make it to managerial positions. (Interview No. A-2)

I worked in a Jewish firm for several years as the only non-Jewish partner. I watched over forty people [get] fired by the firm. I do not like my future being controlled by someone else. I believe I should shift to [the] Chinese market for long-term gain. (Interview No. A-11)

To be self-employed in an ethnic market, despite its heavier work-load and riskier environment, is believed to offer an opportunity to turn ethnic background and connections into assets, and put the workers in control of their own future. With intense market competition fuelled by the growing number of firms, Chinese CPAs are forced to become more sophisticated and to explore specialized services. Interviews suggest that international services are among the fastest-growing sectors in their profession. Many identify international finance and taxation as their major services. The most profitable clients for Chinese CPAs are those immigrant entrepreneurs who have international business backgrounds, own businesses or have other investments overseas, since they are likely to be involved in large projects financed by overseas capital. As over-seas investments from Taiwan and Hong Kong increase steadily in Los Angeles, Chinese accountants become important agents in guiding this capital into a variety of industrial and commercial activities and ensur-ing that these activities conform to the American accounting and regu-latory systems. In their words, the major role of Chinese accounting firms is to 'baby-sit' these new arrivals, starting with explaining the US tax code and accounting system, and later plotting tax strategies and providing investment and financial consulting. Some 36 per cent of the respondents to my survey claimed that they have close relations with overseas business associates, most of which are located in Taiwan, Hong Kong, mainland China, and some Southeast Asian countries. In recent years, TNCs from mainland China have also become very visible. Many accountants in my interviews suggested that they have taught tax laws to visitors from mainland China or have growing mainland companies as their clients. Many accountants viewed the international connections being the major advantage of doing business in Los Angeles. As two CPAs suggested:

Here, no matter what kinds of business you are doing, you must focus on the two sides of the Pacific. Although the US is in bad shape right now [1992–3], if the other side is changing and rolling, Chinese busi-ness here will follow them to change and roll. (Interview No. A-5)

I believe Chinese CPAs are better situated than their American coun-terparts. We are bilingual and bicultural. Globalization integrates US and the Chinese Rim [usually used to refer to mainland China,

Taiwan, and Hong Kong and some Southeast Asian countries where Chinese is influential in the economy]. Our client base will expand as the global economy grows. Every week, one or two of my clients fly across the Pacific. There is so much demand for us to help them with their tax and accounting system. (Interview No. A-10)

Chinese accountants make frequent trips to East Asian countries, although not as frequent as their counterparts in computer firms; 43 per cent of respondents visit mainland China, Hong Kong, Taiwan or Singapore at least once every one to two years. The different accounting systems limit their ability to apply their skills in other countries, so they tend to focus on local transnational firms rather than working directly for overseas firms. Gradually they have cultivated a niche to take advantage of their cross-cultural knowledge and networks. Providing accounting, consulting and information services to Chinese firms interested in investing in America, and American firms interested in doing business in China is seen by many Chinese accountants as their ideal market niche. In the maze of international business, they are capable agents guiding transnational firms to become incorporated into American business frameworks.

## BANKING

A brochure tells a story of the experience of Henry Hwang, the chairman of the board in Far East National Bank, one of the oldest Chinese banks in Los Angeles:

Henry Hwang was born in a merchant's family in China, having had his education in Shanghai and Taiwan. When he arrived in Oregon from Taiwan in 1950, he was a young man with no relatives or friends in the U.S., a few bucks in his pocket, and did not speak English. After he finished college in Oregon, he was unemployed and hung around in San Francisco. He finally found a job in Los Angeles and later on opened a laundry shop as many Chinese did then. While he worked in the laundry, he enrolled in a master's program in accounting at the University of Southern California. In 1960, he got his CPA title and opened the first Chinese CPA office in Los Angeles's Chinatown. During the next ten years, he became known in the community and made a good number of entrepreneur friends in southern California. In 1973, he gathered a ten-person investment group to apply for a federal chartered bank. He received approval quickly, but went through considerable trouble to finally collect US$1.5 million in capital from 300 share owners. In the first four years of operation, the bank ran into many problems. Leadership was inadequate and there were scandals involving senior officials. Hwang was kidnapped and released only after paying a huge sum of money. Several board members asked to quit. In 1978, Hwang decided to become involved directly in the operation of the bank as the CEO, and sold his CPA business. At the end of that year, he turned this failing bank around. During the 1980s, the bank enjoyed rapid growth and a stable financial condition. The bank received the best rating during most of the 1980s. At the end of 1992, the bank's total assets reached US$400 million. (Translated from Hwang, 1992)

Banking is the key institution for the circulation of capital. The globalization of Chinese business relies to a large extent on the development of Chinese-owned financial institutions in different countries. Yet, as the above quote illustrates, the route to establishing a successful bank is not a straightforward one for Chinese immigrants. Traditionally, banking is an industry avoided by immigrant communities. The huge capital requirements, considerable liabilities, sophisticated operations, and the highly regulated and bureaucratic structure contrast sharply with the small, low-cost, little-regulated and flexible sectors with which immigrant communities are most familiar. Yet, banking is also a very important sector for the development of the ethnic economy and communities (Y. Zhou, 1998b). Dymski and Veitch (1995) argue that a well-established financial infrastructure is critical to generating and speeding up economic dynamism at the community level. Without a reliable financial infrastructure, it is extremely hard to circulate and use the painfully accumulated resources within marginal communities. Mainstream banks, although well-established and widely present in ethnic communities, often fall short of the needs of immigrants (Dymski and Veitch, 1995; Light, 1972; Pollard, 1996).

Mainstream American banks have been operating in Chinese immigrant communities for a long time to take advantage of their higher savings rates. Despite being low-income neighbourhoods, Chinatowns in many cities have plenty of mainstream bank branches staffed by Chinese-speaking employees in an attempt to attract deposits. While ethnic Chinese may have good access for depositing their savings, they face great difficulties in obtaining loans from mainstream banks. The language barriers and bureaucratic and discriminatory practices of these banks are very discouraging. The fact that immigrants often have lower incomes, shorter credit histories and a tendency to invest in sectors with low profit margins and high risk makes it more likely that they will have their loan requests refused. Pollard (1996) suggests that, during the 1980s, major Los Angeles banks centralized their loan processing centres from branches to a loan hub. As a result, loan decisions were made outside local communities according to uniform standards and policies. This made it even harder for immigrants to meet loan requirements, and even Chinese-speaking staff in the mainstream banks could not overcome this. In addition, ethnic economies often display an economic cycle that is not entirely consistent with mainstream trends. For example, Chinese real estate investment increased substantially in value during the early 1990s when the rest of the Los Angeles economy went into recession. All these factors make it very hard for mainstream banks to assess accurately the creditworthiness of their ethnic clients.

Not able to rely on mainstream banks, Chinese immigrants have developed their own informal financial arrangements. For example, the rotating credit system (*Hui*) is an informal association to collect capital and to circulate it among the members (Light, 1972). These informal organizations help many small businesses, but their limitations also become more salient over time. The operation of rotating credit systems relies heavily on trust and close ties among participants, which are increasingly difficult to maintain as the Chinese community becomes more heterogeneous. The size of each *Hui* is usually too small to generate enough capital for larger projects such as shopping malls. Therefore, while clearly contributing to the development of Chinese business, informal credit systems cannot replace the full functions of formal banks. Interviews in the Chinese community in Los Angeles in the early 1990s also suggested that such informal institutions were in sharp decline.

Since the 1950s, Chinese merchants in Los Angeles have struggled hard to establish formal Chinese financial institutions. Their request for a charter was turned down repeatedly until the first Chinese–American bank in Southern California, Cathay Bank, opened in 1962 (Cathay Bank Corp, 1992). By 1979, there were six Chinese banks in Southern California. Throughout the 1960s and 1970s, Chinese banks remained small, inexperienced, managed by non-professionals and slow-growing. They were able to survive, however, by relying on the strong savings tradition and conservative investment patterns of Chinese small businesses. The pattern changed dramatically during the 1980s, when the establishment of Chinese banks speeded up with the opening of twelve of the twenty-three Chinese financial institutions[2] in Los Angeles County. Another five opened between 1990 and 1992 (*Findley Reports*, 1992). By 1992, the total assets of Chinese-owned banks headquartered in Los Angeles and Orange County had reached US$5.6 bn, roughly equivalent to the assets of the eighth largest bank in California. East–West Federal Bank, a savings and loan institution established in the early 1970s, became the largest Chinese financial institution, having twenty-one branches and over US$1 bn in assets in 1992. Two other Chinese commercial banks were among the top thirty banks in California. The rapid development of Chinese banking in Los Angeles can be seen even more clearly in comparison with the New York Chinese community of comparable population size. In 1995, there were only ten such Chinese financial institutions in New York with less than a third of the number of establishments and a quarter of the total assets (Y. Zhou, 1998b). The linkage between the Chinese banking industry in Los Angeles and the globalization of Chinese business can be analyzed in two aspects: the capital sources and the market.

**Capital Sources**

Commonly known as Chinese capital banks, the twenty-four banks listed in Table 8.2 can be further divided into three groups with different capital sources; all of them create linkages for the globalization of Chinese business. The first type is those earlier Chinese banks built on small capital holdings of *Hua Qiao* (overseas Chinese), most of whom were earlier immigrants who had accumulated capital through working in small businesses. These banks are more likely to be retail banks, targeting small businesses as their major market. The founders and board members of these banks are typically ethnic Chinese merchants and some professionals. They generally have no affiliation with other large corporations within or outside the USA, but can be interlinked by mutual stockholdings. For example, the owner of Cathay Bank used to be a major stockholder in the East–West Federal Bank before it was purchased by an Indonesian Chinese financial group.

The second type of Chinese bank was established largely during the 1980s, catering mainly to the growing Taiwanese immigrant population and their ventures in Los Angeles. The largest of such banks is General Bank, established in 1980 by the Wu family, one of the richest financial groups in Taiwan. By the end of the 1980s it had grown to become the largest Chinese commercial bank in Los Angeles. According to General Bank's financial report,

*Table* 8.2   Chinese-owned financial institutions headquartered
in Los Angeles County

| Name | Type | No. of branches | Total assets (US$ 1000s) | No. of employees | Date opened** |
|---|---|---|---|---|---|
| American International Bank | Bank | 8 | 482 482 | 204 | Jul. 1978 |
| Asian Pacific Thrift & Loan Co. | Thrift & Loan | 0 | 10 176 | 8 | Aug. 1990 |
| Cathay Bank | Bank | 8 | 757 776 | 324 | Apr. 1962 |
| East–West Federal Bank | S&L | 15 | 1 045 995 | – | Jun. 1972 |
| Eastern International Bank | Bank | 2 | 99 964 | 52 | Jun. 1985 |
| Far East National Bank | Bank | 9 | 354 373 | 129 | Dec. 1974 |
| First Central Bank | Bank | 5 | 132 964 | – | |
| First Continental Bank | Bank | 1 | 33 762 | 17 | Mar. 1991 |
| First Public Savings Bank | S&L | 4 | 229 621 | – | Aug. 1979 |
| General Bank | Bank | 10 | 798 888 | 193 | Mar. 1980 |
| Golden Security Thrift & Loan Assn. | Thrift& Loan | 1 | 35 202 | – | 1981 |
| Grand National Bank | Bank | 1 | 61 482 | 31 | Feb. 1990 |
| International Bank of California | Bank | 7 | 175 555 | – | 1980 |
| Lippo Bank | Bank | 4 | 133 079 | 141 | Nov. 1989 |
| Los Angeles National Bank | Bank | 4 | 81 976 | 51 | Dec. 1982 |
| Omni Bank | Bank | 3 | 151 438 | 82 | Feb. 1990 |
| Preferred Bank | Bank | 1 | 20 952 | 16 | Dec. 1991 |
| Standard Savings Bank | S & L | 4 | 317 737 | – | 1981 |
| Trans-national Bank | Bank | 5 | 103 810 | 73 | Apr. 1978 |
| Trust Saving Bank | S & L | 8 | 124 371 | – | Apr. 1981 |
| United American Bank* | Bank | 2 | 33 685 | 31 | Jun. 1983 |
| United National Bank | Bank | 5 | 131 754 | 100 | Jun. 1983 |
| United Pacific Bank | Bank | 2 | 53 176 | 37 | May 1982 |
| Universal Savings Bank | S & L | 7 | 252 135 | – | 1990 |
| **Total** | **24** | **116** | **5 622 353** | – | |

* United American Bank's headquarters is located in Orange County.
** Date opened or purchased by Chinese capital.
*Sources*:   *Findley Reports* (1992) for annual financial reports of banks 1992–3,
see National Associations of Chinese American Bankers (1992; 1993)

General Bank was organized by a group of people who immigrated
from Taiwan. Most of such persons were educated and had business
experience in both the U.S.A. and Taiwan. The majority of the
Bank's executives and officers were also educated and had business
experience in both countries. (General Bancorp, 1992)

Differing from the first type of bank, these newly-founded banks are
orientated primarily towards new immigrants, who are generally better-

educated and in some cases have substantial capital. These banks also tend to have closer ties with banks or financial groups in Asian countries. A good proportion of their stockholders are investors or banks in Taiwan or Southeast Asia, with extensive commercial and financial interests in that region. Some of these banks are wholesale banks (for example, General Bank), targeting mainly at commercial and industrial investment by large Chinese financial groups. Others are retail-orientated, targeting smaller immigrant businesses. During the 1980s, this type of bank was among the fastest-growing in Los Angeles.

The third group of banks has grown dramatically since the late 1970s. Previously owned either by ethnic Chinese or non-Chinese, they have been acquired by Chinese financial groups from such Asian economies as Taiwan, Indonesia and the Philippines. For example, Bank of Trade, one of the oldest Chinese banks founded in San Francisco, was purchased by the Lippo Group, a financial and banking giant in Indonesia, which changed the name to Lippo Bank. East–West Federal Bank was purchased by Nuri Investment, an enterprise run by one of the richest families in Indonesia. The company also controls United Pacific Bank, a commercial bank in Los Angeles. Omni Bank, a former Japanese bank, was purchased by Taiwan's Wang family. International Bank of California was acquired by the Filipino Chinese Zheng family, and United National Bank was bought by the Tsai family in Taiwan (*Findley Reports*, 1992). All these families represent major financial groups in Asia. Like the case of the second type of bank, these banks can be either retail or wholesale, but they have a special mission in co-ordinating investments and trade activities for particular financial groups.

The growth of the second and third types of Chinese banks shows substantial capital input from overseas Chinese financial groups in several Southeast Asian countries to the Los Angeles area. These Chinese financial groups have traditionally used transnational ethnic networks to diversify their investments geographically in an attempt to gain greater political security in Southeast Asian countries. Such diversification has recently reached North America, which offers several strategic advantages as a location. First, the return of Hong Kong to mainland China in 1997 created uncertainty not only for Hong Kong, but also for Chinese businesses in the surrounding countries. North America was commonly believed by the Chinese to be a secure place, far away from the possible turmoil in Southeast Asia. Second, the USA is the primary market for export-driven economies in Southeast Asia. As these developing countries improve their economic strength, their industrialists are seeking more active roles in trade, which to date has been dominated by TNCs from developed countries. Los Angeles is a financial capital of the Pacific Rim and a major gateway to the US market. By setting up banks in Los Angeles, industrialists in Asian countries occupy a strategic position to control trade and investment flows. Third, by locating in the USA, Taiwanese capitalists have a safe and advantageous position from which they can co-ordinate their activities in mainland China. They are prohibited from doing so in Taiwan and feel that it may be risky to do so in post-1997 Hong Kong; they are also restricted from doing so in other Southeast Asian countries.

In addition, there are overseas branches of foreign banks that are not included in Table 8.2. Banks from mainland China, Hong Kong and Taiwan have branches in Los Angeles to co-ordinate financial activities and to assist trade with their respective countries. Among them, banks from Taiwan are particularly active. 'Going global' has become highly fashionable in the Taiwan banking industry in the late 1990s. Los Angeles, which has the largest concentration of Taiwanese in the USA, is certainly a focal point. In September 1992, interviews with a Chinese banker's association suggested that four Taiwanese banks were applying to establish branches in addition to four other banks that already had branches in Los Angeles. The primary task of these Taiwanese banks is to assist Chinese merchants in international trade. Since foreign banks are restricted in their domestic activities, especially from taking deposits, these banks do not compete directly with local Chinese banks, except in some trading functions. It should also be noted that the above subdivision mainly characterizes the differences in capital sources of Chinese banks. It does not necessarily differentiate their operations, which are related directly to the size and type of bank – that is, commercial banks versus savings and loans. Except for the last group (that is, foreign banks), most local Chinese banks operate within a relatively well-defined ethnic market. Their capital outlet shows clear transnational linkages.

**Loan Markets**

The representatives of most Chinese banks I interviewed estimated that their Chinese customers comprise 50–90 per cent of their total clients, cutting across the four different types of bank. Most of their loans go to the Chinese community. As a result, they run into considerable trouble with the Federal Community Reinvestment Act.[3] Chinese banks are more able to capture the Chinese market than better-capitalized mainstream banks because of their intimate knowledge of, and connections with, the Chinese community. They can design their products and loans programmes specifically to the profiles and needs of immigrants. This is explained by the manager of General Bank:

> The advantages we have over other mainstream banks is that we are more flexible. American banks are doing [loans] mainly on cash flow. If you do not have enough cash flow, they will not loan to you. We look at the secondary sources, such as your collateral and your character. Many of our customers are from Taiwan. Since we have many ties with banks in Taiwan, we can do credit and reference checking in the customer's bank in Taiwan. If this person has nothing here [in the USA], we may also use his credit in Taiwan in the form of a letter of credit to guarantee the lending. Most of our senior managers are bankers from Taiwan, as are many of the employees. We know everything that is happening there, politically and economically. (Interview No. B-5)

Two capital outlets are particularly important for the Chinese banks: real estate and international trade. Real estate provided the first opportunity for Chinese banks to take off. During the 1980s, California's 'bubble economy' was characterized by a frantic escalation of real estate values, and most California banks invested considerably in this market. Between 1987 and 1990, Californian banks' residential real-estate loans grew at an average rate of 37.9 per cent annually (Dymski and Veitch, 1995). In the Los Angeles Chinese community, the real estate boom was accompanied by a sharp increase of new immigrants and the sudden availability of large amounts of overseas capital. In the 1980s, fierce land speculation took place in Monterey Park and surrounding neighbourhoods, where Chinese had a strong presence. This led to a boom in construction and an unprecedented escalation of property values (Fong, 1994). In 1986, Taiwan relaxed its rigid foreign currency control. For the first time in forty years, Taiwanese people could transfer their money abroad easily. This real estate opportunity and the relaxed monetary policy attracted immense capital from Asia to Chinese-owned banks. Many banks generated their initial profits on real-estate lending. If we examine the percentage of real-estate loans among all loans and the portion of commercial real estate in all real-estate lending in 1992, we find a median of 74.4 per cent for Chinese banks (*Findley Reports*, 1992) compared with a median of 44.8 per cent in real-estate loans for California banks (*U.S. Bank Performance Profile*, 1991).

Since the early 1990s, severe defence cutbacks and a national recession have triggered a crash of the real-estate market in Southern California.

Some banks failed, and others reduced their number of branches. The number of FDIC-insured banks in California dropped from 176 in 1992 to 169 in 1993. Total establishments decreased from 1320 to 1169 (Federal Deposit Insurance Corporation, 1982–1993). The Chinese real estate market, however, did not suffer as much as the state in general. Since most Chinese real-estate investment capital came from abroad, the economic recession in the USA did not affect these income sources. For many Chinese real-estate investors, the primary purpose of their investment was to secure a place in Southern California for the long run rather than to obtain a quick profit. They were therefore likely to hold on to their investments despite their temporary loss of value. The tradition of high savings rates also helped Chinese households and enterprises to weather the recession.

The second major market speciality for Chinese banks is financing international trade, particularly those with the Pacific Rim countries. Many Chinese banks have close relations with banks in Asia through mutual stockholding and movement of bank personnel. Some are direct subsidiaries of financial groups in Asia. These give them unique advantages in international trade. In the annual meeting of Chinese-American bankers in 1993, president Henry Hwang's speech illustrated the position of Chinese banks in international trade:

> There is a bright side to the economy in California that should have our Chinese-American bankers brimming with optimism, namely, Pacific-Rim trade. Nobody knows Pacific-Rim banking, commerce and industry like we do. From Seoul to Singapore, Manila to Hong Kong and Jakarta to Shanghai – very few bankers in the world can match us. (*Bird's Eye View*, 1993, vol. 4–2, p. 2)

International trade with the Pacific Rim countries has grown rapidly in Los Angeles, with mainland China, Taiwan and Hong Kong ranking among California's top four trading partners after Japan. Many Chinese entrepreneurs are involved in trading activities with these countries (Tseng, 1994b). Through their linkages with East Asian countries, Chinese banks have captured this market very well. Chinese banks are usually staffed with immigrants from Southeast Asian export-orientated countries who are very familiar with the financial needs and procedures of international trade. In contrast, staff in US banks are much less knowledgeable about such transactions. One Taiwanese interviewee commented with some exaggeration that 'if you grabbed an old lady in the mountains of Taiwan, she would know what a letter of credit means.

But if you ask a staff [*sic*] in Bank of America, he/she would have no idea what you are talking about'. With their good connections with banks and enterprises-at-large in East Asia, Chinese banks can usually handle international trade finance and related issues much faster and more efficiently than can conventional American banks. For example, East–West Federal Bank has an affiliated joint-venture bank in Vietnam with the Vietnamese government, the first of its kind in Vietnam. With this connection, money can be transferred to Vietnam within 24 hours (*Chinese Daily News*, 3 February 1994). Throughout California's recession in the early 1990s international trade was an area that most Chinese banks strove to hold on to and to expand.

## COMPUTER DISTRIBUTION

Mr A is an owner of a computer firm in northern Orange County:

I came from Taiwan as a student to study computer science in the US twenty years ago. It was a hot subject then. After I got my Ph.D. degree, I worked on mini-computers in some large US corporations, including Intel. I was the general designer very early on. Then I was transferred to marketing. In 1983, Taiwan got World Bank funding for universities to purchase computer systems. I visited Taiwan and became connected with people in the Taiwan computer industry at that time. While I was working for Intel in Oregon, I made some investments in this business – a branch of a Taiwan computer manufacturer managed by my friends. I joined them eventually and so this firm became a joint venture. Last year, we were separated from the manufacturer and became an independent firm. (Interview No. C-1)

Mr B owns a computer accessory firm in El Monte:

I studied for an MBA after I came from Taiwan. My family had factories in Taiwan, but they did not do computer-related products. After I graduated, I sent them some product samples of computer accessories, asking them to produce them. They manufactured the products and I sold them here. Now, most of my manufacturing facilities are in mainland China. My brother and I have businesses in Shen Zhen, Shanghai, Beijing and Weifang. I have many relatives occupying high government positions in the mainland. So I got to set up these factories to lower my costs further. (Interview No. C-6)

The above quotes illustrate two typical, but different, paths of Chinese entrepreneurs involved in the computer business. One started with a technical background and established his firm by connecting with Taiwanese manufacturers later on. The other started with a family connection and switched to the computer business as a design and marketing agent for family enterprises in Taiwan. Both went into this business through their international connections.

Computer distribution is different from accounting and banking as it deals with tangible goods rather than information and capital. Producer service literature always includes wholesale/distribution (Marshall, 1988) among its categories. In particular, I selected this sector to illustrate the role of Chinese firms in international trading. If Chinese accounting firms provide guidance on business regulation and tax matters for transnational firms, and Chinese banks facilitate the international circulation of capital, Chinese computer distributors are engaging in the global chain of manufacturing and marketing commodities (Y. Zhou, 1996, 1998a). Chinese involvement in the personal computer industry started soon after this industry emerged in the early 1980s. While some large computer corporations were created by Chinese immigrants, such as Wang and AST, Chinese-owned firms have concentrated more on the smaller end of the size spectrum of this industry. In Southern California, Chinese involvement in the computer sector has grown dramatically. In 1984, only a handful of Chinese firms existed in California, with twenty-four listed in the *Chinese Yellow Pages/Southern California* (1985). By the early 1990s, it was estimated that between 800 and 1200 Chinese-owned firms were involved in the computer industry in Southern California (*Computer Directory*, Southern California Chinese Computer Association, 1992–3). Compiling data from *Dun & Bradstreet Microcosm* (1992), two Chinese Yellow Pages and the membership list of the Southern California Chinese Computer Association, I identified 493 Chinese-owned computer distribution firms in Los Angeles County alone. My survey suggests that 81 per cent of these firms opened after 1986. Most Chinese computer firms in Los Angeles concentrate on trade in the IBM-compatible hardware market. The vast majority of them are distributors and wholesalers. There is also a small number of retailing or software development companies. If we take *Dun & Bradstreet Microcosm, Los Angeles* (1992) as a single source and use owners' last names to identify their ethnicity, Chinese firms make up 25 per cent of computer wholesalers, 9 per cent of retailers and 2 per cent of software companies in Los Angeles County, a region in which the Chinese population constituted about 3 per cent of the total in 1990.

The concentration of Chinese firms in the personal computer industry is closely linked to the globalization of the computer industry and the emergence of Taiwan as one of the leading exporters of computer products to the world market. In recent years, Taiwan has become the world's largest producer of many computer hardware products. According to the Taipei Institute of Information Industry, Taiwan produced US$9.7 bn-worth of computer hardware in 1993. It has more than 50 per cent of the world market share in such computer hardware as monitors, motherboards, scanners, keyboards and mice (*Chinese Daily News*, 29 January 1994). Angel and Engstrom (1995) found that Taiwan is the largest supplier of digital computers to the USA, accounting for 36 per cent of total imported units in 1991 (5.69 million units), and 23.4 per cent of the total imported value (US$3.98 bn). More than half of the Taiwan-made products bear foreign brand names, marketed as OEM (Original Equipment Manufacturer) through large corporations such as IBM. Others are marketed through Taiwanese computer companies (Engardio and Gross, 1993).

Chinese firms in Los Angeles are heavily involved in marketing products from Taiwan. Many firms started by supplying clone products at half the market price of the named brands. The low prices helped them to establish a nationwide customer base. The high profitability of the early days quickly drew more Chinese into the computer business. To solve the problem of insufficient capital, many immigrants exploited linkages with their home country. Some obtained capital support from their families, but more were involved in marketing products made by Taiwanese factories affiliated with their families, relatives or friends. In many cases, they were allowed to pay back loans after the products were sold, a credit arrangement that greatly encouraged the growth of Chinese computer firms. As one interviewee explained:

> There are many immigrants from Taiwan. Almost every Taiwanese manufacturer has relatives or friends in the US. This kind of case is particularly common in LA. For example, I manufacture this product in Taiwan and you are my friend. Then you go to rent a warehouse and sell my products... Business relies on personal relations and payment can be easily delayed since we all are Chinese. (Interview No. C-12)

At a time when computer-product turnover was fast, if some suppliers were willing to grant credit, little initial capital was needed to start a computer distribution firm. Since computer manufacturers in Taiwan during the 1980s were typically small firms as well (Ben, 1992), they had to have sufficient trust in those overseas firms to grant them credit. Without any economic or political means of supervising or sanctioning overseas marketing firms, Taiwan manufacturers resorted to social relationships to ensure responsible and reasonable behaviour, first with family ties, then with close relatives or close friends. For firms in Los Angeles, such social ties win them the trust they could never expect from mainstream banks and manufacturers. These ties also provide them with negotiating ground so they can have longer credit terms or better prices.

Direct access to manufacturing firms in Asia also benefits Chinese firms in the areas of price competition and information flow. Since most Chinese firms operate at the lower end of the personal computer market, where price competition is intense, they are very sensitive to even the smallest price differences. As one interviewee explained:

> In our business, the only competitive advantages we have with the named brands is price. The price gap has to be large enough to attract customers. Therefore, since the beginning, we have tried very hard to save pennies. We would shop around to find the lowest price possible, often ending up with Chinese firms. (Interview No. C-10)

Chinese firms are able to offer lower prices because, first, immigrant firms in general are more ready to accept a lower profit margin than are mainstream firms. Second, their direct access to manufacturers in Taiwan, Singapore, Malaysia or mainland China enable them to charge lower prices by eliminating middlemen. Such access also benefits information flows. Their overseas correspondent manufacturers are well-connected in Taiwan and other major computer-manufacturing countries. Despite their small size, Chinese firms in Los Angeles are thus well informed of market conditions worldwide and can adjust their strategies accordingly. For example, an item out of date in Southern California may still be in great demand in the Midwest or in Europe, and an uncompetitive price in Los Angeles could be competitive elsewhere. One Anglo interviewee in a Chinese firm suggested that having access to local as well as to rerouted overseas information is the key to Chinese firms' success.

The survey gives some indication of the scale of international networks and the frequency of interactions among Chinese computer firms. Of ninety-six responding firms, at least 45 per cent reported that the proprietors owned computer or other business establishments overseas; 61 per cent of the firms had closely-related overseas associates. The overseas locations were concentrated in Taiwan and the Pacific Rim countries, with some in Europe. The frequent connections of Chinese business people with East Asian countries were also shown by their frequency of travel to this region: 27 per cent of surveyed firms have official visits to Taiwan, mainland China, Hong Kong or Singapore at least three times a year in the five years before the survey. Another 24 per cent visited twice a year, an unusually high frequency for casual visits. Only 15 per cent of the surveyed firms made no such visits during this period.

## CONCLUSIONS AND IMPLICATIONS

The globalization literature has prioritized the role of large TNCs in providing transnational business services. Previous studies on ethnic communities have also paid little attention to the economic connections between immigrant communities and their places of origin. In particular, both the producer-service literature and the ethnic-study literature have ignored the role of immigrant-run producer services. By examining the development of Chinese producer-service firms in Los Angeles, and in particular the accounting, banking and computer distribution sectors, this chapter highlights the fact that ethnic economic activities are in many ways closely tied to the larger process of globalization. Since the late 1970s, numbers of Chinese immigrants and investments have grown rapidly in Los Angeles, while the globalization process has linked the US economy more closely with mainland China, Taiwan, Hong Kong and other Southeast Asian countries. Chinese producer-service firms are key agents in facilitating and monitoring transnational economic activities within the Chinese community, a service that has been poorly provided by mainstream establishments. The research findings suggest that many firms in the three sectors are deeply involved in the international flows of information, capital and commodities. Each sector examined performs somewhat different functions in such interactions. Chinese accounting firms assist newly-established Chinese enterprises in Los Angeles, many of which are branches of transnational firms, in adapting to the host business environment and in conforming to the American accounting system. Banks facilitate the international circulation of capital and channel this capital into investments within the Chinese community. Computer firms are directly involved in the global manufacturing and distribution networks of the electronics industry by marketing products manufactured in East Asia.

Differing from large TNCs, the operations of Chinese producer services tend to be decentralized and highly dependent on social relationships.

Ethnic networks extend access and provide an informal regulating mechanism for long-distance co-ordination. Accounting firms depend on Chinese ethnic networks to obtain and establish a client base; banks use ethnic networks to gain capital and investment access to ethnic and international markets; and computer firms rely on ethnic linkages to initiate their enterprises and secure a competitive edge. In general, reliance on social relationships and ethnic networks have enabled small Chinese producer-service firms to organize in a fashion that best complements the size of Chinese firms and their needs in globalization. As some Asian companies, such as Acer, have become quite large, a vertically integrated transnational structure has emerged that requires services provided by large TNCs. Yet, at the most popular level, informal social connections remain the only feasible way for small firms to take full advantage of globalization.

**Notes**

1. Big Six refers to the six top accountancy firms in the USA: Touche Ross Intl; Cooper & Lybrand; Grant Thornton; Price Waterhouse; Ernst & Young; and Deloitte Haskins Sells.
2. Chinese financial institutions are defined as those banks in which ethnic Chinese control over 50 per cent of the total shares.
3. Community Reinvestment Act (CRA) requires banks to give loans proportionally according to the ethnic make-up of their physical communities. It creates a major problem for Chinese capital banks, whose capital sources and historical legacy are entirely based in the Chinese community.

# 9 Chinese Business Networks and the Globalization of Property Markets in the Pacific Rim

Katharyne Mitchell and Kris Olds

## INTRODUCTION

In analyzing the extension of Chinese firms across space, one of the key industries to lend insight to this process is unquestionably the real-estate industry. While much of the vast 'overseas Chinese' literature has focused on the articulation of production networks, sub-contracting connections, and flexible accumulation and credit practices, relatively little attention has been paid to the property development process. This is a serious omission, for two reasons. First, it has become increasingly apparent that Chinese firms are currently among the foremost players involved in the development and acquisition of both commercial and residential projects worldwide; this includes mammoth urban development schemes in cities as diverse as Singapore, Vancouver, Sydney and Shanghai (Mitchell, 1995; Olds, 1995, 1998), and smaller projects throughout East and Southeast Asia (Yoshihara, 1988; Smart, 1997). Second, recent globalizing trends that have been studied in the areas of production, finance, migration, information and culture have also had a great impact on the property development industry, yet have not received the same degree of scholarly attention (Beauregard and Haila, 1997; Haila, 1997; Olds, 1995). The contemporary globalization of property markets affects key cities around the world, and is changing both the form and process of the development and marketing of real estate. By extension, it is also changing the overall shape of the cities, and engendering urban social change (and social conflict) (see Mitchell, 1993a; Ley, 1995). Despite this, however, little research has been devoted to the factors facilitating and shaping the globalization of property markets.

In this chapter we shall address these two theoretical lacunae by examining the dynamics associated with the *early stages* of large-scale overseas property investment commitments made by Hong Kong-based Chinese entrepreneurs. In the late 1980s and early 1990s huge swathes of downtown Vancouver were acquired by some of the most powerful and well-known Chinese property tycoons operating in Asia. The large-scale delocalization of Vancouver's downtown core was initiated by Hong Kong-based property tycoon Li Ka-shing, in association with fellow tycoons, Lee Shau Kee and Cheng Yu Tung. Their investment in one large-scale residential redevelopment project on the former Expo '86 site subsequently spurred other investment flows from small- and large-scale property developers based in various parts of Asia: people such as the Hong Kong-based Kwok family (associated with Sun Hung Kai Properties), and the Malaysia-based developer Robert Kuok quickly followed Li's lead in extending their property interests in Canada. While property investment flows controlled by all these actors have clearly diminished in the late 1990s (for a variety of reasons), an analysis of the earliest stage of this wave of investment can shed some light on the factors underlying the deepening of trans-Pacific connections in the sphere of property.

Following this introduction, the second section of this chapter will focus on the recent globalization of property markets, especially within a Pacific Rim context. What is a global property market, and how does it differ from real-estate investment and activities of the past? Are there differences between commercial and residential property markets, and within these markets? If so, is this linked with particular types of international investment and its emphasis on specialized niches within the real estate industry? In this section we outline how these global markets function, and why they are important contemporary processes within the global economy.

In the third section, we examine how and why 'overseas Chinese' business networks have become such major players in the contemporary development of property markets worldwide (see Mitchell, 1997; Hamilton, 1996a; Gutstein, 1990). One of the major features that characterizes global networking in real estate is the increasing speed and accuracy of information processing. For overseas transactions involving investment in residential or commercial property, including the purchase of property for ownership, rental, sale or development, the accessibility of quick and *reliable* information is absolutely crucial. Recent research into Chinese business firms has shown that the manner in which information is shared between networked members (in, for example, the real-estate industry) is often both more particularist (involving specific, relational ties) and more flexible than in non-Chinese business firms, and may lend an advantage to Chinese firms operating within this sector (Mitchell, 1995; Redding, 1990 and Chapter 2 in this volume; Yeung, 1998b). Chinese property entrepreneurs, especially those with strong links to cities such as Hong Kong, Singapore and Taipei possess abundant forms of 'network capital' (Wong and Salaff, 1998; Wong, 1999). This network capital facilitates their 'global reach' as they weigh overseas investment options, including those in Vancouver, our case study city.

Other areas in which Chinese businesses might have an edge in global property investment relate to the familial nature of the firm. Family ties are defined quite broadly, extending from the immediate family to include in-laws, distant relations, and even college classmates. The use of the extended family in the management and organization of small and medium-sized Chinese firms is important in areas such as credit pooling, the maintenance of personal relations in business – even across long distances – and in the circulation of capital on a long-term basis. We believe that these types of cultural articulations have had an important positive effect on the success of many Chinese business firms in the burgeoning area of overseas investment in property.

Despite these broad claims, however, it is evident that investing in property on a global scale is heavily dependent on understanding the local, regional and national factors that shape the property development process. Local authorities in particular posses a myriad of means to regulate the development process because of property's fixed nature in space. This power becomes significantly more important to investors when the scale of investment commitments rise, and when investors commit to long-term, large-scale property development projects. Such commitments open up even the largest of Chinese firms to the possibility of capital loss and damage to reputation. A key question is, therefore, how do Chinese business firms with property interests deepen and enhance their knowledge of the overseas contexts in where they seek to invest on a relatively large scale for the first time? In particular, how do Asia-based Chinese entrepreneurs ensure that the *formative* early stages of overseas development processes are handled in accordance with their objectives? It is this question we address in the fourth section of the chapter, when we highlight the key role played by Vancouver-based actors in acting as 'bridges' between the Hong Kong-based investors, and the Vancouver-based institutions responsible for regulating the development process (see also Chapter 8 in this volume).

## THE GLOBALIZATION OF RESIDENTIAL PROPERTY MARKETS

Property markets have traditionally been analyzed from local and national perspectives, and regulations shaping property markets have been developed predominantly within the purview of local and national actors and institutions. As John Logan notes (1993, p. 35), real estate investment (and speculation) has historically 'attracted a largely parochial crowd, investors of a modest scale whose knowledge of the local market and connections to local officials gave them a competitive edge in this lucrative but risky business'. Of course, overseas (foreign) property investment has been occurring for hundreds of years (for example, Manhattan was a speculative investment), but the major forces shaping property markets in most Western cities have been characteristically local/national.

While the local/national specificity of property markets in most cities continues to be remarked upon by analysts of contemporary urban transformations, be they critical (for example, Harvey, 1994) or supportive (for example, Economist Intelligence Unit, 1997) of the workings of capitalist markets, most analysts recognize that urbanization processes and urban forms are being transformed increasingly by *globalizing* forces (for example, see Sassen, 1991, 1994; Douglass, 1998). Clearly, land and buildings are fixed in space, and subject to resolutely territorial forms of governance and politics. But while historical and national contexts 'continue to differentiate both the processes of urbanization and the specific nature of urban issue that will be confronted in the future', cities, regions and nations are becoming 'more tightly integrated through trade, investment, political arrangements, and cultural inter-penetration' (Douglass, 1989, p. 10). In such a context 'the processes of urbanization' are becoming more 'internationally interdependent' (ibid.). Urbanization and urban redevelopment processes are being reshaped by globalizing processes; processes that are generating deeper linkages across space, thereby opening cities up to the shifting agendas of distant actors and institutions.

In the Pacific Rim the forces of globalization have spurred on changes in the urban and regional space economy. Overall, the changing spatial order exhibits five emerging forms of development (after Douglass, 1998, and Rimmer, 1994) that are nested in terms of scale: (i) urban mega-projects (UMPS), usually situated within (ii) world/global cities, which are a component of (iii) extended metropolitan regions, which can be part of (iv) transborder regions (for example, growth triangles) and/or (v) international 'development corridors'. These five forms of development are associated with the restructuring or completely new development of large-scale modern seaports and airports. In short, the spatial order of the Pacific Rim is being reworked at a rapid (and volatile) pace: it reflects the burgeoning influence of transnational actors and forces, the adoption of neo-liberal development policies that favour facilitating the workings of private sector actors, and the delimitation of constraints on material and non-material flows.

Property markets, one of the key forces underlying urban change in the Pacific Rim, are also being globalized. However, in contrast to 'goods' such as securities, or sectors such as manufacturing, the transformation of property markets has received little relatively academic attention. This is unfortunate as property makes up one of three major factors in the production process (land, labour and capital), real estate represents much of the world's wealth (somewhere between 20 per cent and 60 per cent according to Mueller, 1992), and the 'real estate or property sector is of central importance' to foreign direct investment flows, making up some 5–20 per cent of total world-wide FDI flows (Economist Intelligence Unit, 1997). Given that a significant proportion of transnational flows of capital into property are not captured in official FDI data,[1] it is safe to say transnational property investment flows are one of the most understated yet significant forms of investment capital in existence. Today one cannot make sense of specific sectors of property markets (for example, Class A commercial space), or development dynamics in specific geographic locations (for example, central business districts, gentrified districts, 'Edge Cities') without 'taking sophisticated account of the very complex fiscal and investment flows' that link national economies through a 'global grid of currency speculation and capital transfer' (Appadurai, 1990, p. 8).

What are the key forces behind the globalization/delocalization of property markets in some cities? Logan (1993, p. 36), for example, identifies two significant phenomena that underlie the globalization of property markets: 'The first is the increasing linkage between the financing of real estate development and the broader capital markets. This has occurred simultaneously with the trend toward the internationalization of capital markets. The second is the emergence of new kinds of organizations to plan and execute development projects.' Haila (1997) concurs with Logan, though she differentiates a series of different, albeit overlapping factors: (i) the operation of global actors (for example, architects, developers and planners) who create an international image for cities; (ii) the spread of similar methods of finance and construction;

(iii) foreign investment flows and the integration of markets; and (iv) buildings as signs. The first three factors are relatively self-evident, while the last refers to the growing trend in which buildings are constructed and purchased for their 'sign value' – that is, their ability to convey and represent fame, prestige, exclusivity, dominance and modernity for their owners, and sometimes for the various levels of government that are responsible for the territory in which these buildings are constructed. Other writers (including the Economist Intelligence Unit, 1997; Olds, 1995; Thrift, 1987) highlight the importance of a variety of similar (interrelated) factors: shifting political values resulting in the liberalization of foreign investment regulations; the development of incentive schemes to attract foreign investment into cities; the emergence of a global corps of professional property consultants working for transnational firms such as Jones Lang Lasalle; and migration.

Regardless of which specific factors are highlighted, the overall point is that macroeconomic restructuring and transnational flows of people (via short- and long-term migration) underlie the supply of, and demand for, specific forms of property in cities. However, the impact of the globalization of property markets is not indiscriminate or homogeneous across space. Rather, it is felt in the cities (and sections of cities) that are most closely integrated with the historic and contemporary 'global space of flows' (Castells, 1989). For example, in a global city context, commercial office space is both funded and utilized by firms linked to transnational finance and production chains. As Sassen (1991, pp. 185–7) notes:

> The rapid growth in the number of financial firms, services firms, and high-income workers concentrated in major cities has contributed to rapid growth of a high-price real estate market. The concentration of major firms and markets in New York, London, and Tokyo in particular has raised the importance of locating in these cities and has been a key factor in the development of massive construction projects. The active participation of foreign firms as investors and as buyers and users of real estate in these three cities has contributed to the formation of an international property market... The central areas of these cities have become part of an international property market; and conversely, these central areas account for much of the international property market that has developed since the 1970s... But it would seem that other conditions had to come together for an international property market to come about. It is the existence of a multiplicity of other markets, and particularly leading markets, that

raises the value of land in the leading financial centres. It is the highly international character of these markets and of the bidders that differentiates this property market and differentiates these cities from other major cities with desirable building stock.

Apart from the globalization of commercial property markets, it is also apparent that some predominantly 'local' *residential* markets in a selection of different types of global cities have 'gone global' (to varying degrees). This is true of London, Paris and New York, as well as key cities in the Pacific Rim (for example, Vancouver, Melbourne, Sydney and Singapore) (Olds, 1995, 1998; Berry, 1994; Stillwell, 1996). In short, global cities are becoming differentially integrated into (and integrated by) what could be deemed a *global residential property market*.[2]

A global residential property market (GRPM) can be said to have two key characteristics. First, there is a significant level of overseas investment in residential property. This can take at least three forms: first, as a purchase for the owner's own use; second, as purchase for rental letting; and third, as direct investment in construction for sale or rental (the focus of this chapter). The second key characteristic is international residential migration (either permanent or temporary) which may be linked to the purchase of property for the owner's specific use, or as part of a wider rental market within cities (for example, a Hong Kong dweller moving to Toronto to rent a privately owned condominium for a temporary period of time).

In operational terms, the existence of a GRPM would be characterized by one or more of the following: first, a significant proportion of sales and or rental lettings within specific sub-sectors or areas of a city to overseas buyers/renters; second, by a significant level of sales to overseas buyers for rental investment; and third, by some degree of overseas-funded new build (the focus of this chapter) or conversion for sale or rent. The second and third criteria are most directly linked to international capital flows.

Since the 1980s there has been considerable media attention on the growth of overseas Chinese investment in the luxury end of residential property markets in cities such as Vancouver, London, Sydney, Auckland and Toronto. In the case of London, individual Chinese investors, primarily from Hong Kong and Singapore, are actively purchasing apartments in Westminster, Kensington, the Docklands and other areas, including Hampstead. While some of these apartments have previously been occupied, it is suggested that many of them are conversions or new build, and that many are bought off plan. London Residential Research (1997) suggest, for example, that the value of residential developments under construction in London in mid-1997 was £2.7 billion and that at least 40 per cent by volume of the units have been or are being sold to overseas buyers. They also claim that over 50 per cent of sales by volume, and more by value, are to South-east Asian buyers, particularly from Hong Kong and Singapore. This is a significant example of overseas Chinese investment in the UK (and the EU); one that is not captured, to any significant degree, by official FDI statistics.

Apart from the direct and indirect demand for overseas property by individuals, Chinese business firms are increasingly involved in the production of residential property, in terms of both individual buildings, and larger-scale property (re)development projects. Numerous condominium projects have been developed in cities such as London, Sydney, Auckland and Vancouver. Large-scale residential (re)development projects are currently being tackled by overseas Chinese business firms in Asia, North America and Australia. Hong Kong-based firms and actors in particular are playing a key role in the globalization of residential property markets, both through the export of their expertise in large-scale, high-density residential development projects, and through the investment capital they are directing and leveraging into cities such as Vancouver.

While overseas Chinese property development firms are becoming more active in transnational investing practices, it is important to be sensitive to the specificities of overseas Chinese business practices, the familial nature of most Chinese firms, the nature of key concepts such as 'trust' and *guanxi*, and the overall role of personalized social relations in guiding the investment process. In the case of the property development process, for example, most analyses are reflective of Western perspectives on development processes. The vast majority of neo-classical property market analyses (for example, Baum and Scofield, 1991; Royal Institution of Chartered Surveyors, 1993) are rooted in the catechisms of self-equilibrating markets, the workings of 'natural' laws, and efficient price-setting markets (Harris, 1994). However, the applicability of universal and overly abstract approaches to property development projects driven by Hong Kong-based developers needs to be questioned. In the remaining sections of this chapter, we shall address some key features of Chinese business networks, and some important aspects related to the extension and deepening of Chinese business networks across space, from Hong Kong to Vancouver.

## CHINESE BUSINESS NETWORKS

The theme of global restructuring since the 1970s is usually premised on fundamental shifts in economic systems world-wide, particularly in the organization of both finance and production. Recent research has shown that the new, increasingly flexible production and circulation systems that characterize much of the recent restructuring are based largely on sub-contracting networks of various kinds (Piore and Sabel, 1984; Gertler, 1988; Beaverstock, 1996; Suarez-Villa, 1996). Despite earlier conceptualizations of these types of networks as being inherently local in operation, they have been shown to continue smoothly and efficiently across international borders (Gereffi, 1996; Gereffi and Hamilton, 1990). The successful functioning of these flexible, high-speed networks relies, at least partially, on social relations characterized by long-term bonds of understanding, trust and reciprocity. We argue that those operating in societies in which these types of social relations are culturally prominent, rather than being disadvantaged, are likely to have an edge in property development within the modern global economy.

The importance of social relations for businesses is manifested in the kind of long-term, inter-firm connections that bind together increasingly flexible production networks around the world.[3] Long-term relations between contractors and subcontractors rely on personal trust and generate high standards of behaviour and feelings of obligation and reciprocity. These social qualities often mitigate against opportunism better than the structures of autocratic authority necessary to control opportunistic behaviour in hierarchically-organized firms. The idea of social relations as an important and powerful glue for the smooth functioning of markets and production is in direct contradiction to traditional theories of the firm. Williamson (1975), for example, argues that organizational forms arise as a result of superior efficiency in reducing economic transaction costs. In this view, transactions that are uncertain and frequently recurring, and which require considerable investment of money or time in specific, non-transferable areas, are more likely to take place within hierarchically organized firms (see Granovetter, 1985, p. 493). With the application of this logic to sub-contracting, a hierarchical, depersonalized structure would eventually arise and supplant earlier structures as the superior organizational form. Yet, in Chinese business, this has not happened; in fact, quite the reverse.[4]

Recurring patterns within Chinese firms include the proliferation of small and medium-sized enterprises owned and managed by family members, a relatively *low* level of vertical and horizontal integration within firms, a large number of subcontracting operations character-ized by personalistic networks linking firms backwards to sources of supply and forward to consumers, and great speed and flexibility within these networks. These types of patterns are evident in the business organization and functioning of Chinese societies in Taiwan, Hong Kong, Singapore, Malaysia, the Philippines, Thailand and Vietnam (see Chapter 1 in this volume).[5] The networked relationships within which business people operate are elastic, flexible, shifting and overlapping – with the norms and obligations of individuals defined in relation to others within the network. The most central relational ties involve fam-ily, and the family operates as a system of contacts as well as an emo-tional unit.[6]

How are these relational networks central to the successful function-ing of modern Chinese economic practices in the area of property development? One crucial feature of the centrality of the relational core is the degree to which ownership, management and control of the business remains within the family. Nearly 90 per cent of business in Taiwan, for example, is family-owned, and management is largely con-ducted by family members (Lin, 1996). Even in large business groups such as the ones associated with the restructuring of Vancouver's down-town area, the 'core group is usually constituted by family members, good friends or old colleagues' (Kao, 1996), a point worth keeping in mind when reading the case study.[7] Extensive family ownership and management is also documented in studies of Chinese business practices in Hong Kong (Lau, 1982; Wong, 1985, 1988; Redding, 1990); South Vietnam (Barton, 1983); the Philippines (Lim, 1983, 1991); and Thai-land (Gray, 1988). According to these studies, when large-scale opera-tions are extended overseas, some successful entrepreneurs may hire professional managers to take care of various aspects of the business, yet the general pattern is for the 'core deal-making' to be conducted in the 'traditional' (family-managed) way.[8]

The emphasis placed on family control is evident in the effort to establish one's own family as a nodal point in the network web. This is most obviously manifested in the rapid turnover of employees who leave the parent firm in order to establish another, usually related, business.[9] The succession of sub-divisions resulting from these actions, rather than leading to cut-throat competition and chronic disputes and bank-ruptcies, has been an important means for extending networks and leading to new business ties and opportunities.[10] The growth of these networks extends *guanxi* (personal ties or connections) in the business world. We argue that in the fast-moving world of property development, the extension of *guanxi* is crucial for the dissemination and reception of business information, as well as for the expansion of contacts and opportunities. According to Gary Hamilton, employers will sometimes even provide the capital necessary for a former employee to get started in a spin-off (sub-contracting) firm. The new owner-manager is then bound through ties of obligation and reciprocity to the former employer, whose *guanxi* network is thereby enlarged and enriched.[11]

A fundamental tenet of this system is trust. The ethic of trust is absolutely central to the business success of Chinese entrepreneurs in Hong Kong, Taiwan, and in many overseas communities (see Chapter 4 in this volume).[12] In order for the established norms of obligation and reciprocity to operate effectively, businesspeople must trust that the other players involved in business transactions will uphold certain expectations, including the expectation to maintain and continue a given moral order.[13] The greater trust accorded to family members and those of the same native place within this moral order is implicit; not only do consanguineous bonds (including those extended in space) form a firmer basis for trust and information-sharing, but because of the threat of communal sanctions, they are also crucial as a means of control over those who do not conform. Finally, by relying largely on the trust inherent in close relationships, it is possible to justify keeping economic benefits within a relatively tight (albeit shifting) community network.

Within the extended moral economy of trust, with loans often based on the implicit assumption of reciprocity or obligation, the policing of behaviour through information-sharing, through the news about someone's good or bad deeds, through *reputation*, is absolutely vital for the successful operation of the whole system. The sharing of information continues long after a partnership is secured, and serves to cement the specific relationship as well as aid in business intelligence useful in more general endeavours. Using information to solidify relational ties and to maintain the moral economy through enforcing communal behaviour, has had numerous repercussions in the delicate negotiations involving money and credit in the world of real estate high finance.

The accumulation of capital through private means, usually through family or friends, is particularly common in countries such as Taiwan, where state control of the banking industry has produced a lethargic and conservative venture capital programme.[14] As the public or formal financial sector is slow or blocked, capital 'circulates by way of informal channels and instruments'.[15] Many businessmen rely on mutual aid associations (*hui*) for venture capital (see Chapter 5 in this volume).

These mutual aid groups are characterized by a strong reliance on personal trust, and by the predominance of friends or relations within the group. In these groups, there are rarely formal laws or administrative agencies used to enforce behaviour; the norms and obligations of appropriate economic behaviour are implicit. Since the accumulation of savings in Taiwanese society has been extraordinarily high since the 1970s, family savings and other informal-sector poolings represents a major source of capital formation.[16] Where this capital goes is based largely on the networks and channels of trust formed through long-term relationships.

By pooling funds and obtaining capital through informal channels, the bulk of the principle necessary for a business venture can often be accumulated *before* the business venture is initiated. In terms of the repayment of interest on the principle, the amount of time taken to repay is less crucial than the eventual success of the business operation, since success adds another nodal point in the expanding business web of all the players involved. This type of 'long-term' debt, in which the obligations of repayment are based on personal relations and are implicit, but are not necessarily regularized in exact measurements of time or money, allows for different strategies of capital utilization by the debtor. The money may or may not be called upon to produce more money within a set amount of time, but this rate of interest is set by the consensus of the family or informal group rather than by an average, standardized or 'going' rate of interest.

These general points regarding the nature of Chinese business networks apply to the Chinese-controlled property development industry. The vast majority of property development firms are still controlled and often managed by family members, with the patriarch responsible for key decisions. Even the large corporate groups situated in Hong Kong and Singapore, with major property development arms, are ultimately guided by the patriarch. Obviously, succession is a key organizational concern and, whenever possible, children (especially sons) are raised to eventually take over responsibility for various arms (often segmented) of the organization. Social relationships, trust and *guanxi* also play key roles in the expansion of property firms, both through the raising of capital, and through the identification of new development opportunities. In the context of the Asian 'economic miracle' in the 1980s, the rapid growth of Chinese-controlled property firms (especially conglomerates with listed arms), the planned return of Hong Kong to Chinese control in 1997, and major migration flows across the Pacific, Chinese business networks stretched out across the Pacific to connect with social formations in cities such as Vancouver and Toronto.

In the next section of this chapter, we shall develop a short case study of *how* social relationships were extended across space, with the aim of guiding property investment flows and building up a long-term North American base for the family and friends of Hong Kong-based property tycoon Li Ka-shing. By focusing on the factors underlying the stretching of such socioeconomic relationships across space in the pursuit of property development opportunities, we hope to shed some light on the globalization of Chinese business networks.

## BRIDGE-BUILDING ACROSS THE PACIFIC: A VANCOUVER CASE STUDY

In 1987 the British Columbia provincial government in Canada decided to sell 204 acres (80 hectares) of land that it owned in downtown Vancouver (see Fig. 9.1). This land (the former Expo '86 site) was put up for sale as part of a newly-initiated privatization programme. The subsequent acquisition of this land in May 1988 for CDN$320 m from the provincial government is the result of the decision of Li Ka-shing, Hong Kong's richest, most powerful and well-connected property tycoon, to deepen his linkages with Vancouver as an individual, as a father, and as patriarch of the Li Group. Fellow tycoons Cheng Yu-Tung and Lee Shau Kee were also drawn into the project in 1988, diversifying their portfolio in a geographic sense, and 'cushioning' their holdings in Hong Kong and China in the context of political and economic uncertainties. As Li Ka-shing's son (Victor Li) put it in 1992, while Canada may not 'offer a very high immediate return, it's an essential part of a healthy, balanced portfolio, providing good mid- to long-term asset growth' (Li, 1992, p. 3).[17] This is particularly the case given that the land could be acquired so cheaply (in a relative sense) on a Pacific Rim scale.

The rationale for the investment, and the broad forces underlying the investment process, have been well covered elsewhere (for example, see Gutstein, 1990; Mitchell, 1993b, 1995; Olds, 1998; Thrift and Olds, 1996). Suffice to say, the Pacific Place project (as it has come to be known) represented a timely opportunity to further a variety of familial and corporate goals related to succession plans within the Hong Kong-based Li Group. Pacific Place was effectively used as an educational tool to enhance the skills, reputation and confidence of Li Ka-shing's

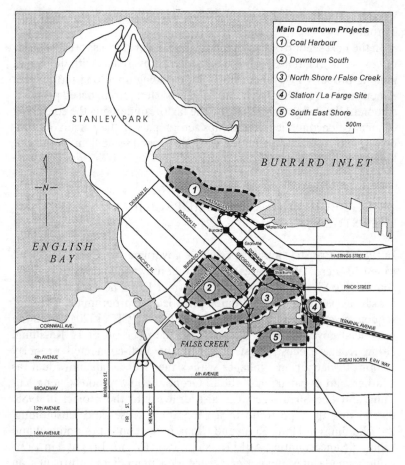

*Figure* 9.1 Pacific Place on the former Expo '86 site (North Shore/False Creek)

eldest son, Victor Li, in the large-scale property development industry. The acquisition of such a large, high-profile site in Vancouver enabled Victor to be 'groomed' in a strategic non-Hong Kong locale for his eventual (1993) appointment as a Cheung Kong (Holdings) Ltd executive. The purchase of 80 hectares of Vancouver's central city also enabled the Li Group to use Pacific Place as a vehicle to establish a 'bolt hole' in North America: Vancouver now acts as a base for development activities in cities across Canada (including Vancouver) and the USA. The city is effectively the Canadian base for a cosmopolitan and globally mobile family of entrepreneurs. And finally, simple material goals also inspired the Li Group to extend their reach over space: the Pacific Place project enabled Li and a small circle of Hong Kong-based property tycoons to diversify their property portfolio while enjoying steady (if unspectacular by Asian standards) returns.[18]

While the rationale for the investment process is now clear, and the broad forces underlying the restructuring of downtown Vancouver have also been examined (see Ley, 1996), little attention has been devoted to the *critical* 'bridge-building' phase – namely, the period in which Li Ka-shing and family finalized their decision to purchase the site, and then formulated a strategy to pursue the development project. In short, how do such actors reach across space to effectively pursue multiple development objectives, especially ones so critical to the issue of succession within the Li Group, and via a project subject to *complex* local government regulations because of the fixed nature of property?

To discuss the critical bridge-building phase, it important for us to backtrack in time to the early 1980s. It was at this time that BC premier, W. Bennett, suffering through a 'crisis in political support' (Ley, 1987, p. 50), announced his 'vision for the future, a vision to build a great meeting place for all our people that we would call British Columbia Place'. The government assembled a package of land on the north shore of False Creek with the intention of hosting an international exhibition on the site, and later redeveloping it into a high-density, high-rise commercial and residential project. In August 1980 a provincial crown corporation (BC Place Ltd) was formed (through provincial legislation) to redevelop the North Shore of False Creek. As a crown corporation, BC Place had:

> the powers of a private corporation, additional privileges and fewer legal restrictions. It represents the extension of the centralized administrative model advocated by Progressive reformers early in this century, and is a vivid illustration of the argument of Weber, Habermas and others concerning the range of social control exercised by the modern bureaucracy. The corporate model gives maximum discretion and minimum disturbance to technical specialists acting as the agents of a central executive. As one corporate planner observed, 'The Cabinet are our shareholders.' (Ley, 1987, p. 53)

BC Place's senior corporate officers and board of directors were many of Vancouver's most powerful business elites. Amongst the ten-person board of directors in 1981 was Stanley Kwok, President of Pendero

Development Co., a Hong Kong immigrant who landed in Canada in 1968, a period characterized as the 'first wave' of Hong Kong immigrants to Canada (following changes in immigration policy and regulations). Further details on Stanley Kwok are presented in Box 9.1.

---

*Box* 9.1    Brief Profile of Stanley Tun-li Kwok

Stanley Tun-li Kwok was born in China in 1928. He was educated in architecture at St. John's University in Shanghai, where he graduated in 1948 (one year before the Communists seized power in China). He fled to Hong Kong in 1949 where he began working for the well-known Hong Kong design firm Eric Cumine and Associates. Kwok lived in Hong Kong for nineteen years until 1968, when he reached the top of the Hong Kong architectural hierarchy (as director and president of the Hong Kong Institute of Architects). During this time he worked for many of Hong Kong's real-estate tycoons including Stanley Ho, Run Run Shaw, Fok Ying Tung and Kwok Tak Seng. He also met the three eventual main shareholders of Concord Pacific – Li Ka-shing, Cheng Yu Tung and Lee Shau Kee.

One year after the Hong Kong riots of 1967 (which were related to the Chinese cultural revolution) Kwok migrated to Canada. As he commented, 'I saw 1997 written on the wall' and I was 'young enough [then 40] and daring enough' to start a new life in Canada (quoted in Williamson, 1992, p. B2). Skill and connections led Kwok to a series of senior positions with three property development firms:

1968–70 – Vice-President, Grosvenor International;
1970–79 – Vice-President, Canadian Freehold Properties;
1980–84 – President, Pendero Development Company Ltd.

During this time he also served on various City of Vancouver committees which addressed issues related to the City's property development planning process.

Kwok was brought onto the board of directors of BC Place in 1981, where he was the only senior BC Place official of Chinese descent. Following the death of BC Place chairman, Alvin Narod, and the resignation of the BC Place president, Gil Hardman, in 1984, he was appointed president and chief executive officer. Kwok also served on the Expo '86 board of directors. Kwok remained as chairman of BC Place until April 1987, when the provincial government abandoned plans to redevelop the Expo '86 site and advertise the site internationally.

Kwok was 61 years old when he was recruited by Li Ka-shing and his son Victor to become director and senior vice-president of Concord Pacific Developments Ltd (see below for further details). Kwok served in this position from September 1987 to April 1993, when he stepped down to make way for Terry Hui, the 29-year-old son of K. M. Hui (another Concord shareholder). Kwok is now president of Amara International Investment Corp., and also practices architecture with Davidson Yuen Simpson, one of the firms that worked on the BC Place and Pacific Place projects. Directorships include Cheung Kong (Holdings) Ltd [he is the only overseas member], the Bank of Montreal Asian Advisory Panel, the BC Business Council, the Canadian Chamber of Commerce, the Downtown Vancouver Association, BC Hydro, the Pacific Rim Council on Urban Development, the Vancouver Urban Development Institute, the Vancouver Foundation, and KCTS- 9 (Seattle public television).

*Sources*:  S. Kwok, interview, February 1994; Edwards, 1992; Shaw, 1993; Williamson, 1992.

After several months of negotiations, BC Place acquired 176 acres (a figure that later increased to 224 acres) on the North Shore of False Creek in November 1980 from Marathon Realty for $30 m in cash and $30 m in downtown building sites. BC Place Ltd was restructured in 1984, and Stanley Kwok was appointed as the corporation's president and chief executive officer. BC Place adopted a new phased approach, concentrating on planning 'North Park' – a 75-acre sub-area of the larger site, close to the edge of Chinatown and Gastown in Vancouver. Kwok and the City's mayor (Michael Harcourt – who later became provincial premier in 1992) developed a trusting relationship through work and through their frequent chance meetings on Sunday morning strolls along the South Shore of False Creek seawall. These random events allowed the pair to swap 'visions' for the North Shore while gathering knowledge about each other, and the institutions they represented (Williamson, 1992). It is this type of everyday action in 'concrete social situations' which highlights the codeterminative nature of structure and action (Boden, 1994, pp. 4–7). These 'tiny, local' moments of 'human intercourse' laid part of the foundation which would eventually transform Vancouver, and help connect the city to the powerful flows of capital being directed out of Hong Kong.

Eventually a world's fair was held on the site from May to October 1986, and an election was held one month after the fair ended (which returned the ruling Social Credit party to power). Within two months of the election, the provincial government announced a moratorium on the development of the BC Place site, including the North Park sub-area. In March 1987, the Minister of Economic Development, Grace McCarthy, notified the public and the City of Vancouver that the BC Enterprise Corporation (BCEC) would be created to take control over various provincial assets (including BC Place), and then sell them. In a political context marked by a desire for a fast-track privatisation pro-gramme, and a desire to attract foreign investment into the province, BCEC recommended in August 1987 that the site be sold in one piece, and advertised worldwide (a decision endorsed by the Socred cabinet). This decision effectively excluded small-scale developers with low cap-italization levels, so the field of prospective buyers was narrowed to consortiums and large-scale international property developers.[19]

The actual sale of the North Shore of False Creek lands is a long and complex story – clearly detailed in Leslie (1991), Matas (1989a, 1989b), Matas and York (1989), and a series of consultants' reports (KPMG Peat Marwick Stevenson & Kellog/Peat Marwick Thorne, 1992) released by a newly-elected New Democratic Party provincial government in March 1992. Readers are directed to these sources should they wish to invest-igate the subject in any detail. Suffice it to say, an official process was followed between April 1987 and May 1988 which resulted in the land being acquired by Concord Pacific Developments Ltd, a private Cana-dian company controlled by Li Ka-shing (the majority shareholder), Lee Shau Kee and Cheng Yu-Tung (key secondary shareholders) and a variety of minority shareholders including the Canadian Imperial Bank of Commerce (CIBC). Concord's only serious competitor was the Van-couver Land Corporation, a consortium of local investors whose proposal came in at around C\$30–\$40 m less than the amount offered by Con-cord (with the added disincentive of dependence on the Vancouver stock market for a large proportion of development capital).

During the course of evaluating whether a Li-backed bid should pro-ceed for the site, information on a suitable bid approach was gathered by the Li Group. The key to a successful proposal to the provincial gov-ernment was the identification of an organizer with the knowledge and skills to structure a successful process, while also meeting the needs of the main Chinese backers of the project. In practice, this person had to be able to pull together the relevant professionals (for example, architects), while also subtly maneuvering themselves through a highly-charged political milieu. As John Markoulis of Concord Pacific suggested to one of us (Olds), it was critical that this person also agreed with and implemented Li Ka-shing's 'trademark' process – that is, one which is 'non-confrontational', while delivering 'benefits to all partners', 'generating money', and producing a result that would build onto Li's reputation (interview, March, 1994).

Fortunately for the Li family, Stanley Kwok had announced publicly that he was stepping down from the Board of BCEC in April 1987 after the provincial government halted the North Park planning process. Following his April announcement (which he had been contemplating since the autumn of 1986) Kwok began preparing a return to the architectural profession, and he made some arrangements to practice with the Vancouver firm, Davidson Yuen. However, Kwok was unable officially to leave the board because it was not until August 1987 'that a replacement had been found for him' (Hume, 1988). During this transition period Kwok also met Victor Li for the first time, at a luncheon engagement (S. Kwok, interview, February 1994). Soon after, Li Ka-shing 'flew him out here [to Hong Kong]'. Kwok was taken on a boat trip to discuss a variety of issues, and he was quickly offered the role of coordinating the Li proposal being made to the provincial government (G. Magnus, interview, April 1994). Kwok was selected by Li (and Magnus) because he 'knew the site', he 'knew people', he 'was an architect', he 'was Chinese', and he knew 'our people' (ibid.).[20]

The opportunity to get involved in this project was also enticing from Kwok's perspective, for it allowed him to 'fulfil his dream of planning and designing a major portion of a city' (quoted in Shaw, 1993, p. C6). Obviously, Kwok was honoured to have Hong Kong's most powerful family put 'their trust' in him to play such a prominent role in this project, particularly given its role as Victor's educational tool. He began working for the Li family in 'about July 1987', even though he did not officially begin working for them until September 1987.[21] In fact, Kwok was their first Vancouver employee. He came to them soon after working for BCEC designing the process for marketing the site. While Kwok never broke any conflict of interest regulations in BC, such a shift in roles highlights the relative laxity of the provincial government's regulations on an international scale. If a more stringent regulatory regime was in place, the whole complexion of the subsequent bid and development process would have changed quite significantly (assuming that the Li family proceeded with a bid).

Stanley Kwok had excellent connections with all Vancouver's key political and business elites, as well as with the Provincial cabinet and the BCEC Board – the people who would ultimately decide which proposal wins the right to develop the Expo site. His prior development experience ensured that he understood the financial aspects of large-scale property redevelopment projects. As Kwok himself put it, 'I just happen to be an architect who understands money' (Williamson, 1992). Kwok also understood the fine details of the City of Vancouver's planning process for large-scale mixed-use redevelopment projects (through his involvement with the BC Place and North Park proposals), and he had built up close and trusting relations with the city manager and several key city planners (the people who would eventually process the development proposal).

At a personal level, Kwok's excellent reputation in Vancouver played an important role in his being entrusted with a project that could quite significantly damage Victor Li's reputation were it not handled well. In business and political circles, Kwok was (and is) associated with qualities of integrity and dependability. He is also a determined, self-effacing, soft-spoken man who was also old enough in 1987 (sixty-one) to be viewed as a 'wise' man, while being young enough to command the full attention and confidence of Hong Kong financiers (including Victor Li).

At the local level, Kwok knew how best to manage community opposition to the proposal. The Pacific Place site is adjacent to a highly-organized, low-income residential community. Organizations such as the Downtown Eastside Residents Association (DERA) were worried about Pacific Place's negative social impacts, particularly in the aftermath of the Expo '86 mass evictions (Beazley, Loftman and Nevin, 1995; Hulchanski, 1989; Ley, 1994; Mitchell, 1993a). Equally important, Kwok had an astute sense of how to manage local media coverage of property development issues. These were skills which Kwok had fine-tuned during his time guiding the development of the North Park proposal, and Expo '86. This deep level of local knowledge and connections was particularly important at the initial stages of the development process because the City had not yet confirmed what its policies for the site were. Civil society in Canada (and Vancouver) is more developed than in Hong Kong. The nature of civil society is reflected in Vancouver's planning system, which is much more community-based in comparison to the technocratic Hong Kong system. Local citizens' groups, critical politicians (on the city council), and the local media can force issues into the public sphere, and push for changes that the developers must sometimes agree to. This is a form of civil society that Hong Kong-based Chinese developers absolutely detest. Rather, their experience (and preference) is to operate in a society characterized by deference to authority, the strong admiration of wealthy people, a closed legal system, and opaque information flows. Given the importance of this project to the Li family, Stanley Kwok was the perfect person for the job. Kwok could (better than anyone else) massage the process to ensure that the developers achieved their goals, while also structuring a process (and a public relations approach) that would quell the concerns of the majority of the interested public.[22]

In this manner, Stanley Kwok functioned as the perfect intermediary in a process involving global and local processes. The mesh between the global and the local is dependent on cultural hybrids such as Kwok, who use their expert knowledge to interpret local conditions and negotiate cultural differences for the geographically distant capitalists and financiers. He is one of the true transnational 'cosmopolitans', a person able to manage meaning strategically in ever-shifting and diverse circumstances. Hannerz (1990, p. 246) writes of this group: 'Their decontextualized knowledge can be quickly and shiftingly recontextualized in a series of different settings... What they carry, however, is not just special knowledge, but also that overall orientation toward structures of meaning to which the notion of the "culture of critical discourse" refers'. Cosmopolitans, ever savvy to the world of cultural negotiation, occupy an important niche in the contemporary global economy; they are particularly significant for the global property industry, which requires an extremely rapid inscription and re-inscription of culturally coded informational bartering and exchange (see Mitchell, 1995). As Kwok himself stated:

> Sometimes there are insights into certain situations that maybe someone who has been living in both worlds can understand. We have very basic cultural differences. Although it is the same problem and the same issue, you can approach it from a different way. And it's useful for each side to see how the other would have approached it. That's how you bridge things. (Quoted in Edwards, 1992).

Former Socred cabinet minister, Grace McCarthy, made the same point *vis-à-vis* Kwok's role as intermediary between both communities and cultures: 'Stanley is a terrific bridge between the Chinese and Canadian business communities. He bridges it well and he brings them together, and that's very important (quoted in Williamson, 1992, p. B2).

As a self-described bridge-builder and hybrid figure, Stanley Kwok facilitates the political and economic connections necessary for capital to shift rapidly between global, national and local scales and, even more importantly, he also facilitates the cultural connections that enable capital*ists* to interrelate in a profitable, long-term manner. Kwok serves as a cultural and economic point man – a key player aiding capital accumulation around the globe, yet seldom appearing in the media or the public eye. The ability to operate in the interstices of cultural, political and economic structures enables individuals such as Kwok to wield considerable power, yet to be rendered opaquely, indeed almost invisibly, in the overall image of global business deals and general capital articulations. For this reason, their role is often underplayed in broad-based analyses of globalization processes and/or the workings of global property markets.

CONCLUSION

We have devoted considerable space to the events through which the Hong Kong financiers came to be aware of the Vancouver property site, the complex rationale behind their decision to invest in it, and the perceived logic of using Stanley Kwok as both local a co-ordinator and a human bridge between Hong Kong and Vancouver. Our emphasis is part of a deliberate attempt to refocus attention on the particulars of global processes: the role of family, of culture and of individuals. In this chapter we, like many scholars, have discussed the numerous ways in which the structure of financial systems and global property markets are implicated in the types and amounts of investment that flows from one site to another. Also acknowledged is the key role of the state – in Hong Kong, and at all three levels of government in Canada. But these structural factors tell only part of the story; often left undiscussed is the absolutely crucial role of various actors and networks operating within these broader systemic constraints. It is the role of these 'various actors and networks' that we have attempted to elucidate here.[23]

By analyzing the early, formative stages of specific globalization processes and by emphasizing particular sectors within those processes (such as the global property market), the role of family networks, and even individual agents of change, can be more easily disclosed. The emphasis, for example, on *why* Li Ka-shing invested in Vancouver and *who* helped him to obtain information about the local political, economic and cultural situation there, aids us in avoiding economistic accounts or an overarching structural emphasis on the globalization process and what impacts it has or will have on local environments. Local cultures and even individuals are able to exert tremendous influence on the ways in which global structures play out on the ground. Rather than depicting globalization as a vague, formless and faceless process, where tidal waves of capital flow into and through cities, and goods fly formlessly through the void, we have tried to locate it in the geographies and histories of specific places and people.

Chinese business networks are a perfect vehicle for rendering specific the ways in which various aspects of globalization occur in the property market. Some of the key features of these networks (as outlined in this chapter) include the importance of extended family ties, the role of trust and reputation in business dealings, the extension of informal credit lines, the exchange of culturally-inscribed information, and the role of key 'facilitators' in almost all large-scale property transactions. These factors have aided in the extension of property investment flows across space and are highly particular, contingent and changeable. They are, furthermore, absolutely central to the ways that property investment and development have taken place in the Pacific Rim since the 1970s.

### Notes

1. FDI flows into real estate can take many different forms; forms that are not factored-in when governments produce FDI data. For example, individuals may invest overseas in property for their own use; global pension funds may invest into American property via stocks in property firms and this is classified as portfolio investment; or multinational firms may aquire property for a factory, or lease buildings. On this issue, see Economist Intelligence Unit (1997, pp. 28–31).
2. Many of the ideas and text related to 'global residential property markets' are derived from a joint research proposal that was prepared by Chris Hamnett (King's College London) and Kris Olds.
3. In the discussion below we shall focus on the success of these systems in Taiwanese, Hong Kong and overseas Chinese societies. Empirical studies from other regions of the world, however, have shown similar phenomena. See, for example, the study of construction sub-contracting in Massachusetts by Eccles, 1981, reported in Granovetter, 1985, p. 498.
4. In later work, Williamson amended his views to accommodate 'relational contracting' as an intermediate form between the large firm and the market.

5. There have been numerous recent overviews and case studies of the importance of relational ties in Chinese economic practices in East and Southeast Asia. See Redding (1990) and Yoshihara (1988; ch. 3) for general overviews. Case studies can be found in Hamilton (1996a) and in Lim and Gosling (1983). For some excellent older studies, see Willmott and Crissman (1972).

6. Matthew Montagu-Pollock (1991) 'All the Right Connections', *Asian Business*, vol. 27, p. 1.

7. Of the hundred largest firms in Taiwan (controlling 20 per cent of the country's GDP), all but two are owned by either one person, by close partners, or by a family. Of the two exceptions, one is foreign-owned and the other is union-owned. See *Asian Business*, p. 23.

8. *Asian Business*, 1991, p. 23.

9. This pattern has occurred with great regularity in Taiwan and Hong Kong, with the proliferation of small businesses in similar lines (such as wigs in Hong Kong or plastic flowers in Taiwan). In interviews with seventy-two Chinese businessmen from Hong Kong and Singapore, Gordon Redding noted that the most intense and often expressed drive was the desire to be one's own boss. See the interviews in Redding (1990, pp. 88–94).

10. This practice of subdivision and spin-off operates in family concerns as well, where different family members may run different enterprises, even with separate sets of accounts – but within the connected *guanxi* web. Hamilton and Biggart (1988, pp. S83–85) link this tendency to the cultural practice of patrilineage and equal inheritance among sons. Assets within a Chinese family are always considered to be divisible (among surviving sons), but the decisions about these assets are expected to be made in light of long-term family interests.

11. For some recent studies on the importance of *guanxi* in Chinese business practice, see Numazaki (1996), and Yang (1994).

12. Case studies documenting the importance of trust in Chinese business relations in Hong Kong include: Silin (1972), Wong (1988), Sit and Wong (1989). See, in particular, Wong (1996); and Kao (1996).

13. Wong (1991) defines the expectations that social actors have of one another within a system of personal trust as the continuity of the natural and moral order, technical competence, and fiduciary responsibility.

14. All the banks in Taiwan are under the control of the central and provincial governments. Bank managers are considered to be conservative, generally preferring to 'maintain stability, rather than foster development' (Kao, 1991).

15. The underground financial sector in Taiwan has been particularly voluminous and volatile since the late 1980s (Lin, 1996).

16. In the 1970s, Taiwan's savings rate (over 30 per cent) was among the highest in the world. The rate of savings in 1986 was 50.15 per cent. See Lin (1991).

17. The gradual diversification of Li's corporate assets continues to the present day. Moreover, in June 1995, Li raised considerable speculation about Hong Kong's future by placing his 34.95 per cent controlling interest in Cheung Kong in a Cayman Islands trust ('Li Ka-shing Unity Holdings'). While his rationale was that he sought to avoid inheritance tax (for his sons' sake), the action was seen as embarrassing for Li given his excellent connections in Beijing (Holberton, 1993, 1995).

18. At the time of writing (December 1998), rumours are circulating in development circles in Vancouver that the Li family has sold all its shares in Concord Pacific (Chow, 1998). If they have done so, this is a sign that the Li family is withdrawing from substantial involvement in the Canadian property industry, concentrating instead on their core profit centres throughout East and Southeast Asia.

19. Kevin Murphy, the official in charge of the sale process for BCEC, informed Kris Olds (in 1994) that they were well aware of the 'small club' of international property developers who had access to sufficient capital and organizational resources to acquire and develop the site. BCEC contacted all these firms to inform them of the site's availability in August and September 1987. However, it is also important to keep in mind that the recession during the first half of the 1980s narrowed this club's size. Furthermore, the global stock market crash of 19 October 1987 forced some of the companies who had expressed interest in the site to shelve their investment plans.

20. Jon Markoulis suggested similar reasons for choosing Stanley. Markoulis also noted that they considered other people in Vancouver, but none came close to matching Stanley Kwok's qualities (interview, March 1994).

21. There is some discrepancy about when Stanley Kwok started working for Concord. Jon Markoulis suggested it was 'about July' (interview, March 1994) while Stanley noted it was in September (interview, February 1994). We have not had an opportunity to confirm the correct date. Kwok did inform Kris Olds that he was very careful about a potential conflict of interest, and his action was 'cleared' in accordance with provincial government regulations. Like may global property developers, Li Ka-shing has previously attempted to hire well-placed government officials with important knowledge and contacts (Gutstein, 1990, p. 139).

22. Every single Vancouver interviewee noted Kwok's deft skills at handling the Pacific Place planning process for the developer (even those who fundamentally disagreed with the nature of the process). Kwok's retirement celebration (after he left Concord Pacific in 1993) was held in an Expo '86 legacy building, and drew over 500 people, including local and provincial politicians of disparate ideologies. Obviously, Kwok was allocated his power by the Li family, and he had a wealth of resources to draw upon if needed; however, it takes considerable skill to carry out the instructions he was given by the financial backers of Concord.

23. By focusing on individuals such as Stanley Kwok, for example, it quickly becomes apparent that particular actors do not just operate within broader structures, but in fact influence, in certain contexts, how these systems work. For example, Kwok's connections to both the local and provincial governments in Vancouver and British Columbia influenced the manner in which the BC Place land was assembled, disassembled and marketed; his further connections with the Li family influenced the way in which Li Ka-shing purchased and developed the property.

# 10 The Internationalization of Singaporean Firms into China: Entry Modes and Investment Strategies

Chia-Zhi Tan and Henry Wai-chung Yeung

## INTRODUCTION

The promotion of overseas investment was mounted when, in 1985, Singapore registered its first GDP decline since independence. At that time, the Economic Committee for Overcoming Recession (ECOR) identified overseas investment and the development of offshore business opportunities as a long-term solution to the lack of investment opportunities in Singapore. One basic rationale for the need of overseas investment by Singaporean firms is that geographic and demographic factors are limiting domestic economic growth potential (*Asian Intelligence*, 1993; Régnier, 1993; Tan, 1995; Yeung, 1998a, 1999b). Singapore is limited by its small population size and small market, as well as limited labour and land. Hence there is a need to develop an 'external economy' for Singapore. The plan in 1985 was to globalize Singaporean firms into Europe and North America. By the early 1990s, however, there was a change in the geographical focus of overseas investment from an international to a regional scale because of the lack of success in Singapore's globalization drive and the emergence of the growth potential in many East Asian and Southeast Asian countries. As a result, it was considered wise to promote Singaporean investments in Asian 'countries with which Singapore has close historical and cultural links, which are achieving steady economic growth, and which have adopted policies welcoming foreign investment' (Kanai, 1993, p. 21).

Meanwhile, China has been a significant destination for inward foreign direct investments since it began its open-door policy in 1979 (see Chapters 1 and 11 in this volume). The opening of China's economy to foreign technology and investments and improved Sino-Singapore relations since 1979 have encouraged Singaporean companies to venture more into direct investment projects in China. Many earlier investments were concentrated spatially on the southern coastal cities and special economic zones (SEZs). The high concentration of Singaporean firms in Guangdong and Fujian provinces reflects in part the close family and business ties Singaporean business people have in these two provinces (Pang and Komaran, 1985a; Lu and Zhu, 1995). In this chapter, we aim to examine the organization of Singaporean investments in another province of southern China – Hainan. We have chosen Hainan because earlier studies of Singaporean investments in China focused exclusively on Guangdong, Fujian and Jiangsu provinces (see Cartier, 1995; Willis and Yeoh, 1998). Another reason is that no empirical studies have been conducted on Singaporean investments in Hainan province, despite the strong ethnic linkages between Singaporean Hainanese and their birthplace.

Based on personal interviews with twenty-two Singaporean companies in Hainan, we argue that their investments in Hainan are often embedded in social and ethnic ties with the ancestral homes of their Hainanese owners. Their social organization of internationalization into Hainan resembles some key attributes of Chinese business firms – strong role of familism and kinship relations, and the reliance on political-economic alliances (see Chapters 2 and 4 in this volume). These Singaporean firms have constructed intricate intra-firm networks and ownership bonds based on lineage, regional loyalty and dialect affiliations. These network linkages have underscored their reliance on joint ventures and partnership as the key entry modes to invest in Hainan. In fact, the growth of Singaporean investments in Hainan's economy began shortly after China's open-door policy in the late 1970s and the establishment of Hainan as a province in 1988 as part of an attempt by Beijing to resolve its 'Hainan problem' (Feng and Goodman, 1995). Hainan was previously one of the most underdeveloped provinces in China. It accounted for only half a percentage point of the nation's GDP. The Beijing government attempted to emulate the success of other SEZs in Hainan by following an export-orientated development strategy and by carrying out advanced market-orientated reforms. It also intended to make Hainan a 'testing ground for many of the comprehensive, market-based reforms whose implementation throughout China is planned over the medium term' (Cadario *et al.*, 1992, p. vii).

To date, ethnic Chinese abroad were the most important source of foreign capital in Hainan even before the establishment of the People's Republic of China (PRC) (Xing *et al.*, 1991; *Dangdai Zhongguo de Hainan*, 1993; Feng and Goodman, 1995, 1997). Apart from enjoying all privileges available to the other SEZs, Hainan was bestowed with extra 'freedom' that went beyond the other SEZs and was allowed to adopt a more liberal economic system. This is because the Beijing government wanted to attract as many foreign investors as possible to help resolve Hainan's sluggish economy. Hainan was encouraged to have a 'small government and large society', implying fewer state-owned enterprises and minimal government intervention in the economy (Cadario *et al.*, 1992). A 'large society' in Hainan SEZ refers to the larger realm of the business community in comparison to the smaller domain of the provincial government. Business people and enterprises in Hainan could enjoy more economic freedom than elsewhere in China, and had to deal with much less bureaucracy and fewer government authorities (that is, a 'small government'). For example, in order to set up a new firm in the late 1990s, an investor in Hainan needs only to register once at the Administrative Bureau of Industry and Commerce, without the problems of having to seek approval from other ministerial units (Feng and Goodman, 1995, p. 24). Another example is that a developer can buy a piece of land below 100 *mu* (approximately 6.67 hectares) directly from the county government without prior approval from the provincial government (field interview, February 1998). Basically, Hainan has been given the flexibility to function primarily by following market principles.

This chapter begins with an historical account of the relationships between Singaporean Hainanese and Hainan province. This is followed by a brief analysis of the characteristics of Singaporean firms in Hainan. We then examine their various modes of entry into Hainan: personal direct investments, wholly-owned subsidiaries, and joint ventures. The penultimate section discusses the two main types of investment strategy: market seekers; and factor seekers.

## SINGAPOREAN HAINANESE LINKAGES WITH HAINAN PROVINCE

Singaporean Hainanese have a long history of various social and economic linkages with Hainan province that can be traced back to the early twentieth century. The first Hainanese arrived in Singapore as early as the mid-nineteenth century. Hainanese immigrants migrated to Southeast Asia and other parts of the world largely in an attempt to escape from a war situation, or for poverty reasons, while some were deceived or forced to work as coolies overseas (*Dangdia Zhongguo de Hainan*, 1993). There are now more than two million overseas ethnic Chinese

*Table* 10.1   Estimated overseas Chinese
population of Hainan origin by country

| Country | Population |
|---------|-----------|
| Thailand | 1 000 000 |
| Malaysia | 700 000 |
| Singapore | 280 000 |
| Hong Kong and Macau | 200 000 |
| Indonesia | 150 000 |
| North America | 60 000 |
| Others | 50 000 |

*Source*: *Dangdai Zhongguo de Hainan* (1993, p. 353).

with ancestral origin from Hainan. Singapore has the third largest concentration of ethnic Hainanese, after Thailand and Malaysia (see Table 10.1).

Singaporean Hainanese are well known to possess very deep ethnic feelings or 'a sense of belonging' to their ancestral roots, and they have maintained very strong links with their kin back in Hainan (Xing *et al.*, 1991). These strong relationships can be seen from their continuous 'exports' such as remittances, donations and contributions in kind, such as sewing machines, bicycles, old clothing, medicines and other daily necessities back to Hainan. These transactions are handled by a few Hainanese transportation agencies that have good connections in Hainan to manage the delivery of the cargo. These agencies have been largely responsible for the arrangements for the movement of people and goods between the two places for four generations, since the late nineteenth century (interview in Singapore, 7 January 1998).

In recent years, with the opening-up of China's economy and improved political relations between China and Singapore, an increasing number of Singaporean Hainanese join 'home-visiting' tours to return and stay at their ancestral houses in the villages. As the economy and living standards of Hainan province have greatly improved since 1988, the form of assistance by Singaporean Hainanese has taken on a different character. Most of the remittances from the Hainanese outside mainland China (as with Singaporean Hainanese) are used to rebuild or renovate ancestral houses and temples. Donations are also made to improve public institutions such as hospitals and schools, to construct public amenities such as road and bridges, and to set up study awards for top students in the local schools (Xing *et al.*, 1991). The number of Singaporean direct

*Table* 10.2 Singapore's contracted FDI value and number of projects approved in Hainan (US$ millions)

|  | 1990 | 1991 | 1992 | 1993 | 1994 | 1995 | 1996 |
|---|---|---|---|---|---|---|---|
| *Contracted FDI value* | 16.2 | 11.9 | 67.2 | 155.1 | 151.7 | 2092.5* | 22.8 |
| *Number of projects approved* | 4 | 17 | 54 | 120 | 53 | 35 | 26 |

*Note*: *1995 value appears to be erroneous.
*Source*: *Hainan Jingji Nianjian*, various years.

*Table* 10.3 Hainan's realized foreign investment from Asian countries (US$ millions)

| Country | 1996 | Rank | 1995 | Rank |
|---|---|---|---|---|
| Hong Kong | 376.6 | 1 | 564.4 | 1 |
| Japan | 146.9 | 2 | 189.8 | 2 |
| Singapore | 83.8 | 3 | 73.8 | 4 |
| Taiwan | 79.9 | 4 | 78.7 | 3 |
| Thailand | 19.8 | 5 | 22.9 | 5 |
| Korea | 11.9 | 6 | 14.1 | 7 |
| Malaysia | 9.5 | 7 | 16.1 | 6 |
| Indonesia | NA | 8 | 1.7 | 8 |
| Total | 1 189.6 |  | 1 455.0 |  |

*Note*: NA = Not available.
*Source*: *Hainan Jingji Nianjian*, various years.

investments in Hainan have also increased more than tenfold since 1990 (see Table 10.2). The number of enterprises, amount of contract-ed and realized capital or investment by ethnic Chinese abroad now account for more than 80 per cent of total investment in Hainan (Feng and Goodman, 1995, p. 76). In terms of realized foreign investment, Singapore was ranked third in 1996 among the other Asian economies (see Table 10.3). What, then, are the characteristics of these Singa-porean Chinese firms in Hainan?

## CHARACTERISTICS OF SINGAPOREAN CHINESE FIRMS IN HAINAN[1]

We have classified our twenty-two case studies into two broad categor-ies: small and medium-sized enterprises (SMEs); and large corporations. A small or medium-sized enterprise (SME) is a company with not more than S$8 million in net fixed asset investment (for manufacturing companies), or employs not more than fifty workers (for firms in the service industries) (SME Committee, 1989, p. 9). A total of fifteen sampled firms are SMEs, three of which do not have any other business in Singapore or elsewhere other than in Hainan (for example, the Jinghua Hotel, the Eastern Park Hotel, and the SINFenghuang Hotel). Their relatively small assets in Hainan are their sole foreign investments from Singapore. In terms of ownership, all except two belong to Hainanese owners. Of the two non-Hainanese-owned SMEs, one is of Hokkien origin (Hoe Leong), while the other is a joint venture with a mix of majority Hainanese shareholders and other dialect-group shareholders (Haixin Investment). The majority of Hainanese owners in these SMEs reflect the close relationship between their ethnicity and investment strategies in Hainan (see below). Among the large corporations, only one has some form of ethnic relationship with Hainan province. While only the Hainan-registered Zilong Group Company is owned by a Hainan-born Singaporean owner, the remaining six corporations are not owned by any Hainanese. In any case, these seven companies are either listed companies or private companies having more than S$15 m in assets. These large corporations usually have complex organizational structures, unlike those of the leaner SMEs, which have a more informal organizational structure managed largely by the entrepreneurs themselves. Although most of these large companies are run in a corporatized manner by professional managers, some of the board chairpersons and directors are the founder-entrepreneurs themselves (for example, Asia Pulp and Paper, Hainan Zilong, Prime Group International).

In terms of management style, the smaller SMEs are largely managed in a simple manner by the entrepreneurs themselves, or by later-generation members of the founder-owner's family. These firms exhibit largely ethnic-based personalistic and paternalistic features in its management style. The internal dynamics of these paternalistic firms are characterized by family-bound values such as patriarchal loyalty, filial piety and strong mutual personal relationships (Jamann, 1994; Redding, 1990; see also Chapter 2 in this volume). Hence, the entrepreneur-founder of the firm is usually the top decision-maker, who decides the direction in which the firm should be heading. However, as the family-owned Chinese firms expand their portfolios and establishments into larger corporations, an increasing professionalization of the management function is needed for more complex business operations. For example, Pang (1994, p. 177) has pointed out another reason for the professionalisation of Singaporean Chinese firms: 'in many cases, the professional managers were recruited to revitalise companies that were once thriving but had since encountered problems because their founders failed to adjust their personalistic management styles to changing times'. One Hong Kong consultant was quoted recently as saying that 'the growth of the companies and sharper competition requires delegation, financial controls and man management [in Chinese business]. It might well be that the founder is not best equipped to deal with this' (quoted in *Financial Times*, 5 March 1998).

In terms of their industrial distribution, the twenty-two Singaporean firms belong to three broad types of industry: property; industrial; and service industries. The majority of Singaporean investments in Hainan are found in the property industry, with most of these firms being engaged in property developments such as hotels, resorts or apartment blocks. This phenomenon coincides with Hainan's rapid and enormous real-estate development since 1989, which reached a peak during the period 1992–3. Hainan's real-estate business was ranked fifth among China's thirty provinces and provincial-level units and contributed to more than 20 per cent of the province's annual financial income (Feng and Goodman, 1995, p. 64). One of the key reasons for this real estate boom was the establishment of Hainan as a separate province from Guangdong in 1988, which boosted its tourist trade and industrialization. The growth in these two industries has, in turn, resulted in an increased demand for hotels, office blocks, factories and residential buildings. Another reason that attracts foreign investors to invest in Hainan's property is its special seventy-year land lease on large areas of land – twenty years longer than in other SEZs.

In the *industrial* sector, Singapore Power's and Choo's investments are in the form of a joint venture 150 MW power facility and a wholly-owned water treatment plant respectively. Both projects belong to the privatized public utilities industry. From a Hainan field trip, we discovered that Mr Choo also owns a recently completed office block which happens to be the tallest building in the Qionghai City centre. Similarly, both owners of Arklight Engineering and Great Link Investment have engaged in real-estate business, although they have their own primary businesses in Hainan (see below). These examples have demonstrated the overwhelming attraction of the real-estate boom in Hainan in motivating Singaporean business people to diversify their portfolios outside their familiar trade. Other Singaporean transnational corporations (TNCs), such as Asia Pacific Breweries Ltd (APB) and Asia Pulp and Paper Co. Ltd (APP), are engaged largely in production operations in green-field or newly-established manufacturing plants. Both TNCs intend to build their own new facilities because of the lack of such industries and manufacturing plants in Hainan. APP plans to build a wholly-owned plant, whereas APB has an 80 per cent stake in its current operational brewery. The reasons for these two TNCs to engage in different methods of foreign entry will be discussed later. The remaining three SMEs in the industrial sector are engaged in a variety of different industries ranging from construction (for example, SINGlass Holding) to machinery engineering (for example, Arklight Engineering and Hoe Leong). Finally, two sampled case studies are grouped under *service* industries. Sam Son Travel Service has a representative office in Haikou which helps to manage Singaporean tour groups in Hainan and to arrange for the local Hainanese in 'relative-visiting' tours to Singapore. Great Link Investment is a Singapore-based company which provides a consultancy service for potential Singaporean investors to Hainan. Its owner, Mr Leong, is well known in both Singapore and Hainan's communities, and has several personal and joint venture investments in Hainan province.

In terms of their geographical spread in Hainan, there is some degree of correlation in the location of some of the investment projects and the ancestral homes of their Hainanese owners (see Figure 10.1). Among the small hotels, all of them are found in smaller towns near to their ancestral villages. Other properties and offices are built in either Wenchang City centre or Qionghai City centre, depending on the owner's ancestral place of origin. One of the reasons for this spatial clustering phenomena is that the owners are more familiar with these places than other locations because of their personal experience of having once lived there. Good connections (*guanxi*) with the local authorities because of their ancestry affiliation with the location is another motivation. Some of these *guanxi* may be established long ago when both parties were once classmates or friends from the same locality or area. Despite this, it is still typical for most firms to set up their subsidiary 'headquarters' offices in Haikou – the capital city of Hainan province. This is because of the administrative, telecommunications and financial facilities available there.[2] Because of the large space requirements and the nature of operations, some firms built their manufacturing facilities in such special economic or industrial developmental zones as the Qinglan Economic Development Zone (for example, Arklight Engineering, Singapore Power), Haikou Jinpan Industrial Development Zone (for example, APB) and Yangpu Economic Developmental Zone (for example, APP). One major tourism project – PSC's Sanya Fudao Tourism – is located at the designated Yalong Bay National Holiday Zone (see Figure 10.1).

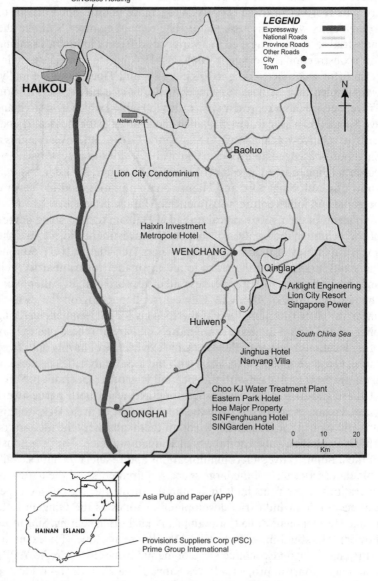

Arklight Engineering
Hainan Asia Pacific Breweries
Hainan Mandarin Hotel
Hainan Zilong
Hoe Leong
Sam Son Travel
SINGlass Holding

HAIKOU

LEGEND
Expressway
National Roads
Province Roads
Other Roads
City
Town

N

Meilan Airport

Baoluo

Lion City Condominium

Haixin Investment
Metropole Hotel

WENCHANG

Qinglan

Arklight Engineering
Lion City Resort
Singapore Power

Huiwen

South China Sea

Jinghua Hotel
Nanyang Villa

Choo KJ Water Treatment Plant
Eastern Park Hotel
Hoe Major Property
SINFenghuang Hotel
SINGarden Hotel

QIONGHAI

0      10      20
Km

HAINAN ISLAND

Asia Pulp and Paper (APP)

Provisions Suppliers Corp (PSC)
Prime Group International

*Figure* 10.1   Location of Singaporean investments in China

The placement of investments in these designated developmental zones is to reap the benefits of the preferential economic and land-lease incentives as well as their more comprehensive 'built-for-industrial-use' infrastructure.

## MODES OF ENTRY OF SINGAPOREAN FIRMS IN HAINAN

Based our interviews, four main modes of foreign entry by Singaporean business people and firms are found: (i) personal direct investments; (ii) wholly-owned subsidiaries; (iii) joint ventures; and (iv) multiple entry modes. Figure 10.2 shows the distribution of various modes of entry by Singaporean firms.

### Personal Direct Investments

Among Singaporean investors in Hainan, many have their own businesses in Singapore. However, some of their investments in Hainan are not affiliated to any of their Singapore-based firms. Their ventures in Hainan are totally different from their main lines of business in Singapore. For example, Mr Han, owner of a ship-building engineering company (Arklight Engineering Pte Ltd) in Singapore, has established Qiangda (Hainan) Travel and Trading company to manage his diversified investment projects in Hainan. The trading company also helps to facilitate easier accounting for his properties in Hainan under one 'umbrella firm'. On the other hand, Mr Leong, owner of Great Link Investment (an investment consultancy firm) and Method Engineering (an air-conditioning business) in Singapore, started a farming business in Hainan because he believed in the factor advantages of Hainan's agriculture resources (interview in Singapore, 30 December 1997). A cheap and abundant agricultural workforce and resources are easily available in Hainan. In 1992, agricultural labourers accounted for about 70 per cent of the total work force in Hainan (Feng and Goodman, 1995). Another factor is that some officials and economists have proposed a development strategy to promote the agricultural sector to become the leading sector in the province.

Of these personal direct investments, some business people may not own any businesses in Singapore, apart from their Hainan properties (for example, the Eastern Park, SINFenghuang and Jinghua hotels). These sole property assets mainly belong to older Singaporean Hainanese retirees. One special case here is Hainan Zilong Group Co.'s founder, Mr Wu,

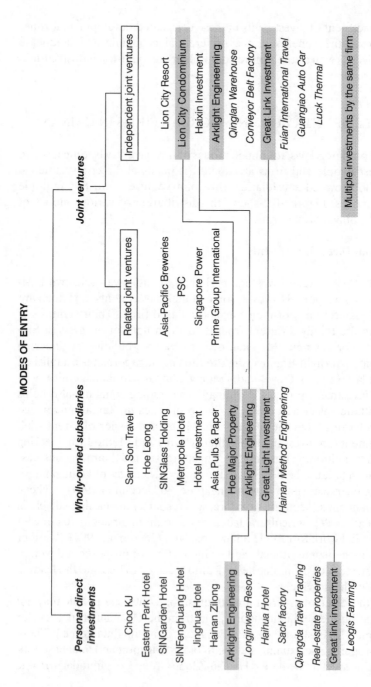

*Figure* 10.2   Modes of entry of Singaporean investments in Hainan

Owner: **WU QINGHAI**

   *(Chairman of Board of Directors – Hainan Zilong Group)*
   *(Vice Chairman of Hainan Enterprises Association)*

HAINAN *Subsidiaries*:

   Hainan Zi Long Industry & Commerce Co. Ltd.
   Hainan Zi Long International Tour Service Co. Ltd.
   Hainan Zi Long Construction Co. Ltd.
   Hainan Zi Long Catering & Entertainment Co. Ltd.
   Hainan Zi Long Real Estate Development Co. Ltd.
   Hainan Zi Long Pawn & Auction Co. Ltd.
   Hainan Zi Long Restaurant
   China Hainan Peace Republic School
   China Hainan Peace Republic School (Sanya Branch)

CHINA *Subsidiary*:

   Huifeng City Credit Bank, Xi Ning, Qinhai Province

OVERSEAS *Subsidiary*:

   Zi Long Export & Import Co., Philippines

*Figure* 10.3   Hainan Zilong Group Co.

who does not own any firms in Singapore. However, his Hainan-based parent enterprise has multiple holdings of diversified portfolios in different parts of China and overseas (see Figure 10.3). Mr Wu was born in Hainan and migrated to Singapore at the age of thirteen. He received some education in Singapore before returning to Hainan in 1988 to help his adoptive father's friend there. He started from the bottom of the corporate ladder as an office boy before rising to management level, and had shown great entrepreneurship in starting Hainan Zilong in 1993. At that time, he took the opportunity to acquire his former employer's failing business in Hainan. Because of his familiarity with Hainan's institutional environment (both socio-cultural and political), he was able to restructure the failing business and to diversify his portfolio. Today, Mr Wu is the chairman and general manager of the four-hundred-million *yuan* (RMB) Hainan Zilong Group, which has subsidiaries in other parts of China and the Philippines (interview in Hainan, 17 February 1998).

**Wholly-Owned Subsidiaries**

Seven SMEs and two large corporations have wholly-owned subsidiaries in Hainan (see Figure 10.2). Most of the SMEs (except the Metropole

Hotel) operate representative offices to manage their businesses in Hainan. Most of these subsidiaries in Hainan are engaged in higher-end value chain functions such as marketing, sales, distribution and services. These SMEs aim to utilize their presence in Hainan better to capture the local and China's market. As some of these firms work mainly on a project basis (for example, Arklight Engineering, Method Engineering of Great Link Investment, and SINGlass Holding), their representative offices in Hainan are practically inactive when there is no ongoing project. Among the large corporations, Hotel Investment is the investment holding company of its wholly-owned Hainan Mandarin Hotel in Haikou. On the other hand, APP plans to built a wholly-owned green-field manufacturing plant. The Hainan authority has recently approved a US$1.2 bn investment by APP to develop a paper mill at Yangpu Economic Development Zone (*Lianhe Zaobao*, 3 December 1997). APP's decision to establish a wholly-owned subsidiary plant is contrasted with another TNC: APB's joint venture brewery. The main reason for a TNC not to engage in joint ventures during their FDI is the fear of interference by the local partner in certain critical decision areas (Hooijmaijers, 1995; Beamish and Killing, 1997). However, APB deems its foreign partners to be a key attribute to a more successful foreign entry for its industry (see below).

**Joint Venture Investments**

Joint ventures are common among Singaporean investments in China. They are either related to the existing businesses of their parent companies in Singapore or independent ventures unrelated to any Singapore-based businesses (see Figure 10.2). For related-business joint ventures in Hainan, Singaporean firms have joined forces with either local Chinese partners, foreign firms or other Singaporean investors. Two of our case studies cover local (that is, Hainan) government-linked units in their joint ventures. Hainan Asia Pacific Brewery Co. Ltd (HAPCO) is a green-field investment by APB (80 per cent interest) and Hainan Brewery Co. Ltd (20 per cent of the shares) to produce the popular Tiger and Anchor beer for China's vast market. APB mentioned the advantage or necessity of engaging a government partnership for such a large, risky business as the alcohol industry. Similarly, Provisions Suppliers Corporations (PSC) has a 40 per cent shareholding in its Hainan joint venture, whereas its Hainan's partner – the State Economic Commission – has a majority 60 per cent of the shares in Sanya Fudao Tourism.

In the second type of related-business joint venture, a foreign company is preferred in the partnership. Singapore Power International chose to take a 50 per cent stake with a foreign partner (US Enron Corporation) in a large infrastructure investment in Hainan Meinan Power Facility. One reason behind the preference for a foreign partner in this case is that Hainan's units or enterprises may not have the technological expertise to engage in such large-scale infrastructure development. The third type of joint venture subsidiary involves partnership among Singaporean firms. According to newspaper reports, Prime Group International and Singapore Technologies planned to invest S$67 m in an orchid farm and a holiday resort (*Lianhe Zaobao*, 13 July 1997; *The Business Times*, 26 August 1997). However, this investment project has not yet been finalized, according to our brief telephone interviews with top management executives from both parties. Singapore Technologies denied its involvement in the project; and Prime Group International did not wish to have further publicity about this project and declined to be interviewed.

Joint ventures by Singaporean Chinese firms in Hainan can also take the form of separate and *independent* investments which are unrelated to the core business of their shareholders in Singapore. Joint ventures with two or more shareholders are not uncommon when the investment is large or risky. Three such ventures involved mainly Singaporean shareholders and another two involved Chinese partners. For example, Lion City Holiday Resort in Gaolong Bay is a joint venture by two Singaporean Hainanese. One of them is in the food and beverage business and the other a retired teacher. Of larger investments such as the Lion City Condominium project, it is a joint venture project with twenty-one shareholders. Moreover, Haixin Investment has ten shareholders investing in the Mandarin Garden industrial-cum-residential project. Two prominent business people who have excellent local contacts are involved in joint-venture projects with Chinese partners. In one example, Mr Leong (of Great Link Investment) has a personal share in the Hainan Fu'an International Travel Plaza project, which includes local Chinese partnership. Apparently, his Chinese partners are influential governmental officials, as he chose not to reveal much during the interview except to mention that they come from certain government units. In another example, Mr Han (owner of Arklight Engineering) was invited by the local Wenchang City's mayor to develop jointly a warehouse in the newly-established Qinglan International Harbour.

**Multiple Modes of Foreign Entry**

Apart from the above modes of entry by Singaporean Chinese firms in Hainan, we note that there is another complex pattern of investments in Hainan. Some of the business people have their own personal direct investments, subsidiaries of their Singapore-based parent firms, as well as joint-venture investments (see Figure 10.2). For example, three prominent businesspeople among the Hainanese community are involved in such multi-modal investments: Mr Leong of Great Link Investment; Mr Han of Arklight Engineering; and Mr Hoe of Hoe Major Property. Table 10.4 shows a detail representation of the multiple modes of entry by these three individuals.

Mr Leong's Method Engineering Pte Ltd deals in air-conditioning and has a subsidiary in Hainan. His private investments in Hainan include three associated Singaporean firms in which he has shares; one joint venture project with local Hainan authorities; and a wholly-owned farming company in Hainan. One additional investment that is not considered to be a Singaporean investment in Hainan *per se*, is a Singapore-registered investment consultancy company which acts as an 'exchange-point' for Singaporean and Chinese Hainanese business people. Mr Han runs a ship-engineering company in Singapore and has owned a subsidiary in Hainan since 1984. He has also invested US$3 m in a separate trading/ investment company in Hainan. This company has several other investment projects in its name. One of these is a sack-making factory in the Qinglan Economic Development Zone. The third businessman, Mr Hoe, owns a property firm in Singapore and has an associated company in Hainan – Hainan International Foreign Investment Consultancy Company. He is also one of the major shareholders of Singapore Guiliyang Holdings Pte Ltd, which developed a condominium project – Lion City Condominium, near Hainan's future Meinan International Airport. Apart from having their own subsidiaries in Hainan, these three businesspeople are involved in other investments and businesses apart from their core businesses in Hainan. These different modes of foreign entry show *how* Singaporean Hainanese have made their investments in Hainan. The question of *why* they have chosen to invest in Hainan, however, is not reflected in their preferred modes of investments. The next section aims to identify the economic motivation and investment strategies of these Singaporean Hainanese firms in Hainan.

## INVESTMENT STRATEGIES OF SINGAPOREAN FIRMS IN HAINAN

Our case studies of Singaporean firms in Hainan show two main types of investment strategy: market seekers; and factor seekers (see Dunning, 1993b; 1998). Among the market seekers, three variants of strategy are identified: (i) expansionary market seekers; (ii) 'beach-head' strategy; and (iii) 'first-timer' strategy. Each of these motivations differs slightly from the others, but seeking a market is still their main strategic consideration (see Yeung, 1994a, 1998b). However, the two types, market seekers and factor seekers, are not mutually exclusive (see Table 10.4). It is noted that firms may possess a combination of market strategies. Some of the market seekers are also concurrently factor seekers.

In this study, all twenty-two case studies are fundamentally motivated by *market access*. Market-seeking investors generally set up businesses or produce in a foreign market 'either to satisfy local demand or to export to markets other than their domestic market' (Hooijmaijers, 1995, p. 69). Generally, hotels and resorts aim to tap into the lucrative tourism industry in the host market (that is, Hainan province). The tourism industry is one of the major prospects for foreign investors in Hainan SEZ (Cadario *et al.*, 1992; East Asia Analytical Unit, 1995; Feng and Goodman, 1995, 1997). Hainan's tourism industry has gained support from both the provincial and Beijing governments. The provincial government intends to turn Hainan into an international resort destination (East Asia Analytical Unit, 1995). At the national level, Hainan is 'identified as one of the seven major national tourism districts and the only nationally designated winter resort in China' (Feng and Goodman, 1997, p. 71). Major players such as Hotel Investment's Hainan Mandarin Hotel, PSC's Sanya Fudao Tourism, and Prime Group's Orchid Farm and Holiday Resort proposal are generally seeking profits from this industry.

At a more local level, smaller hotels (for example, the Hainan Metropole Hotel, Eastern Park Hotel, SINGarden Hotel, Jinghua Hotel and Arklight Engineering's Haihua Hotel) and apartment developments (for example, the Lion City Condominium) in small towns and cities are targeting 'overseas Chinese' tourists returning to their ancestral villages and do not wish to stay in the less sophisticated countryside. Concurrently, they also provide a cheaper alternative for local people and mainland China tourists. Lion City Resort's development has heeded one of the business recommendations offered by the Singapore Chinese Chamber of Commerce and Industry (SCCCI) to capture the potential Singaporean market: 'Hainan is the nearest Chinese province to Singapore. The proximity between the two areas opens up opportunities such as the export of fresh primary products to Singapore or the island as a new getaway for urban Singaporeans' (SCCCI, 1995, p. 2).

In the manufacturing and other industrial sectors, the investment strategy is to manufacture products to satisfy local demand and to take

*Table* 10.4   Investment strategies of Singaporean firms in Hainan

| Case study company name | Market seekers | | | Factor seekers |
|---|---|---|---|---|
| | Expansionary | 'Beach-head' strategy | 'First-timer' strategy | |
| Lion City Resort | | ✓ | | ✓ cheap labour |
| Great Link Investment | ✓ | | | ✓ farming |
| SINGlass Holding | ✓ | | | |
| Haixin Investment | | ✓ | | |
| Sam Son Travel | ✓ | | | |
| Arklight Engineering | ✓ | | | ✓ ship engineering |
| Hoe Leong | ✓ | | | |
| Hoe Major Property | ✓ | | | |
| Lion City Condominium | | ✓ | | |
| Choo KJ | ✓ | | | ✓ water treatment |
| Metropole Hotel | ✓ | | | |
| Hotel Investment | ✓ | | | ✓ 5-star hotel |
| Jinghua Hotel | | ✓ | | |
| SINGarden Hotel | | ✓ | | |
| Eastern Park Hotel | | ✓ | | |
| SIN Fenghuang Hotel | | ✓ | | |
| Hainan Zilong | | ✓ | | |
| Asia Pacific Breweries (ABP) | ✓ | | ✓ | ✓ |
| Singapore Power | ✓ | | | |
| Prime Group International | ✓ | | | ✓ |
| Provisions Suppliers Corporation (PSC) | ✓ | | | |
| Asia Pulp and Paper (APP) | ✓ | | ✓ | ✓ |
| **Total** | **14** | **8** | **5** | **5** |
| Percentage (of 22 case studies) | 63.6 | 36.4 | 22.7 | 22.7 |

the opportunity to penetrate the larger mainland market from their Hainan bases. Market is a major strategic consideration for both APB and APP.

APB's Hainan subsidiary is the 'first step of the Long March', according to Mr Dennis Li, GM of HAPCO (HAPCO, 1997, p. 2). He also added, 'I always emphasise the point that our brewery is built not only for Hainan. Now it has become our urgent need to "go to the Mainland"' (HAPCO, 1997, p. 2). APP operates several facilities in China (for example, in Ningbo, Zhenjiang, Jiangsu, Suzhou and Shanghai) and has proposed a new green-field manufacturing plant in Hainan. The main reason for starting these investment projects in China is 'to establish a base in the country which provides many stimuli for the launch of new products and designs aimed at the huge China market – the second largest market in the world' (Asia Pulp and Paper, 1998, p. 20).

Most of the subsidiary firms belong to the *market-expansionary strategy* group. Generally, they operate in a similar manner to that of their parent firms' main business lines elsewhere. Firms employing the *'beachhead' strategy* differ from the former group in that their investments are usually unrelated to the original businesses of their parent firms and owners. In the case of both the Lion City Condominium and Haixin Investment, a number of their shareholders intend to use these real-estate developments as stepping stones to enter China's market. They want to get some sort of foothold in Hainan first, before they consider establishing their own lines of business there. The third variant of market seekers, *'first-timer'* Singaporean investors, have specific reasons for investing in Hainan. To a large extent, they want to capitalize on their proprietary expertise ahead of competitors by ensuring their presence in Hainan. For example, Mr Tan, general manager of Hotel Investment (the parent company of the Hainan Mandarin Hotel), said 'when we were there [in Hainan], there weren't any five-star hotels. Now they do have five-star hotels, but still we are the first foreign-managed five-star hotel' (interview in Singapore, 4 February 1998). APB echoed a similar sentiment. Malcom Tan, marketing manager of Hainan ABP, noted that 'there weren't any good breweries in Hainan . . . Hainan is a large province. Many provinces in China have their own breweries, but Hainan does not have one' (interview in Hainan, 18 February 1998).

On the other hand, *factor-seekers* are attracted by factors of production such as cheap labour, long land leases and the availability of raw materials. For example, Mr Leong of Great Link Investment has a personal investment in such resource-rich primary industries as agriculture (for example, Leong's Farm owned by GL Investment). Some property developers (for example, the Lion City Resort and Lion City Condominium) have mentioned the availability of cheap labour and land as two of the reasons for their real-estate developments in the area. APB and APP have also considered the availability of competitive factors in Hainan, compared to other regional locations. However, their intention of penetrating China's vast market is not to be overlooked. It is therefore clear that factor-seekers are not limited exclusively to manufacturing firms, although in our study there are fewer manufacturers than service-orientated Singaporean firms in Hainan. Another point to be noted is that even though an entrepreneur- or owner-run Singaporean firm may have chosen to invest in Hainan for factor-costs reasons, the motivation of the entrepreneur or owner may not be clear until we examine the broader set of contextual factors. This is our task in the penultimate section below.

## EXPLAINING SINGAPOREAN INVESTMENTS IN HAINAN

From the above analysis, it is evident that the different types of investment strategy are not mutually exclusive (see Table 10.4). We have so far looked only at the economic and strategic objectives of Singaporean investments in Hainan. However, as noted by Hooijmaijers (1995, p. 69), 'foreign investments are usually motivated by a wider and more complicated set of strategic, behavioural, and economic considerations'. Three main macroeconomic circumstances have stimulated increasing Singaporean investments into China since the early 1980s. First, China's economic reform and its modernization programme since 1979 are an important contextual factor in influencing Singaporean investments in China. The new open-door policy of China's economy offers great investment opportunities, which come with a large consumer and factor market, as well as numerous economic incentives to foreign investors, including Singaporean firms and businesspeople (Pang and Komaran, 1985b; Kanai, 1993; Lee, 1994). The designation of SEZs and 'open cities' in the provinces of Guangdong and Fujian is deliberate. They are aimed at complementing the sociohistorical reasons mentioned earlier, and attracting 'overseas Chinese' investors whose ancestral roots originate largely from there (Pang and Komaran, 1985a; Kanai, 1993; Liu, 1998b).

Second, the Singapore economy experienced a recession during the mid-1980s and the government, as a strategy to sustain its economic growth and to diversify firms' portfolios, has since encouraged Singaporean firms to expand overseas. The regionalization drive launched in 1993 through which the Singapore government offers taxation incentives and financial assistance to firms has played an important role in motivating Singaporean investments in China (Kanai, 1993; Lu and Zhu,

1995; Willis and Yeoh, 1998; Yeung, 1998a, 1999b). 'Push' factors such as the land constraint factor and increasing labour costs and a policy shift discouraging labour-intensive manufacturing processes, have forced some labour-intensive operations from Singapore to relocate to China and other countries in the region where there is abundant cheap labour (Kanai, 1993; Ho, 1994; Lee, 1994; Pang, 1995; Chiu *et al.*, 1997).

The political determinants of Singaporean FDI in China have been most evident since the early 1980s. Chin (1988) has recognized the significance of institutional forces such as the Bank of China and later the Trade Mission Representative Offices in driving the commercial activities between the two countries before 1990. The establishment of official diplomatic relations between the two countries in 1990 is a major political reason for the growing Singaporean investments in China (Lu and Zhu, 1995; Liu, 1998b). Another factor is the regionalization drive initiated by the Singapore government in 1993. Later Singaporean investments in non-traditional emigrant regions such as North-eastern economic zones (for example, Shanghai, Suzhou and Wuxi in Jiangsu Province; Ningbo in Zhejiang Province; and Qingdao in Shangdong Province) and Inner Economic regions (for example, Sichuan and Yunan Province) reflect further political co-operation between the two governments (see Cartier, 1995; Lu and Zhu, 1995; Tan, 1995; Yong, 1995; Yeung, 1998a). For example, the Singapore government has made it a top priority to encourage Singaporean firms to invest in China through spearheading government-led large-scale infrastructural investments in those regions (for example, the infamous Suzhou–Singapore Industrial Park in Jiangsu province). Numerous ministerial visits by Singapore's senior politicians, together with the personal ethnic and social linkages of Singaporeans, have reduced substantially the uncertainty and risks of investment projects in China. As a result, many earlier studies have ascribed the Singapore government to be one of the most important institutional forces behind Singaporean investments in China. Similarly, Yeung (1998a) has proposed the term 'political entrepreneurship' to describe the involvement of Singapore's key politicians in opening up business opportunities in China for government-linked companies and private enterprises from Singapore.

Third, a majority of Singapore's FDI in China belongs to Singaporean Chinese firms and business people. These firms portray characteristics of the Chinese business system. A typical Chinese business system is made up of family-based enterprises run on a paternalistic basis. On unique characteristic that separates Chinese business firms from other 'family-type' enterprises is its personalistic network relationships.

Networks are an essential characteristic and ingredient of the success of ethnic Chinese in the global economy, and particularly in China (Kotkin, 1992; Weidenbaum and Hughes, 1996; see also Chapter 1 in this volume). These networks relationships exist in intra-, inter-, or extra-firm linkages, and are based on trust. Trust, an important element when conducting business dealings over long distances, is found among kinship, common dialect and origin in a clan or village (*Economist*, 1992; Sender, 1991; Yeung, 1997a; 1998b; Tong and Yong, 1998).

Within a firm, the internal core of the Chinese enterprise is 'cemented' by family ties that have the highest degree of trust. Apart from family lineage, kin with the same ancestry from a region and schoolmates are also generally considered to be more trustworthy than unfamiliar 'outsiders' in inter-firm transactions. These personalized relationships can be translated into connections or *guanxi* – a crucial business advantage, particularly when they are extended extra-firm arrangements such as political alliances or trade associations. Other characteristics of this ethnic advantage include the commonality of language, cultural and intrinsic skills in making connections and networking. Linguistic and cultural familiarity has reduced commercial barriers for Singaporean firms in China (Pang, 1995, p. 176). A dense web of connections or *guanxi* emanates from this ethnicity linkage and this has ensured preferential treatments towards friends, relatives and acquaintances when doing business. In sum, personalistic relationships are important in Chinese business organizations, regardless of whether they are found in internal intra-firm hierarchical relationships, inter-firm networks, or extra-firm connections. These ethno-social characteristics have facilitated Singaporean Hainanese investments in Hainan province.

## CONCLUSION

In this chapter, we have described and explained the organizational characteristics, entry modes and business strategies of twenty-two Singaporean companies in Hainan, China. Specifically, we found that the majority of these companies have invested in the property and service industries. This reflects the wider Chinese business system in which property and service industries are preferred because of their lower technological requirements and faster turnover time (for example, Heng, 1997). Some of these Singaporean investment projects in Hainan are also located close to the ancestral homes of their Hainanese owners. In terms of entry modes, Singaporean investments in Hainan are not much different from their predecessors elsewhere in China in that they prefer joint ventures with local firms (see Pang and Komaran, 1985b; also Yeung, 1994a). Since wholly-owned investment projects are allowed in many sectors in China, this preference for joint ventures implies that Singaporean Hainanese possess good connections or *guanxi* with their local partners which can be tapped to facilitate their cross-border operations. These connections are often embedded in ongoing personal relationships between the founders or entrepreneurs and their Chinese counterparts. Their strategic orientation in Hainan is primarily aiming at the burgeoning domestic market, particularly after Hainan was redesignated as a SEZ in 1988.

In order to explain their entry mode and business strategies, we argue that Singaporean investments in Hainan are often guided by the socio-cultural principles of being ethnic Chinese. During our interviews, the ethno-social rationale often cited for their investments in Hainan reveals the close ethnic relationships and emotional attachment Singaporean Hainanese have towards their ancestral homeland. At the micro level, the principle of familism and kinship relations instituted in these ethnic Chinese abroad are used to uphold the hierarchical nature of intra-firm networks and ownership bonds. This institutional system is extended into lineage, regional loyalty and dialect affiliations. As ethnic Chinese who have little dependence on family or lineage support in a foreign country, many Singaporeans have turned to such institutions as clan associations (founded on the principles of ethnicity and dialect affiliation), formal business societies, and other informal social groupings, to cultivate a vast network of connections or *guanxi* among ethnic Chinese outside mainland China. As a result, a Singaporean-specific Chinese business system has evolved with its configurations of trust and *guanxi* relationships. These network linkages or inter-firm networks, as evident in numerous joint ventures and partnerships explained in this chapter, reflect the role of ethnicity and social organization in facilitating business among Singaporean Chinese in China.

The influence of political considerations on cross-border transactions such as FDI cannot be overlooked in this case. The political institutional setting can shape the extent and characteristics of investment strategies. Our comparative examination of case studies in this chapter has suggested that political connection is an important advantage and a powerful element contributing to a higher successful rate among Singaporean investment projects in Hainan. Some projects by Singaporean firms, in particular those by government-linked companies, are also influenced by the ongoing political agenda of the Singapore government. In sum, an understanding of the institutional settings and decision-making processes of entrepreneurs and firms is essential to providing good insights into the globalization of Chinese business firms. This chapter marks just the beginning of such an important intellectual endeavour.

## Notes

1.  We used a qualitative personal interview method to collect data and a case study approach to analyse it. Yin (1994, p. 3) remarks that the case study 'allows an investigation to retain the holistic and meaningful characteristics of real-life events'. We have therefore selected multiple case studies to carry out a comparative analysis of multi-level phenomenon. Each case was analyzed carefully, and cases that reflected similar results or reasons were grouped together to draw meaningful conclusions. In the preliminary selection, a list of twenty-three firms was compiled from a commercial directory (*Singapore-China Trade and Investment Directory 96/97*, 1997), various newspaper articles, the Internet and through personal contacts. After telephone surveys were conducted to verify these firms, however, seventeen firms were identified, along with their relevant person-in-charge. Personal interviews were conducted with top executives from parent firms in Singapore (and in Hainan Province if the key executive was personally managing the operations there). The selection of top executives, such as chairmen, managing directors, chief executive officers and general managers, for interview was necessary because they were often the initiators of investment strategies and the decision-makers in the operational processes. This ensured more accurate information about the real motivation for their investments and the nature of their operations in Hainan. During the interviews, a tape recorder was used wherever possible, with the permission of the respondents. This allowed unobstructed conversation without the distraction of the interviewer writing notes. It also enabled the researcher to capture fully the wealth of qualitative information for accurate presentation of data in the writing-up later. Ten transcripts were made in total. At the end of the interview, permission was sought from the interviewees for one of the authors to visit their business sites and to interview their local managers in Hainan in February 1998. From the initial list of seventeen firms, all except three granted personal interviews. During the interviewing process, three further contacts were recommended and all granted interviews. In total, sixteen interviews were conducted. The remaining sampled firms used in this study were drawn from information provided by local people, personal observations during Hainan field trips and printed materials such as newspapers and annual reports. A total of twenty-two firms were compiled for use as case studies in this chapter.
2.  In Haikou, the Hainan Mandarin Hotel (a wholly-owned subsidiary of Hotel Investment) is one of the first buildings constructed at the new *Binghai Dadao* (Marina Boulevard), which is quite a distance from the city centre. This is a strategic position because the Marina Area is the newly-designated commercial heart of Haikou City. The Hainan Mandarin Hotel

has the advantage of being one of the first five-star hotels in Haikou capable of hosting important and affluent business executives from large corporations visiting Hainan. Similarly, another Singaporean joint venture – the Lion City Condominium project, is building an eighteen-storey condominium near Haikou's new international airport in Meilan Town. The project's early entry and proximity to the new airport is explained by the perceived advantage of future economic development and improved transportation network in that area (interview, Singapore, 26 January 1998).

# 11 Failures and Strategies of Hong Kong Firms in China: An Ethnographic Perspective

Alan Smart and Josephine Smart

## INTRODUCTION

There has been a great deal of scholarly and journalistic interest in the remarkable accomplishments of business firms controlled by ethnic Chinese outside the People's Republic of China, and the distinctive organizational and strategic features of these firms in comparison to Western enterprises. A central narrative theme in these accounts revolves around 'success', both for individual firms and for the societies where these firms are concentrated (Cumings, 1993; Dirlik, 1997; Nonini and Ong, 1997). While some analysts have discussed whether the features that have served small and medium enterprises well will undermine their viability once they become large corporations (Redding, 1990), in general there has been very little study of occasions when ethnic Chinese firms have not achieved success or have completely failed. Is there something to be learned from the failures that inevitably beset firms run by Chinese entrepreneurs, just like any others? This chapter begins an exploration of the experience, discourse and implications of failure for an understanding of the nature of ethnic Chinese-operated businesses.

In examining the issue of the implementation of strategies such as reliance on kinship ties, the development of trust, and the mobilization of *guanxi* (social connections) by Hong Kong entrepreneurs operating across the border in China, we suggest that the economic success of a firm is strongly influenced by the complex interplay between management expertise and socio-cultural knowledge as played out in the daily decision-making processes and operational management undertaken by key individuals in the firm. Context (such as the set of available resources and the current business climate) is also critical. Strategies that work in one set of circumstances may be disastrous in another set, or in the same situation at a later date. Space does not allow for an examination of such contextual factors (see Chapters 1 and 4 in this volume), but we simply want to suggest that even where circumstances were similar, and comparable strategies adopted, the skill with which the strategies were implemented would still have a critical impact.

We concentrate on production across the Hong Kong–China border. Hong Kong investment has accounted for the majority of foreign direct investment since the opening of China in 1979, and nearly 85 per cent of cumulative foreign investment between 1979 and 1993 came from Hong Kong, Taiwan, Macao, Singapore and Thailand (Christerson and Lever-Tracy, 1997, p. 576). Hong Kong companies were pioneers in this process, becoming heavily involved well before the rules were clearly laid out, and when the rules that did exist were widely seen as being serious obstacles to the profitable operation of capitalist enterprises. These ventures were organized through the use of principles and strategies distinct from those used by foreign multinationals, and involved making arrangements through local rather than central authorities, reliance on pre-existing social connections, the development of trust as a substitute for carefully negotiated contracts (Hsing, 1998), and an emphasis on the factor complementarities of Hong Kong and China: available capital and managerial knowledge of world markets versus cheap labour and land (Naughton, 1997). One result is the concentration of foreign investment in the provinces from which most emigration occurred: Guangdong, Hainan and Fujian (Hsing 1998, p. 22). Table 11.1 illustrates the unevenness of distribution, with Guangdong receiving 24.2 per cent of all foreign investment in 1997, while Fujian received a further 7.6 per cent. Statistics from earlier periods provide an even stronger picture of concentration of foreign investment in emigrant-producing provinces (Smart and Smart, 1991). Only Jiangsu and Shanghai, the heartland of vibrant domestic manufacturing, received more. When the proportion of foreign capital in provincial GDP is compared to the national average of foreign capital as 6.6 per cent of GDP, the three provincial sources of emigration stand out again, with Hainan weighted at 289.2 per cent of the average, Guangdong at 254.6 per cent, and Fujian at 198.8 per cent. These high levels of foreign capital are approximated only in the province-equivalent cities of Shanghai and Tianjian.

At the heart of these investment practices was a process of brokerage or arbitrage (Sung, 1991) in which entrepreneurs created linkages across a divide between two radically different political economies (Jin

*Table* 11.1  Provincial distribution of foreign capital in PRC (1996)

| | Total realized foreign capital (billion US$) | % of total foreign capital in PRC | % of provincial GDP compared to national average* |
|---|---|---|---|
| National | 54.8 | | |
| Beijing | 1.7 | 3.1 | 133.2 |
| Tianjin | 2.2 | 4.1 | 254.3 |
| Hebei | 0.9 | 1.7 | 33.4 |
| Shanxi | 0.2 | 0.4 | 19.2 |
| I. Mongolia | 0.2 | 0.4 | 29.2 |
| Liaoning | 1.9 | 3.4 | 74.9 |
| Jilin | 0.6 | 1.1 | 58.0 |
| Heilongjiang | 0.8 | 1.5 | 43.8 |
| TCShanghai | 4.8 | 8.8 | 208.7 |
| Jiangsu | 5.5 | 10.0 | 114.5 |
| Zhejiang | 1.6 | 3.0 | 49.2 |
| Anhui | 0.7 | 1.4 | 39.6 |
| Fujian | 4.1 | 7.6 | 198.8 |
| Jiangxi | 0.3 | 0.6 | 26.6 |
| Shandong | 0.3 | 0.5 | 6.0 |
| Henan | 0.8 | 1.4 | 26.5 |
| Hubei | 1.1 | 2.0 | 46.4 |
| Hunan | 0.8 | 1.4 | 35.9 |
| Guangdong | 13.3 | 24.2 | 254.6 |
| Guangxi | 0.8 | 1.4 | 52.2 |
| Hainan | 0.9 | 1.6 | 289.2 |
| Sichuan | 0.6 | 1.1 | 18.7 |
| Guizhou | 0.3 | 06 | 59.1 |
| Yunnan | 0.1 | 0.1 | 6.3 |
| Tibet | 0.0 | 0.0 | 4.6 |
| Shaanxi | 0.4 | 0.7 | 39.4 |
| Gansu | 0.2 | 0.4 | 38.6 |
| Qinghai | 0.0 | 0.0 | 6.8 |
| Ningxia | 0.0 | 0.1 | 31.7 |
| Xinjiang | 0.3 | 0.5 | 38.8 |

* Foreign capital as a percentage of provincial GDP divided by foreign capital as a percentage of national GDP.
*Source*:  Goodman *et al.*(1998, p. 90).

and Haynes, 1997). Bridging the divide between these societies offered the possibility of substantially boosted profit margins (given the factor complementarities and the large supplies of underemployed labour and land), but at the expense of high levels of risk. Every investor knows, of course, that there is usually a trade-off between the potential for higher-than-average profits and increased risks. Yet, in the literature, the considerable hyperbole about the remarkable successes achieved by these entrepreneurs and the contributions they have made to their home territories is accompanied by very little attention to the large numbers of failures and losses that accompany high-risk activities such as those involved in brokering across borders and pioneering new markets and product niches. Strategies such as relying on social connections and trust more than on legal contracts may offer substantial savings in transaction cost, but simultaneously heighten risk. Given this risk, effective performance and tactical moves can mean the difference between a remarkably successful strategy and a disastrous one.

The financial crises in Asia since 1997 have started to shift the focus from success to failure (Emmerson, 1998). Although the new pessimism has concentrated on the mistakes of national economies and politicians more than on firms, the problems stemmed initially from private rather than public debt (Wade and Veneroso, 1998). The degree of ease with which firms can fail in each country has been seen by some economists as being closely related to the speed with which each economy has bounced back from its problems: the harder it is to close a business, the more prolonged the crisis. Conversely, an economy which is flexible enough to make it easy for 'troubled businesses to die and new ones to spring up' makes it easier for economies such as Taiwan and Hong Kong to adjust to turbulent circumstances (*Economist*, 3 January 1998, p. 73). Low failure rates and high barriers to entry inhibit the kind of creative destruction that Joseph Schumpeter saw as the driving force of economic growth under capitalism, and which involves repeated waves of business failures (Magnusson, 1994, p. 3).

The lack of attention in studies of Chinese business firms paid to failures and to implementation resembles the majority of policy studies, where most of the work is devoted to the study of problems and prescribing policy solutions, rather than studying the actual implementation of the policies, and how this implementation process might have an independent effect on outcomes.[1] Similarly, studies of Chinese business firms have relied on either aggregate data or on interviews with owners/managers of the businesses. While it is clear from the aggregate statistics that large numbers of Chinese-operated businesses fail and disappear, field research has (naturally) concentrated on the businesses that survive. Furthermore, researchers have relied primarily on interviews with managers and/or owners of enterprises, and thus are likely to get more information on strategies and intentions rather than on the implementation of those practices. In addition, it is a standard methodological problem that interviews tend to elicit normative accounts (what it is thought *should be*) rather than descriptive accounts (what, in fact, *is*). Participant observation research is one way of avoiding the normative bias and facilitating the study of implementation of practices and strategies rather than just their expression in the abstract. Observations allow the researcher to prompt the informant for explanations and elaborations of happenings on site that have been omitted by the informant. Longitudinal research over a substantial period of time is also required for the careful study of implementation, since the practices themselves take time, and the outcomes may not be apparent for some time.

We have been conducting research on a number of Hong Kong enterprises for as long as nine years, including cases where informants were involved in a previous research project dating back to 1983. Field observations have been carried out by one of us almost every year since 1987. However this time-depth and intensity of investigation limits the number of enterprises that can be studied. Our most detailed ethnographic material has come from only two enterprises, but we have also conducted interviews and, in some cases site visits, of greater or lesser intensity with informants from several dozen other Hong Kong enterprises that have been conducting business across the border in China.

## CHINESE BUSINESS STRATEGIES AND THE DISCOURSE OF SUCCESS

The globalization of Chinese business is hardly a new thing. After all, Chinese enterprises have often been examined in the context of middlemen minorities or, going back to Max Weber, as 'pariah capitalism', enterprises that cut across societal or cultural boundaries and are seen as corrupting or dangerous. Many times in history, 'merchants and traders were outsiders' (Oxfeld, 1993, p. 13), and overseas Chinese were frequently used by British colonizers to serve such roles in Southeast Asia and the Caribbean. Until the Chinese Revolution in 1949, Hong Kong operated essentially as an entrepôt for co-ordinating trade between China and the rest of the world, and this role has been re-emerging as a result of China's open-door policy since 1978. Most past commentators, including Weber, saw such patterns as being exceptional and not very relevant to the main course of capitalist development, which involved the increasing rationalization of both enterprises and state institutions to allow the increase of productivity, rational accounting and the elaboration of the division of labour eventually into Fordist patterns of mass production and mass consumption.

The proclivity of Chinese enterprises to operate across national boundaries has attracted a new kind of attention in a world preoccupied with global competition, marketing and production systems, and with elaborating the kinds of supranational institutions (such as Free Trade Agreements and the World Trade Organization) that can facilitate a smooth transition to the global scope of economic activities (Dirlik, 1997; Ong, 1993, 1997). Following the discovery of Japan as 'number one', the rapid growth of the 'Four Little Dragons' and the next wave of newly-industrializing countries in the Association of South East Asian Nations (ASEAN) drew attention to the role of overseas Chinese in the rapid growth of the Pacific Rim. Standard figures of speech in what Bruce Cumings (1993, p. 30) calls 'Rimspeak' include 'miracle'[2] as well as 'dynamism'. However, the 'miracles' of the rim 'do not truck with Joseph Schumpeter's notion that capitalism's dynamic is through waves of creation and destruction: it is all on the up-and-up, a whoosh of progress transforming the region' (Cumings, 1993, p. 30). China is among the latest entrants into the 'miracle-of-the-month' club, and here the role of the overseas Chinese is seen as being particularly crucial, since the economy is still dominated by state-owned enterprises. In William Overholt's (1993, p. 197) words: 'Hong Kong became the nuclear reaction at the core of the Chinese economic explosion.'

A variety of features have been identified that make the overseas Chinese style of business so distinctive (see Chapters 1 and 2 in this volume). This discussion will be brief and concentrate on those points that will be examined in the case studies below. According to Redding (1990, p. 3) what is special about Chinese business organization is that 'it retains many of the characteristics of small scale, such as paternalism, opportunism, flexibility, even to very large scale. It does not follow the Western pattern of professionalization, bureaucratization, neutralization to anywhere near the same extent'. A main theme of his 1990 book is that this form of organization is 'peculiarly effective and a significant contributor to the list of causes of the East Asia miracle' (Redding, 1990, p. 4). Social networks are constructed and mobilized to develop particularistic interpersonal forms of trust, which encourages 'co-operation, loyalty, obedience, duty, stability, adaptiveness and legitimacy in the short and long term' (Thrift and Olds, 1996, p. 324). Yeung (1998, p. 219) sees network relationships and co-operative synergy as the inherent competitive advantage of ethnic Chinese transnational corporations, 'which many Western firms have grave difficulty in matching'. Personal obligations and paternalism are also often emphasized in labour relations (Kipnis, 1997, p. 152), although Wong (1988, p. 142) found that Shanghainese cotton-mill operators tried to avoid employing relatives who were not immediate members of the family. Many other studies have pointed to the frequent occurrence of the family enterprise among overseas Chinese and the strengths offered by the overlap between household and enterprise (Redding, 1990, p. 143; Hamilton and Biggart, 1992; Castells, 1996, p. 181).

Yeung (1994, p. 1939) has criticized studies of Hong Kong-based transnational corporations for ascribing causal status to their motivations in explaining their operations. Such studies have failed to 'stipulate the causal mechanisms through which transnational operations by HK-TNCs are made possible', and not just desired. Similarly, in this chapter, we are sceptical about the tendency to accept the *strategies* adopted by Hong Kong entrepreneurs as adequate explanations for their successes. While we would accept that their strategies (and those of other overseas Chinese businesses) might contribute to their successes, we argue that simply attending to the strategies themselves is incapable of identifying the causal mechanisms through which these successes are accomplished. Our reservations are because of the undeniable, if largely ignored, fact that large proportions of entrepreneurs following such strategies fail to accomplish their goals, resulting in lower profits than had been expected, high levels of difficulty in managing enterprises, or failure and even bankruptcy. If the same kinds of strategy are adopted by those who fail as well as those who succeed, then strategy alone cannot explain success. Instead, there must be other factors needing attention, including the resources available to the respective entrepreneurs, the conditions in which strategies are adopted, and the skill with which strategies are pursued. In general, we argue that the effectiveness and utility of a strategy is an accomplishment, not a necessary outcome of its use in the context of particular cultural norms and features (Smart and Smart, 1993).

Gordon Redding is one of the few researchers of Chinese business organization to give serious attention to their failures as well as their successes. He argues that organizational features 'which in one context can be strengths can in another be weaknesses' (1990, p. 210). For example, cultural norms about the normality of inequality make it relatively easy for an organization to establish stable hierarchies and willing compliance on the part of subordinates. But these features can also stifle initiative (1990, p. 208). We agree with this general observation, but would suggest that it does not go far enough. We believe that even the strengths of Chinese organizational features such as mobilization of networks can fail if they are not implemented effectively enough in practice. A strategy that can offer a competitive advantage can also result in disaster. Using the example of the normality of hierarchy, Redding suggests that in overseas Chinese organizations, 'Discipline is already there; it does not need to be injected' (1990, p. 208). But while there may be norms supporting compliance and a greater degree of comfort with hierarchical relationships within an organization, this does not mean that discipline cannot easily be lost, as any Chinese manager would surely admit. Maintaining cultural resources like these requires effective practices: they can be wasted as easily and as quickly as any other kind of resource.

It might be said that these reservations are obvious and rather trivial (at least if we do not proceed to specifying in useful detail what form such other factors must take to achieve success), but both academic and popular literature has paid remarkably little attention to them, emphasizing instead a kind of triumphalist narrative of remarkable accomplishments, leavened perhaps with forebodings about the future and the chances of continued success. Here, the literature is consistent with Chinese entrepreneurs' own narrative preferences, where failures are rarely mentioned except as evidence of moral character through the ability to overcome such difficulties (Chan and Chiang, 1994). Some danger lies in the uncritical acceptance of the effectiveness of some of these strategies and their adoption in circumstances where they might not be suitable.

There is a more general reason, though, for greater attention to the circumstances in which characteristically Chinese business strategies might fail. And that is because many of these strategies rely on a kind of balancing act. They are high-risk manoeuvres which may lead to higher profits and competitive advantages, but at the cost of a heightened probability of catastrophe. In the next section, we first offer some initial explorations of the role of failure in the political economy of Chinese businesses, particularly in terms of flexibility and the extension of production chains across the Hong Kong–China border. Following that, we review some of the known meanings that failure and the risk of failure hold for Chinese entrepreneurs. Neither of these tasks can be attempted in a definitive manner, but are intended simply to indicate the significance of failure in the firms and economies where Chinese entrepreneurs are predominant.

## THE POLITICAL ECONOMY AND EXPERIENCE OF FAILURE

Despite the relative lack of attention to failure, it is clearly a common experience for Chinese business outside China,[3] particularly for small, family-run businesses (Greenhalgh, 1994). High rates of turnover in the predominantly small-scale manufacturing sector in Hong Kong are related to patterns of rapid, opportunistic movement into new markets: when the market for a product contracts, the smallest businesses fold or move into new products (Sit *et al.*, 1979, p. 309). These very small businesses are usually either sub-contractors or dependent on orders from large import–export firms (the successors to the mercantile trading firms), and act as a buffer between volatile market demand and the large, well-established businesses (Lin *et al.*, 1980, p. 23). The speed with which such firms are established, change direction or fail is a part of the famed flexibility and hyper-competitiveness of Hong Kong's economy (Christerson and Appelbaum, 1995; Enright *et al.*, 1997). Hamilton and Water (1997), for example, have demonstrated that different strategies were responsible for the success of Chinese entrepreneurs in Thailand at different points in history. But rather than a case of the same individuals changing strategies, more commonly the result was failure, followed by new groups adopting new ways of doing business.

In 1982, 966 Hong Kong businesses failed (a ratio of 92 per 10 000 firms), rising to 4953 failed firms in 1991 (158 per 10 000) – see Figure 11.1 – although these numbers are still dwarfed by the 12 679 and 48 163 new firms registered, respectively, in these two years (Hong Kong Registrar General Annual Departmental Reports). This data fails to register the large number of informally-operated family firms (A. Smart, 1992; J. Smart, 1989). Taiwan also has a high rate of bankruptcy among its predominantly small-scale enterprises (Hamilton and Biggart, 1992, p. 193). In the chemical industry, for example, 40 per cent of the industry's ouput in 1991 came from firms that did not exist in 1986, while the firms that had produced 58 per cent of the ouput of chemicals in 1981 had left the industry by 1991. The same pattern was even stronger in other fields: 'Four out of five firms that manufactured clothing, metal products, textiles and plastics in 1981 either closed or changed lines of business over the next decade' (*Economist*, 3 January 1998, p. 73). Hsing (1998, p. 50) found that there were several periods in which a substantial fraction of Taiwan's shoe manufacturers were shut down.

Established since the 1950s, these patterns have been transformed by the opening of China and the rapid increase in Hong Kong's affluence (with its impact on labour and land costs for production within Hong Kong). There has been a strong trend towards deindustrialization in Hong Kong. For example, employment in the electronics industry peaked in 1988 at 109 677 but dropped to 71 466 by 1991 (Chiu *et al.*,

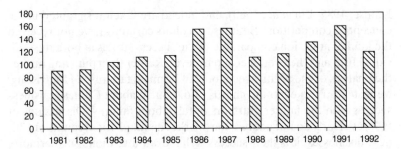

*Figure* 11.1   Number of failures per 10 000 firms in Hong Kong, 1981–92
*Source*:   Hong Kong Government, Registrar General Annual Departmental
Reports, various issues.

1997). As Hong Kong manufacturers take advantage of the opportunities to relocate production into China, they have generally not been upgrading production within Hong Kong (Salaff 1995, p. xv; Tuan and Wong, 1993). The close and convenient availability of cheaper labour and land has meant that Hong Kong has moved into technology-intensive manufacturing much less than has Taiwan (Tuan and Ng, 1994, 1995). It is not clear, however, how many of the disappearing enterprises are being relocated, and how many are failing. Enright *et al*. (1997, p. 21) point out as well that when companies transfer their manufacturing processes offshore, their remaining local staff become reclassified as service workers, reinforcing the statistical decline of employment in industry. Hong Kong seems to be in the process of becoming a centre for the coordination of the international division of labour, concentrating managerial and administrative functions, and complementing this with a rapid development of its financial sector (Yeung, 1998). The garment industry has had more restrictions on its ability to transfer production than has electronics, because of trade quotas (Sung, 1997). Garment producers have drawn upon their strong ties within the commercial subcontracting network of global capitalism and an industry structure characterized by small firms interconnected through the subcontracting network to maintain flexibility in production (Lui and Chiu, 1994, p. 62). Quota systems on garments have limited the option of relocation to China and elsewhere, so that the path of development has been one that has increasingly locked garment manufacturers into 'a system of flexible production for volatile export markets' (ibid.).

Business closures in Hong Kong enterprises have not been ignored then; they have been incorporated into accounts of Hong Kong's success that focus on flexibility and market-driven responsiveness (for example,

Krause, 1985; Lin *et al.*, 1980), and indeed are taken for granted in the
concept of competition. But these accounts certainly have not received
the kind of attention comparable to the success stories at both the individual firm and the overall economy level. Rather than pursuing further
the analysis of the political economy of business failures in Hong Kong,
we instead try to echo the chorus of discourse about Chinese business
success with the fainter murmurs of talk about failures. Discussions of
failures clearly do not address the 'market demand' for accounts of Chinese businesses: it is their successes that draw attention. Furthermore,
Chinese entrepreneurs are generally reluctant to talk about their failures. If interviews are conducted with business operators, those whose
firms have already collapsed will obviously be undersampled or missed
entirely. As Chan and Chiang (1994, p. 264) note:

> entrepreneurial setbacks were numerous although not many were in
> fact recorded in the interview transcripts. This reluctance to talk about
> one's 'failures' was understandable in a culture concerned with image
> and 'face-keeping'. What was important was not how and why they
> failed in some business ventures but whether they bounced back
> quickly enough and recovered from the crises. It was this ability to
> learn from experience, to acquire insights from events of adversity,
> which constituted a key attribute of entrepreneurs.

One prominent way of talking about failures was in terms of 'luck'
and 'fate'. For an effort to be rewarded with success, it had to be
'matched with good foresight and sound judgement. Sometimes it
depended on good connections or even luck. The more risks an entrepreneur had taken, the more chances of failures there would be; yet,
the more failures entrepreneurs had confronted and rebounded from,
the more experienced they would become' (Chan and Chiang, 1994,
p. 264). One entrepreneur who had lost money in a film business venture commented:

> I felt that since I did not bring any money to this world, the fact that I
> am making money now must be attributed to fate. In fact what I had
> lost in my business was not because I was not capable or lacking in
> good judgement. I attributed my failure to fate as well and that made
> me feel at peace with myself... When there are difficulties, you have
> to be calm, think hard, then you will find a resolution. Do not fret
> over your losses... If you become overly distressed, nothing could be
> done properly. (Chan and Chiang, 1994, p. 265)

Failure, and how both to avoid and explain it, is an important concern for Chinese business operators, if not as much for researchers of these businesses. Reference to luck and fate serves to externalize failure from the performance of those failing; it also identifies appropriately the importance of conditions and unpredictable events. The adoption of risky strategies involves a fundamental reliance on conditions that cannot be fully controlled. Wong (1988, p. 166) found that the decline of cotton mills was most often attributed to 'mismanagement and personnel problems', including conflict among directors and factionalism. This account is closer to the ones we shall offer below based on our ethnographic research. Firms fail despite favourable conditions, if performance causes problems, and skilled management of difficult conditions can lead ultimately to success.

The overwhelming attention given to the success stories of overseas Chinese business, be it driven by popular interest or the result of methodological biases, encourages the tendency to under-report the tensions and fractures within overseas Chinese family businesses. Indeed, there is a general assumption that the internal co-operation and management within the family business are a given 'by virtue of the small scale of the organizations, and the clear sense of who is in charge' (Redding, 1990, p. 214). In reality, the observable characteristics of peace and harmony in a family business are the products of ongoing contestation and compromises. Rarely is it the case that the interests and visions of a family business head are equally shared and accepted by other members of the family, nor is his/her authority automatically accepted without challenge all the time. Furthermore, there is a common, though misleading, impression that 'workers and owner/managers naturally ... tend to be similar socially, in terms of their values, their behaviour, their needs, and their aspirations. In consequence, one of the major weaknesses found in many Western organizations, that of the management/worker divide, may be largely discounted in the Overseas Chinese case' (Redding, 1990, p. 209). These impressions are boosted by the uncritical acceptance of the significance of Confucianism in Asian values and behaviour. Discourse on Asian values has taken a circuitous route. First seen as an obstacle to successful modernization, Confucianism later became an explanation for the 'Asian miracle'. Most recently, Confucian values are being used to account for the spectacular collapses of 1997 through the medium of replacing 'relationships' and 'strong family ties' with 'crony capitalism' and 'nepotism' (*Economist*, 25 July 1998, p. 23). These reversals miss the point that vague over-generalizations such as 'Asian values', or more specific cultural features such as an emphasis on cultivating personal relationships, do not of themselves produce determinate outcomes. Instead, they are resources and strategies that must be enacted in particular circumstances, and in doing so, outcomes may vary dramatically.

We shall use ethnographic data to illustrate these arguments more concretely through an examination of two issues. First, we examine reliance on social relationships more than on formal contracts to support business deals, and the potential risks and problems involved in this strategy. Second, we open up the 'black box' of the cohesive family enterprise, to look at the internal strains and frictions, and the ways in which these strains can undermine the effective operation of a cross-border investment. Problems of internal cohesion among family members who share the ownership and management of the family business, and the problems of internal co-operation between business owners and employees are common contributing factors in Chinese business failures.

## RELIANCE ON SOCIAL RELATIONSHIPS RATHER THAN CONTRACTS

We have elsewhere discussed the character and implications of Hong Kong investment in China since 1978 (Smart and Smart,1991, 1992, 1993). We shall only briefly set out the context here. It is important, though, to stress that discussions of these processes have commonly emphasized the same narrative elements of success through the mobilization of cultural commonalities and characteristics of Chinese business strategies, and that we have not been immune to this tendency in our own accounts. While there are many persuasive accounts of how the mobilization of social relationships has underpinned business success and rapid economic growth (Hsing, 1997; Yeung, 1998b), we argue in this section that reliance on social relationships is a strategy that requires considerable skill in its implementation if it is not to have negative results. There is a considerable variety of potential pitfalls which can lead to disaster if situations are not carefully handled.

When China opened its doors to foreign investment in 1978, there was a palpable wave of desire for the mythical Chinese market of a billion consumers. However, the obstacles to investment by capitalist enterprises were also immense: only the sketchiest of regulations and guidelines existed, and even these were hardly sturdy legal supports like those that had become routine in the developed economies. It became expected that in order to do business in China, an investor had to be patient, endure difficult and protracted negotiations, and concentrate on the long-term by building relationships, rather than expecting short-term profits. Only the largest transnational corporations could afford this kind of adventure, so it was a surprise for us to discover that large numbers of small and medium-sized enterprises from Hong Kong were establishing factories in China. They did so, for the most part, by building on social connections (*guanxi* in Chinese) that existed or that could be asserted by reference to shared identities such as kinship or a common native home town (Smart and Smart, 1998). Rather than going through the centralized mechanisms co-ordinated by national and provincial ministries, they made deals at the local level, often in the rural townships of the Pearl River Delta in Guangdong province. These deals relied less on clear contracts and firm legal guarantees, and more on social relationships that either could be trusted, or were developed into trustworthy relations gradually through the very medium of business partnership itself (Christerson and Lever-Tracy, 1997, p. 576).

Given the complexities of going through the formal mechanisms of investment, and the lack of security offered even when apparently tightly-drafted contracts were finally accomplished, we and others argued that reliance on social connections could reduce transaction costs, get an enterprise up and running more quickly, and the profits would allow the participants subsequently to solve any problems that might arise (Lin, 1997; Hsing, 1997). In practice, this meant that Hong Kong investors regularly went beyond what was officially permitted by the regulations, or even by the national constitution, although rules were sometimes subsequently altered to legitimize the ways in which investors had been 'pushing the envelope' (A. Smart, 1998). The argument, then, is that Hong Kong entrepreneurs have generally used a strategy of relying on social connections more than legal and contractual guarantees. Furthermore, this strategy is consistent with a tendency identified for Chinese businesses in other contexts, and not just where legal property rights are seriously underspecified and uncertain (King, 1994; Wong, 1991; Yeung, 1994, p. 1940). Reliance on these kinds of relationship is seen as being important enough to warrant discussion of a distinctive variety of economic organization found among ethnic Chinese and sometimes known as *guanxi* capitalism (Tu, 1994, p. 7), or more formally as a reliance on network forms of governance. Outside China, the utilization of *guanxi* has been more commonly seen in a context of the desirability of maintaining flexibility and being rapidly able to respond to changes in market demand. However, it is clear that reliance on law or networks is not an either/or kind of situation. Networks can still be important where legal protection is reasonably unambiguous, and legal protection can be pursued when social relationships are the main source of reliable interaction. In certain cases, the availability of a reliable rule of law may facilitate the development of *guanxi* rather than inhibit it.

The construction of *guanxi* networks is accomplished by discovering and asserting a basis for inclusion of counterparts in an 'us', sharing some form of identity such as kin, classmates, or coming from the same region. Once established, *guanxi* links are maintained and reinforced through a continuing sequences of reciprocal exchanges of gifts and favours (Yang, 1994; Yan, 1996b; Kipnis, 1997). A variety of authors, including ourselves, have argued that the cultivation of social connections has played an important part in the rapid expansion of China's economy and in particular its exports to the developed economies since its opening up to the world economy (see, for example, Hsing, 1998; Weidenbaum and Hughes, 1996). Recently, however, the emphasis on *guanxi* has been subject to some important empirical and theoretical criticisms. We shall consider two of these studies at some length, because they allow us to place the use of *guanxi* connections in an appropriate context, and serve to demonstrate the importance of seeing such social interactions as being situated accomplishments, subject to failure and a variety of negative possibilities.

Eng and Lin (1996) used a large dataset of information from 9325 industrial firms in China with foreign investment to test hypotheses about whether overseas-Chinese-invested firms (with presumably better social connections) had better profit rates than firms with investment from other sources.[4] They found that overseas-Chinese-invested firms did not outperform other firms, and 'their overall profitability may even be poorer' (p. 1134). Based on these results plus interviews they concluded that knowledge of the Chinese language and pre-existing social ties did not necessarily generate a competitive advantage. The absence of pre-existing ties did not prevent non-Chinese foreign investors from dealing effectively with the state apparatus through the cultivation of networks. Their results give strong indications that reliance on connections can easily fail to achieve the desired results. Can we conclude from them that the cultivation of *guanxi* is an ineffective strategy? Clearly not. The foreign-invested firms run by non-Chinese often have financial and technological advantages that make the development of personal ties with them very advantageous for Chinese officials and organizations. There is substantial anecdotal evidence that Western and Japanese managers have learnt to mobilize the social networks of local and Hong Kong managers to engage in the gift economy of cultivating *guanxi*. Furthermore, our argument is that reliance on social connections is a potentially profitable, but high-risk, strategy. Lower average profitability does not disprove this claim, since those who succeed may have much greater profitability, while those who slip and fail may have much greater losses.

Douglas Guthrie (1998) has argued that rather than increasing with economic reforms since 1978, as Mayfair Yang (1994) claimed, the significance of *guanxi* has in fact declined during China's economic transition. His argument is restricted to the urban industrial economy, which is still dominated by state-owned enterprises, and thus is not strictly comparable to the growing factory towns where we conducted our research, and where the majority of Hong Kong investment has been concentrated. Based on his interviews in Shanghai in 1995, he suggests that although *guanxi* connections are still important in doing business, *guanxi* practices (*guanxi xue* – literally the study of *guanxi*) had diminished in importance. The distinction between the two for Guthrie is that '*guanxi* is the set of relationships, while *guanxi xue* is the practice and technique of using and manipulating these relationships for specific ends' (Guthrie, 1998, p. 262). His interviewees repeatedly assert that relationships are important in any market economy, as they still are in urban China, but that the use of connections to get around procedures is increasingly rare. While the uncertainty of the first years of reform may have created an appearance of a trend towards greater reliance on connections, Guthrie finds that the Chinese government's efforts to construct a 'rational-legal system that will govern the decisions and practices of economic actors' (ibid., p. 281) has been influential if not complete, and this is particularly true for large-scale organizations that are more closely monitored by the administration. In support of this, Li (1998) argues that a new emphasis on the rule of law has emerged recently in Guangdong province, despite its previous fame for 'flexibility'. Their argument is important and reflects widespread sentiments within China. However, we are sceptical about some of the dualisms implicit in Guthrie's argument: between instrumental and expressive (friendship) ties, and between the market efficiency in 'rational-legal' procedures versus inefficiency in *guanxi* practices. Distinctions between 'good' and 'bad' versions of *guanxi* are far from new developments, and are often tied to comparisons between what we do (supportive relationships) and what others do (bribing and cheating the system). Everyone agrees that corruption is bad; the question revolves around what should be considered corrupt.

In recent books on *guanxi* and the gift economy, Kipnis (1997) and Yan (1996b) suggest that urban *guanxi* in China is more instrumentally orientated than it is in the villages, and that it can shade into loosely-disguised bribery, as it does frequently in interactions between Chinese and Western businesses. Making a sharp separation between instrumental and expressive dimensions of relationships, as they and Guthrie do, misses an important aspect of the nature of *guanxi* as an idiom of interaction. The apparent conflict between the instrumental and the affective valuation of a relationship is overcome through *guanxi* as an idiom that 'acknowledges the legitimacy both of seeking the accomplishment of instrumental aims through friends and of building relationships through support and exchange', as long as the instrumental use remains subordinated to the cultivation of the relationship (A. Smart, 1993, p. 404). It may be that it is not *guanxi* as an idiom or a form of relationship/interaction that changes so much as the context: in the largely closed community setting of China's villages, short-term manipulation of the idiom of *guanxi* is less likely to be effective and more likely to have repercussions than in urban contexts where relationships can be neglected or discarded with greater impunity. Similarly, the changes that Guthrie documents as a decline in the significance of *guanxi* may more accurately represent more effective controls on blatantly manipulative forms of *guanxi* practice related to cadre power. Guthrie's study demonstrates that in the urban industrial economy, *guanxi* practices that allow actors to get around the law and grossly manipulate institutional procedures are now more likely to result in reprobation and failure, but this does not mean that *guanxi* is certain to fade away as China's economy converges with the West. After all, *guanxi* is far from insignificant in Hong Kong and Taiwan; it has simply been domesticated in such a way as to be more or less limited by the rule of law and concern for economic efficiency. If we do not assume a definition of *guanxi* as being negative and detrimental, then a decline in the 'bad' forms of *guanxi* practice need not imply a decline in the significance of *guanxi*.

Guthrie (1998, p. 274) suggests that one main reason for the decline in importance of *guanxi* practice is that 'the competitive forces of the emerging market economy are driving economic and political actors to focus on quality and service instead of the norms of *guanxi* practice for economic decision-making in the reform era'. The assumption here that the elaboration of 'rational-legal' institutions within economic organizations will ensure greater economic efficiency is rather surprising in an era where bureaucratic procedures have been under attack as inflexible and insufficiently responsive in China, in the former Communist economies (Pickles and Smith, 1998b), and in the advanced capitalist economies. The emergence of regimes of flexible accumulation and network forms of governance (Yeung, 1998b) seems to suggest that a properly disciplined version of *guanxi* may have a great deal to offer towards economic efficiency (A. Smart, 1998), if it is carried out effectively. Our argument here is that while strategies of reliance on personal relationships may not always succeed, neither are negative outcomes certain.

In relationships that cross boundaries separating political economies as distinct as those of China and Hong Kong, the use of gift exchange to build relationships that can help to circumvent red tape and bureaucratic delays and obstacles can easily become perceived and sanctioned as bribery. Jin and Haynes (1997) suggest that China's reforms have operated at the edge of order and chaos, a potentially disastrous situation that has nevertheless managed to produce remarkable results. While the way things are done within your own society or context can be seen as reasonably orderly and predictable, the practices across a boundary of radical disjuncture seem chaotic and uncontrollable. Also, the resources that each agent brings to the deal are differentially evaluated in the distinct social and economic systems.

Boundaries have always generated risk and potential profit simultaneously, and those who can manage the risk effectively have been able to profit handsomely from their brokerage or arbitrage across those borders. When chaotic conditions are managed skilfully, they can be turned from threat to risky opportunity (A. Smart, 1998). But getting things done across borders requires *tact*, and this is certainly the case in China. Tact, of course, is embedded in expectations about interactional proprieties and etiquette, which must be accomplished, and not just submitted to as cultural determinism would suggest (A. Smart, 1993). When tact and agreement are absent or fail, brokerage across borders can have less positive outcomes (Smart and Smart, 1993), including failed endeavours; pariah status for the brokers; corrupt and illegal activities; and reliance on coercion, as in colonialism. Hong Kong entrepreneurs who pioneered foreign investment in China did not always succeed, but they had a variety of symbolic, social and cultural resources that made operating across boundaries somewhat less risky, and helped to legitimate the conduct of capitalist practices within a socialist polity. Hong Kong and Macao residents, for example, were not 'foreigners' but *tong bao* – compatriots – and could thus contribute to national modernization in a way that was less threatening than assistance from capitalists who were also non-Chinese, but not part of an imagined cultural/racial '*us*' (Smart and Smart, 1998).

Common understanding or interactional practices that allow those on opposite sides of a border to live with distinct interpretations of the situation can smooth out rough edges, and may thus reduce transaction costs, but it can also empower agents to manipulate the local system in detrimental ways. One of us has argued elsewhere (A. Smart, 1993) that the social boundary (as opposed to the formal legal definition) between a gift and a bribe in the Chinese context is related to whether or not the instrumental motivation for an exchange is seen as being more important than the relationship in itself. To put it the other way, someone is offering a bribe rather than a gift if the development of the relationship is being subordinated to the practical goal, so that it is a means rather than an end.[5] The reason why this is relevant here is that the perception of a social exchange as a bribe is partially related to effective performance, the enactment of the expectations of *guanxi* and interpersonal relationships. The vocabulary and practices of *guanxi* can be powerful resources for reducing the transaction costs and potential risks of capitalist investment in China. But the vocabulary and practices of gifts and *guanxi*:

> cannot simply be exploited or manipulated in a short-term maximization of the investor's self-interest. The effectiveness of the idiom and the relationships built on it are dependent on adherence to the forms and social etiquette, as well as on the expectation that the building of the relationship will be treated as the primary objective, not just an incidental expense or inconvenience (A. Smart, 1993, p. 404).

Despite the overall situation of successes involved in the strategy of using trustworthy relationships as a substitute for costly and uncertain legal guarantees, it is clearly also a risky proposition, and effective performance can mean the difference between profits and disaster, as the following case should indicate. A Hong Kong entrepreneur who invested in a factory in Shenzhen where eighty-seven people were burnt to death in 1993 was sentenced to a two-year jail sentence for breaching fire regulations. The factory's mainland manager received six years, and two firemen charged with receiving bribes from them were sentenced to seventeen years and ten years (*South China Morning Post*, 14 December 1994, p. 1). The fire did not happen because there were no fire regulations, but because the negotiation of arrangements with local counterparts is much more important than are formal rules (see also R. Levy, 1995). The same situation applies in the case of labour and environmental protection regulations: the weaknesses are not in the legislation, but in the enforcement (or lack thereof), leading to considerable exploitation and environmental damage (Neller and Lam, 1994). One

Hong Kong informant involved with investment in China did not feel that the case would lead to any significant changes in management practices. This informant thought that the imprisoned investor's mistake had been to return to China after the disaster. The informant suggested that a safer strategy would have been to send a manager to negotiate compensation, and only return after an agreement had been reached. Another informant agreed with this assessment, and pointed out that the greatest protection in China was not obtained by following the rules, but through good contacts. When asked why this one investor had found himself in trouble (although rather minimal trouble in comparison with his mainland counterparts), the informant suggested that perhaps he did not have good enough links, but also was unlucky enough to have had the fire at a time when there had been a series of well-publicized disasters and a scapegoat was necessary. He noted that comments in the press were already indicating that the investor had health problems, and speculated that once attention had moved elsewhere, an early compassionate release would be likely.

We have selected this example from a variety of others that could have presented the development and mobilization of trustworthy relations in a more positive light – for example, as heightening efficient economic organization in the context of underspecified property rights, or as promoting the construction of a civil society as not completely penetrated by state power. This choice was made because we are concerned about the tendency to romanticize trust. Trust is a tool, something that certainly can promote co-operation, but before we can assess it, we need to know what kind of co-operation is being promoted. As Gambetta (1988) points out, there are many forms of co-operation based on trust that we would prefer to do without, such as that involved in organized crime or in collusion between government officials and lobbyists. After all, trust is intimately involved in the kind of rent-seeking that economists have analyzed as 'directly unproductive activity'. Thus we would be inclined to disagree with the assumption in Fukuyama's (1995) thesis that can be boiled down to 'the more trust, the better'. It really depends on what kind of trust, how it is distributed, and what it is being used to accomplish.

The more general point for this chapter, of course, is that since the reliance on *guanxi* and trust rather than on law and contracts is a potentially risky strategy, it needs to be done with a great deal of sophistication and sensitivity, or it can easily backfire in disastrous ways. As this example suggests, the disaster can be both for the entrepreneur and for society as a whole. If, as Guthrie (1998) and Li (1998) suggest, the rule of law is increasingly being applied in a predictable rather than a flexible manner, the risks of using social connections to circumvent the rules may become ever more risky and lead to greater failures among small-scale entrepreneurs whose willingness to rely on social protection has been an important part of their competitive advantage.

## ALL IS NOT WELL WITHIN THE FAMILY

One of the strengths of Chinese business systems has been seen as the ability of family firms to tap into the solidarity and co-operative capacity of kin. For example, Weidenbaum and Hughes (1996, p. 54) note the common beliefs that 'the only people you can trust are family members. An incompetent relative in the family business is considered to be more reliable than a competent stranger'. The centralized patriarchal authority 'avoids many of the "agency" problems that Western businesses must overcome in ensuring that managers promote the interests of the owners rather than themselves' (Weidenbaum and Hughes, 1996, p. 54). Greenhalgh (1994, p. 750) convincingly criticizes scholars of the Chinese family firm for adopting a romantic perspective in which political economy stops at the boundary of the family, so that 'within the family, relationships remain traditional, Western influences are kept at bay, and people are diligent, selfless, and good to one another'. Her analysis sees the family firm instead as suffering deep conflicts, and based on a patriarchal form of accumulation – inequalities and the ability of the family/firm head to control material and discursive resources. Yet, while Greenhalgh delineates some of the costs of this form of family business, particularly for women, she does not touch on the possibility that such internal conflict might lead to inefficiencies and business failures. In what follows, we analyze a case where such tensions have endangered both the family and the firm, although business collapse has not yet been the outcome. If the management of the fused family and firm, or family *as* firm, is crucial to the competitive advantage of small and medium Chinese firms, and if trust and co-operation are not automatically forthcoming, then familial mismanagement is likely to undermine the effectiveness of an enterprise. The extension of Hong Kong production systems into China seems to have exacerbated some of these tensions, and might be intensified even more in cases of cross-border investment where easy daily or weekly movement back and forth is not possible.

The steady injection of Hong Kong investment into China since 1978, especially in the province of Guangdong, has created millions of jobs in

China, a proportion of which directly benefit Hong Kong workers who are hired to work as managers, technicians, foremen, accountants and other highly skilled positions in Hong Kong factories throughout the south-eastern parts of the Pearl River Delta. A significant number of Hong Kong investors, especially among the smaller investors, station themselves nearly permanently in China, overseeing every aspect of the production and management of the enterprise in China, making regular trips to Hong Kong for marketing, purchasing and banking purposes. This parallel relocation of residence from Hong Kong to China creates fewer problems for single investors or workers, than it does for married ones.

The single biggest problem confronting Hong Kong investors/workers in their decision regarding residence relocation is the issue of their children's education. The curriculum, school facilities and qualifications of teachers in China are regarded as inferior to those provided by Hong Kong public and private schools. This poor impression of the school system in China is shared by both Hong Kong Chinese and mainland Chinese. There is not a single Hong Kong resident we spoke to in our more than ten years of research who supported the idea of having his/ her child(ren) educated in China. Yet, leaving children in Hong Kong raises problems of the adequacy of supervision, particularly for those smaller family firms where both husband and wife are actively involved.

The most common solution to this problem is the formation of 'twin households' or 'split households'. In the sociological literature, this kind of household arrangement is sometimes called 'mutilated households' – we avoid using this label because it carries the assumption that the household structure is 'incomplete', 'pathological', 'sick', or 'unhealthy'. The more neutral label of 'twin' household serves to emphasize the interconnections between the two household segments. Typically, it is the husband who travels frequently between China and Hong Kong to bridge his business and familial obligations/duties while his the wife and children remain living in Hong Kong. It is common for the husband and wife to develop a new division of labour on relocating their production to China. The husband spends most of his time in China overseeing the production and on-site management of the business, while the wife maintains an active office in Hong Kong to handle buyers' orders, banking needs, production contracts, and local and cross-border transportation arrangements for the transport of raw materials and finished goods, as well as the management of the household with or without the aid of hired help. Everything up to this point is consistent with a selfless attitude towards the maximization of the collective/familial interest by all concerned. This indeed appears to be so on the surface until one probes deeper into the many instances of disagreement and tension within the household that arise from and affect individual and household economic decisions.

In one case, the wife fought for many years against the husband's plan to set up production in China. This created a great deal of tension in their marital relationship, particularly since the workshop in Hong Kong was under ever-increasing competitive pressure because of the higher costs of rent and labour in Hong Kong. They have five children, and concern about their education was the main reason for the wife's reluctance to relocate into China, a sentiment that was initially shared by the husband but which dimmed as the children grew up and left school. None of the children did well in school; one daughter ran away from home at the age of 15 and left school after completing the equivalent of grade 7. Tension continued to mount within the household under the strain of economic disagreement between husband and wife concerning the direction and location of their business investment and the ongoing rebellion and misconduct of the runaway daughter. She forged her mother's cheques to support the purchase of expensive accessories and to pay for entertainment expenses with her friends. The husband resented his wife's resistance to his business expansion plan. The wife was caught in a no-win situation in which she would not allow her husband to be a 'bachelor' in China running his business without the family,[6] yet at the same time she could not find a solution for the care of the two youngest children who were still in school should she accompany her husband in his investment to China. Violent verbal disputes broke out between the couple on a regular basis, which escalated into near-violence with knives and blunt objects on more than one occasion. The wife took to staying out late playing mahjong, and her functional role in the family business became a routine rather than a motivating force behind hard work and a source of satisfaction. Eventually the wife agreed to her husband's investment plan only after the husband's widowed mother and several of his sisters had volunteered to take in their school-age children (aged 15 and 7 in 1996) so that they could continue their education in Hong Kong while the parents and older siblings set up a factory and household in China.

Of the five children in this family, two are of school age and live with paternal relatives in Hong Kong, seeing their parents either in Hong Kong or in China on weekends and holidays. The eldest daughter is mildly mentally retarded: she helps out at the family factory in China doing unskilled work and is often the cause of embarrassment and irritation to her parents and siblings because of her underdeveloped social skills. She tends to be overly 'friendly' with the workers and hired help, and now she is in her early twenties she is showing a keen interest in the opposite sex. This new sexual awakening is a major concern to her parents, whose ultimate fear is that some local man or migrant worker will 'sweet talk' her into marriage in order to get his hands on the family wealth. The eldest son finished high school with difficulty and has been working as an apprentice in a tool-and-die shop in Hong Kong for a few years. He shares a rented flat with friends. His boss is a family friend. The parents suggest that it is always difficult to train one's children; that they learn better under non-family supervision and instruction. They hope the son will eventually return to the family business, but it is unclear what role he might assume. The parents would like him to take on a management role, but they are painfully aware that he does not have the personality or strategic thinking to be a successful entrepreneur. The daughter who dropped out of junior high school was invited to become an active participant in the family business when it became clear that she was determined to keep herself out of school at the age of 15. The parents were bitterly disappointed with her academic failure and her disobedience. They consider her participation in the family business as a last resort to create an economic niche for a daughter who has little education and no particular skills. They also think of it as an effective measure to control her tendency to run away from home. She later brought her boyfriend, also a school dropout, into the family business.

By the time this daughter was 16, she and her boyfriend were living together like husband and wife in an apartment with her parents and other siblings in China. After working in the family business for more than two years, the young couple still do not have a definite rank or position in the family business. The workers know them as 'the boss's daughter' and 'the boss's daughter's boyfriend'. They do not receive a fixed salary or wage rate – they are paid in 'pocket money' and subsistence support. From the parents' perspective, this arrangement is more than generous on their part, given that the young couple are highly unreliable and lazy in their work habits. They commonly sleep in until noon , work only when they please, and take off for Hong Kong whenever they like without advance notice and with little certainty about when they will return to work in China. From the young couple's perspective, life in China is extremely dull and boring. They have very little in common with the Chinese workers, and they can hardly do the kind of things they enjoy with the girl's parents or her siblings. The most readily accessible entertainment of the kind they can relate to are Hong

Kong television programmes and they do spend a great deal of time watching television whenever they are not working.

In public, the family described above appears always as a unified social unit. Beneath a veneer of happiness and prosperity is an intense case of marital and intergenerational tension and conflict that are present in all families to varying degrees. For a family business, such disharmony among the family members can have direct and long-term impacts on the direction and viability of the family enterprise. On a number of occasions, tensions among family members have influenced the management of the business. After an expansion of the labour force, the number of workers has more recently been reduced because of a variety of problems. While the enterprise is still operating, it appears to be on a downward spiral, and it is only the fusion of firm and household that seems to keep things afloat: household maintenance costs are much lower in China than in Hong Kong.

## CONCLUSION

The emphasis on the remarkable business successes achieved by Chinese entrepreneurs, and of the economies where they are concentrated, is understandable. Academics who offer clues to competitive advantages based on highlighting success stories will probably always receive more attention than those who concentrate on the mundane reality of failures, conflicts and muddling through. But we have suggested in this chapter that there needs to be more careful analysis of these failures and the mechanisms and skilled performance involved in securing the benefits of potentially useful strategies. Sensible, even brilliant, strategies by themselves do not guarantee success, because the tactical practices of implementing these strategies require great skill. The current Asian financial crisis also reminds us how quickly success can be transformed into disaster. By focusing only on success, we become unprepared for responding to failure, or even to start to make sense of it. Clearly, changing conditions and 'luck' will have an influence on which enterprises survive or even thrive in the much harsher current business climate, but the degree of skill with which common strategies are implemented and monitored will also serve to separate out successful firms from those which fail.

At a higher level of analysis, the readiness with which enterprises fail or become established is starting to be seen as crucial to the extent of disruption caused by the current crises, and the rapidity with which economies recover from their devastation. Reluctance to allow Japanese banks to fail is widely seen as contributing to the prolongation of difficulties in the financial sector. The history of Hong Kong and Taiwan's economic development since the Second World War has demonstrated repeatedly how failure has led eventually to stronger and more competitive industries, while protection in other contexts generally produces weak firms that cannot compete without continued support. While the literature on flexibility clearly emphasizes success, failure is a crucial aspect of economic dynamism based on rapid response to market signals. Creative destruction may unfortunately be destructive, but its contribution to creativity is also undeniable. Grabher and Stark (1998) argue that situations where firms all adopt the most efficient forms and strategies to exploit current circumstances may become ill-suited to respond to changes in circumstances, because diversity has been lost. Instead, they suggest that when some developmental paths 'produce ineffective solutions and sup-optimal outcomes' this is not 'an indication of evolutionary failure but a precondition for evolutionary selection: no variety, no evolution. Hence, the evolutionary process necessarily entails development through failure' (p. 57).[7]

To emphasize the importance of failure to political economies is not to suggest that the more failure there is, the better. Rather, it is to recognize that fear of failure is a crucial motivator in a capitalist economy, and one that deserves more scholarly analysis. The methodology of most research on firms has made it much harder to obtain solid information on failure, and this chapter has attempted to take some steps towards identifying the significance of failure for both economies and entrepreneurs. Gordon Redding (1990) has paid considerable attention to the weaknesses as well as the strengths of the distinctive features of overseas Chinese business organization. However, he seems to see both strengths and weaknesses as being more or less automatic outcomes of the features, and it is the context that determines whether the feature is for that purpose a strength or a weakness. Our approach is different in asserting that even strengths can be squandered and dissipated through incompetence, and that weaknesses may not necessarily appear if the pitfalls are carefully negotiated and challenges properly managed. Cultural features are resources that can be mobilized, not invariant outcomes.

We have also suggested that the dimension of skilled practical accomplishment is of particularly great significance for Chinese businesses because many of the strategies that have allowed them their successes have involved high levels of risk. Reliance on social connections more than on legal guarantees in investing across the border in China, for example, can sidestep troublesome red tape and get things done quickly, cheaply and expeditiously, but doing so also exposes the investor to potential jeopardy. Avoiding the dangers involved in practicing the art of *guanxi* requires very careful monitoring of the environment, and skilful management of interpersonal relationships. As Guthrie (1998) and Li (1998) indicate, the dangers of reliance on *guanxi* to sidestep rules are currently increasing in China, and the recent sentencing of Beijing's former mayor to sixteen years in prison for corruption appears to signal the need for caution at all levels of the political hierarchy. Similarly, while for many analysts family enterprises draw on the solidarity and commitment of the family/household, we have argued that this ignores the internal dynamics of the household. In reality, solidarity and co-operation cannot be taken for granted, but are practical accomplishments, and these accomplishments are always at risk from changes in the future. Divisions and resentment within families and households are just as characteristic, as are co-operation and commitment. Failures, then, cannot be ignored without misinterpreting the successes, because the courting of an increased risk of failure is an integral part of the success.

## Notes

1. The same kind of comment can be made about mainstream economic analysis, where assumptions such as the no-cost enforcement of contracts serve the same kind of fictitious (and misleading) role as do non-existent frictionless planes in physics.
2. Paul Krugman (1994) has argued that economic miracles do not and cannot exist, and that East Asia represents a rather mundane example of the mobilization of underutilized factors of production, particularly labour and capital, but without substantial increases in total factor productivity, so that the limits to rapid growth are predictably being reached in all the miracle economies, with Japan being the first illustration.
3. The possibility of failure is increasingly a reality in China, even for state-owned enterprises, but particularly for private, individual and collective ones. As yet, we know even less about failure in China than we do for Chinese entrepreneurs outside China.
4. There are, of course, a variety of problems with the use of official statistics in China. Most significant for the issue at hand is the definition of a 'foreign-invested firm'. Generally, domestic enterprises that engage in export-processing contracts with foreign firms do not fit into this category. However, this is one of the most common forms of co-operation with small and medium sized Hong Kong enterprises, and the domestic company is sometimes a 'shell' firm disguising an operation that is completely managed by the Hong Kong investors. This may be one reason why Eng and Lin (1996, p. 1128)

did not find any evidence of what we earlier described as a 'guerrilla strategy' by Hong Kong firms to set up several small investments rather than
one larger entity, in order to reduce risk (Smart and Smart, 1991). Another
factor is that our account concerned the early 'pioneer' phase of Hong
Kong investment, when entrepreneurs were 'testing the water' and the regulatory climate was much less certain than it was by the early 1990s.

5.  Rubert Hodder (1996, pp. 64–9) has criticized this approach to *guanxi* as a
'cultural determinist' argument in which A. Smart (1993) treats trust as a
'moral absolute' and is reluctant to 'ascribe to others the deliberate and
manipulative use of relationships'. This seems to be a misreading of the
argument, and another instance of the instrumental/expressive dualism
examined above in reference to Guthrie's article. The point is not that partners in a *guanxi* relationship never use the relationship for instrumental
ends, but rather that if it becomes apparent that the relationship is being
subordinated to an immediate goal rather than the favour or service being
part of the cultivation of a long-term relationship, the nature of the interaction changes. It is not that trust is a moral absolute (although we do believe
that it is an influential value in Chinese societies), but that there are interactional expectations in *guanxi* as an idiom of interaction. If people explicitly
or implicitly treat others as negotiating partners or as individuals who can
be bribed to advantage, then different kinds of exchange relationships will
be perceived. Hodder (1996, p. 69) states that the 'main question which
Smart has failed to address is whether or not reciprocity works for or cor-
rupts the prosecution of trade'. The answer is that 'it depends'. *Guanxi* is a
mechanism, a way of interacting or getting things done, and its outcomes
are influenced by context, and by the intentions of those who utilize the
interactional possibilities that it affords. Far from being an argument based
on cultural determinism and the attribution of moral absolutism, the avoidance of the dualistic distinction between instrumental and expressive goals
in A. Smart's (1993) treatment of *guanxi* involves moral and methodological agnosticism.

6.  In recent years, many marriage break-ups in Hong Kong have been attributed to affairs and permanent relationships that Hong Kong male workers
have begun with young women in China. The increasingly common phenomenon of Hong Kong married men keeping mistresses in China has
come to the attention of law-makers and social service workers in both
Hong Kong and China. For details, see Lang and Smart (n.d.) and *The
China Times Magazine* (in Chinese) January 1995, no. 161–2, pp. 71–5.

7.  A more elaborate examination of evolutionary and neo-Schumpeterian
approaches to political economy would provide a stronger theoretical
foundation for our argument about the importance of failure and the high-
risk strategies characteristic of Chinese entrepreneurs. Because of limited
space, we have taken the alternative path of trying to draw out the meaning
of failure for Chinese entrepreneurs themselves, and looked at the contribution of performance and skills in reducing the chances of failure when
adopting high-risk strategies.

# Part 3
# Implications

# 12 Epilogue
## Henry Wai-chung Yeung and Kris Olds

Through its interdisciplinary contributions, this book, we hope, has advanced our understanding of the nature and processes of Chinese business firms that are venturing increasingly into the global economy. In particular, the book has shed theoretical light not only on the nature and social organization of Chinese family businesses, but also on the dynamic and institutional aspects of their globalization processes. We think these theoretical insights are important because so much of the previous research into Chinese business has focused too narrowly on their home-country operations. We hope future studies into the cross-border operations of Chinese business firms will apply and extend some of these theoretical insights. Though we do not intend to argue for an ethnocentric model to understand the globalization of Chinese business firms, we do advise future studies of these ethnic firms to take into account the peculiar historical and geographical contexts in which their globalization takes place. In addition, this book has brought together some very useful empirical studies of how globalizing Chinese business firms are managing their operations across borders. The chapters in Part 2 have identified various problems and strategies of Chinese business firms in their globalization drive. We hope their findings offer some important lessons for Chinese business entrepreneurs and managers, academic researchers and policy-makers in different institutions.

Although these empirical examples cover both North America and Asia, none of them has addressed explicitly how Chinese business firms manage their European operations. The globalization of Chinese business firms is therefore clearly an unfinished business, in two ways. In a material sense, few Chinese business firms are really *global* in their cross-border operations, despite the fact that some ethnic Chinese entrepreneurs have built truly global networks of social relationships. There is still much more scope for the globalization of these ethnic firms in the future. In a discursive sense, much has been said about the importance and dominance of the 'overseas Chinese' in East and Southeast Asia. However, little detailed *empirical research* has been done on the 'global reach' of these ethnic Chinese and their business firms. In ending this book with a short epilogue, we aim to propose some ideas for future research on the globalization of Chinese business firms. These ideas also originate from the inherent weaknesses of this collection.

First, future studies need to examine the *impact* of Chinese business firms on host countries (and cities) *outside* East and Southeast Asia. When these ethnic-based firms venture into Western countries (and cities), it would be useful to find out: (i) how they seek (and sometimes manage) to transfer their competitive advantage based on largely monopolistic positions in their home countries; (ii) how they seek (and sometimes manage) to adapt their managerial practices and organizational structures to compete successfully in the host countries (and cities); and (iii) how their business practices transform the *status quo* of the business and political community in the host countries (and cities). Some recent studies have indicated that a number of Chinese business firms have succeeded in transferring their competitive advantage embedded in business networks and personal relationships (see Chapter 9 in this volume; Olds, 1998). How far does this transplanting process succeed in facilitating the globalization of Chinese business firms? Another dimension of this type of impact study might examine the extent to which Chinese business firms lose their distinctiveness in the globalization process. The emphasis on family networks and informal personal relationships in Chinese business is not much different from the business practices of early family firms in Britain and America (see Chandler, 1990), except that these British and American family firms transformed themselves into professionally-managed corporations through globalization.

Second, if the *family* remains central to our understanding Chinese business firms in their global context, we need to analyze its nature and examine how the family resolves challenges and contradictions inherent in the globalization process. One of the critical issues is succession in family business (see Aronoff and Ward, 1995; Greenhalgh, 1994; Handler, 1994). To what extent are Chinese business firms successful in accomplishing globalization on the one hand, and succession of the family firm on the other? This question requires answers that address the practices of employing family members, the retention of non-family members, changing gender roles and relations, family conflict, the delegation of authority and responsibility, and the procedures for evaluating family employees (see Hoy and Verser, 1994).

Third, the *role of entrepreneurship* continues to be an important focus of research into the globalization of Chinese business firms. Its importance is underscored by the perceived need to sustain globalization through continuous innovation and entrepreneurial activities. Entrepreneurship is important to any TNC, irrespective of its country of origin. The research question remains how best to encourage entrepreneurship and how to create an 'entrepreneurial' transnational corporation in which every employee is an 'entrepreneur' capable of innovation, risk-taking and adaptation. To a certain extent, the emergence of global product mandates in certain TNCs has promoted intra-TNC entrepreneurship (see Roth and Morrison, 1992; Birkinshaw, 1996).

Fourth, very little research has been conducted on the development of *'situated support'* (Smart, 1995) for Chinese business firms in non-Asian countries. It is clear from recent research in Vancouver (Mitchell, 1993a, 1995; Olds, 1998) that the development of a plethora of institutions focused around the discourse of the 'Pacific Rim' have worked hard to facilitate ethnic Chinese investment flows into the city (and the incorporation of the city into powerful personalistic networks). However, it is unclear what the actual impact of this situated support is, how significant the support is to different types of overseas Chinese investors, and how conflict over the nature of this support (and a city's development path) can be resolved in a democratic and participative fashion. Case studies in specific places (for example, Pacific-Rim cities such as Vancouver or Sydney), or on specific sectors (for example, property or telecommunications) would enable complementary angles to be pursued on this topic. This research topic should also be linked to deepening our understanding of the relationship between immigration, economic development and urban change.

Fifth, much more research needs to be conducted on the nature of the relationships between *Western financial institutions* and *ethnic Chinese entrepreneurs*. It is clear that Western financial institutions are targeting leading Chinese entrepreneurs and attempting to form long-term relationships of mutual benefit/exploitation. The underexamined relationship between the Canadian Imperial Bank of Commerce and Li Ka-shing is a case in point, as is the strategy of HSBC Holdings on this matter. In relation to this topic, which links Chinese business firms and the international financial community, we need more research into how the ongoing Asian economic crisis is (re)shaping the dynamic transformations of 'Chinese' business networks and, for that matter, the practices associated with Chinese capitalism. The Asian crisis, for example, led to the reworking of state–business relations in Indonesia in 1998, leading some analysts to note that 'Indonesia's Chinese conglomerates . . . may soon be relegated to becoming bit players in the new economic landscape' (*Business Times*, 5 October 1998, p. 1). The ongoing severing of networks between the state and Chinese business has occurred in the context of economic crisis, the IMF's stringent bail-out and reform packages, and the linked demise of the Suharto regime. In effect, this externally-driven multilateral agent has challenged significantly the constituency of pre-existing Chinese business networks in Indonesia. However, in other contexts, such researchers as Hamilton (1998) note that some countries may in fact be less crisis-affected because of the dominance of their economies by flexible production systems co-ordinated by ethnic Chinese manufacturers and distributors. Others have noted how economic globalization has presented tremendous opportunities to Chinese business in Southeast Asia (Yeung, 1999e). In short, what effect is the crisis having on Chinese business networks and specific Chinese-controlled firms?

Last but not least, we need to know more about how *representations* of the effectiveness of Chinese business networks and *guanxi* have an impact on the *actual operation* of these networks. How do global financial analysts and writers for the global business media form their opinions, and what are the material and discursive impacts of these opinions on the financial resources available to Chinese entrepreneurs? How do Chinese firms develop and implement strategies to persuade the people creating these representations that networks and reputation are effective in facilitating long-term economic growth?

Taken together, we know that Chinese business firms are beginning to globalize their operations. We have observed drastic changes in the management practices and organizational structures of Western firms during their globalization drive. We need much more time and research effort to explore the challenges of globalization to Chinese business firms and the problems they encounter in their globalization process. We also need to know how best these Chinese business firms can manage the globalization process and whether they remain as a distinctive species of capitalist institutions. Research efforts need to explore the challenges of globalization to Chinese business firms and their role in facilitating (both directly and indirectly) the emergence of a tangled web of sociocultural and economic networks which are unevenly incorporating the globe.

The globalization of Chinese business firms appeared unthinkable in the 1970s. As we approach the new millennium, however, we appear to be witnessing the emergence of new and much larger groups of Chinese business firms globalizing to win a bigger share of the ever-competitive world economy. The key question is, of course, whether they will continue to exhibit the characteristics needed to withstand the volatilities associated with a globalizing political and economic context.

# Bibliography

Abegglen, J. C. (1994) *Sea Change: Pacific Asia as the New World Industrial Center* (New York: The Free Press).

Aldrich, H. and Zimmer, C. (1986) 'Entrepreneurship Through Social Networks', in D. Sexton and R. Smilor (eds), *The Art and Science of Entrepreneurs* (Cambridge, Mass.: Ballinger).

Amin, A. and Thrift, N. (1994) 'Living in the Global', in A. Amin and N. Thrift (eds), *Globalization, Institutions, and Regional Development in Europe* (Oxford: Oxford University Press).

Amsden, A. (1989) *Asia's Next Giant: South Korea and Late Industrialization* (New York: Oxford University Press).

Angel, D. P. and Engstrom, J. (1995) 'Manufacturing Systems and Technological Change: The U.S. Personal Computer Industry', *Economic Geography*, vol. 71, pp. 79–102.

Anonymous (1887) 'Chinese Partnerships: Liability of the Individual Members', *Journal of the China Branch of the Royal Asiatic Society*, New Series, vol. 22, p. 41.

Anxi Association (1994) *Singapore Ann Kway Association 70th Anniversary in Conjunction with the World Ann Kway Convention* (in Chinese) (Singapore: Singapore Ann Kway Association).

Appadurai, A. (1990) 'Disjuncture and Difference in the Global Cultural Economy', *Public Culture*, vol. 2, no. 2, pp. 1–24.

Appadurai, A. (1991) 'Global Ethnoscapes: Notes and Queries for a Transnational Anthropology', in R. Fox (ed.), *Recapturing Anthropology: Working in the Present* (Santa Fe, New Mexico: School of American Research Press).

Appelbaum, R. P. and Henderson, J. (eds) (1992) *States and Development in the Asian Pacific Rim* (Newbury Park, Calif.: Sage).

Aronoff, C. E. and Ward, J. L. (1995) 'Family-owned Businesses: A Thing of the Past or a Model for the Future?', *Family Business Review*, vol. 13, no. 2, pp. 121–30.

*Asia, Inc.*, various issues.

*Asian Intelligence* (1993) 1 December 1993, p. 400.

Asia Pulp and Paper (1998) *APP Corporate Profile* (Singapore: APP).

Bartlett, C. A. and Ghoshal, S. (1989) *Managing Across Borders: The Transnational Solution* (London: Century Business).

Bartlett, C. A. and Ghoshal, S. (1995) *Transnational Management: Text, Cases, and Readings in Cross-Border Management*, 2nd edn, (Chicago: Irwin).

Barton, C. (1983) 'Trust and Credit: Some Observations Regarding Business Strategies of Overseas Chinese Traders in South Vietnam', in L. Lim and P. Gosling (eds), *The Chinese in Southeast Asia* (Singapore: Maruzen Asia).

Baum, A. and Schofield, A. (1991) 'Property as a Global Asset', Working Papers in European Property, Centre for European Property Research, University of Reading, March.

Beamish, P. W. and Killing, J. P. (eds) (1997) *Cooperative Strategies: Asia-Pacific Perspectives* (San Francisco: New Lexington Press).

Beauregard. R., and Haila, A. (1997) 'The Unavoidable Incompleteness of the City', *American Behavioural Scientist*, vol. 41, no. 3, pp. 327–41.

Beaverstock, J. (1996) 'Subcontracting the Accountant! Professional Labour Markets, Migration, and Organizational Networks in the Global Accountancy Industry', *Environment and Planning A*, vol. 28, no. 2, pp. 303–24.

Beazley, M., Loftman, P. and Nevin, B. (1995) 'Community Resistance and Mega-project Development: An International Perspective', Paper presented to the British Sociological Association Annual Conference, Leicester, 10–13 April.

Ben, X. S. (1992) 'Bian Zhong Qu Sheng Bu Jin Ze Tui' (To win in a changing environment – the achievement of Taiwan's computer industry in the last ten years), *Management Magazine*, March, pp. 82–97.

Benton, G. (1997) *The Chinese in Europe* (London: Macmillan).

Berger, P. L. (1986) *The Capitalist Revolution* (New York: Basic Books).

Berle, A. A. (1954) *The Twentieth Century Capitalist Revolution* (New York: Harcourt Brace).

Berry, M. (1994) 'Japanese Property Development in Australia', *Progress in Planning*, vol. 41, no. 2, pp. 113–201.

Beyers, W. (1991) 'Trends in Producer Services in the USA: The Last Decade', in P. W. Daniels (ed.), *Services and Metropolitan Development* (London: Routledge).

Biers, D. (1995) 'Staying the Course: Mainland Upsets Don't Faze Overseas-Chinese Investors', *Asian Wall Street Journal*, 19 July.

Biggart, N. W. and Hamilton, G. G. (1992) 'On the Limits of a Firm-Based Theory to Explain Business Networks: The Western Bias of Neoclassical Economics', in N. Nohria and R. G. Eccles (eds), *Networks and Organisations: Structure, Form, and Action* (Boston, Mass.: Harvard Business School Press).

*Bird's-Eye View: Newsletter of National Association of Chinese American Banks* (1989–93) (Los Angeles: NACAB).

Birkinshaw, J. M. (1996) 'How Multinational Subsidiary Mandates Are Gained and Lost', *Journal of International Business Studies*, vol. 27, no. 3, pp. 467–95.

Björkman, I. and Kock, S. (1995) 'Social Relationships and Business Networks: The Case of Western Companies in China', *International Business Review*, vol. 4, no. 4, pp. 519–35.

Boddewyn, J. J. (1988) 'Political Aspects of MNE Theory', *Journal of International Business Studies*, vol. 19, no. 3, pp. 341–64.

Boden, D. (1994) *The Business of Talk: Organizations in Action* (Cambridge: Polity Press).

Boisot, M. (1986) 'Markets and Hierarchies in a Cultural Perspective', *Organisation Studies*, vol. 7, no. 2, pp. 135–58.

Bonacich, E., Ong, P. and Cheng, L. (eds) (1994) *The New Asian Immigration in Los Angeles and Global Restructuring* (Philadelphia: Temple University Press).

Bond, M. H. (ed.) (1986) *The Psychology of the Chinese People* (Hong Kong: Oxford University Press).

Bond, M. H. (1996) *The Handbook of Chinese Psychology* (Hong Kong: Oxford University Press).

Bourdieu, P. (1989) 'Social Space and Symbolic Power', *Sociological Theory*, vol. 7, no. 1, pp. 14–25.

Boyer, R. and Drache, D. (eds) (1996) *States Against Markets: The Limits of Globalization* (London: Routledge).

Brook, T. and Luong, Hy V. (eds) (1997) *Culture and Economy: The Shaping of Capitalism in Eastern Asia* (Ann Arbor, Mich.: University of Michigan Press).

Brown, R. A. (ed.) (1995) *Chinese Business Enterprise in Asia* (London: Routledge).

Brown, R. A. (1998) 'Overseas Chinese Investments in China – Patterns of Growth Diversification and Finance: The Case of Chareoen Pokphand', *The China Quarterly*, no. 155, pp. 610–36.

Buckley, P. J. (1991) 'The Frontiers of International Business Research', *Management International Review*, Special Issue; vol. 31, pp. 7–22.

Buckley, P. J. and Casson, M. (1976) *The Future of Multinational Enterprise* (London: Macmillan).

Buckley, P. J. and Casson, M. (1988) 'A Theory of Co-operation in International Business', in F. J. Contractor and P. Lorange (eds), *Cooperative Strategies in International Business* (Lexington, Mass.: Lexington Books), pp. 31–53.

Burnham J. (1941) *The Managerial Revolution* (New York: John Day).

Burt, R. S. (1992) 'The Social Structure of Competition', in N. Nohia and R. G. Eccles (eds), *Networks and Organisations: Structure, Form, and Action* (Boston, Mass.: Harvard Business School Press), pp. 57–91.

*Business Times, The* (1997) 26 August.

Cadario, P. M., Ogawa, K. and Wen, Yin-Kann (1992) *A Chinese Province as a Reform Experiment: The Case of Hainan* (Washington DC: World Bank).

Campbell, J. P., Dunnette, M. D., Lawler, E. E. and Weick, K. (1970) *Managerial Behavior, Performance and Effectiveness* (New York: McGraw-Hill).

*Capital* (1994) Hong Kong, June.

Cartier, C. L. (1995) 'Singaporean Investment in China: Installing the Singapore Model in Sunan', *Chinese Environment and Development*, vol. 6, pp. 117–44.

Casson, M. (1990) *Enterprise and Competitiveness: A Systems View of International Business* (Oxford: Clarendon Press).

Casson, M. (1995) *The Organisation of International Business: Studies in the Economics of Trust*, vol. 2 (Aldershot: Edward Elgar).

Casson, M. and Cox, H. (1992) 'Firms, Networks and International Business Enterprises', Paper presented at the Annual Meeting of the European International Business Association, 13–15 December.

Castells, M. (1989) *The Informational City* (Oxford: Basil Blackwell).

Castells, M. (1996) *The Rise of the Network Society* (Oxford: Basil Blackwell).

Cathay Bankcorp, Inc. (1992) *Annual Report* (Los Angeles: Cathay Bankcorp, Inc.).

Caves, R. E. (1996) *Multinational Enterprise and Economic Analysis*, 2nd edn (Cambridge: Cambridge University Press).

Census and Statistics Department (1998) *Estimates of Gross Domestic Product 1961–1997* (Hong Kong: Government Printers).

Chan, K. B. and Chiang, S.-N. C. (1994) *Stepping Out: The Making of Chinese Entrepreneurs* (Singapore: Simon and Schuster).

Chan, W. K. (1991) *The Making of Hong Kong Society* (Oxford: Clarendon Press).

Chan, W. K. K. (1982) 'Organizational Structure of the Traditional Chinese Firm and Its Modern Reform', *Business History Review*, vol. 56, no. 2, pp. 218–35.

Chan, W. K. K. (1995) 'The Origins and Early Years of the Wing On Company Group in Australia, Fiji, Hong Kong and Shanghai: Organisation and Strategy of a New Enterprise', in R. A. Brown (ed.), *Chinese Business Enterprise in Asia* (London: Routledge), pp. 80–95.

Chan, W. K. K. and McElderry, A. (eds) (1998) 'Historical Patterns of Chinese Business', *Journal of Asian Business*, Special Issue, vol. 14, no. 1.

Chandler, A. D., Jr (1977) *The Visible Hand: The Managerial Revolution in American Business* (Cambridge, Mass.: Harvard University Press).

Chandler, A. D., Jr (1990) *Scale and Scope: The Dynamics of Industrial Capitalism* (Cambridge, Mass.: Harvard University Press).

Chang, C.-Y. (1989) 'Localization and Chinese Banking in Southeast Asia', in Mee-kau Nyaw and Chak-yan Chang (eds), *Chinese Banking in Asia's Market Economies* (Hong Kong: Overseas Chinese Archives, Chinese University of Hong Kong).

Chang, T.-L. (1990) *The Competitive Strategies of Firms in their Internationalization Process: The Case of Taiwanese Firms in the Information Industry*, Unpublished Ph.D. Thesis, George Washington University (Ann Arbor, Mich.: University Microfilms International).

Chen, C.-H. (1994) *Xieli wangluo yu shenhuo jiegou: Taiwan zhongxiao qiye de shehui jiji fenxi* (Mutual aid networks and the structure of daily life: A social economic analysis of Taiwan's small and medium-sized enterprises) (Taipei: Lianjing).

Chen, C.-H. (1995) *Huobi wangluo yu shenhuo jiegou: Difang jinrong, zhongxiao qiye Taiwan shisu shehui zhi zhuanhua* (Monetary networks and the structure of daily life: Local finances, small and medium-sized enterprises, and the transformation of folk society in Taiwan) (Taipei: Lianjing).

Chen, Che-hung (1986) 'Taiwan's Foreign Direct Investment', *Journal of World Trade Law*, vol. 20, pp. 639–64.

Chen, H.-M. and Chen, T.-J. (1998) 'Network Linkages and Location Choice in Foreign Direct Investment', *Journal of International Business Studies*, vol. 29, no. 3, pp. 445–68.

Chen, M. (1995) *Asian Management Systems: Chinese, Japanese and Korean Styles of Business* (London: Routledge).

Chen, T.-J. (1992) 'Determinants of Taiwan's Direct Foreign Investment: The Case of a Newly Industrializing Country', *Journal of Development Economics*, vol. 39, pp. 397–407.

Chen, T.-J. (ed.) (1998) *Taiwanese Firms in Southeast Asia: Networking Across Borders* (Cheltenham: Edward Elgar).

Chen, T.-J. *et al.* (ed.) (1995) *Taiwan's Small- and Medium-sized Firms' Direct Investment in Southeast Asia* (Taipei: Chung-Hua Institution for Economic Research).

Chen, X.-M. (1994) 'The New Spatial Division of Labor and Commodity Chains in the Greater South China Economic Region', in G. Gereffi and M. Korzeniewicz (eds), *Commodity Chains and Global Capitalism* (Westport, Conn.: Praeger), pp. 165–86.

Chen, X.-M. (1996) 'Taiwan Investments in China and Southeast Asia', *Asian Survey*, vol. 36, no. 5, pp. 447–67.

Chen, Y.-S. (1990) Shanglu Shengya Bushi Meng (Life in business is not a dream)(Hong Kong: Fanrong Publishing Co.).

Cheng, L.-K. (1985) *Social Change and the Chinese in Singapore* (Singapore University Press).

Chin, K. W. (1988) 'A New Phase in Singapore's Relations with China', in J. K. Kallgren, N. Sopiee and S. Djiwandono (eds), *ASEAN and China: An Evolving Relationship* (Berkeley, Calif.: Institute of East Asian Studies, University of California), pp. 274–91.

China Credit Information Service (1998) *Business Groups in Taiwan 1998/1999* (Taipei: China Credit Information Service).

*China Times Magazine* (Hong Kong), in Chinese.

*Chinese Consumer Yellow Pages, Los Angeles* (1993).

*Chinese Daily News (World Journal)* (1992–4) (Monterey Park, Calif.: Chinese Daily News).

*Chinese Yellow Pages/Southern California* (1985–93) (Monterey Park, Calif.: Asia System Media, Inc.).

Chirot, D. and Reid, A. (eds) (1997) *Essential Outsiders: Chinese and Jews in the Modern Transformation of Southeast Asia and Central Europe* (Seattle: University of Washington Press).

Chiu, S. W. K., Ho, K. C. and Lui, T.-L. (1997) *City-States in the Global Economy: Industrial Restructuring in Hong Kong and Singapore* (Boulder, Col.: Westview Press).

Chow, W. (1998) 'Expo Site Purchaser Li Ka-shing Sells Out', *Vancouver Sun*, 5 December, p. B1.

Chu, G. C. and Ju, Y.-N. (1993) *The Great Wall in Ruins: Communication and Cultural Change in China* (Albany, NY: State University of New York Press).

Christerson, B. and Appelbaum, R. P. (1995) 'Global and Local Subcontracting: Space, ethnicity, and the Organization of Apparel Production', *World Development*, vol. 23, no. 8, pp. 1363–74.

Christerson, B. and Lever-Tracy, C. (1997) 'The Third China? Emerging Industrial Districts in Rural China', *International Journal of Urban and Regional Research*, vol. 21, no. 4, pp. 569–88.

Chung, C. (1997) 'Division of Labor Across the Taiwan Strait: Macro Overview and Analysis of the Electronics Industry', in B. Naughton (ed.), *The China Circle: Economics and Technology in the PRC, Taiwan, and Hong Kong* (Washington DC: Brookings Institution Press).

Clifford, J. (1994) 'Diasporas', *Cultural Anthropology*, vol. 9, no. 3, pp. 302–38.

Coffey, W. J. and Bailly, A. S. (1991) 'Producer Services and Flexible Production: An Exploratory Analysis', *Growth and Change*, vol. 22, pp. 95–117.

Cohen, M. (1976) *House United, House Divided, The Chinese Family in Taiwan* (New York: Columbia University Press).

Cohen, R. (1997) 'Diasporas, the Nation-State, and Globalisation', in Wang Gungwu (ed.), *Global History and Migration* (Boulder, Col. and Oxford: Westview Press).

*Computer Directory* (1992, 1993) (City of Industry, Calif.: Southern California Chinese Computer Association).

Cox, K. R. (ed.) (1997) *Spaces of Globalization: Reasserting the Power of the Local* (New York: Guilford).

Cumings, B. (1993) 'Rimspeak', in A. Dirlik (ed.), *What is in a Rim? Critical Perspectives on the Pacific Region Idea* (Boulder, Col.: Westview).

Cushman, J. W. and Wang, Gungwu (eds) (1988) *Changing Identities of the Southeast Asian Chinese Since World War II* (Hong Kong: Hong Kong University Press).

*Dangdai Zhongguo de Hainan* (Hainan Today) (1993) (Beijing: Dangdai Zhongguo Chubanshe (Hainan Today Publishing)).

Daniels, P. W. (1985) *Service Industries: A Geographical Appraisal* (London: Methuen).

DeGlopper, D. R. (1995) *Lukang, Commerce and Community in a Chinese City* (Albany, NY: State University of New York).

Demsetz, H. (1988) 'The Theory of the Firm Revisited', *Journal of Law, Economics and Organisation*, vol. 4, no. 1, pp. 141–61.

DeMont, J. and Fennell, T. (1989) *Hong Kong Money: How Chinese Families and Fortunes are Changing Canada* (Toronto: Key Porter Books).

Dicken, P. (1998) *Global Shift: Transforming the World Economy*, 3rd edn (London: Paul Chapman).

Dirlik, A. (1997) *The Postcolonial Aura: Third World Criticism in the Age of Global Capitalism* (Boulder, Col.: Westview Press).

Dixon, C. (1991) *South East Asia in the World Economy: A Regional Geography* (Cambridge: Cambridge University Press).

Dobson, W. and Chia, S. Y. (eds) (1997) *Multinationals and East Asian Integration* (Ottawa: International Development Research Centre).

Doremus, P. N., Keller, W. W., Pauly, L. W. and Reich, S. (1998) *The Myth of the Global Corporation* (Princeton, NJ: Princeton University Press).

Douglass, M. (1989) 'The Future of Cities on the Pacific Rim', in M. P. Smith (ed.), *Pacific Rim Cities in the World Economy: Comparative Urban and Community Research*; vol. 2 (New Brunswick and London: Transaction Publishers).

Douglass, M. (1998) 'World City Formation on the Asia Pacific Rim: Poverty, 'Everyday' Forms of Civil Society and Environmental Management', in M. Douglass and J. Friedmann (eds), *Cities for Citizens* (Chichester: John Wiley).

*Dun & Bradstreet Microcosm* (1992) (Los Angeles County: Dun & Bradstreet Inc.).

Dunning, J. H. (1993a) *The Globalization of Business* (London: Routledge).

Dunning, J. H. (1993b) *Multinational Enterprises and the Global Economy* (Reading, Mass.: Addison Wesley).

Dunning, John H. (1995) 'Reappraising the Eclectic Paradigm in an Age of Alliance Capitalism', *Journal of International Business Studies*, vol. 26, no. 3, pp. 461–91.

Dunning, J. H. (ed.) (1997) *Governments, Globalization and International Business* (Oxford: Oxford University Press).

Dunning, J. H. (1998) 'Location and the Multinational Enterprise: A Neglected Factor?', *Journal of International Business Studies*, vol. 29, no. 1, pp. 45–66.

Drucker, P. (1994) 'The New Superpower: The Overseas Chinese', *Asian Wall Street Journal*, 21 December.

Dymski, G. A. and Veitch, J. M. (1995) 'Financial Transformation and the Metropolis: Booms, Busts, and Banking in Los Angeles', Paper presented at the Association of American Geographers, Chicago.

East Asia Analytical Unit (1995) *Overseas Chinese Business Networks in Asia* (Parkes, Australia: Department of Foreign Affairs and Trade).

*Economic News* (1993) Hong Kong, 2 February.

*Economist, The* (1992) 'The Overseas Chinese', 18 July, pp. 21–3.

*Economist, The* (1996) 'The Limits of Family Values', 9–15 March, pp. 10–14.

*Economist, The* (1998) 3 January, p. 73; 25 July, p. 23.

Economist Intelligence Unit (1997) *Global Direct Investment and the Importance of Real Estate* (London: EIU).

Edwards, I. (1992) 'Quiet Clout', *Business in Vancouver*, 8–14 December, pp. 8–9.

Ellis, P. (1998) 'Johnson Electric', *Asian Case Research Journal*, vol. 2, pp. 53–66.

Emmerson, D. K. (1998) 'Americanizing Asia?', *Foreign Affairs*, vol. 77, no. 3, pp. 46–56.

Elvis, P. (1998) 'Strategic Evolution in Large Chinese Business Groups', Working paper, Asian Management Research Centre, School of Business, University of Hong Kong.

Eng, I. and Lin, Y. (1996) 'Seeking Competitive Advantage in an Emergent Open Economy: Foreign Direct Investment in Chinese Industry', *Environment and Planning A*, vol. 28, pp. 1113–38.

Engardio, P. and Gross, N. (1993) 'Taiwan: The Arms Dealer of the Computer War', *Business Week*, 28 June, pp. 51–4.

Enright, M. J., Scott, E. E. and Dodwell, D. (1997) *The Hong Kong Advantage* (Hong Kong: Oxford University Press).

Eriksson, K., Johanson, J., Majkgard, A. and Sharma, D. D. (1997) 'Experiential Knowledge and Cost in the Internationalisation Process', *Journal of International Business Studies*, 2nd quarter, pp. 337–60.

Faison, S. (1996) 'Riady's China Technique: Local Ties', *International Herald Tribune*, 21 October.

Fallows, J. (1995) *Looking at the Sun: The Rise of the New East Asian Economic and Political System* (New York: Vintage Books).

*Far Eastern Economic Review*, various issues, Hong Kong.

Faure, D. (1989) 'The Lineage as Business Company: Patronage versus Law in the Development of Chinese Business', *Proceedings of the Second Conference on Chinese Economic History*, 5–7 January (Taipei: Institute of Economics, Academia Sinica).

Faure, D. (1997) *A Documentary History of Hong Kong* (Hong Kong: Hong Kong University Press).

Federal Deposit Insurance Corporation (1982–93) *Databook: Summary of Deposits in all FDIC-insured Commercial and Savings Banks and U.S. Branches of Foreign Banks* (San Francisco California).

Fei, X.-T. (1953) 'Peasantry and Gentry: An Interpretation of Chinese Social Structure and Its Changes', *American Journal of Sociology* (1946), reprinted in R. Bendix and S. M. Lipset (eds), *Class, Status and Power: A Reader in Social Stratification* (Glencoe: Free Press).

Fei, X.-T. (1992) [1947] *From the Soil: The Foundations of Chinese Society*, Trans., Introduction and Epilogue by G. G. Hamilton and Wang Zheng (Berkeley, Calif.: University of California Press).

Feng, Chongyi and Goodman, D. S. G. (1995) *China's Hainan Province: Economic Development and Investment Environment* (Perth: University of Western Australia Press).

Feng, C.-Y. and Goodman, D. S. G. (1997) 'Hainan: Communal Politics and the Struggle for Identity', in D. S. G. Goodman (ed.), *China's Provinces in Reform: Class, Community and Political Culture* (London: Routledge), pp. 53–87.

*Financial Times* (1998) London, 5 March.

Findley Reports, Inc. (1992) *The Findley Reports* (Brea, Calif.: Findley Reports, Inc.).

Fitzgerald, R. (ed.) (1994) *The State and Economic Development: Lessons from the Far East* (London: Frank Cass).

Fladmoe-Lindquist, K. and Tallman, S. (1992) *Resource-based Strategy and Competitive Advantage Among Multinationals*, Paper presented at the AIB Annual Meeting, Brussels, 21–22 November.

Fligstein, N. (1990) *The Transformation of Corporate Control* (Cambridge, Mass.: Harvard University Press).

Florin, J. M. (1996) *Neither Markets nor Hierarchies: Non-equity Co-operative Arrangements as Efficient Models of Organisation*, Paper presented at the Conference on Global Perspectives on Co-operative Strategies, London, Ontario, March.

Fong, T. P. (1994) *The First Suburban Chinatown* (Philadelphia: Temple University Press).

*Forbes* (1992) Hong Kong, August.

Forsgren, M., Holm, U. and Thilenius, P. (1994) *Network Infusion and Subsidiary Influence in the Multinational Corporation*, Unpublished paper, Uppsala University.

Fung, V. (1995) *Evolution in the Management of Family Enterprises in Asia*, Lecture delivered at the Unversity of Hong Kong, 11 November.

Fukuyama F. (1995) *Trust: The Social Virtues and the Creation of Prosperity* (New York: Free Press).

*Fuoji Chaoxu* (TIC Bulletin), nos 18/19 (1996), p. 6.

Gambetta D. (1988) 'Fragments of an Economic Theory of the Mafia', *European Journal of Sociology*, vol. 29, pp. 127–45.

Gates, H. (1987) *Chinese Working-Class Lives: Getting by in Taiwan* (Ithaca, NY: Cornell University Press).

Geertz, C. (1963) *Peddlers and Princes: Social Development and Economic Change in Two Indonesian Towns* (Univerity of Chicago Press).

Geertz, C. (1973) *The Interpretation of Cultures* (New York: Basic Books).

General Bancorp (1992) *Annual Report* (Los Angeles: General Bancorp).

Gereffi, G. (1994) 'The International Economy and Economic Development', in N. Smelser and R. Sweldberg (eds), *The Handbook of Economic Sociology* (Princeton, NJ: Princeton University Press).

Gereffi, G. (1996) 'Commodity Chains and Regional Divisions of Labour in East Asia', *Journal of Asian Business*, vol. 12, no. 1, pp. 75–112.

Gereffi, G. and Hamilton, G. (1990) *Modes of Incorporation in an Industrial World: The Social Economy of Global Capitalism*, Institute of Government Affairs, Program on East Asian Business and Development, Working Paper Series No. 34.

Gereffi, G. and Korzeniewicz, M. (eds) (1994) *Commodity Chains and Global Capitalism* (Westport, Connc.: Greenwood Press).

Gertler, M. (1988) 'The Limits to Flexibility: Comments on the Post-Fordist Vision of Production and its Geography', *Transactions of the Institute of British Geographers*, vol. 13, no. 4, pp. 419–32.

Ghoshal, S. and Bartlett, C. A. (1990) 'The Multinational Corporation as an Interorganisational Network', *Academy of Management Review*, vol. 15, no. 4, pp. 603–25.

Go, F. M. and Pine, R. (1995) *Globalization Strategy in the Hotel Industry* (London: Routledge).

Godley, M. R. (1989) 'The Sojourners: Returned Overseas Chinese in the People's Republic of China', *Pacific Affairs*, vol. 62, no. 3, pp. 330–52.

Goldberg, M. A. (1985) *Chinese Connections: Getting Plugged Into Pacific Rim Real Estate Trade and Capital Markets* (Vancouver: University of British Columbia Press).

Goodman, B. (1996) *Native Place, City, and Nation: Regional Networks and Identities in Shanghai, 1853–1937* (Berkeley, Calif.: University of California Press).

Goodman, D. S. G., Hendrischke, H., and Underdown, M. (1998) 'The 1997 Statistical Yearbook in Provincial Perspective', *Provincial China*, vol. 5, pp. 68–96.

Grabher, G. and Stark, D. (1998) 'Organising Diversity: Evolutionary Theory, Network Analysis and Post-Socialism', in J. Pickles and A. Smith (eds), *Theorising Transition: The Political Economy of Post-Communist Transformation* (London: Routledge), pp. 54–75.

*Grand Meeting in Macau* (1997) (Hainan: Hainan Overseas Chinese Newspaper Bureau).

Granovetter, M. (1985) 'Economic Action and Social Structure: The Problem of Embeddedness', *American Journal of Sociology*, vol. 91, no. 3, pp. 481–510.

Granovetter, M. (1991) 'The Social Construction of Economic Institutions', in A. Etzioni and P. R. Lawrence (eds), *Socio-Economics: Toward a New Synthesis* (Armonk, NY: M. E. Sharpe), pp. 75–81.

Gray, C. (1988) 'Empires Beyond Kingdoms: The Thai Buddhist King and his Chinese Bankers', Conference paper delivered at New York University, 28 September–3 October.

Greenhalgh, S. (1988) 'Families and Networks in Taiwan's Economic Development', in E. A. Winckler and S. Greenhalgh (eds), *Contending Approaches to the Political Economy of Taiwan* (New York: M. E. Sharpe).

Greenhalgh, S. (1994) 'De-Orientalizing the Chinese Family Firm', *American Ethnologist*, vol. 21, no. 4, pp. 746–75.

Guthrie, D. (1998) 'The Declining Significance of *Guanxi* in China's Economic Transition', *The China Quarterly*, no. 154, pp. 254–82.

Gutstein, D. (1990) *The New Landlords: Asian Investment in Canadian Real Estate* (Victoria: Porcépic Books).

Haggard, S. and MacIntyre, A. (1998) 'The Political Economy of the Asian Economic Crisis', *Review of International Political Economy*, vol. 5, no. 3, pp. 381–92.

Haila, A. (1997) 'The Negelected Builder of Global Cities', in O. Källtorp, I. Elander, O. Erricsson, M. Franzén (eds), *Cities in Transformation – Transformation in Cities: Social and Symbolic Change of Urban Space* (Aldershot: Avebury).

*Hainan Jingji Nianjian* (Hainan Yearbook), various issues, 1989–97 (Hainan: Hainan Nianjianshe).

Hakka Association (1998) *The 13th World Hakka Reunion, November 1996, Singapore* (in Chinese) (Singapore: Nanyang Khek Community Guild).

Haley, G. T., Tan, Chin-Tiong and Haley, U. C. V. (1998) *The New Asian Emperors: The Overseas Chinese, Their Strategies and Competitive Advantages* (Oxford: Butterworth-Heinemann).

Hamilton, G. G. (1985) 'Why No Capitalism in China?', *Journal of Developing Societies*, vol. 2, pp. 187–211.

Hamilton, G. G. (ed.) (1991a) *Business Networks and Economic Development in East and South East Asia* (Hong Kong: Centre of Asian Studies, University of Hong Kong).

Hamilton, G. G. (1991b) 'The Organizational Foundation of Western and Chinese Commerce: A Historical and Comparative Analysis', in G. G. Hamilton (ed.), *Business Networks and Economic Development in East and South East Asia* (Hong Kong: Centre of Asian Studies, University of Hong Kong).

Hamilton, G. G. (1994) 'Civilizations and the Organization of Economies', in N. Smelser and R. Swedberg (eds), *The Handbook of Economic Sociology* (Princeton, NJ: Princeton University Press).

Hamilton, G. G. (ed.) (1996a) *Asian Business Networks* (Berlin: Walter de Gruyter).

Hamilton, G. G. (1996b) 'Overseas Chinese Capitalism', in W. M. Tu (ed.), *Confucian Traditions in East Asian Modernity* (Cambridge, Mass.: Harvard University Press), pp. 328–42.

Hamilton, G. G. (1996c) 'Competition and Organization: A Re-examination of Chinese Business Practices', *Journal of Asian Business*, vol. 12, no. 1, pp. 7–20.

Hamilton, G. G. (1997) 'Organisation and Market Processes in Taiwan's Capitalist Economy', in M. Orrù, N. W. Biggart and G. G. Hamilton (eds), *The Economic Organization of East Asian Capitalism* (Thousand Oaks, CA.: Sage).

Hamilton, G. G. (1998) '*Asian Business Networks in Transition*', paper presented at the Workshop on 'Asian Business Networks', Department of Sociology, National University of Singapore, 31 March–2 April 1998.

Hamilton, G. G., and Biggart, N. W. (1988) 'Market, Culture and Authority: A Comparative Analysis of Management and Organization in the Far East', *American Journal of Sociology*, vol. 94 (Supplement), pp. S52–94.

Hamilton, G. G. and Kao, C. S. (1990) 'The Institutional Foundations of Chinese Business: The Family Firm in Taiwan', *Comparative Social Research*, vol. 12, pp. 135–51.

Hamilton, G. G. and Waters, T. (1995) 'Chinese Capitalism in Thailand: Embedded Networks and Industrial Structure', in E. K. Y. Chen and P. Drysdale (eds), *Corporate Links and Foreign Direct Investment in Asia and the Pacific*, (Sydney: Harper Educational), pp. 87–111.

Hamilton, G. G. and Waters, T. (1997) 'Ethnicity and Capitalist Development: The Changing Role of the Chinese in Thailand', in D. Chirot and A. Reid (eds), *Essential Outsiders: Chinese and Jews in the Modern Transformation of Southeast Asia and Central Europe* (Seattle: University of Washington Press).

Handler, W. C. (1994) 'Succession in Family Business: A Review of the Research', *Family Business Review*, vol. 7, no. 2, pp. 133–57.

Handley, P. (1997) *De-mythologising Charoen Pokphand: An Interpretive Picture of the CP Group's Growth and Diversification*, Paper presented at the Chinese Business in Southeast Asia Conference, Kuala Lumpur, 23–25 June.

Hannerz, U. (1990) 'Cosmopolitans and Locals in World Culture', *Theory, Culture and Society*, vol. 7, no. 2–3, pp. 237–52.

Hansen, N. (1990) 'Do Producer Services Induce Regional Economic Development?', *Journal of Regional Science*, vol. 30, pp. 465–76.

HAPCO (Hainan Asia Pacific Brewery Company Ltd) (1997) *High Point*, October.

Harrington, J. W. (1995) 'Producer Services in U.S. Regional Studies', *Professional Geographers*, vol. 47, no. 1, pp. 82–7.

Harris, R. (1994) 'Office Property Development and the Role of Marketing Research', Unpublished paper (London: Stanhope Properties plc).

Harrison, B. (1994) *Lean and Mean: The Changing Landscape of Corporate Power in an Age of Flexibility* (New York: Basic Books).

Harvey, D. (1994) 'The Invisible Political Economy of Architectural Production', in O. Bouman and R. van Toorn (eds), *The Invisible in Architecture* (London: Academy Editions).

Hawes, G. and Liu, H. (1993) 'Explaining the Dynamics of the Southeast Asian Political Economy: State, Society and the Search for Economic Growth', *World Politics*, vol. 45, pp. 629–60.

He, Wenxiang (1992) *Xianggang Xingui* (The Newly Rich in Hong Kong) (Hong Kong: Ming Bao Press).

Hedlund, G. (1986) 'The Hypermodern MNC-A Heterarchy', *Human Resource Management*, vol. 25, no. 1, pp. 9–35.

Hefner, R. W. (ed.) (1998) *Market Cultures: Society and Values in the New Asian Capitalisms* (Singapore: Institute of Southeast Asian Studies).

Heng, P. K. (1997) 'Robert Kuok and the Chinese Business Network in Eastern Asia: A Study in Sino-capitalism', in T. Brook and Hy V. Luong (eds), *Culture and Economy: The Shaping of Capitalism in Eastern Asia* (Ann Arbor, Mich.: University of Michigan Press), pp. 155–81.

Hennart, J. F. (1982) *A Theory of Multinational Enterprise* (Ann Arbor, Mich.: University of Michigan Press).

Hennart, J. F. (1988) 'A Transaction Cost Theory of Equity Joint Ventures', *Strategic Management Journal*, vol. 9, pp. 319–32.

Hennart, J. F. (1990) 'Is Internalisation Theory a General Theory of the MNE? The Case of "Capital-exporting Firms"', Proceedings EIBA Annual Conference 1990 Madrid.

Hicks, G. L. (ed.) (1993) *Overseas Chinese Remittances from Southeast Asia 1910–1940* (Singapore: Select Books).

Hirst, P. and Thompson, G. (1996) *Globalization in Question: The International Economy and the Possibilities of Governance* (Cambridge: Polity Press).

Ho, K. C. (1994) 'Industrial Restructuring, the Singapore City-State, and the Regional Division of Labour', *Environment and Planning A*, vol. 26, no. 1, pp. 33–51.

Ho, Yin-Ping (1992) *Trade, Industrial Restructuring and Development in Hong Kong* (London: Macmillan).

Hobday, M. (1998) 'Latecomer Catch-up Strategies in Electronics: Samsung of Korea and Acer of Taiwan', *Asia Pacific Business Review*, vol. 4, no. 2/3, pp. 48–83.

Hodder, R. (1996) *Merchant Princes of the East: Cultural Delusions, Economic Success and the Overseas Chinese in Southeast Asia* (Chichester: John Wiley).

Hodgson, G. M. (1988) *Economics and Institutions: A Manifesto for a Modern Institutional Economics* (Cambridge: Polity Press).

Hofstede, G. (1980) *Culture's Consequences* (London: Sage).

Hofstede, G. (1992) *Cultures and Organizations: Software of the Mind* (London: McGraw-Hill).

Holberton, S. (1993) 'HK's Superman Finds Warmer Winds from China', *Financial Times*, 23 June, p. 30.

Holberton, S. (1995) 'Mr. Li Sets Hong Kong a Puzzle', *Financial Times*, 6 June, p. 26.

Hollingsworth, J. R. and Boyer, R. (1997) *Contemporary Capitalism: The Embeddedness of Institutions* (Cambridge: Cambridge University Press).

Hong Kong Cotton Spinners Association (1988) *Forty Years of The Hong Kong Cotton Spinning Industry* (Hong Kong: Hong Kong Cotton Spinners Association).

Hong Kong Government (various dates) *Registrar General Annual Departmental Report*.

Hooijmaijers, M. (1995) 'Foreign Direct Investment in China', in H. Marcel, C. van der Bergh and S. Jella (eds) *Dancing with the Dragon: Backgrounds, Strategies and Practices for Business Success in China* (Amsterdam: Thesis Publishers).

Houston, P. (1985) 'Impossibility of the Bee', *Open Places*, no. 38/39 (Spring), p. 209.

Howlett, B. (ed.) (1997) *Hong Kong 1997: A Review of 1996* (Hong Kong: Information Services Department).

Hoy, F. and Verser, T. G. (1994) 'Emerging Business, Emerging Field: Entrepreneurship and the Family Firm', *Entrepreneurship Theory and Practice*, vol. 19, no. 1, pp. 9–23.

Hsing, You-tien (1996) 'Blood Thicker Than Water: Interpersonal Relations and Taiwanese Investment in Southern China', *Environment and Planning A*, vol. 28, pp. 2241–61.

Hsing, You-tien (1997) 'Building *guanxi* across the Straits: Taiwanese Capital and Local Chinese Bureaucrats', in A. Ong and D. Nonini (eds), *Ungrounded Empires: The Cultural Politics of Modern Chinese Transnationalism* (New York: Routledge), pp. 143–64.

Hsing, You-tien (1998) *Making Capitalism in China: The Taiwan Connection* (New York: Oxford University Press).

Hu, Yao-Su (1992) 'Global Firms are National Firms with International Operations', *California Management Review*, vol. 34, no. 2, pp. 107–26.

Hu, Yao-Su (1995) 'The International Transferability of the Firm's Advantages', *California Management Review*, vol. 37, no. 4, pp. 73–88.

Hulchanski, J. D. (1989) 'Low Rent Housing in Vancouver's Central Area: Policy and Program Options', Report prepared for the Central Area Division, City of Vancouver, September.

Humes, S. (1993) *Managing the Multinational: Confronting the Global–Local Dilemma* (New York: Prentice Hall).

Hwang, D. (1992) *Far East National Bank and Henry Hwang*, Brochure of Far Eastern National Bank, Los Angeles.

Hwang, Kwang-kuo (1984) 'Rujia lunli yu qiye zuzhi xingtai' (Confucian theory and types of enterprise organization), in *Zhongguo shi guanli* (Chinese-style Management) (Taipei: Gongshang Shibao).

Hwang, Kwang-kuo (1987) 'Face and Favor: The Chinese Power Game', *American Journal of Sociology*, vol. 92, no. 4 (January), pp. 944–74.

Jacobs N. (1985) *The Korean Road to Modernization and Development* (Urbana, Ill.: University of Illinois Press).

Jamann, W. (1994) *Chinese Traders in Singapore: Business Practices and Organisational Dynamics* (Saarbrücken: Verlag für Entwicklungspolitick Breitenbach GmbH).

Jansson, H. (1994) *Transnational Corporations in Southeast Asia: An Institutional Approach to Industrial Organisation* (Cambridge: Edward Elgar).

Jessop, B. (1999) 'Some Critical Reflections on Globalization and Its Illogic(s)', in K. Olds, P. Dicken, P. F. Kelly, L. Kong and H. W. C. Yeung (eds), *Globalisation and the Asia Pacific: Contested Territories* (London: Routledge).

Jesudason, J. V. (1989) *Ethnicity and the Economy: The State, Chinese Business and Multinationals in Malaysia* (Singapore: Oxford University Press).

Jesudason, J. V. (1997) 'Chinese Business and Ethnic Equilibrium in Malaysia', *Development and Change*, vol. 28, no. 1, pp. 119–41.

Jin, Dengjian and Haynes, K. E. (1997) 'Economic Transition at the Edge of Order and Chaos: China's Dualist and Leading Sectoral Approach', *Journal of Economic Issues*, vol. 31, no. 1, pp. 79–101.

Johanson, J. and Vahlne, J. E. (1977) 'The Internationalisation Process of the Firm: A Model of Knowledge Development and Increasing Foreign Market Commitments', *Journal of International Business Studies*, vol. 8, no. 1, pp. 23–32.

Johanson, J. and Mattsson, L.-G. (1988) 'Internationalisation in Industrial Systems: A Network Approach', in N. Hood and J.-E. Vahlne (eds) *Strategies in Global Competition* (New York: Croom Helm).

Jomo, K. S. (1988) *A Question of Class: Capital, the State, and Uneven Development in Malaya* (New York: Monthly Review Press).

Jones, G. R. and Hill, C. W. L. (1988) 'Transaction Cost Analysis of Strategy–Structure Choice', *Strategic Management Journal*, vol. 9, pp. 159–72.

Kanai, T. (1993) 'Singapore's New Focus on Regional Business Expansion', *NRI Quarterly*, vol. 2, no. 3, pp. 18–41.

Kao, C.-S. (1996) '"Personal Trust" in the Large Businesses in Taiwan: A Traditional Foundation for Contemporary Economic Activities', in G. Hamilton (ed.), *Asian Business Networks* (Berlin: Walter de Gruyter).

Kao, C.-S. (forthcoming) *Sociability and Profit: The Social Foundations of Taiwan's Export Economy* (in Chinese) (Taipei: Lianjing).

Kao, J. (1993) 'The Worldwide Web of Chinese Business', *Harvard Business Review*, March–April, pp. 24–36.

Kearney, M. (1995) 'The Local and the Global: The Anthropology of Globalization and Transnationalism', *Annual Review of Anthropology*, vol. 24, pp. 547–65.

Keister, L. A. (1998) 'Social Ties and the Formation of Chinese Business Groups', *Sociological Analysis*, vol. 2, pp. 99–118.

Kelly, P. F. (1999) 'The Geographies and Politics of Globalization', *Progress in Human Geography*, vol. 23, no. 3, pp. 379–400.

Kim, T. J., Knaap, G. and Azis, I. (1992) *Spatial Development in Indonesia: Review and Prospects* (Aldershot: Avebury).

King, A. Yeo-chi. (1985) 'The Individual and Group in Confucianism: A Relational Perspective', in D. Munroe (ed.) *Individual and Holism* (Ann Arbor, Mich.: Center for Asian Studies, University of Michigan).

King, A. Yeo-chi. (1991) 'Kuan-hsi and Network Building: A Sociological Interpretation', *Daedalus*, vol. 120, no. 2, pp. 63–84.

King, A. Yeo-chi (1994) 'Kuan-hsi and Network Building: A Sociological Interpretation', in Tu Wei-ming (ed.), *The Living Tree: The Changing Meaning of Being Chinese Today* (Stanford, CA: Stanford University Press).

Kipnis, A. B. (1997) *Producing Guanxi: Sentiment, Self, and Subculture in a North China Village* (Durham, NC: Duke University Press).

Kirby, W. C. (1995) 'China Unincorporated: Company Law and Business Enterprise in Twentieth-Century China', *Journal of Asian Studies*, vol. 54, no. 1 (February), pp. 43–63.

Ko, A. C. K. (1998) 'Strategy and Performance of Listed Firms in Hong Kong 1975–1994', Unpublished doctoral dissertation. School of Business, University of Hong Kong.

Kondo, D. K. (1990) *Crafting Selves: Power, Gender, and Discourses of Identity in a Japanese Workplace* (Chicago: Chicago University Press).

Kotkin, J. (1992) *Tribes: How Race, Religion and Identity Determine Success in the New Global Economy* (New York: Random House).

KPMG Peat Marwick Stevenson & Kellog/Peat Marwick Thorne (1992) 'British Columbia Financial Review: The Issue of Disposal and Valuation of Assets', Report to the Province of British Columbia, 5 March.

Kraar, L. (1993) 'Importance of Chinese in Asian Business', *Journal of Asian Business*, vol. 9, no. 1, pp. 87–94.

Krause, L. B. (1985) 'Introduction', in W. Galenson (ed.), *Foreign Trade and Investment: Economic Development in the Newly Industrializing Asian Countries* (Madison: University of Wisconsin Press) pp. 3–41.

Krugman, P. (1994) 'The Myth of Asia's Miracle', *Foreign Affairs*, vol. 73, no. 6, pp. 62–78.

Kwok, S. (1994) Interview with K. Olds, February.

La Croix, S. J., Plummer, M. and Lee, K. (eds) (1995) *Emerging Patterns of East Asian Investment in China: From Korea, Taiwan, and Hong Kong* (Armonk, NY: M. E. Sharpe).

Landa, J. T. (1991) 'Culture and Entrepreneurship in Less-Developed Countries: Ethnic Trading Networks as Economic Organizations', in B. Berger (ed.), *The Culture of Entrepreneurship* (San Francisco: ICS Press).

Landa, J. T. (1994) *Trust, Ethnicity, and Identity: Beyond the New Institutional Economics of Ethnic Trading Networks, Contract Law, and Gift-Exchange* (Ann Arbor, Mich.: University of Michigan Press).

Lane, C. and Bachmann, R. (eds) (1998) *Trust Within and Between Organizations: Conceptual issues and Empirical Applications* (Oxford: Oxford University Press).

Lang, G. and Smart, J. (n.d.) 'Industrialization, Migration and the "Second Wife" in South China', unpublished manuscript.

Larson, A. (1992) 'Network Dyads in Entrepreneurial Settings: A Study of the Governance of Exchange Relationships', *Administrative Science Quarterly*, vol. 37, pp. 76–104.

Lasserre, P. (1988) 'Corporate Strategic Management and the Overseas Chinese Groups', *Asia Pacific Journal of Management*, vol. 5, no. 2, pp. 115–31.

Lasserre, P. and Schütte, H. (1995) *Strategies for Asia Pacific* (London: Macmillan).

Lau, S.-K. (1982) *Society and Politics in Hong Kong* (Hong Kong: Chinese University Press).

Lau, H.-F. (1991) 'Development Process of the Hong Kong Manufacturing Companies: with Special Reference to the Garment Firms', in E. K. Y. Chen, Mee-Kau Nyaw and T. Y. C. Wong (eds), *Industrial and Trade Development in Hong Kong* (Hong Kong: Centre of Asian Studies, University of Hong Kong).

Lee, T. Y. (1994) *Overseas Investment: Experience of Singapore Manufacturing Companies* (Singapore: McGraw-Hill).

Leslie, G. (1991) *Breach of Promise: Scored Ethics Under Vander Zalm* (Madeira Park, BC: Harbour Publishing).

Lever-Tracy, C., Ip, D., Kitay, J., Phillips, I. and Tracy, N. (1991) *Asian Entrepreneurs in Australia: Ethnic Small Business in the Indian and Chinese Communities of Brisbane and Sydney* (Canberra: Australian Government Publishing Service).

Lever-Tracy, C., Ip, D. and Tracy, N. (1996) *The Chinese Diaspora and Mainland China: An Emerging Economic Synergy* (New York: St Martin's Press).

Levy, R. (1995) 'Corruption, Economic Crime and Social Transformation since the Reforms', *Australian Journal of Chinese Affairs*, no. 33, pp. 1–25.

Lévy, B. (1995) 'Globalization and Regionalization: Toward the Shaping of a Tripolar World Economy?', *The International Executive*, vol. 37, no. 4, pp. 349–71.

Lewis, J. D. (1995) *The Connected Corporation: How Leading Companies Win Through Customer–Supplier Alliances* (New York: The Free Press).

Ley, D. (1987) 'Styles of the Times: Liberal and Neo-conservative Landscapes in Inner Vancouver, 1968–1986', *Journal of Historical Geography*, vol. 14, pp. 40–56.

Ley, D. (1994) 'The Downtown Eastside: "One hundred years of struggle"', in S. Hasson and D. Ley, *Neighbourhood Organizations and the Welfare State* (Toronto: University of Toronto Press).

Ley, D. (1995) 'Between Europe and Asia: The Case of the Missing Sequoias', *Ecumene*, vol. 2, no. 2, pp. 185–210.

Ley, D. (1996) *The New Middle Class and the Remaking of the Central City* (Oxford: Oxford University Press).

Li, L. C. (1998) 'Guangdong: From "Machiavellian" Flexibility towards the Rule of Law', *Provincial China*, vol. 5, pp. 1–17.

Li, V. T. K. (1992) 'Why We Invest in Canada', *Dialogue* (Asia Pacific Foundation of Canada), vol. 6, February 3, 8.

Liao, C.-Y. (1997) 'Chinese Social Organisations and Trading Networks in Japan: Fujian Clan Association of Nagasaki, 1860–1950s', (in Japanese), *Toyo Bunka Kenkyu Kiyo*, no. 134, pp. 109–73.

*Lianhe Wanbao*, 6 November 1994.

*Lianhe Zhaobao*, 13 July 1997, 3 December 1997. 20/24, November, 27 January 1993, 27 November 1992.

Light, I. (1972) *Ethnic Enterprise in America: Business and Welfare among Chinese, Japanese, and Blacks* (Berkeley, Calif.: University of California Press).

Lim, L. Y. C. (1991) *The New Ascendancy of Chinese Business in Southeast Asia: Political, Cultural, Economic and Business Implications*, Paper presented at the 43rd Annual Meeting of the Association for Asian Studies, New Orleans, April.

Lim, L. Y. C. (1996a) 'The Evolution of Southeast Asian Business Systems', *Journal of Southeast Asia Business*, vol. 12, no. 1, pp. 51–74.

Lim, L. (1996b) 'Southeast Asian Business Systems: The Dynamics of Diversity', in A. E. Safarian and W. Dobson (eds), *East Asian Capitalism: Diversity and Dynamism*, Hong Kong Bank of Canada Papers on Asia, vol. 2 (Toronto: University of Toronto Press).

Lim, L. Y. C. (1997) 'The Southeast Asian Currency Crisis and its Aftermath', *Journal of Asian Business*, vol. 13, no. 4, pp. 65–83.

Lim, L. and Gosling, P. (eds) (1983) *The Chinese in Southeast Asia* (Singapore: Maruzen Asia).

Lim, L. Y. C. and Gosling, P. (1997) 'Strengths and Weaknesses of Minority Status for Southeast Asian Chinese at a Time of Economic Growth and Liberalization', in D. Chirot and A. Reid (eds), *Essential Outsiders: Chinese and Jews in the Modern Transformation of Southeast Asia and Central Europe* (Seattle: University of Washington Press), pp. 285–317.

Limlingan, V. S. (1986) *The Overseas Chinese in ASEAN: Business Strategies and Management Practices* (Manila: Vita Development Corporation).

Lin, P.-A. (1996) 'The Social Sources of Capital Investment in Taiwan's Industrialization', in G. Hamilton (ed.), *Asian Business Networks* (Berlin: Walter de Gruyter).

Lin, T. B., Mok, V. and Ho, Y. P. (1980) *Manufactured Exports and Employment in Hong Kong* (Hong Kong: Chinese University of Hong Kong Press).

Lin T.-C. (1997) *The Man Crossing the Bridge: An Autobiography of an Overseas Chinese through the Turbulent Years* (in Japanese) (Kobe: Epic Press).

Liu, H. (1998a) 'Think Locally, Act Regionally: Singapore Chinese Chamber of Commerce and Industry as an Institutional Nexus of Asian Chinese Business Networks', Paper presented at the international workshop, Asian Business Networks, Singapore, 31 March–2 April.

Liu, H. (1998b) 'Old Linkages, New Networks: The Globalization of Overseas Chinese Voluntary Associations and its Implications', *The China Quarterly*, no. 155, pp. 582–609.

Liu H. (1999a) 'From Two-Way Communications to Multi-dimensional Networks: The Singapore Chinese Chamber of Commerce and Industry and Singapore–Malaysian Socio-economic Interactions' (in Chinese), in E. C. Tan (ed.), *Studies in the History and Literature of Chinese in Singapore and Malaysia* (Singapore: Island Society).

Liu, H. (1999b) 'Bridges Across the Sea: Chinese Social Organizations in Southeast Asia and the Links with *Qiaoxiang*, 1900–1949', in L. Douw, C. Huang and M. Godley (eds), *Chinese Transnationalism: Cultural and Economic Dimensions* (London: Kegan Paul International).

Liu, J. M. and Cheng, L. (1994) 'Pacific Rim Development and the Duality of Post-1965 Asian Immigration to the United States', in P. Ong, E. Bonacich and L. Cheng (eds), *The New Asian Immigration in Los Angeles and Global Restructuring* (Philadelphia: Temple University Press).

Liu, P. C., Liu, Y.-C., and Wu, H.-L. (1993) 'Manufacturing Enterprise and Management in Taiwan', Discussion paper no. 9304 (Taipei: Institute of Economics, Academia Sinica).

Logan, J. (1993) 'Cycles and Trends in the Globalization of Real Estate', in P. Knox (ed.), *The Restless Urban Landscape* (Englewood Cliffs, NJ: Prentice Hall).

London Residential Research (1997) *Residential Development in Central and Inner London* (London: LRR).

Low, L., Ramstetter, E. D. and Yeung, H. W. C. (1998) 'Accounting for Outward Direct Investment from Hong Kong and Singapore: Who Controls What?', in R. E. Baldwin, R. E. Lipsey and J. D. Richardson (eds), *Geography and Ownership as Bases for Economic Accounting* (Chicago: University of Chicago Press).

Lu, D. and Zhu, G.-T. (1995) 'Singapore Direct Investment in China: Features and Implications', *ASEAN Economic Bulletin*, vol. 12, no. 1, pp. 53–63.

Lui, T.-L. (1998) 'Trust and Chinese Business Behaviour', *Competition and Change*, vol. 3, no. 3, pp. 335–57.

Lui, T.-L. and Chiu, S. (1994) 'A Tale of Two Industries: The Restructuring of Hong Kong's Garment-Making and Electronics Industries', *Environment and Planning A*, vol. 26, no. 1, pp. 53–70.

Luo, Q. and Howe, C. (1993) 'Direct Investment and Economic Integration in the Asia Pacific: The Case of Taiwanese Investment in Xiamen', *The China Quarterly*, no. 136, pp. 746–69.

Lynn, P. (ed.) (1998) *The Encyclopedia of Chinese Overseas* (Singapore: Archipelago Press).

Mackie, J. (1988) 'Changing Economic Roles and Ethnic Identities of the Southeast Chinese: A Comparison of Indonesia and Thailand', in J. W. Cushman and Gungwu Wang (eds), *Changing Identities of the Southeast Asian Chinese Since World War II* (Hong Kong: Hong Kong University Press).

Mackie, J. (1992a) 'Overseas Chinese Entrepreneurship', *Asia-Pacific Economic Literature*, vol. 6, pp. 41–64.

Mackie, J. (1992b) 'Changing Patterns of Chinese Big Business in Southeast Asia', in R. McVey (ed.), *Southeast Asian Capitalists* (Ithaca, NY: Southeast Asia Program, Cornell University), pp. 161–90.

Mackie J. (1995) 'Economic Systems of the Southeast Asian Chinese', in L. Suryadinata (ed.), *The Ethnic Chinese in the ASEAN States* (Singapore: Institute of Southeast Asian Studies), pp. 33–65.

Mackie J. (1998) 'Business Success Among Southeast Asian Chinese: The Role of Culture, Values, and Social Structures', in R. W. Hefner (ed.), *Market Cultures: Society and Morality in the New Asian Capitalisms* (Boulder, Col.: Westview Press), pp. 129–46.

Magnus, G. (1994) Interview with K. Olds, April.

Magnusson, L. (1994) 'The Neo-Schumpeterian and Evolutionary Approach to Economics – An Introduction', in L. Magnusson (ed.), *Evolutionary and Neo-Schumpeterian Approaches to Economics* (Boston: Kluwer Academic Publishers), pp. 1–8.

Magretta, J. (1998) 'Fast, Global, and Entrepreneurial: Supply Chain Management, Hong Kong Style: An Interview with Victor Fung', *Harvard Business Review*, vol. 76, no. 5, pp. 103–14.

Markoulis, J. (1994) Interview with K. Olds, March.

Malnight, T. W. (1995) 'Globalization of an Ethnocentric Firm: An Evolutionary Perspective', *Strategic Management Journal*, vol. 16, pp. 119–41.

Mark, L. Li (1972) *Taiwanese Lineage Enterprises: A Study of Familial Entrepreneurship*, Unpublished dissertation, University of California at Berkeley.

Marshall, G. (1994) *Oxford Concise Dictionary of Sociology* (Oxford: Oxford University Press).

Marshall, J. N. (1988) *Services and Uneven Development* (Oxford: Oxford University Press).

Matas, R. (1989a) 'Mystery, Unanswered Questions Remain About B.C.'s Land Deal of the Century', *The Globe and Mail*, 17 June, pp. A1, A7.

Matas, R. (1989b) 'BC Government Lost Millions in Rush to Sell Waterfront Land', *The Globe and Mail*, 20 June, pp. A1, A8.

Matas, R. and York, G. (1989) 'Expo Site Project Rolling on Fast Track', *The Globe and Mail*, 19 June, pp. A1, A8.

Mathews, J. A. (1997) 'A Silicon Valley of the East: Creating Taiwan's Semiconductor Industry', *California Management Review*, vol. 39, no. 4, pp. 26–54.

Mathews, J. A. (1999) 'A Silicon Island of the East: Creating a Semiconductor Industry in Singapore', *California Management Review*, vol. 41, no. 2, pp. 55–78.

Mathews, J. A. and Snow, C. C. (1998) 'A Conversation with the Acer Groups' Stan Shih on Global Strategy and Management', *Organizational Dynamics*, vol. 27, no. 1, pp. 65–74.

McVey, R. (ed.) (1992) *Southeast Asian Capitalists* (Ithaca, NY: Cornell University Southeast Asia Program).

Menkhoff, T. (1993) *Trade Routes, Trust and Trading Networks – Chinese Small Enteprises in Singapore* (Saarbrucken: Verlag Breitenback).

Min, P. G. (1987) 'Factors Contributing to Ethnic Business: A Comprehensive Synthesis', *International Journal of Comparative Sociology*, vol. 28, pp. 173–91.

Mitchell, K. (1993a) 'Multiculturalism, or the United Colors of Capitalism?', *Antipode*, vol. 25, no. 4, pp. 263–94.

Mitchell, K. (1993b) *Facing Capital: Cultural Politics in Vancouver*, Unpublished Ph.D. dissertation, University of California at Berkeley.

Mitchell, K. (1995) 'Flexible Circulation in the Pacific Rim: Capitalisms in Cultural Context', *Economic Geography*, vol. 71, no. 4, pp. 364–82.

Mitchell, K. (1997) 'Transnational Discourse: Bringing Geography Back In', *Antipode*, vol. 29, no. 2, pp. 101–14.

Mitchell, K. and Hammer, B. (1997) 'Ethnic Chinese Networks: A New Model?', in A. E. Safarian and W. Dobson (eds), *The People Link: Human Resource Linkages Across the Pacific* (Toronto: Centre for International Business, University of Toronto).

Mittelman, J. H. (ed.) (1996) *Globalization: Critical Reflections* (Boulder, Col.: Lynne Rienner).

Montagu-Pollock, M. (1991) 'All the Right Connections', *Asian Business*, vol. 27, no. 1, pp. 20–4.

Moran, R. T. and Riesenberger, J. R. (1994) *The Global Challenge: Building the New Worldwide Enterprise* (London: McGraw-Hill).

Morishima M. (1982) *Why Has Japan Succeeded?* (Cambridge: Cambridge University Press).

Mueller, G. (1992) 'Watching Global Real Estate Markets', *Urban Land*, March, pp. 30–2.

Nathan, A. (1993) 'Is Chinese Culture Distinctive?', *Journal of Asian Studies*, vol. 52, no. 4, pp. 923–36.

National Association of Chinese American Bankers (1992, 1993) *5th and 6th Annual Convention and Banquet Publication* (Los Angeles: American International Bank).

Naughton, B. (ed.) (1997) *The China Circle: Economics and Technology in the PRC, Taiwan, and Hong Kong* (Washington, DC: Brookings Institution).

Neller, R. J. and Lam K. C. (1994) 'Environment', in Y. Yeung and D. Chu (eds), *Guangdong* (Hong Kong: Chinese University of Hong Kong Press), pp. 401–28.

Nevitt, C. E. (1996) 'Private Business Associations in China: Evidence of Civil Society of Local State Power?' *The China Journal*, vol. 36, pp. 25–46.

*Next Magazine, The* Hong Kong, various issues.

Ng, L. F.-Y. and Tuan, C. (eds) (1996) *Three Chinese Economies – China, Hong Kong and Taiwan: Challenges and Opportunities* (Hong Kong: Chinese University of Hong Kong Press).

Nohria, N. and Eccles, R. G. (1992) (eds) *Networks and Organisations: Structure, Form, and Action* (Boston, Mass.: Harvard Business School Press).

Nohria, N. and Ghoshal, S. (1997) *The Differentiated Network: Organizing Multinational Corporations for Value Creation* (San Francisco: Jossey-Bass).

Nonini, D. M. and Ong, A. (1997) 'Chinese transnationalism as an alternative modernity', in A. Ong and D. M. Nonini (eds), *Ungrounded Empires* (London: Routledge).

North, D. C. (1990) *Institutions, Institutional Change and Economic Performance* (Cambridge: Cambridge University Press).

Numazaki, I. (1991a) *Networks and Partnerships: The Social Organization of The Chinese Business Elite in Taiwan*, Unpublished dissertation, Michigan State University.

Numazaki, I. (1991b) 'The Role of Personal Networks in the Making of Taiwan's *Guanxiqiye* (Related Enterprises)', in G. Hamilton (ed.), *Business Networks and Economic Development in East and Southeast Asia* (Hong Kong: Centre of Asian Studies, University of Hong Kong).

Numazaki, I. (1993) 'The Tainanbang: The Rise and Growth of a Banana-Bunch-Shaped Business Group in Taiwan', *The Developing Economies*, vol. 31, no. 4, pp. 485–510.

Numuzaki, I. (1996) 'The Role of Personal Networks in the Making of Taiwan's *Guanxiqiye* (Related Enterprises)', in G. Hamilton (ed.), *Asian Business Networks* (Berlin: Walter de Gruyter).

Numazaki, I. (1997) 'The Laoban-led Development of Business Enterprises in Taiwan: An Analysis of Chinese Entrepreneurship', *The Developing Economies*, vol. 35, no. 4 (December), pp. 440–57.

Nyaw, M.-K. (1996) 'Investment Environment: Perceptions of Overseas Investors of Foreign-funded Industrial Firms', in Yue-man Yeung and Yun-wing Sung (eds), *Shanghai: Transformation and Modernization Under China's Open Policy* (Hong Kong: Chinese University of Hong Kong Press).

Ohmae, K. (1985) *Triad Power: The Coming Shape of Global Competition* (New York: Free Press).

Ohmae, K. (1990) *The Borderless World: Power and Strategy in the Interlinked Economy* (London: Collins).

Ohmae, K. (1995) *The End of the Nation State: The Rise of Regional Economies* (London: HarperCollins).

Olds, K. (1995) 'Globalization and the Production of New Urban Spaces: Pacific Rim Mega-projects in the Late 20th Century', *Environment and Planning A*, vol. 27, pp. 1713–43.

Olds, K. (1998) 'Globalization and Urban Change: Tales from Vancouver via Hong Kong', *Urban Geography*, vol. 19, no. 4, pp. 360–85.

Olds, K. (2000) *Globalization and Urban Change: Capital, Culture and Pacific Rim Mega Projects* (New York: Oxford University Press).

Olds, K., Dicken, P., Kelly, P., Kong, L. and Yeung, H. W. C. (eds) (1999) *Globalisation and the Asia Pacific: Contested Territories* (London: Routledge).

Olds, K. and Yeung, H. W. C. (1999) '(Re)shaping "Chinese" Business Networks in a Globalising Era', *Environment and Planning D: Society and Space*, vol. 17.

Ong, A. (1993) 'On the Edge of Empires: Flexible Citizenship among Chinese in Diaspora', *Positions*, vol. 1, no. 3, pp. 745–78.

Ong, A. (1997) '"A Momentary Glow of Fraternity": Narratives of Chinese Nationalism and Capitalism', *Identities*, vol. 3, no. 3, pp. 331–66.

Ong, A. and Nonini, D. (eds) (1997) *Ungrounded Empires: The Cultural Politics of Modern Chinese Transnationalism* (New York: Routledge).

Ong, P. and Azores, T. (1994) 'Asian Immigrants in Los Angeles: Diversity and Divisions', in P. Ong, E. Bonacich and L. Cheng (eds), *The New Asian Immigration in Los Angeles and Global Restructuring* (Philadelphia: Temple University Press).

Orrù, M., Biggart, N. and Hamilton, G. G. (1997) *The Economic Organization of East Asian Capitalism* (London: Sage).

Ouchi, W. G. (1980) 'Markets, Bureaucracies, and Clans', *Administrative Science Quarterly*, vol. 25, pp. 129–41.

Ouchi, W. G. (1981) *Theory Z* (Reading, Mass.: Addison-Wesley).

Overholt, W. H. (1993) *The Rise of China* (New York: W. W. Norton & Co).

Oxfeld, E. (1993) *Blood, Sweat and Mahjong: Family and Enterprise in an Overseas Chinese Community* (Ithaca, NY: Cornell University Press).

Pack, H. (1992) 'New Perspectives on Industrial Growth in Taiwan', in G. Ranis (ed.), *Taiwan, from Developing to Mature Economy* (Boulder, Col.: Westview Press).

Pan, L. (1991) *Sons of the Yellow Emperor* (London: Mandarin Paperbacks).

Pananond, P. and Zeithaml, C. P. (1998) 'The International Expansion Process of MNEs from Developing Countries: A Case Study of Thailand's CP Group', *Asia Pacific Journal of Management*, vol. 15, pp. 163–84.

Pang, E. F. (1994) 'Chinese Business Enterprise in Singapore and Southeast Asia: Adjusting to New Challenges at Home and Abroad', in R. Brown (ed.), *Culture, Politics, and Economic Growth: Experiences in East Asia* (Williamsburg, Va: Department of Anthropology, College of William and Mary).

Pang, E. F. (1995) 'Staying Global and Going Regional: Singapore's Inward and Outward Direct Investments', in *The New Wave of Foreign Direct Investment in Asia* (Singapore: Nomura Research Institute and Institute of Southeast Asian Studies).

Pang, E. F. and Komaran, R. V. (1985a) 'Singapore Firms in China', *Singapore Business*, vol. 9, no. 9, pp. 12–15.

Pang, E. F. and Komaran, R. V. (1985b) 'Singapore Multinationals', *Columbia Journal of World Business*, vol. 20, no. 2, pp. 35–43.

Pascale, R. T. and Athos, A. G. (1981) *The Art of Japanese Management* (New York: Simon and Schuster).

Peng, M. W. (1997) 'Firm Growth in Transitional Economies: Three Longitudinal Cases from China, 1989–96', *Organization Studies*, vol. 18, no. 3, pp. 385–413.

Penrose, E. (1995) *The Theory of the Growth of the Firm*, 3rd edn (Oxford: Oxford University Press).

Perlmutter, H. V. (1969) 'The Tortuous Evolution of the Multinational Corporations', *Columbia Journal of World Business*, January–February, pp. 9–18.

Pickles, J. and Smith, A. (eds) (1998) *Theorizing Transition: The Political Economy of Post-Communist Transformations* (London: Routledge).

Piore, M., and Sabel, C. (1984) *The Second Industrial Divide: Possibilities for Prosperity* (New York: Basic Books).

Pollard, J. (1996) 'Banking at the Margins: A Geography of Financial Exclusion in Los Angeles', *Environment and Planning A*, vol. 28, no. 7, pp. 1209–33.

Priebjrivat, V. and Rondinelli, D. A. (1994) 'Privatizing Thailand's Telecommunications Industry: A Case Study of Politics and International Business', *Business & the Contemporary World*, vol. 6, no. 1, pp. 70–83.

Pura, R. (1994) 'A Breed Apart: Stamina and Success Mark Fuzhou Chinese Diaspora', *Asian Wall Street Journal*, 8 June.

Putnam, R. D. (1993) *Making Democracy Work* (Princeton, NJ: Princeton University Press).

Ramstetter, E. D. (1996) 'Trends in Production in Foreign Multinational Firms in Asian Economies: A Note on an Economic Myth Related to Poor Measurement', *Kansai University Review of Economics and Business*, vol. 24, no. 1/2, pp. 49–107.

Redding S. G. (1990) *The Spirit of Chinese Capitalism* (New York: de Gruyter).

Redding, S. G. (1991) 'Weak Organizations and Strong Linkages: Managerial Ideology and Chinese family business networks', in G. G. Hamilton (ed.), *Business Networks and Economic Development in East and South East Asia* (Hong Kong: Centre of Asian Studies, University of Hong Kong).

Redding S. G. (1993) 'Comparative Management Theory: Jungle, Zoo, or Fossil Bed?', *Organization Studies*, vol. 15, no. 3, pp. 323–60.

Redding, S. G. (1994) 'Determinants of the Competitive Power of Small Business Networking: The Overseas Chinese Case', in H. Schütte (ed.), *The Global Competitiveness of the Asian Firm* (New York: St. Martin's Press).

Redding, S. G. (1995) 'Overseas Chinese Networks: Understanding the Enigma', *Long Range Planning*, vol. 28, no. 1, pp. 61–9.

Redding, S. G. (1996) 'Weak Organizations and Strong Linkages: Managerial Ideology and Chinese Family Business Networks', in G. G. Hamilton (ed.), *Asian Business Networks* (New York: de Gruyter), pp. 27–42.

Redding, S. G. and Tam, S. (1993) 'The Impact of Colonialism on the Formation of an Entrepreneurial Society in Hong Kong', in S. Birley and I. C. McMillan (eds), *Entrepreneurship Research: Global Perspectives* (Amsterdam: North-Holland), pp. 158–76.

Redding, S. G. and Wong, G. Y. Y. (1986) 'The Psychology of Chinese Organisational Behaviour', in M. H. Bond (ed.), *The Psychology of the Chinese People* (Oxford: Oxford University Press), pp. 267–95.

Régnier, P. (1993) 'Spreading Singapore's Wings Worldwide: A Review of Traditional and New Investment Strategies', *The Pacific Review*, vol. 6, no. 4, pp. 305–12.

Reid, A. (ed.) (1996) *Sojourners and Settlers: Histories of Southeast Asia and the Chinese* (Sydney: Allen & Unwin).

Reid, A. (1997) 'Entrepreneurial Minorities, Nationalism, and the State', in D. Chirot and A. Reid (eds), *Essential Outsiders: Chinese and Jews in the Modern Transformation of Southeast Asia and Central Europe* (Seattle: University of Washington Press).

Remmer, K. (1997) 'Theoretical Decay and Theoretical Development: The Resurgence of Institutional Analysis', *World Politics*, vol. 50, no. 1, pp. 34–61.

Rimmer, P. (1994) 'Regional Economic Integration in Pacific Asia', *Environment and Planning A*, vol. 26, no. 11, pp. 1731–60.

Robison, R. (1986) *Indonesia: The Rise of Capital* (Sydney: Allen & Unwin).

Rodan, G. (1989) *The Political Economy of Singapore's Industrialization: Nation State and International Capital* (Kuala Lumpur: Forum).

Rohlen, T. P. (1974) *For Harmony and Strength* (Berkeley, Calif.: University of California Press).

*Rong Qing* (Newsletter of the International Federation of Fuging Clans) No. 22 (1994), p. 6.

Rosenberger, L. R. (1997) 'Southeast Asia's Currency Crisis: A Diagnosis and Prescription', *Contemporary Southeast Asia*, vol. 19, no. 3, pp. 223–51.

Roth, K. and Morrison, A. J. (1992) 'Implementing Global Strategy: Characteristics of Global Subsidiary Mandates', *Journal of International Business Studies*, vol. 23, no. 4, pp. 715–35.

Roy, W. G. (1997) *Socializing Capital: The Rise of the Large Industrial Corporation in America* (Princeton, NJ: Princeton University Press).

Royal Institution of Chartered Surveyors (1993) *Understanding the property cycle*, Working Paper no. 2 (London: The Royal Institution of Chartered Surveyors), March.

Rugman, A. M. (1980) 'Internalisation as a General Theory of Foreign Direct Investment: A Re-Appraisal of the Literature', *Weltwirtschaftliches Archiv*, vol. 116, pp. 365–79.

Said, E. S. (1978) *Orientalism* (New York: Random House).

Salaff, J. W. (1995) *Working Daughters of Hong Kong: Filial Piety or Power in the Family* (New York: Columbia University Press).

Sassen, S. (1988) *The Mobility of Labor and Capital: A Study in International Investment and Labor Flow* (New York: Cambridge University Press).

Sassen, S. (1989) 'Finance and Business Services in New York City: International Linkages and Domestic Effects', in L. Rodwin and H. Sazanami (eds) *Deindustrialization and Regional Economic Transformation* (London: Unwin Hyman).

Sassen, S. (1991) *The Global City* (Princeton, NJ: Princeton University Press).

Sassen, S. (1994) *Cities in a World Economy* (Thousand Oaks, CA: Pine Forge Press).

Sassen, S. (1996) *Losing Control? Sovereignty in an Age of Globalization* (New York: Columbia University Press).

Saxenian, A. L. (1994) *Regional Advantage: Culture and Competition in Silicon Valley and Route 128* (Cambridge, Mass.: Harvard University Press).

Saxenian, A. L. (1998) 'Silicon Valley's New Immigrant Entrepreneurs and their Asian Networks', Paper presented at the International Conference on Business Transformation and Social Change in East Asia, 22–23 May, Tunghai University, Taiwan.

SCCC (Singapore Chinese Chamber of Commerce) (1931) *Singapore Chinese Chamber of Commerce Special Commemorative Publication* (in Chinese), (Singapore: SCCC).

SCCCI (Singapore Chinese Chamber of Commerce and Industry) (1991) *1st World Chinese Entrepreneurs Convention: A Global Network* (Singapore: SCCCI).

SCCCI (Singapore Chamber of Chinese Commerce and Industry) (1995) 'Why Hainan?', Unpublished article.

Scott, A. (1997) *The Limits of Globalization* (London: Routledge).

Scott, A. J. (1993) *Technopolis: High-Technology Industry and Regional Development in Southern California* (Berkeley, Calif.: University of California Press).

Seagrave, S. (1995) *Lords of the Rim: The Invisible Empire of the Overseas Chinese* (New York: G. P. Putnam's Sons).

Semkow, B. W. (1994) *Taiwan's Capital Market Reform: The Financial and Legal Issues* (Oxford: Oxford University Press).

Sender, H. (1991) 'Inside the Overseas Chinese Network', *Institutional Investor*, August, pp. 29–45.

Serrie, H. (1985) 'The Familial and the Familiar: Constancy and Variation in Chinese Culture with Reference to the Hsu Attributes', *Journal of Comparative Family Studies*, Special Issue, Summer, pp. 271–92.

Shanghai Academy of Social Sciences (ed.) (1981) *Shanghai Yongan Gongsi de Chansheng, Fazhan wo Gaizao* (The Birth, Development and Reconstitution of the Shanghai Wing On Company) (Shanghai: Renmin Chubanshe).

Shaw, G. (1993) 'It's Back to the Drawing Board for Stanley Kwok', *Vancouver Sun*, 18 September, p. C6.

Shieh, G. S. (1992) *'Boss' Island: The Subcontracting Network and Micro-Entrepreneurship in Taiwan's Development* (New York: Peter Lang).

Shikatani, T. (1995) 'Corporate Finances of Overseas Chinese Financial Groups', *Nomura Research Institute Quarterly*, vol. 4, no. 1, pp. 68–91.

Silin, R. (1972) 'Marketing and Credit in a Hong Kong Wholesale Market', in W. Willmott and L. Crissman (eds) *Economic Organization in Chinese Society* (Stanford, CA: Stanford University Press).

*Sinchew Jitpoh*, 8 October 1996, 1 January 1996.

*Singapore Business*, various issues.

*Singapore–China Trade & Investment Directory 1997/1998, 3rd edn*. (1997) (Singapore: Longkin Consultants & Publishers Pte Ltd.).

Sinn, E. (1995) 'Emigration from Hong Kong before 1941: General Trends' and 'Emigration from Hong Kong before 1941: Organization and Impact', in R. Skeldon (ed.), *Emigration from Hong Kong* (Hong Kong: Chinese University of Hong Kong Press).

Sinn, E. (1997) *'Xin Xi Guxiang*: A Study of Regional Associations as a Bonding Mechanism in the Chinese Diaspora. The Hong Kong Experience', *Modern Asian Studies*, vol. 31, no. 2, pp. 375–97.

Sit, V. F. S., Siu-lun Wong and Kiang T. S. (1979) *Small-scale Industry in a Laissez-faire Economy* (Hong Kong: Centre of Asian Studies, University of Hong Kong).

Sit, V. and Wong, S.-L. (1989) *Small and Medium Industries in an Export-Oriented Economy: The Case of Hong Kong* (Hong Kong: Centre of Asian Studies, University of Hong Kong).

Skeldon, R. (ed.) (1994) *Reluctant Exiles? Migration from Hong Kong and the New Overseas Chinese* (Armonk, NY: M. E. Sharpe).

Skeldon, R. (1995) *Emigration from Hong Kong* (Hong Kong: Chinese University of Hong Kong Press).

Smart, A. (1992). *Making Room: Squatter Clearance in Hong Kong* (Hong Kong: Centre of Asian Studies, University of Hong Kong).

Smart, A. (1993) 'Gifts, Bribes and *guanxi*: A Reconsideration of Bourdieu's Social Capital', *Cultural Anthropology*, vol. 8, no. 3, pp. 388–408.

Smart, A. (1995) '*The Social Construction of Markets in China: State and Society in Transformation*', unpublished manuscript.

Smart, A. (1998) 'Economic Transformation in China: Property Regimes and Social Relations', in J. Pickles and A. Smith (eds), *Theorizing Transition: The Political Economy of Post-Communist Transformations* (London: Routledge), pp. 428–50.

Smart, A. and Smart, J. (1992) 'Capitalist Production in a Socialist Society: The Transfer of Manufacturing from Hong Kong to China', in F. Rothstein and M. Blim (eds), *Anthropology and the Global Factory* (New York: Bergin & Garvey).

Smart, A. and Smart, J. (1998) 'Transnational Social Networks and Negotiated Identities in Interactions between Hong Kong and China', in M. P. Smith and L. E. Guarnizo (eds), *Transnationalism from Below* (New Brunswick: Transaction Publishers), pp. 103–29.

Smart, J. (1989) *The Political Economy of Street Hawkers in Hong Kong* (Hong Kong: Centre of Asian Studies, University of Hong Kong).

Smart, J. and Smart, A. (1991) 'Personal Relations and Divergent Economies: A Case Study of Hong Kong Investment in South China', *International Journal of Urban and Regional Research*, vol. 15, no. 2, pp. 216–33.

Smart, J. and Smart, A. (1993) 'Obligation and Control: Employment of Kin in Capitalist Labour Management in China', *Critique of Anthropology*, vol. 13, no. 1, pp. 7–31.

SME Committee (1989) *Report on Enterprise Development* (Singapore: Economic Development Board).

Sohn, D. J. H. (1994) 'Social Knowledge as a Control System: A Proposition and Evidence From the Japanese FDI Behaviour', *Journal of International Business Studies*, vol. 25, no. 2, pp. 295–324.

*South China Morning Post* (various dates), Hong Kong daily newspaper.

Stillwell, F. (1996) 'Globalization: Reshaping Australian Cities', Unpublished MS.

*Straits Times, The,* Singapore, various issues.

Suarez-Villa, L. and Karlsson, C. (1996) 'The Development of Sweden's R&D-Intensive Electronics Industries: Exports, Outsourcing, and Territorial Distribution', *Environment and Planning A*, vol. 28, no. 5, pp. 783–818.

Suehiro, A. (1985) *Capital Accumulation and Industrial Development in Thailand* (Bangkok: Chulalongkorn University Social Research Institute).

Suehiro, A. (1992) 'Capitalist Development in Postwar Thailand: Commercial Bankers, Industrial Elites, and Agribusiness Groups', in R. McVey (ed.), *Southeast Asian Capitalists* (Ithaca, NY: Cornell University Southeast Asia Program).

Suehiro, A. (1998) *Modern Family Business and Corporation Capability in Thailand: A Case Study of the CP Group*, Paper presented at the Workshop on Asian Business Networks, National University of Singapore, 31 March–2 April.

Sung, Y.-W. (1991) *The China–Hong Kong Connection* (Cambridge: Cambridge University Press).

Sung, Y.-W. (1996) '"Dragon Head" of China's Economy?', in Yue-man Yeung and Yun-wing Sung (eds), *Shanghai: Transformation and Modernization Under China's Open Policy* (Hong Kong: Chinese University of Hong Kong Press).

Sung, Y.-W. (1997) 'Hong Kong and the Economic Integration of the China Circle', in B. Naughton (ed.), *The China Circle* (Washington: Brookings Institution Press), pp. 41–80.

Suryadinata, L. (1988) 'Chinese Economic Elites in Indonesia: A Preliminary Study', in J. W. Cushman and Gungwu Wang (eds), *Changing Identities of the Southeast Asian Chinese Since World War II* (Hong Kong: Hong Kong University Press).

Suryadinata, L. (ed.) (1995) *Southeast Asian Chinese and China: The Political-Economic Dimension* (Singapore: Times Academic Press).

Suryadinata, L. (ed.) (1997) *Ethnic Chinese as Southeast Asians* (Singapore: Institute of Southeast Asian Studies).

Swedberg, R. (1990) *Economics and Sociology: Redefining their Boundaries: Conversations with Economists and Sociologists* (Princeton, NJ: Princeton University Press).

Szczepanik, E. (1958) *The Economic Growth of Hong Kong* (London: Oxford University Press).

*Sunday Times, The,* 17 April 1994.

Tan, C. H. (1995) *Venturing Overseas: Singapore's External Wing* (Singapore: McGraw-Hill).

Teece, D. (1986) 'Transactions Cost Economics and the Multinational Enterprise', *Journal of Economic Behaviour and Organisation*, vol. 7, pp. 23–45.

Hong Kong Cotton Spinners Association (1988) *Forty Years of The Hong Kong Cotton Spinning Industry* (Hong Kong: Hong Kong Cotton Spinners Association).

Thrift, N. (1987) 'The Fixers: The Urban Geography of International Commercial Capital', in J. Henderson and M. Castells (eds), *Global Restructuring and Territorial Development* (London: Sage).

Thrift, N., and Olds, K. (1996) 'Refiguring the Economic in Economic Geography', *Progress in Human Geography*, vol. 20, no. 3, pp. 311–37.

Tien, Ju-k'ang. (1953) *The Chinese of Sarawak: A Study of Social Structure* Monographs on Social Anthropology, 12 (London: London School of Economics).

Tong, C. K. (1991) 'Centripetal Authority, Differentiated Networks: The Social Organization of Chinese Firms in Singapore', in G. Hamilton (ed.), *Business Networks and Economic Development in East and Southeast Asia* (Hong Kong: Centre of Asian Studies, University of Hong Kong).

Tong, C. K. and Yong, P. K. (1998) 'Guanxi Bases, Xinyong and Chinese Business Networks', *British Journal of Sociology*, vol. 49, no. 1, pp. 75–96.

Tong-an Association (1994) *A Commemorative Publication for the Founding of World Tong-an Association* (in Chinese). (Singapore: Tong-an Association).

Tsang, E. W. K. (1998) 'Can *Guanxi* Be a Source of Sustained Competitive Advantage for Doing Business in China?', *Academy of Management Executive*, vol. 12, no. 2, pp. 64–73.

Tseng, Y.-F. (1994a) 'Suburban Ethnic Economy: Chinese Business Communities in Los Angeles', Ph.D. dissertation, Department of Sociology, University of California, Los Angeles.

Tseng, Y. -F. (1994b) 'Chinese Ethnic Economy: San Gabriel Valley, Los Angeles County', *Journal of Urban Affairs*, vol. 16, no. 2, pp. 169–89.

Tu, W. M. (1984) *Confucian Ethics Today* (Singapore: Federal Publications).

Tu, W. M. (ed.) (1994) *The Living Tree: The Changing Meaning of Being Chinese Today* (Stanford, CA: Stanford University Press).

Tuan, C. and Ng, L. F.-Y. (1994) 'Economic Liberalization in China and Structural Adjustment of Hong Kong Manufacturing', *Seoul Journal of Economics*, vol. 7, no. 2, pp. 141–60.

Tuan, C. and Ng, L. F.-Y. (1995) 'Manufacturing Evolution under Passive Industrial Policy and Cross-Border Operations in China: The Case of Hong Kong', *Journal of Asian Economics*, vol. 6, no. 1, pp. 71–88.

Tuan, C. and Wong, C.-S. (1993) 'Evolution of Foreign Direct Investment Patterns and Management of TNCs in Hong Kong', *Regional Development Dialogue*, vol. 14, no. 4, pp. 125–45.

Unger, J. (1996) 'Bridges: Private Business, the Chinese Government and the Rise of the New Associations', *The China Quarterly*, no. 147, pp. 795–819.

U.S. Bureau of Census (1990) *Census of Population and Housing* (Washington, DC: US Government Printing Office).

*U.S. Bank Performance Profile: An Index of Banking Performance Service* (1991) (Rolling Meadows, IA: Bank Administration Institute).

United Nations Conference on Trade and Development (1994) *World Investment Report 1994: Transnational Corporations, Employment and the Workplace* (New York: United Nations).

United Nations Conference on Trade and Development (1996a) *World Investment Report 1996* (New York: United Nations).

United Nations Conference on Trade and Development (1996b) *Transnational Corporations and World Development* (London: International Thomson Business Press).

United Nations Conference on Trade and Development (1997) *World Investment Report 1997* (New York: United Nations).

United Nations Conference on Trade and Development (1998) *World Investment Report 1998* (New York: United Nations).

United Nations Center on Transnational Corporations (1992) *World Investment Report 1992: Transnational Corporations as Engines of Growth* (New York: United Nations).

Van Den Bulcke, D. (1995) 'The Strategic Management of Multinationals in A Triad-based World Economy', in A. M. Rugman, J. Van Den Broeck and A. Verbeke (eds), *Global Strategic Management* (London: JAI Press).

Van Den Bulcke, D. and Zhang, H.-Y. (1995) 'Chinese Family-owned Multinationals in the Philippines and the Internationalisation Process', in R. A. Brown (ed.), *Chinese Business Enterprise in Asia* (London: Routledge).

Vogel, E. (1979) *Japan as Number 1: Lessons for America* (New York: Harper & Row).

Wade, R. (1990) *Governing the Market: Economic Theory and the Role of Government in East Asian Industrialization* (Princeton, NJ: Princeton University Press).

Wade, R. and Veneroso F. (1998) 'The Asian Crisis: The High Debt Model versus the Wall Street – Treasury – IMF Complex', *New Left Review*, no. 228, pp. 3–23.

Wakeman, F. Jr and Yeh, W.-H. (eds), (1992) *Shanghai Sojourners* (Berkeley, Calif.: Institute of East Asian Studies, University of California).

Waldinger, R. D. and Tseng, Y. F. (1992) 'Divergent Diasporas: The Chinese Communities of New York and Los Angeles Compared', *Revue Europeenne Des Migrations Internationales*, vol. 8, no. 3, pp. 91–116.

Waldinger, R. D. (1986) *Through the Eye of the Needle: Immigrants and Enterprise in New York's Garment Trades* (New York: New York University Press).

Walker, R. (1985) 'Is There a Service Economy: The Changing Capitalist Division of Labor', *Science and Society*, vol. 39, pp. 42–83.

Wang, Gungwu (1981) *Community and Nation: Essays on Southeast Asia and the Chinese* (Singapore: Heinemann).

Wang, Gungwu (1991) *China and the Chinese Overseas* (Singapore: Times Academic Press).

Wang, Gungwu (1997) 'Migration History: Some Patterns Revisited', in Wang Gungwu (ed.), *Global History and Migrations* (Boulder, Col.: Westview Press).

Wang, T. P. (1995) *The Origins of Chinese Kongsi* (Petaling Jaya: Pelanduk Publications).

Wang, Z. M. (1994) 'Culture, Economic Reform, and the Role of Industrial and Organizational Psychology in China', in H. C. Triandis, M. D. Dunnette and L. M. Hough (eds), *Handbook of Industrial and Organizational Psychology*, vol. 4 (Palo Alto, Calif.: Consulting Psychologists Press), pp. 689–726.

Weidenbaum, M. and Hughes, S. (1996) *The Bambook Network: How Expatriate Chinese Entrepreneurs are Creating a New Economic Superpower in Asia* (New York: The Free Press).

Weiss, L. (1998) *The Myth of the Powerless State: Governing the Economy in a Global Era* (Cambridge: Polity Press).

Wells, L. T., Jr (1992) 'Mobile Exporters: New Foreign Investors in East Asia', in K. A. Froot (ed.), *Foreign Direct Investment* (Chicago: University of Chicago Press).

Wickberg, E. (1965) *The Chinese in Philippine Life, 1850–1898* (New Haven, Conn.: Yale University Press).

White, L. T., III (1989) *Shanghai Shanghaied? Uneven Taxes in Reform China* (Hong Kong: Centre of Asian Studies, University of Hong Kong).

Whitley, R. (1990) 'East Asian Enterprise Structures and the Comparative Analysis of Forms of Business Organization', *Organization Studies*, vol. 11, no. 1, pp. 47–74.

Whitley, R. (1991) 'The Social Construction of Business Systems in East Asia', *Organization Studies*, vol. 12, no. 1, pp. 1–28.

Whitley, R. (1992) *Business Systems in East Asia: Firms, Markets and Societies* (London: Sage).

Whitley, R. (1994) 'The Internationalization of Firms and Markets: Its Significance and Institutional Structuring', *Organization*, vol. 1, no. 1, pp. 101–24.

Whitley, R. (1998) 'Internationalization and Varieties of Capitalism: The Limited Effects of Cross-national Coordination of Economic Activities on the Nature of Business Systems', *Review of International Political Economy*, vol. 5, no. 3, pp. 445–81.

Whyte, M. K. (1996) 'The Chinese Family and Economic Development: Obstacle or Engine?', _Economic Development and Cultural Change_, vol. 45, no. 1, pp. 1–30.

Willcocks, L. and Choi, C. J. (1995) 'Co-operative Partnership and "Total" IT Outsourcing: From Contractual Obligation to Strategic Alliance?', _European Management Journal_, vol. 13, no. 1, pp. 67–78.

Williamson, O. E. (1975) _Markets and Hierarchies_ (New York: The Free Press).

Williamson, O. E. (1985) _The Economic Institutions of Capitalism_ (New York: The Free Press).

Williamson, O. E. (1991) 'Comparative Economic Organisation: The Analysis of Discrete Structural Alternatives', _Administrative Science Quarterly_, vol. 36, no. 2, pp. 269–96.

Williamson, O. E. (1993) 'Calculativeness, Trust, and Economic Organisation', _Journal of Law and Economics_, vol. 36, no. 1, pp. 453–86.

Williamson, R. (1992) 'Kwok's Connections Open Doors to Asia,' _Globe and Mail_, 6 April, pp. B1–B2.

Willis, K. D. and Yeoh, B. (1998) 'The Social Sustainability of Singapore's Regionalisation Drive', _Third World Planning Review_, vol. 20, no. 2, pp. 203–21.

Willmott, W. and Crissman, L. (1972) _Economic Organization in Chinese Society_ (Stanford, CA: Stanford University Press).

Windolf, P. and Beyer, J. (1996) 'Co-operative Capitalism: Corporate Networks in Germany and Britain', _British Journal of Sociology_, vol. 47, no. 2, pp. 205–31.

Winn, J. K. (1994) 'Relational Practices and the Marginalization of Law: Informal Financial Practices of Small Businesses in Taiwan', _Law and Society Review_, vol. 28, no. 2, pp. 193–232.

Wong, B. (1988) _Patronage, Brokerage, Entrepreneurship and the Chinese Community of New York_ (New York: AMS Press).

Wong, G. (1996) 'Business Groups in a Dynamic Environment: Hong Kong 1976–1986', in G. Hamilton (ed.), _Asian Business Networks_ (Berlin: Walter de Gruyter).

Wong, S.-L. (1985) 'The Chinese Family Firm: A Model', _British Journal of Sociology_, vol. 36, no. 1, pp. 58–72.

Wong, S.-L. (1988) _Emigrant Entrepreneurs: Shanghai Industrialists in Hong Kong_ (Hong Kong: Oxford University Press).

Wong, S.-L. (1995) 'Business Networks, Cultural Values and the State in Hong Kong and Singapore', in R. Ampalavana Brown (ed.), _Chinese Business Enterprise in Asia_ (London: Routledge).

Wong, S.-L. (1996a) 'Chinese Entrepreneurs and Business Trust', in G. Hamilton (ed.), _Asian Business Networks_ (Berlin: Walter de Gruyter).

Wong, S.-L. (1996b) 'Chinese Entrepreneurship and Economic Development', in J. Unger and B. McCormick (eds), _China's Prospects: Lessons From Eastern Europe and East Asia_ (New York: M. E. Sharpe).

Wong, S.-L. (1996c) 'The Entrepreneurial Spirit: Shanghai and Hong Kong Compared', in Yue-man Yeung and Yun-wing Sung (eds), _Shanghai: Transformation and Modernization Under China's Open Policy_ (Hong Kong: Chinese University of Hong Kong Press).

Wong, S.-L. (1997) 'Trust and Prosperity: The Role of Chinese Family Enterprise in Economic Development', T. T. Tsui Lecture in Asia Pacific Business, University of Hong Kong, 3 February 1997.

Wong, S.-L. (1999) 'Deciding to Move, Deciding to Stay, Deciding Not to Decide', in G. Hamilton (ed.), *Cosmopolitan Capitalists: Hong Kong and the Chinese Diaspora at the End of the 20th Century*. (Seattle: University of Washington Press).

Wong, S.-L. and Salaff, J. W. (1998) 'Network Capital: Emigration from Hong Kong', *British Journal of Sociology*, vol. 49, no. 3, pp. 358–74.

Wong, T. W. P. (1991) 'Inequality, Stratification and Mobility', in Siu-kai Lau, Ming-kwan Lee, Po-san Wan and Siu-lun Wong (eds), *Indicators of Social Development: Hong Kong 1988* (Hong Kong: Hong Kong Institute of Asia-Pacific Studies, Chinese University of Hong Kong).

Woon, Y.-F. (1989) 'Social Change and Continuity in South China: Overseas Chinese and the Guan Lineage of Kaiping County, 1949–87', *The China Quarterly*, no. 118, pp. 324–44.

Wu, F. and Duk, S. Y. (1995a) 'Hong Kong and Singapore: "Twin Capitals" for Overseas Chinese Capital', *Business & The Contemporary World*, vol. 7, no. 3, pp. 21–33.

Wu and Duk (1995b) '(Overseas) China, Inc.', *International Economy*, January/February, pp. 33–5.

Wu, Y. L. and Wu, C. H. (1980) *Economic Development in Southeast Asia: The Chinese Dimension* (Stanford, Calif.: Hoover Institution).

Xing, Y. S., Han, Q. Y. and Huang, L. J. (1991) *Ups and Down of Overseas Hainanese* (Hainan: Nanhai chuban gongsi).

Yan, Y.-X. (1996a) 'The Culture of *Guanxi* in a North China Village', *The China Journal*, no. 35, January, pp. 1–25.

Yan, Y.-X. (1996b) *The Flow of Gifts. Reciprocity and Social Networks and a Chinese Village* (Stanford, CA.: Stanford University Press).

Yang, M. (1994) *Gifts, Favors, and Banquets: The Arts of Social Relationships in China* (Ithaca, NY: Cornell University Press).

Yao, Souchou (1997) 'The Romance of Asian Capitalism: Geography, Desire and Chinese Business', in Mark T. Berger and Douglas A. Borer (eds), *The Rise of Asia: Critical Visions of the Pacific Century* (London: Routledge).

Yeung, H. W. C. (1994a) 'Transnational Corporations from Asian Developing Countries: Their Characteristics and Competitive Edge', *Journal of Asian Business*, vol. 10, no. 4, pp. 17–58.

Yeung, H. W. C. (1994b) 'Third World Multinationals Revisited: A Research Critique and Future Agenda', *Third World Quarterly*, vol. 15, no. 2, pp. 297–317.

Yeung, H. W. C. (1994c) 'Critical Reviews of Geographical Perspectives on Business Organisations and the Organisation of Production: Towards a Network Approach', *Progress in Human Geography*, vol. 18, no. 4, pp. 460–90.

Yeung, H. W. C. (1996) 'The Historical Geography of Hong Kong Investments in the ASEAN Region', *Singapore Journal of Tropical Geography*, vol. 17, no. 1, pp. 66–82.

Yeung, H. W. C. (1997a) 'Cooperative Strategies and Chinese Business Networks: A Study of Hong Kong Transnational Corporations in the ASEAN Region', in P. W. Beamish and J. P. Killing (eds), *Cooperative Strategies: Asia-Pacific Perspectives* (San Francisco: New Lexington Press), pp. 22–56.

Yeung, H. W. C. (1997b) 'Business Networks and Transnational Corporations: A Study of Hong Kong Firms in the ASEAN Region', *Economic Geography*, vol. 73, no. 1, pp. 1–25.

Yeung, H. W. C. (1998a) 'The Political Economy of Transnational Corporations: A Study of the Regionalisation of Singaporean Firms', *Political Geography*, vol. 17, no. 4, pp. 389–416.

Yeung, H. W. C. (1998b) *Transnational Corporations and Business Networks: Hong Kong Firms in the ASEAN Region* (London: Routledge).

Yeung, H. W. C. (1998c) 'Transnational Economic Synergy and Business Networks: The Case of Two-way Investment between Malaysia and Singapore', *Regional Studies*, vol. 32, no. 8, pp. 687–706.

Yeung, H. W. C. (1999a) 'The Internationalization of Ethnic Chinese Business Firms from Southeast Asia: Strategies, Processes and Competitive Advantage', *International Journal of Urban and Regional Research*, vol. 23, no. 1, pp. 103–27.

Yeung, H. W. C. (1999b) 'Regulating Investment Abroad? The Political Economy of the Regionalisation of Singaporean Firms', *Antipode*, vol. 31, no. 3, pp. 245–73.

Yeung, H. W. C. (1999c) 'Neoliberalism, *laissez-faire* Capitalism and Economic Crisis: The Political Economy of Deindustrialisation in Hong Kong', *Competition and Change*, vol. 4, no. 2, pp. 1–49.

Yeung, H. W. C. (1999d) 'Service Transnational Corporations from Hong Kong: An Emerging Competitor in the Regional and Global Marketplace', *International Business Review*, vol. 6.

Yeung, H. W. C. (1999e), 'Under Siege? Economic Globalisation and Chinese Business in Southeast Asia', *Economy and Society*, vol. 28, no. 1, pp. 1–29.

Yin, R. K. (1994) *Case Study Research* (Thousand Oaks, CA: Sage Publications).

Yong, P. A. (1995) 'Singapore's Investment in China,' in L. Suryadinata (ed.), *Southeast Asian Chinese and China: The Politico-Economic Dimension* (Singapore: Times Academic Press), pp. 249–54.

Yoshihara, K. (1988) *The Rise of Ersatz Capitalism in South East Asia* (Singapore: Oxford University Press).

Yoshihara, K. (1994) *The Nation and Economic Growth: The Philippines and Thailand* (Singapore: Oxford University Press).

Zhang, G. and Sjoberg, O. (1992) 'Institutions and Managerial Strategies in China', Research Report No. 13, Economic Research Institute, Stockholm School of Economics.

Zhou, M. (1992) *Chinatown: The Socioeconomic Potential of an Urban Enclave* (Philadelphia: Temple University Press).

Zhou, Y. (1996) 'Inter-Firm Linkages, Ethnic Networks and Territorial Agglomeration: Chinese Computer Firms in Los Angeles', *Papers in Regional Science*, vol. 75, no. 3, pp. 265–91.

Zhou Y. (1998a) 'Beyond Ethnic Enclaves: Location Strategies of Chinese Producer Services Firms in Los Angeles', *Economic Geography*, vol. 74, no. 3, pp. 228–51.

Zhou Y. (1998b) 'How Do Places Matter? Comparative Studies of Chinese Ethnic Economies in Los Angeles and New York', *Urban Geography*, vol. 19, no. 6, pp. 531–53.

# Name Index

Abegglen, J.C. 57
Aldrich, H. 171
Amin, A. 27
Amsden, A. 83
Angel, D.P. 191
Appadurai, A. 119, 199
Appelbaum, R.P. 83, 252
Aronoff, C.E. 276
Arrow, K. 123–5
Athos, A.G. 33
Azores, T. 175

Bachmann, R. 15
Bailly, A.S. 169, 175
Bartlett, C.A. 22, 24, 85,
    128, 149
Barton, C. 204
Baum, A. 202
Beamish, P.W. 232
Beauregard, R. 195
Beaverstock, J. 203
Beazley, M. 214
Ben, X.S. 192
Benton, G. 27
Berger, P.L. 32
Berle, A.A. 36
Berry, M. 201
Beyer, J. 15
Beyers, W. 169
Biggart, N.W. 59, 76, 129, 131,
    168, 218, 250, 252
Birkinshaw, J.M. 277
Björkman, I. 15
Boddewyn, J.J. 131
Boden, D. 211
Boisot, M. 128, 132
Bond, M.H. 17, 35
Bourdieu, P. 120
Boyer, R. 27, 59
Brook, T. 82
Brown, R.A. 11, 18, 21, 27, 71, 76,
    81, 108, 113, 126, 134
Buckley, P.J. 127, 128

Burnham, J. 36
Burt, R.S. 131

Cadario, P.M. 221, 222, 235
Campbell, J.P. 35
Cartier, C.L. 221, 239
Casson, M. 21, 127, 129, 131, 134
Castells, M. 15, 129, 200, 250
Caves, R.E. 21
Chan, K.B. 16, 17, 251, 254
Chan, W.K. 153
Chan, W.K.K. 5, 11, 80, 87–9, 163
Chandler, A.D., Jr 58, 59, 81, 276
Chang, C.-Y. 163
Chang, T.L. 83
Chearavanont, D. 4, 71, 73
Chen, Che-hung 83
Chen, Chieh-hsuan 65
Chen, H.M. 83
Chen, M. 64, 65, 80
Chen, T.-J. 64, 70, 72, 83
Chen, X.-M. 61, 63, 65, 78, 83
Chen, Y.-S. 163
Cheng, L. 173
Cheng, L.-K. 109
Cheng, Y.T. 91, 196, 207, 210, 212
Chai, E.C. 92
Chia, S.W. 92
Chia, S.Y. 70, 72
Chiang, S.-N.C. 16, 17, 251, 254
Chin, K.W. 239
Chirot, D. 37
Chiu, S. 253
Chiu, S.W.K. 83, 239, 252
Choi, C.J. 27
Chou, W.H. 154
Chow, C.-K. 90
Chow, W. 219
Chow, W.-H. 90
Chu, G.C. 161
Chua, L.K. 121
Christerson, B. 245, 252, 257
Chung, C. 70

Chung, W.-K. 74
Clifford, J. 120
Coffey, W.J. 169, 173
Cohen, R. 67, 124
Cox, H. 129
Cox, K.R. 27
Crissman, L. 218
Cumings, B. 244, 249
Cushman, J.W. 18

Daniels, P.W. 169
DeGlopper, D.R. 65
Demsetz, H. 128
DeMont, J. 173
Deng, X.P. 160
Dicken, P. 2, 27, 75, 77, 167
Dirlik, A. 9, 11, 13, 105, 244, 249
Dixon, C. 5
Dobson, W. 70, 72
Dodwell, D. 160, 253
Doremus, P.N. 27
Douglass, M. 198
Drache, D. 27
Drucker, P. 114
Duk, S.Y. 8, 92
Dunning, J.H. 21, 75, 82, 234
Dymski, G.A. 181, 187

Eccles, R.G. 128, 129, 217
Edwards, I. 211, 215
Ellis, P. 27
Emmerson, D.K. 28, 247
Elvis, P. 38
Eng, I. 258, 270
Engardio, P. 191
Engstrom, J. 191
Enright, M.J. 160, 252, 253
Eriksson, K. 132, 133

Faison, S. 121
Fallows, J. 57
Faure, D. 67, 153
Fei, X.T. 61, 62, 63, 154, 155
Feng, C.-Y. 221, 222, 224, 226, 229, 235
Fennell, F. 173
Fitzgerald, R. 83
Fligstein, N. 59
Florin, J.M. 130

Fok, Y.T. 210
Fong, T.P. 170, 174
Forsgren, M. 129
Fung, V. 27
Fukuyama, F. 41, 57, 58, 123, 263

Gambetta, D. 43, 263
Gates, H. 67
Geertz, C. 65, 124
Gereffi, G. 59, 203
Gertler, M. 203
Ghoshal, S. 22, 24, 85, 128, 149
Go, F.M. 97
Godley, M.R. 163
Goldberg, M.A. 168
Goodman, B. 109
Goodman, D.S.G. 221, 222, 224, 226, 229, 235, 246
Gosling, P. 35, 107, 218
Grabher, G. 269
Granovetter, M. 79, 203, 217
Gray, C. 204
Greenhalgh, S. 11, 13, 59, 60, 65, 66, 252, 264, 276
Gross, N. 191
Guo, L. 88
Guthrie, D. 15, 259, 260, 263, 270, 271
Gutstein, D. 196, 207, 219

Haggard, S. 28
Haila, A. 195, 199
Haley, G.T. 15, 76
Haley, U.C.V. 15, 76
Halim, R. 108
Hamilton, G.G. 1, 11, 12, 15, 17, 22, 23, 35, 38, 59, 63, 65, 67, 68, 70, 71, 74, 76, 92, 105, 124, 129, 131, 168, 196, 203, 205, 218, 250, 252, 278
Hamnett, C. 217
Han, Q.Y. 221, 223
Handler, W.C. 276
Handley, P. 27
Hannerz, U. 215
Hansen, N. 169
Harcourt, M. 211
Hardman, G. 210
Harrington, J.W. 169

Harris, R.   202
Harrison, B.   59
Harvey, D.   198
Hawes, G.   123
Haynes, K.E.   246, 261
Hedlund, G.   128
Hefner, R.W.   12, 82, 123
Henderson, J.   83
Hendrischke, H.   287
Heng, P.K.   240
Hennart, J.F.   127
Hicks, G.L.   18
Hill, C.W.L.   127
Hirst, P.   27, 75
Ho, K.C.   83, 239, 252
Ho, Y.-P.   83, 252, 254
Hobday, M.   27
Hodder, R.   5, 7, 8, 10, 13, 14, 15,
   76, 80, 82
Hodgson, G.M.   79
Hofstede, G.   34, 40
Holberton, S.   218
Hollingsworth, J.R.   59
Holm, U.   130
Hooijmaijers, M.   232, 235, 238
Houston, P.   56, 74
Howe, C.   78
Howlett, B.   160
Hoy, F.   276
Hsing, Y.-T.   10, 18, 28, 66, 70, 71,
   72, 78, 80, 245, 252, 256–8
Huang, L.J.   221, 223
Hughes, S.   5, 7, 8, 9, 15, 21, 76, 85,
   86, 91, 92, 99, 102, 240, 258, 264
Hu, Y.-S.   24, 87, 100–2
Hui, K.M.   211
Hulchanski, J.D.   214
Huntington, S.   124
Hwang, H.   177, 180, 181, 188
Hwang, K.-K.   58, 62, 63

Ip, D.   108, 164

Jacobs, N.   38
Jamann, W.   66, 225
Jessop, B.   27
Jesudason, J.V.   18, 19, 20, 82
Jin, D.-J.   245, 261
Johanson, J.   130, 133

Jomo, K.S.   20
Ju, Y.-N.   161
Jones, G.R.   127

Kanai, T.   220, 238, 239
Kao, C.-S.   15, 38, 66, 70, 204, 218
Kao, J.   1, 10, 35, 72, 73, 76, 121,
   126, 135
Kearney, M.   105, 124
Keister, L.A.   15
Keller, W.W.   27
Kelly, P.F.   27
Kiang, T.S.   252
Killing, J.P.   232
Kim, T.J.   20
King, A. Yeo-chi   12, 61, 63,
   115, 257
Kipnis, A.B.   63, 249, 259
Kirby, W.C.   74
Kitay, J.   108, 164
Ko, A.C.K.   38
Kock, S.   15
Komaran, R.V.   221, 238, 241
Kondo, D.K.   60
Kong, L.   27
Kotkin, J.   1, 240
Kraar, L.   8
Krause, L.B.   254
Krugman, P.   270
Kuok, R.H.N.   4, 20, 73, 90, 107,
   142, 196
Kwek, L.B.   4
Kwok, S.   209–11, 213–16, 219
Kwok, T.S.   210

La Croix, S.J.   78
Lam, K.C.   262
Landa, J.T.   66, 111
Lane, C.   15
Lang, G.   271
Larson, A.   131
Lasserre, P.   68, 72, 73, 136
Lau, H.-F.   89
Lau, S.-K.   43, 158, 204
Lee, K.   78
Lee, K.Y.   34, 107
Lee, S.-K.   91, 196, 207, 210, 212
Lee, T.Y.   238, 239
Leslie, G.   212

Lever-Tracy, C.   108, 164, 245, 257
Levy, R.   262
Lévy, B.   77
Lewis, J.D.   15, 27
Ley, D.   195, 209, 214
Li, D.-S.   91
Li, K.S.   4, 51, 53, 73, 91, 97, 196, 207, 212, 213, 216, 218, 219, 277
Li, L.C.   259, 263, 370
Li, V.   207, 208, 214
Li, W.-Z.   121
Liao, C.-Y.   109
Light, I.   170, 181, 182
Lim, L.Y.C.   10, 35, 107, 141, 143, 147, 204, 218
Liem, S.L.   4, 20, 50, 53, 73, 107, 108, 114
Limlingan, V.S.   10, 18, 21, 65, 66, 136
Lindquist, F.   128
Lin, P.-A.   204, 218, 270
Lin, T.B.   252, 254
Lin, T.C.   115, 257
Lin, Y.   258
Ling, L.S.   116
Liu, H.   11, 24, 108, 109–12, 115, 119, 120, 123, 238
Liu, J.M.   173
Liu, P.C.   71, 72
Liu, Y.C.   71, 72
Loftman, P.   214
Logan, J.   198, 199
Loke, Y.   27
Low, L.   92
Lu, D.   221, 239
Lui, T.-L.   63, 83, 239, 252, 253
Luo, Q.   78
Luong, Hy V.   82
Lynn, P.   18

MacIntyre, A.   28
Mackie, J.   16, 19, 35, 82, 105, 111, 136, 141
Magnusson, L.   247
Magretta, J.   27
Majkgard, A.   133
Markoulis, J.   213, 219

Malnight, T.W.   85
Mark, L. Li   65
Marshall, G.   124
Marshall, J.N.   167, 190
Matas, R.   212
Mathews, J.A.   27, 79, 83
Mattsson, L.-G.   130
McCarthy, G.   212, 215
McElderry, A.   5, 80
McVey, R.   18, 19, 82, 113
Menkhoff, T.   11, 15, 18, 21
Min, P.G.   170
Mitchell, K.   10, 25, 80, 97, 195–7, 207, 214, 215, 277
Mittelman, J.H.   27
Mohammed Mahathir   90
Mok, V.   252, 254
Montagu-Pollock, M.   218
Moran, R.T.   78
Morishima, M.   33
Morrison, A.J.   277
Mueller, G.   199
Murphy, K.   219

Narod, A.   210
Naughton, B.   70, 245
Neller, R.J.   262
Nevin, B.   214
Nevitt, C.E.   123
Ng, L.F.-Y.   78, 253
Nixon, R.   172
Nohria, N.   85, 128, 129
Nonini, D.M.   11, 13, 21, 244
North, D.C.   63, 112, 124
Numazaki, I.   65, 66, 72, 218
Nyaw, M.-K.   159

Oei, T.H.   27
Ogawa, K.   221, 222, 235
Ohmae, K.   75, 77
Olds, K.   1, 10, 15, 21, 24, 26, 27, 80, 81, 97, 105, 166, 195, 200, 201, 207, 217, 219, 249, 276, 277
Ong, A.   9, 11, 13, 21, 106, 244, 249
Ong, P.   175
Orrù, M.   59, 76
Ouchi, W.G.   33, 131

Overholt, W.H.   249
Oxfeld, E.   248

Pack, H.   66
Pan, L.   58
Pananond, P.   27
Pang, E.F.   221, 225, 238–41
Pangilinan, M.   53
Pao, Y.K.   51, 73
Pascale, R.T.   32
Pauly, L.W.   27
Peng, M.W.   15
Penrose, E.   36, 45
Perlmutter, H.V.   85
Phillips, I.   108, 164
Pickles, J.   260
Pine, R.   97
Piore, M.   59, 203
Plummer, M.   78
Pollard, J.   181, 182
Priebjrivat, V.   81
Pura, R.   107
Putnam, R.D.   41

Quek, L.C.   4

Ramstetter, E.D.   9, 92
Redding, S.G.   10, 12, 15, 17, 18,
    21–3, 35, 39, 40, 47, 58, 72, 76,
    80, 126, 134, 135, 137, 139, 142,
    146, 149, 197, 204, 218, 225, 244,
    249–51, 255, 269
Régnier, P.   220
Reich, S.   27
Reid, A.   5, 10, 27, 157
Remmer, K.   124
Riady, M.   4, 121
Riesenberger, J.R.   78
Rimmer, P.   198
Robison, R.   19
Rohlen, T.P.   33
Rondinelli, D.A.   81
Rong, H.-Y.   89
Rosenberger, L.R.   28
Roth, K.   277
Roy, W.G.   59
Rugman, A.M.   127

Sabel, C.   59, 203

Said, E.S.   59
Salaff, J.W.   164, 197, 253
Sassen, S.   27, 169, 198, 200
Saxenian, A.L.   59, 74
Schofield, A.   202
Schumpeter, J.   247, 249
Scott, A.   27
Scott, E.E.   160, 252, 253
Seagrave, S.   57, 73
Semkow, B.W.   65, 68
Sender, H.   72, 73, 240
Seng, L.C.   117
Serrie, H.   138, 149
Sharma, D.D.   133
Shaw, G.   211, 213
Shieh, G.S.   66, 67
Shikatani, T.   92
Silin, R.   218
Sinn, E.   113, 162
Sit, V.F.S.   218, 252
Sjoberg, O.   32
Skeldon, R.   164
Smart, A.   11, 15, 17, 18, 26, 80, 195,
    245, 250, 252, 256, 257, 260, 261,
    262, 271, 277
Smart, J.   11, 15, 17, 18, 26, 80, 245,
    250, 252, 256, 257, 261, 271
Smith, A.   260
Snow, C.C.   27
Sohn, D.J.H.   131
Sophonpanich, C.   20, 73
Stark, D.   269
Stillwell, F.   201
Suarez-Villa, L.   203
Suehiro, A.   19, 27
Suharto   50
Sung, Y.-W.   159, 245, 253
Suryadinata, L.   9, 18, 19
Susanto, D.   108
Swedberg, R.   125
Szczepanik, E.   162

Tallman, S.   128
Tam, S.   35
Tan, C.H.   220, 239
Tan, C.-T.   15, 76
Tan, C.Z.   25
Tan, L.   4, 20
Tan, M.   237

Tan, S.P. 27
Tay, Z.-N. 112
Techapaiboon, U. 115
Thilenius, P. 130
Thio, T.S. 27
Thompson, G. 27, 75
Thrift, N. 27, 200, 207, 249
Tien, J.K. 65
Tiong, H.K. 107
Tong, C.K. 11, 15, 68, 72, 111, 240
Tong, D. 117
Tracy, N. 108, 164
Tsai, W.-L. 73
Tsang, E.W.K. 15
Tsao, F. 90
Tseng, Y.-F. 170, 171, 173–5, 188
Tu, W.M. 34, 106, 257
Tuan, C. 78, 253

Underdown, M. 287
Unger, J. 123

Vahlne, J.E. 133
Van Den Bulcke, D. 23, 98, 104, 128, 144
Veitch, J.M. 181, 187
Veneroso F. 247
Verser, T.G. 276
Vogel, E. 33

Wade, R. 83, 247
Wakeman, F. Jr 155
Waldinger, R.D. 173
Walker, R. 169
Wang, G.-W. 9, 18, 27, 106, 124
Wang, T.P. 109
Wang, Y.-C. 73
Wang, Z.M. 35
Ward, J.L. 276
Waters, T. 71, 92, 252
Weber, M. 248
Weidenbaum, M. 5, 7–10, 15, 21, 76, 85, 86, 91, 92, 99, 102, 240, 258, 264
Weiss, L. 27
Wells, L.T. Jr 137, 141

Wen, Y.-K. 221, 222, 235
Wickberg, E. 65
White, L.T. 161
Whitley, R. 10, 14, 40, 41, 79, 126, 132, 134, 135
Whyte, M.K. 1, 81
Willcocks, L. 27
Williamson, O.E. 127, 129, 132, 203
Williamson, R. 211, 214, 215
Willis, K.D. 221, 238
Willmott, W. 218
Windolf, P. 15
Winn, J.K. 65
Wong, B. 255
Wong, C.-S. 253
Wong, G. 160, 218
Wong, G.Y.Y. 80
Wong, S.-L. 11, 14, 15, 17, 24, 68, 80, 89, 90, 139, 156, 161, 164, 170, 197, 204, 218, 249, 252
Wong, T.W.P. 161, 218, 257
Woo, P. 100
Woon, Y.-F. 108
Wu, F. 8, 92
Wu, C.H. 144
Wu, H.L. 71, 72
Wu, Y.L. 144

Xing, Y.S. 221, 222

Yan, Y.-X. 63, 258, 259
Yang, M. 114, 218, 258, 259
Yao, S.C. 11, 13
Yeh, A. 91
Yeh, W.-H. 155
Yeoh, B. 221, 239
Yeung, H.W.C. 1, 10, 14–17, 19–21, 23, 25–8, 66, 68, 71, 73, 76, 80–4, 89, 91, 92, 96, 97, 99, 105, 126, 135, 166, 197, 220, 235, 239–41, 249, 250, 253, 256, 257, 261, 278
Yew, S.L. 119
Yin, R.K. 242
Yong, P.A. 72, 239
Yong, P.K. 15, 111, 240
York, G. 212
Yuen, D. 213

Yung, C.C.   163
Yoshihara, K.   18, 19, 20, 56, 58, 82, 124, 195, 218

Zeithaml, C.P.   27
Zhang, G.   32

Zhang, H.-Y.   23, 98, 104, 144
Zhou, M.   170
Zhou, Y.   15, 18, 24, 74, 170, 173, 181, 183, 190
Zhu, G.-T.   221, 238, 239
Zimmer, C.   171

# Subject Index

accounting 176–80
　Certified Public Accountants
　　(CPA) 177–81
　Jewish firms 176, 178
Acer 50, 83, 87, 100, 146
acquisitions 84, 97, 99, 133
agribusiness 92, 102
alliances 38, 43, 53, 65, 70
　cross-border 146–7
　political-economic 12, 16, 18, 20,
　　136, 221, 240
　strategic 99, 128
Altos Computer Systems 100
American banks 181
American Express 168
ancestral origin 110, 221, 223, 227,
　238, 240
Anchor Beer 232
anthropology 34
Anxi 117–19
Anxi Association 112
Argentina 90
Arklight Engineering 226, 227, 229,
　230, 232–6
arm's-length transaction 92
Asia 2, 8, 24, 77, 87, 113, 147,
　202, 275
Asia Pacific Breweries Ltd
　(APB) 225, 230, 232, 236
Asia Pacific region 38, 77, 82,
　105–6, 122
Asia Pulp and Paper (APP) 225–7,
　230, 236, 238
Asian economic crisis 1, 22, 53, 56,
　70, 71, 107, 122, 173, 174, 247,
　268, 277
Asian economic miracle 206
Asian Newly Industrialized
　Economies (NIEs) 82, 87
Asian values 34, 255
Association of South East Asian
　Nations (ASEAN) 135, 136,
　141, 142, 145, 249

associations 205
　Chinese 108, 111, 112, 115–17,
　　119–24
　informal 182
　involuntary 106
　trade 115, 240
AT&T 168, 176
Auckland 201, 202
Australia 88, 113, 164
authoritarianism 43
authority 38, 80, 129–31, 136, 153
　centralized patriarchal 58, 264
　Chinese family 63

bamboo networks 1, 15, 35
Bangkok 107
Bangkok Bank 8
Bangkok Cotton Mill 89
Bank of China 111
Bank of Trade 185
banking 180–9
BC Place Ltd 209–12
Beijing 100, 222, 235
Berli Jucker Co. Ltd 99
Britain 276
Brazil 92
bureaucracy 104, 127, 249
Burma 163
business networks 14, 15, 17, 21, 36,
　37, 109, 115–17, 120, 121, 130–5,
　138, 140, 145, 147, 164, 196, 276
　Chinese 15, 65, 99, 105–24,
　　126–48, 195–217, 278
　cross-border 17
　foreign 133, 143
　institutionalization 122
　internationalized 143
business strategies 15
business system 14

California 59, 99, 182, 187,
　190, 192
Caltech 48

Canada 1, 51, 84, 107, 164, 173, 207, 208, 210, 214
Canadian Imperial Bank of Commerce 212, 277
capital 2, 7, 8, 25, 26, 56, 87, 164, 199, 205
  accumulation 64
  Chinese 50, 108
  non-Chinese 86
capitalism 32, 44, 50, 58–9, 161, 247, 248, 255
  Chinese 2, 12, 35, 38, 40, 123, 277
  ersatz 56
  family 38, 41
  global 13, 253
Caribbean 248
Cathay Bank 182, 183
centrally planned economies 32, 35
*chaebol* 56, 57, 129, 136
Charoen Pokphand Group 20, 82, 92, 97, 142
China 32, 42, 52, 112, 113, 153, 155, 162, 173, 192, 193, 231, 247, 251, 265, 270
  Cultural Revolution 163
  *danwei system* 161
  economic reform 238, 258–9
  entrepreneurs in industrial firms 258
  Hong Kong 244, 256, 265
  investment in 91, 106, 220, 262
  open-door policy 9, 91, 220, 221, 223, 248, 256
  Special Economic Zones (SEZs) 221, 222, 226, 235, 238, 241
Chinese
  associations 108, 110–12, 115–19, 120 (*see also* association)
  banking 183, 185, 186, 188, 190
  chamber of commerce 107, 115
  culture 109, 112
  diaspora communities 108–10, 113, 118–20
  entrepreneurs 107–8, 120, 126, 135, 162, 190, 227, 251
  financial institutions 182, 183
  immigrants 109, 144, 185, 210

  investors 201
  multinational enterprises 126, 127, 135, 139, 144, 146–8
  property tycoons 196, 207, 210
  social networks 138
Chinese-American Bank 182
Chinese business firms 17, 22, 23, 31, 45, 68, 75–104, 82, 100, 202, 275–6
  acquisition 97
  control and co-ordination 102, 103
  competitive advantage 99
  computer industry 189–93
  globalization 2, 21, 81, 105, 124, 143, 175, 181, 248, 276
  growth strategies 20, 101–3
  hierarchical structure 138
  Hong Kong-based 16, 79
  internationalization 77, 79, 80, 85, 86, 105, 142
  investment 16, 20, 70, 89, 91
Chinese business systems 239
Chinese Commercial Bank 111
Chinese Commonwealth 1, 22
Chinese Communist Party 161
Chinese diaspora 106, 108, 109, 115
Chinese family business 31–54, 40, 54, 122, 136–7, 156, 255–6, 275
Chinese People's Consultative Congress 107
Chineseness 22, 31, 33, 115, 120
collaboration 35, 40, 42–3, 99, 130, 135
collective bargaining 123
colonialism 155, 158, 159, 261
commodity chains 50, 52
communist 89, 154, 155, 157, 260
competitive advantage 16, 82, 99, 100, 102, 103, 123, 130, 249, 251, 264, 268, 276
computer distribution 189–193
Concord Pacific Development Ltd 212
Confucianism 12, 14, 39, 43, 112, 164, 255
connections 43, 58, 62, 66, 136, 144, 157, 194, 203–4, 216, 240–1, 244–7, 254, 257–8, 269

control 36, 130
conventions 106, 107
co-operation 135, 139, 249, 264, 270
co-operative agreements 130
co-operative enterprises 91
co-ordination 85, 99, 130, 146
corruption 52–3, 58
cross-shareholding 145
cultural determinism 261
cultural policies 159
culture 35, 41, 86, 113–14, 119, 120, 122, 124, 129, 133, 135, 137, 155, 158, 173, 175, 198, 215, 240

decision-making 36, 50, 68, 80, 103, 132, 138, 241
democracy 53
developing countries 9, 77, 185
Dhamala Group 92
differentiated networks 85
directorships 89, 145
discrimination 99, 102
disintegration 175
Disney 34
distribution linkages 66
diversification 70, 73, 79, 101–2, 127, 136, 174
division of labour 64, 265
Docklands 201
Downtown Eastside Residents Association (DERA) 214
Dragonair 51
DuPont 176

East Asia 1, 5, 14, 123, 134, 173, 193, 220, 275, 276
East Asia miracle 249
East–West Federal Bank 183, 189
Eastern Park Hotel 225, 229, 230, 235
economic development 82, 105
economic dynamism 172, 181
economic geography 2
economic globalization 1
economic institutions 12
economic integration 77
economic policies 20, 99

economic success 73, 126
economic theory 31
economies of scale 73, 99
economies of scope 73
Eli Lilly & Company 85
embeddedness 15, 31, 35, 73
emigration 245
entrepreneurial conglomerates 135–7, 144
entrepreneurship 16, 36, 69, 135, 154–6, 158, 159, 277
  intra-firm 36, 135
  Japanese 73
  political 239
  Western 38
ethnic distribution 5
ethnic linkages 144, 221
ethnicity 86, 121, 241
export-oriented economies 173
export processing zones 144
Europe 70, 113, 144, 192, 193, 275
  Singaporean investment 220
European Union (EU) 91

familial obligation 265
familism 32, 38, 57, 156, 157, 221, 241
family 135, 216, 225, 270, 276
  business 12, 32, 36, 37, 135
  cohesion 256
  connections 144, 190
  control 35–7, 53
  identity 42
  Jewish 37
  ownership 35, 36, 58, 204
  resources 42, 68
  ties 86, 105, 197, 217, 240, 255
family-ization 17
Federal Community Reinvestment Act 186
Fiji Islands 88
filial piety 63, 66, 225
finance 12
financial crisis 56
firm-specific advantages 85, 99, 100, 102, 104, 145, 147
First Pacific Davies 99
flagship company 137, 143
flexible accumulation 260

foreign direct investment (FDI)
145, 168, 199, 232, 241, 244
Japanese 70
Overseas Chinese 93
Taiwanese 83
Western 70
formalization 36, 80
Formosa Plastics 83
*Fortune 500* 52
France 84
free market 36, 46
Free Trade Agreements 249
Fujian 5, 92, 108, 118, 238
emigration 245
Singapore firms 221
Fujian Economic Development
Holdings Company 111
functional integration 1

Gaolong Bay 233
General Bank 183–4
geographical contexts 1, 15
geographical dispersion 139
Chinese entrepreneurs 145
geographical distance 103
geographical proximity 141, 144
global competition 102, 249
global corporations 85
global networking 146–7
global restructuring 202
global space 122
global residential property market
(GRPM) 201
globalization 20, 49, 124, 179, 194,
275, 278
definition 2, 105
Chinese associations 115,
119, 121–3
Chinese business firms 75–104,
146, 147, 175, 181
Chinese producer services
167–94
Chinese social organizations 114,
122, 124
property markets 195–217
Western firms 81
government 102, 136, 141
government-linked
corporations 241

Great Link Investment 226, 227,
229, 230, 232–4, 236
greenfield operation 99, 226, 232
groupism 35
growth triangles 198
Guangdong 5, 9, 92, 107, 108, 112,
154, 157, 159, 171, 226, 238,
257, 264
emigration 245
Singapore firms 221
Guangzhou 88
*guanxi* 12, 15, 58, 62, 66, 72, 80, 81,
82, 102, 114, 115, 204–6, 227, 240,
241, 244, 257–60, 263, 270, 278
*guanxi* capitalism 257

Hagemeyer 99
Haikou 232
Haikou Jinpan Industrial
Development Zone 227
Hainan 25, 220–42
Hainan Asia Pacific brewery Co. Ltd
(HAPCO) 232, 239
Hainan International Foreign
Investment Consultancy
Company 234
Hainan Mandarin Hotel 232,
235, 237
Hampstead 201
Harvard Business School 121
Harvey Nicholas 84
heterarchy 128
hierarchical governance 130
hierarchical relationships 251
hierarchical structure 138
hierarchy 66–7, 70, 129, 132, 138
historical heritage 128
historical regeneration 122
Hoe Leong 227
Hong Kong 2, 5, 7, 9, 14, 20, 24–6,
35, 50, 51, 56, 129, 137, 141,
143, 144, 146, 173, 193, 201,
202, 205, 244
Chinese enterprise
transplants 153–66
deindustrialization 252
development histories 46
economic development 156,
162, 269

Hong Kong (*continued*)
  economy   160, 252
  education   46
  government   158
  industry   89, 156, 253
  industrialization   83–4, 89
  regionalization   101
  service-oriented firms   84
  Special Administrative Region
       (SAR)   155, 159, 162
  stock exchange   52
Hong Kong Cotton Spinners
     Association   90
Hong Kong and Shanghai Hotels
     Ltd   94
Hong Leong Group   20, 82, 92, 142
Hopewell Holdings Ltd   96
housing   46
*huaqiao*   183
*hui*   182
Hui'an Fishing Company   111
Husky Oil   51, 84
Hutchinson Group   53, 146

IBM   176, 191
import-substitution   135
indebtedness   57, 65
individualism   17
Indonesia   19, 20, 39, 56, 113, 135,
     185, 277
  Chinese business   141, 277–8
  market saturation   82
  *pribumi*   16, 82
  privatization   81
  racial violence   163
industrial restructuring   83
industrialization   19, 44, 46, 79,
     89, 226
information costs   132
inheritance   45
institutional configurations   40, 76, 77
institutional environments   79,
     129, 231
institutional structures   16, 20
institutional thickness   15
institutionalization   34, 80, 105–6,
     113, 122–3
  Chinese-owned enterprises
       126–48

institutions   12, 23, 42, 45, 56, 97,
     100, 112, 132, 136, 160, 182,
     277, 278
integration   1, 44, 70, 88, 127, 145,
     200, 204 (*see also* disintegration)
Intel   189
interdependence   77, 130
inter-firm collaboration   135
inter-firm commitments   80
internalization   128, 135
internalization model   127
International Anxi Society   117
International Bank of
     California   185
international division of labour   253
International Federation of Fuqing
     Clans   115, 116
international investment   78
International Jinjiang
     Federation   113
International Monetary Fund
     (IMF)   48, 277
international production   77, 78, 85
international trade   78
internationalization   122, 128, 131,
     133, 134, 139, 147
  capital markets   199
  Chinese business networks
       139–47
  Chinese-owned multinational
       enterprises   126, 147, 148
  ethnic Chinese firms   77, 78, 141
  Singaporean firms   220–42
intra-firm internalization   135
intra-TNC entrepreneurship   277
investment   72, 147
  cross-border   8, 73, 99
  intra-regional   97
  Japanese   70
  liberalization   200
  real-estate   198
  strategy   222
inward foreign investment   141, 142

Japan   14, 45, 84
  banking   269
  business   34
  Chinese in   109
  culture   33

Fujianese businessmen in   115
*keiretsu*   56, 129, 136
organization   33
Jakarta   51
Java   5
Jiangsu   221, 237, 239
Jieyang   112
Jinhua Hotel   225, 229, 230, 235
Jinshanzhuang   88
Jiyou Bank   111
Johannesburg   51
joint ventures   91, 97, 100–4, 130,
      136, 142, 143, 145, 189, 221, 222,
      225, 229, 232
Jones Lang Lasalle   200

Kampuchea   163
Kensington   201
Keppel Group   83
kinship   14, 23, 26, 106, 113, 115,
      116, 120, 121, 131, 138, 221,
      241, 244
knowledge codification   48
Kobe General Association of
      Overseas Chinese   115
*kongsi*   109
Kuok Group   20, 82, 92, 163

labour movement   46, 79
*laissez-faire*   158, 175
Langkawi   107, 118
licensing   130
Li Group   207–9, 212
Liem Group   82, 97, 99
Lippo Group   121, 142, 185
linkages
   backward   204
   business   109, 110, 117, 222
   ethnic   221–2
   inter-firm   126
   intra-firm   126, 137
   intra-diaspora   110
   institutionalized   106
   vertical   108, 112, 113, 123
   horizontal   108, 112,
         113, 123
   space   198
   state–society   122
   transnational   186

Lion City Holiday Resort   230, 233,
      234, 237
*loaban*   67
loans   89, 186–9
local sourcing   144
locality   105, 113, 120
localization   122–4
locational advantage   88, 143, 145
London   9, 51, 200–2
Los Angeles   9, 24, 115
   Chinese producer services in
         167–94
   professional population   171

mistrust   37, 38, 43
Macao   9, 113, 163, 245
Mafia   43
Malacca   107
Malacca Textile   90
Malayan Weaving Mills   90
Malaysia   2, 5, 19, 56, 110, 112, 113,
      119, 135, 192
   *bumiputra*   19, 20, 82
   Chinese associations   117
   Chinese business   141
   Hainanese in   223
   Industrial Coordination Act   19
   market saturation   82
   New Economic Policy   19
   political coalition   18
   privatization   81
   Malaysian International Shipping
         Corporation (MISC)   90
Malaysian Selangor Anxi
      Association   118
managerial capability   78–9
Mandarin Oriental International
      Ltd   94
manufacturing investment   143
market access   235
market governance   129
market hierarchy   129, 130
market imperfection   127
market liberalization   145
marketization   168
mass consumption   248
mass production   248
Meinan International Airport   234
Melbourne   201

mergers and acquisitions 34
Method Engineering 229, 234
Metro Drugs 84
metropolitan regions 198
M-form corporations 99
Microtell 127
migration 84, 155, 157–9, 200, 201
Mitsubishi 161
mobile exporters 137, 143, 144
modernization 40
multinational enterprises
    (MNEs) 32, 49, 59, 85,
    128, 137
    American 142
    Chinese-owned 126, 127, 135,
        139, 144, 146–8
    Japanese 142
    production chains 143
    western 137, 146, 148

Nanyang 5, 37
Nanyang Cotton Mill Ltd 90
national boundaries 1, 20, 77, 83,
    109, 113, 124, 249
nationalism 111
nepotism 43, 255
Netherlands 99
network capital 164, 165
networking 36, 43, 74, 110–11, 116,
    119, 196
networks 8, 16, 41, 43, 58, 64–5,
    68–9, 71–3, 107, 113, 122,
    127–30, 134–5, 168, 205, 216,
    239–40, 261, 275–7 (*see also*
    business networks)
    *chaebol* 57
    Chinese 81, 83
    distribution 66, 88, 101, 141,
        144, 193
    economic 74, 278
    entrepreneurial 126, 131, 132,
        134, 137–40, 142, 147
    ethnic 185, 194
    extra-firm 16
    formation 138
    global 56, 146–7
    informal 99, 123
    inter-firm 59, 77, 80, 240, 241
    internationalized 137, 142

    interpersonal 69, 102, 134
    intra-firm 77, 221
    locality 113
    mobilization 250
    production 138, 141, 142, 195
    social 80, 113, 116, 121, 126–9,
        133, 138, 157, 249, 278
    trans-Pacific 25
    value-added 146
New World Development Co.
    Ltd 95
New York 2, 14, 24, 77, 93, 97,
    200, 201
    business firms 25
    Chinese community in 183
Ningbo 237
North America 99, 103, 113, 144,
    173, 185, 208
    Chinese communities 170
    Chinese producer services 110
    Singaporean investment 220
North American Free Trade Area
    (NAFTA) 78
Nuri Investment 185
NYNEX 92

obedience 63, 69
offshore production 142
Omni Bank 185
opportunism 51, 130, 203, 249
Orange County 183
Oregon 189
original equipment manufacturing
    (OEM) 42, 50, 52, 100,
    137, 191
organization
    business firms 112
    Chinese 61
    multi-unit 89
    political 112
    social 62, 110
    Western 61, 255
organizational efficiency 49
organizational principles 61
organizational scope 44
organizational structures 80, 103,
    130, 225
outward manufacturing
    investment 143

Overseas Chinese 1, 2, 8, 9–14, 17, 107, 110, 111, 118, 183, 195, 255, 275 (*see also* Chinese)
  business firms 91
  capital 91, 118, 162
  investment 25, 202, 238
  social organizations 105
overseas property investment 196
ownership 35–6, 43, 54
ownership advantages 126, 130, 135, 137, 140, 142

Pacific Rim 173, 186, 188, 192, 198, 199, 201, 217, 277
  property markets 195–217
  role of overseas Chinese 249
Pan-Malaya Federation of Taishan Associations 111
Paris 51, 107, 201
partnerships 86, 100, 109, 121, 135, 221, 233, 241
  business 115, 146, 257
  government 232
paternalism 43, 249
patriarchy 67, 69
patrimonialism 38
Pearl River Delta 257, 265
Pendero Development Co. 210
People's Republic of China 89, 172, 221, 244
personal contacts 80, 144
personal support 91
personalism 37, 38, 44
Philippines 8, 113, 135, 185, 231
  Chinese businesses 141
  market saturation 82
  Retail Trade Nationalization Law 19
pluralism 53
political alliances 136
political empowerment 53
political hierarchy 270
political leaders 20
political patronage 99, 135
political support 38, 209
political uncertainty 83
power 35
  Chinese family 63
  decentralization 50

pragmatism 157
Price Waterhouse 176
Prime Group International 225, 233, 235
principle of hierarchy 138
privatization 81, 212
producer services 24, 25
  Chinese 110, 167–94
  definition 167
  globalization 167
  internationalization 167
  in USA 169
product portfolio 136
production systems 59, 203
professionalism 37, 50, 53
professionalization 249
  management 225
  Singaporean Chinese firms 226
property markets 199
Provision Suppliers Corporations (PSC) 227, 232, 235
public ownership 37, 38

Qiangda (Hainan) Travel and Trading 229
*qiaoxiang* 108–11, 113, 114, 117, 118, 121, 122, 124
Qinglan Economic Developmental Zone 227, 234
Qinglan International Harbour 233
Qionghai City 226, 227
Queensland 88

rationalization 84
reciprocation 64
reciprocity 63, 65, 69, 73, 80, 130, 203, 205
Regal Hotels International Holdings Ltd 96
regional boundaries 77
regional connections 157
regional integration 143
regional interdependence 113
regionalization 78, 146
relationships 12, 17, 35, 58, 62, 63, 70, 79, 80, 115, 117, 129, 133, 147, 240, 249, 255, 257, 259, 262
  business 66, 102, 137
  co-operative 15, 40

relationships (*continued*)
  credit 65
  cross-border 128
  ethnic Chinese TNCs 225
  family 63, 80
  government–business 46
  inter-firm 69, 81, 130, 156
  intra-firm 85, 130, 240
  long-term 206
  patron–client 20
  personal 15, 102, 165, 225, 240, 241, 256, 270, 276
  reciprocal 73
  social 61, 73, 102, 122, 193, 206, 207, 256, 258, 275
  state–society 123
*renqing* 63, 64, 69
reputation 65, 130, 156, 205
research and development 58
resource mobilization 138
risk management 79
rotating credit system 182
rural townships 257

Salim Group 142
San Francisco 173, 180, 185
San Gabriel Valley 174, 177
San José 101
Sansui Electric 84
Shanghai 24, 88, 153, 155, 156, 159, 237, 245
Shangri-La International Group 96
Shantou 119
Shantou Chamber of Commerce 112
Shanxi 92
Shen Xin Textile 89
Shenzhen 262
*shetuan* 23, 106, 108–10, 113, 116–22
Siam 5
Sierra Semiconductor Corp. 101
Silicon Valley 96
Sin-Thai Shipping Company 111
Sinar Mas Group 92
SINFenghuang Hotel 225, 229
Singapore 2, 5, 19, 20, 45, 56, 107, 112–13, 144, 192–3, 201, 202, 244
  Central Provident Fund 46
  corporatist state 83

development histories 46
Economic Committee for Overcoming Recession (ECOR) 220
external economy 220
foreign capital 83
GDP 220
globalization drive 220
government 32, 46
government-linked corporations 241
Hainanese in 223
investment in China 25, 220–42
regionalization drive 25, 83, 238
urban development 195
Teochews 119
Singapore Anxi Association 109, 110
Singapore Chinese Chamber of Commerce (SCCC) 109–11, 116, 235
Singapore Fuqing Association 83, 109
Singapore Hui'an Association 111
Singapore Ji Yang Cai Clan Association 121
Singapore Power 226, 227, 232
Singapore Technologies 83, 101
Singapore Tong-an Association 111
Singer Co. 84
SINGlass Holding 227, 231, 232
Single European Market 78
Sino–British Joint Declaration 83, 164, 172
Sino–Singapore relations 220
small and medium enterprises 32, 65, 70, 97, 101, 120, 121, 137, 168, 197, 203, 224, 227, 232
social boundary 262
social conformity 154
social foundation 120
social organizations 109–12, 114, 122, 124, 241, 275
  internationalization 221
  overseas Chinese 105
social protection 264
social space 113, 124
sociology 34, 41, 73
South Africa 113

South China 67, 88, 159, 160
South Korea 174
  *chaebol* 56, 57, 129, 136
  economic strategies 57
  indebtedness 57
South Seas 5
Southeast Asia 1, 2, 110,
    135, 139, 144, 173, 248,
    275–6, 278
  Chinese business
      communities 110, 126, 134,
      135, 140, 141, 180
  economic development 123
  Hainanese immigrants 222
  intra-regional investment 145
  Japanese joint ventures 141
  political security 185
  population 14
  Singaporean investment 220
  Taiwanese investors 142
  Western enterprises 141, 148
Southern California Chinese
    Computer Association 190
space–economy 106
space linkages 198
state interference 45
state ownership 160
state regulation 82
strategic alliances 99, 128, 146
strategic transformation 135
strategies 75–6, 84, 244
  Chinese business 251, 256
  control 102
  co-operative 15, 91, 99
  diversification 101
  market-expansionary 237
  risk 263
subcontracting 46, 66, 101, 143, 159,
    195, 203–5, 253
  accounting work 177
  flexible 160
(sub)culture 119, 121, 124
(sub)ethnicity 116, 120, 121 (*see also*
    ethnicity)
sub-regional integration 78
subsidiaries
  foreign 85, 103
  in Hainan 232
  overseas 102

in Shanghai 160
  wholly-owned 222, 229
Suntec Convention Centre 90
Suzhou 237
Suzhou–Singapore Industrial
    Park 239
Sy Group 20, 82
Sydney 195, 201, 202, 277

Taipei Institute of Information
    Industry 191
Taiwan 5, 7, 9, 14, 20, 56, 113, 129,
    136, 137, 141, 143, 144, 146, 173,
    180, 184, 185, 244
  banking industry 205
  business 65
  capitalist economy 65
  development histories 46
  economic development 173, 269
  government 32
  *guanxi* in 260
  industry 43, 52, 189–93, 252
  national champions 83
  network of production 72
  productivity gains 45
  regionalization 101
  science parks 46
  subsidiaries and incentives 83
technological capability 78
technology transfer 52, 137
Telecom Asia 92
Temasek Holdings 83
Textile Corporation of Malaya 90
Thailand 5, 8, 56, 82, 107, 135, 245
  Chinese business 141
  Chinese entrepreneurs 525
  communications industry 81
  Hainanese in 223
  military patronage 19, 81
  privatization 81
Third-World multinationals 76
Tianjian 245
Tiger Beer 232
Tokyo 106, 200
*tongbao* 261
Toronto 51, 201, 207
totalitarianism 38
tourism 118
trade 5, 109, 116, 118, 253

transaction costs   37, 111, 126, 128,
    132, 133, 203, 245, 257, 262
transaction cost economies
    (TCE)   126–30, 132
transborder regions   198
transnational corporations
    (TNCs)   77, 114, 168, 185,
    193–4, 227, 232, 257, 276
    American   85
    Chinese   2, 20, 21, 75, 77, 85, 107,
        120, 179, 249
    competitive advantage   102
    developed countries   168
    entrepreneurship   277
    Hong Kong-based   81, 250
    globalization   82
    headquarters   175
    Singaporean   226
    Western   81
transnational entrepreneurs   122
transnational ethnic networks   185
transnational finance   200
transnational linkages   186
transnational mobility   106, 108,
    115, 122
transnational social sphere   124
transnationalism   108, 113, 114, 122
transnationalization   21
Triad countries   83, 93, 99
Triad regions   79, 87
Triadization   77
trust   40, 44, 54, 65, 111–13, 115,
    122–3, 129–31, 134, 141, 156–7,
    177, 203, 205–6, 240, 244–5,
    247, 249, 264

U-form structure   135
uneven development   20
Union of Jinjiang Societies   113
United Kingdom   84, 202
United Pacific Bank   185
United Savings Bank   99
University of Southern
    California   180
urban industrial economy   259
urban mega-projects (UMPs)   198
urbanization   198

USEnron Corporation   233
USA   1, 25, 84, 100, 144, 147, 164,
    171, 173–4, 176, 184, 208

value chains   85
value-generation process   128,
    130, 133
Vancouver   25, 107, 195–6, 201–2,
    204, 207–9, 211–12, 214, 216, 277
Vietnam   5, 163, 189

Washington   100
Weberian thesis   1
Wei Sun Knitting Factory   88
Wenchang City   227
Western-centric perspective   22
Western Europe   2, 14, 24, 77,
    93, 99
Western family   138
Western financial institutions   277
Western Imperialism   87
Western influences   264
Westminster   201
Wharf Holdings   95, 100
Wheelock & Co.   100
wholly-owned companies   91
Wing On Company   88, 163
Winsor Industrial Group   90, 154
World Bank   7, 189
World Chinese Business Network
    (WCBN)   116
World Guan Association   107
World Trade Organization   249
Worldwide Shipping   51

*xiao*   63, 66, 69
*xinyong*   111, 114

Yalong Bay National Holiday
    Zone   227
Yangpu Economic Developmental
    Zone   227, 232
youth culture   34

Zhejiang   87, 237
Zhongshan   92
Zilong Group   225, 229–31